THE UNITED STATES
AND MEXICO

AMS PRESS

NEW YORK

THE UNITED STATES
AND MEXICO

By J. FRED RIPPY, A.M., Ph.D.

PROFESSOR OF HISTORY, DUKE UNIVERSITY

REVISED EDITION

NEW YORK · F. S. CROFTS & CO.

MCMXXXI

Reprinted from the edition of 1931, New York
First AMS EDITION published 1971
Manufactured in the United States of America

International Standard Book Number: 0-404-05337-8

Library of Congress Number: 73-137281

AMS PRESS INC.
NEW YORK, N.Y. 10003

TO
MARY D.

PREFACE

The volume here presented is the first general survey of the diplomatic relations of the United States and Mexico that has appeared in any language. The author has tried to set forth in simple narrative designed to appeal to the public as well as to students of college and university rank, the difficulties which have arisen between the two countries, the factors which have produced them, and the spirit in which they have been met.

The three decades subsequent to the Mexican War of 1846–1848 have been treated most fully. The reasons for this procedure will readily appear. The earlier period has already been written upon extensively by others. The thirty years which followed the advent of Porfirio Díaz were marked in general by a pacific intercourse yielding comparatively little for the historian to record. The most important of the sources necessary for the final history of the years following his overthrow are not yet available. I have given my own brief interpretation of this recent period. Whoever desires to make a fuller study will find helpful suggestions in the bibliography.

Like most subjects, this one has its larger aspects and ramifications. The reader will often be reminded of the bearing of a century of United States-Mexican relations upon the recent Caribbean policy of the United States. In many respects Mexico's place and condition have been typical. A weak, turbulent, bankrupt state with varied and valuable natural resources, sometimes menaced by European powers, constantly exposed because of its position to the enterprising and energetic advances of the United States, Mexico has not yet officially and formally lost its independence, but it has been forced to give up a large part of its domain and its autonomy has frequently been threatened. Like the smaller states of the Caribbean area, it has been at once the occasion for American apprehensiveness respecting possible European designs and the object of American benevolence and greed. Indeed, long before Nicaragua, Haiti, Santo Domingo, Cuba, and Panama became protectorates of the United States an analogous state of affairs calling for similar procedure had arisen in Mexico, and no remedy has been applied to these little nations which had not previously been proposed as a solution of the Mexican problem.

This account, as will appear from the foot-notes, is based almost
entirely upon primary materials—upon contemporary newspapers
and periodicals, and upon documents published by the two governments or drawn from their archives. Except for the periods prior to
1848 and subsequent to 1910 and the administrations of Buchanan
and Lincoln, the author has broken virgin soil. In many instances
published documents have been checked with the originals in the
archives, but the former have usually been cited except in cases of
important variation from the originals. It need hardly be remarked
that this has been done because the published documents are more
available to the average reader. Only recently a small volume appeared on the Gadsden Treaty, but this came out after I had
already examined the sources bearing upon this phase of the subject and presented my conclusions in several magazine articles. I
am gratified to note that the work of my colleague and friend, Dr.
Paul Garber, tends for the most part to confirm these conclusions.
I also desire to thank the editors of these magazines—Professor E. C.
Barker, of *The Southwestern Historical Quarterly*, Dr. J. A. Robertson, of *The Hispanic American Historical Review*, and Dr. M. M.
Quaife, of *The Mississippi Valley Historical Review*—for the privilege of using these articles in modified form in this work.

It is a pleasure to acknowledge the kindness and encouragement
of librarians, custodians of manuscripts, teachers, and friends who
have taken an interest in this work. Only those who have attempted
the arduous and often irksome task of perusing the manuscripts
filed in our diplomatic archives or housed in our libraries are capable
of adequately appreciating the time and effort required to examine
the correspondence bearing on the relations of two neighboring nations for three-quarters of a century. To those who have helped to
lighten this task—to the late Mr. Stanton, of the Library of the
Department of State, to Mr. John C. Fitzpatrick, of the Library of
Congress (Division of Manuscripts), to the late Dr. Gaillard Hunt,
Director of the Division of Publications of the Department of State,
and to Dr. William R. Manning, of the same department—the author
is under a very deep obligation. Finally, it is a pleasure to acknowledge the kindly encouragement of Dr. James Alexander Robertson
and Dr. Tyler Dennett, of Washington, D. C., and particularly that
of Professor Herbert E. Bolton and his colleagues and Seminar students at the University of California where these researches were
begun.

J. FRED RIPPY.

CONTENTS

MAPS

CHAPTER I

EARLY RELATIONS; TEXAS AND THE MEXICAN WAR

THE opening years of the nineteenth century revealed little foreboding of the stormy relations which were to mark the intercourse of the United States and its neighbor on the south. On the contrary, they gave fair promise of mutual cordiality and esteem. The struggle for independence in Mexico (1810 ff.), as in the remainder of Spanish America, had awakened interest and sympathy among the people of the United States. Some had offered their money, others their swords in the contest. Still others had championed the cause of the patriots in the press and from the forum. The government itself, although at first restrained by the state of the Florida negotiations, did not long delay announcement of its determination to extend recognition to the new states and oppose European designs of reconquest. Each of the short-lived insurgent governments of Mexico had been prompt to dispatch agents to the United States. Augustín de Iturbide, who finally led the Mexican revolutionary forces to success (1821), not only expressed profound admiration for Henry Clay and appreciation of his services in Congress in Mexico's behalf, but declared his conviction that Mexico and the United States were "destined to be united in the bonds of the most intimate and cordial fraternity." The first republican government of Mexico not only hastened to acknowledge its gratitude to its American sympathizers, but reminded the envoy it sent to Washington of the readiness with which the United States had granted recognition and directed him to avoid every motive for discord or complaint while exercising diligence in cultivating and strengthening relations of friendship.[1]

But harbingers of dissension and trouble soon appeared. The execution of the Florida treaty (1819) had not been effected when the Mexicans achieved their independence. Repeated utterances of dissatisfaction with the western boundary of Louisiana as stipulated in this pact and the operations of Long's American filibusters on the frontier soon attracted the attention of the Mexican government.

---

[1] Manning, *Early Diplomatic Relations between the United States and Mexico*, pp. 1–30, *passim*.

And just as the first faint signs of suspicion became visible, the Spanish Minister at Washington published a very damaging memorial, in which he declared, among other things, that the Americans thought themselves "superior to all the nations of Europe"; that both they and their government believed that their dominion was "destined to extend now to the Isthmus of Panama, and, hereafter, over all the regions of the new world"; that the "whole course of their policy calculates [calculated] upon the illusions of these flattering expectations." [2] The effect of the early boundary issue and of the Spanish memorial is found recorded for the historian in the early despatches of the Mexican envoys and agents in the United States. On December 26, 1822, one of them expressed the conviction that the national army and the militia of the several states of the American Union were to be augmented with the view of occupying Texas. In time, said he, the people of the United States "will be our sworn enemies, and foreseeing this we ought to treat them as such from the present day." "The haughtiness of these republicans will not allow them to look upon us as equals but merely as inferiors; and in my judgment their vanity goes so far as to believe that their capital will be that of all the Americas." [3] This from the pen of the first Mexican minister officially received at Washington within two weeks after his reception!

Nor was the second agent any less apprehensive. On August 21, 1823, he informed his government that the newspapers of the United States were frequently dwelling upon the fertility of the soil of Texas and lamenting the cession of the province to the Spaniards. He pointed out the danger of permitting the Anglo-Saxon element to become preponderant in Texas. In this connection he said:

My opinion is that some agents from New Orleans are intending to plant colonies of Anglo-Americans in Texas with the same object in view which they have accomplished in Baton Rouge, namely, that of acquiring an influence and majority in the population and forcing the inhabitants to declare that they desire to be annexed to the United States . . .[4]

In the following January this agent expressed even greater alarm. He said that he would not be surprised if the troops of the United States on the frontier were ordered to advance into Texas at any time, so unlimited was the desire of the United States for this region.

[2] As quoted in Manning, *op. cit.,* p. 279. This memoir was published in Madrid in 1820, and an English translation was printed in Baltimore the following year.

[3] As quoted in Manning, *op. et loc. cit.*

[4] As quoted in *ibid.,* p. 280, note.

He reported that he had been introduced to General Jackson, who had remarked in his presence that the United States should never have imperiled its opportunity to obtain the province of Texas, and that the best way to acquire territory was to occupy it first and negotiate for it afterwards, as had been done in the case of Florida.[5]

Recent reports from Texas itself had been equally alarming; and in October, 1823, the Mexican *chargé* at Washington was directed to press for a settlement of this boundary issue. Early in 1824 he addressed a formal inquiry to the State Department asking whether the United States were disposed to acknowledge Mexico's title to Texas and to appoint commissioners to run the boundary as laid down in the Florida treaty. For more than a year this note remained unanswered.[6]

Another factor which constituted an ill omen for the future relations of the United States and Mexico was the growing influence of England south of the Rio Grande and the increasing disposition of the British government to use that influence to the detriment of the United States. The announcement of the intention of the United States to recognize the Spanish-American insurgents and the substitution of the Monroe manifesto for a joint declaration with Great Britain against a general European interference in the Spanish colonies added a political motive to the strong commercial interest which England already had in those colonies. George Canning feared that the United States would become the head and sole director of a "Trans-Atlantic League" of "youthful and stirring nations" which would become the rival of the "wornout" monarchal governments of Europe. He had no special fondness for these effete monarchies, but was eager to become the leader of the new Spanish-American nations, or at least to prevent the United States from attaining this leadership. He considered Mexico the key to the success of his policy, and accordingly began the campaign to counteract the influence of the United States. In October, 1823, Canning had warned the French Minister in London that the English government would consider any attempt of the European powers to assist Spain to recover her American colonies as sufficient motive for immediate recognition of the revolutionary governments. At the same time he had dispatched three commissioners to Mexico City with authority to give a pledge that England did not desire any of the former Spanish colonies for herself and that she would not permit their acquisition by any other power. These British agents had evinced great partiality for Mexico, one of them going so far as to guarantee,

[5] *Ibid.,* pp. 281–282.
[6] *Ibid.,* pp. 283–286.

in the name of Great Britain, a loan to the Mexican government.
Early in 1825 Britain extended formal recognition to Mexico, after
a vain effort to induce Spain to follow the same course; and on
April 6 a treaty decidedly favorable to the Aztec republic was negotiated.[7]

Canning did not approve the procedure of the British commissioners without reservations, but his exact attitude was not known
for some time; and England quite naturally stood very high in the
esteem of the Mexican government during these early days. In a
report which the Mexican Minister of Foreign Relations sent to
Congress early in 1825, he spoke in enthusiastic terms of the assistance which Great Britain had given to Mexico, but described the
attitude of the United States in brief and platonic fashion. The
receptions of H. G. Ward, first British *chargé*, and of Joel R. Poinsett, the first American minister to Mexico, presented a still more
vivid contrast in the sentiment which the Mexican government entertained for these respective nations. President Victoria's reply
to Ward alluded to the English as "the great people who sustain
the liberties of the world" and expressed the hope that the
friendship of the two nations might be perpetual, but his response
to the speech of Poinsett was brief, non-committal, and almost cold.
It was evident, as Poinsett remarked, that "the British had made
good use of their time and opportunities." [8]

A third matter which presaged trouble between the two republics
was the Cuban question. The effect which the emancipation movement might have on that island was a subject of much concern to
both. Each feared that the other was planning to seize Cuba, each
was determined to prevent the other from doing so, and each desired if possible to acquire Cuba for itself. Mexico probably desired
to see Cuba independent if she could not acquire the island, but the
United States preferred that it should remain a part of Spain rather
than see it exposed, as an autonomous state, to the dangers of
future European absorption. The United States might accuse Mexico of greed, but Mexico could charge the United States both with
greed and with the cooling of its ardor for liberty! [9]

A fourth factor which gave promise of future trouble was the
trade between Santa Fé, New Mexico, and the frontier of the United
States. "Precarious and fitful" under the colonial régime, this trade
had grown "by leaps and bounds" during the years immediately

[7] Manning, *op. cit.*, pp. 55–66.
[8] *Ibid.*, pp. 52–54, 67–70.
[9] *Ibid.*, p. 89 ff.

following the collapse of Spanish power. The unreasonable and
irritating restrictions which had formerly hampered it had not been
enforced during the period of uncertainty and confusion which attended the overthrow of Iturbide and the establishment of the first
republican government. They had not been removed, however, and
it soon became evident that Mexico heard with uneasiness and dis-
pleasure the "news of the growing intercourse on the far northern
frontier." Indeed, this attitude was revealed very clearly in the
spring of 1825 by the establishment of a consul at St. Louis to keep
a close watch over this trade and to prevent the introduction of
American settlers. It was likewise revealed by Mexico's definite
refusal at that time to issue *exequaturs* to consuls which the United
States had appointed for Santa Fé, Chihuahua City, and Saltillo.
The aggressive Anglo-Saxon frontiersmen were not likely to submit
passively to these irksome limitations.[10]

The stage was therefore set for exciting events when the first
minister of the United States arrived in Mexico in June, 1825. Few
envoys have been called upon to face a greater combination of difficulties. Before Joel R. Poinsett, this first American minister, had
presented his credentials Mexico had come to look upon the United
States as its natural rival and enemy, and he himself had been
represented by the Mexican Minister at Washington as possessing
no "great talents." Two days after his formal reception a man
by the name of Azcarate, who claimed to have been closely associated with the Emperor Iturbide, wrote President Victoria an alarming letter. Azcarate said that during an interview which he had had
with Poinsett in 1822 the latter had pointed to a map which they
had before them and indicated the desire of the United States to
"absorb all Texas, New Mexico, and Upper California, and parts
of Lower California, Sonora, Coahuila, and New Leon." [11] With
the Mexican administration thus prejudiced against both his government and himself, Poinsett was called upon by his instructions,
as Justin H. Smith so well puts it, "to stand for a Protestant power
in a country intensely Roman Catholic, to represent democracy
where the dominant element consisted of aristocrats hoping more
or less generally for a Bourbon king, to support Monroe's doctrine
of America for the Americans against the strength of Europe and
the European affiliations of Mexico, to vindicate the equal position
of the United States where Great Britain had established a virtual

[10] *Ibid.*, p. 166 ff.; Gregg, *Commerce of the Prairies;* Inman, *Old Santa Fé Trail.*
[11] Manning, *op. cit.*, pp. 48, 289–290.

protectorate, to insist upon full commercial privileges when the Spanish-American states favored mutual concessions. . ."[12] If to this long list of duties one adds those of securing arrangements calculated to stimulate the Santa Fé trade when Mexico feared this trade would result in the loss of New Mexico; of acquiring territory when the mere proposal of such a thing confirmed Mexican suspicion, wounded Mexican pride, and intensified Mexican anger; of presenting the complaints of his fellow countrymen against bewildering commercial regulations, and of opposing Mexico's cherished designs regarding Cuba, the enumeration will be for practical purposes complete.[13] What wonder that Poinsett met with little success!

The only achievement of his more than five years in Mexico was the negotiation of two treaties, one of amity and commerce, and the other relating to the boundary, neither of which was ratified until long after his recall. The failure of his mission has been attributed to his "excursion into local politics," to the "amazing impudence" with which he attempted to reorganize Mexican parties and overturn Mexican cabinets; but to the writer it appears that deep-rooted suspicion of the United States in Mexico, the hostile influence and criticism of British agents, and the nature of the task laid upon him, may well have defeated the efforts of a more tactful and gifted minister.[14]

Be this as it may, the relations of the United States and Mexico were in an extremely unsatisfactory state at the close of 1829. Not only had the early apprehension and bitterness in Mexico become more widespread and intense, but the unprecedented treatment accorded Poinsett had left the United States piqued and somewhat angry. And, moreover, that series of domestic disturbances which were to continue for almost a half-century and even to threaten Mexico's national existence had already begun. To handle the situation much sagacity, patience, and tact would be needed.

At least two requirements would be indispensable to the restoration of harmony: a gifted diplomatist, and the suppression, for a time at any rate, of all attempts to acquire territory. But, unfortunately, neither of these was met by the Jackson administration. A spoils politician was sent to Mexico as *chargé d'affaires* and numer-

---

[12] *The War with Mexico,* I, 58.

[13] Manning, *op. cit., passim.*

[14] On Poinsett's mission see, besides Manning, *op. cit.,* Smith, "Poinsett's Career in Mexico," in American Antiquarian Society, *Proceedings,* XXIV (1914), 77 ff; Rives, *The United States and Mexico,* I, 162, *passim;* Reeves, *American Diplomacy Under Tyler and Polk,* p. 61 ff.

ous efforts were made to purchase not only Texas but also an additional strip of territory extending westward to the Pacific and including the Bay of San Francisco. The career of this new agent is set forth in striking fashion by Smith:

> . . . For about six years [subsequent to 1829] the United States had as its representative a friend of Jackson's named Anthony Butler, whose only qualifications for the post were an acquaintance with Texas and a strong desire to see the United States obtain it. In brief he was a national disgrace. Besides having been through bankruptcy more than once, if we may believe the Mexican minister at Washington, and having a financial interest in the acquisition of this Mexican territory, he was personally a bully and a swashbuckler, ignorant . . . of the Spanish language and even of the forms of diplomacy, shamefully careless about legation affairs, wholly unprincipled as to methods, and, by the testimony of two American consuls, openly scandalous in conduct. One virtue, to be sure, according to his own account he possessed: he never drank spirits; but one learns of this with regret, for an overdose of alcohol would sometimes be a welcome excuse for him.
>
> His particular business was to obtain as much of Texas as possible, an enterprise that lay close to Jackson's heart; and he began by visiting the province—about whose loyalty and relations with the United States much concern was already felt at Mexico—when on the way to his post. This promise of indiscretion in office was admirably fulfilled. Maintaining a hold on our President by positive assurances of success, he loafed, schemed, made overtures, threatened, was ignored, rebuffed, snubbed, and cajoled, fancied he could outplay or buy the astute and hostile Alamán, tried to do "underworking" with Pedraza, plotted bribery with one Hernández, the confessor of Santa Anna's sister, grossly violated his conciliatory instructions by engaging in a truculent personal affair with Tornel, and was finally, after ceasing to represent us, ordered out of the country. In short he succeeded only in proving that we had for a minister a cantankerous, incompetent rascal, in making it appear that our government was eager to obtain Mexican territory, and in suggesting —though explicitly and repeatedly ordered to eschew all equivocal methods— that we felt no scruples as to means. On the ground of Butler's connection with disaffected Texas, Mexico politely asked for his recall near the close of 1835, and in December Powhatan Ellis . . . was appointed *chargé d'affaires*.[15]

The only progress made during Butler's residence in Mexico was the ratification of the two treaties negotiated by Poinsett. By the terms of the boundary treaty which the United States had been compelled to accept in order to obtain favorable commercial arrangements, the two powers agreed to acquiesce in the boundary line of 1819. The most important provisions of the commercial pact were: (1) the most favored nation clauses, (2) the sections designed to regulate and promote the Santa Fé trade, and (3) the stipulations regarding the Indians along the international frontier.[16] According to the last provision the contracting parties were bound

15 Smith, *op. cit.*, I, 62–63.
16 Manning, *op. cit.*, pp. 205–276.

to restrain the Indians residing within their respective boundaries and to return all captives found among these Indians. In view of the importance which the matter was to assume in the future, it is worth while to note also that the envoy of the United States had made a vigorous, though vain, effort to write into the commercial treaty an agreement for the rendition of fugitive slaves. And one of the main objections to this provision was its alleged tendency to promote Anglo-Saxon settlements along the international boundary and in Texas.[17]

The Anglo-Saxons in Texas had in fact soon become the victims of Mexico's hostile distrust of the United States and its citizens. These hardy frontiersmen had drifted into the region because of the urge of the westward-moving impulse and the attraction of cheap lands and of political and social conditions which they probably supposed would be in every way satisfactory. They were entirely innocent of conspiracy or of ulterior motives of any sort. The Mexican government, possibly under the illusion that the prospective colonizers and colonists were Catholics who would erect a barrier against the Protestants of their native land, at first gave them a cordial reception. Not only were they furnished huge tracts of land at small cost, but they were exempted from tariffs and permitted to introduce slaves into territory formerly considered free. But the Memorial of de Onis (the Spanish Minister at Washington), the hostile intrigues of the British *chargé* in Mexico City,[18] the errors and improprieties of the United States and its agents, aggressive utterances from the American press and platform, and the ill-timed, ill-fated Fredonian revolt in eastern Texas, eventually brought down upon these settlers the intense suspicion of the formerly friendly Mexican authorities.

Thereafter the Texas revolution was a foregone conclusion. The Mexican government determined to "take order with the Texans." It undertook to exclude further immigration from Anglo-Saxon America, to abolish slavery in Texas, to impose irksome and injurious revenue measures; and in order to insure Mexican predominance in the region, attempted to induce its own nationals to

[17] *Ibid.*, pp. 229–231, 240–242, *passim*.
[18] On the general topic of the early rivalry between the United States and England in Mexico see Manning, *op. cit.*, pp. 55–88; Ward's activities against the Anglo-Americans in Texas are set forth in the following despatches: Ward to Canning, Nos. 32, 54, and 64, Sept. 22, Nov. 15, and Dec. 10, 1825, Public Records Office, London, Foreign Office, 50, Vols. 14 and 15. Ward had several interviews with President Victoria, in which he urged him to be on his guard against the Anglo-American immigrants and to send Mier y Terán into Texas to make a thorough investigation.

seek homes beyond the Rio Grande, dispatched convicts thither, and refused to permit Texas to separate from the much more populous state of Coahuila. Moreover, with the passing of time it became evident that the Texans were bound to be involved in the series of revolutions already well under way in the interior of Mexico. In the winter of 1835 news came that Santa Anna, who had proclaimed a centralized government, had now raised a large army and, breathing fire and threatening destruction, was advancing northward with the avowed purpose of subduing the Texans and supplanting their local autonomy with an agent of military despotism. This proved to be the last straw. Fierce lovers of freedom and stanch opponents of economic restrictions and military authority, men whose ancestors had risked their lives and fortunes to evade the British revenue system and prevent the establishment of British troops in their villages and homes, could hardly have been expected tamely to submit to the more immoderate tyranny of dictators springing from a race which they considered far inferior to their own. The Texans revolted, defeated Santa Anna's army, set up a government of their own and gave evidence of ability to maintain their independence, so that the Texas Republic was soon welcomed into the family of nations by the recognition of the United States, of England, and of France.

Three possibilities were presented to the newly constituted state: continued independence, annexation to the United States, or reconquest by Mexico. Perhaps it would have been the part of wisdom for Mexico, gracefully yielding to accomplished facts, to have acknowledged the independence of Texas. The European powers, anxious to erect a dyke against the Anglo-Saxon flood, urged this course upon the Mexican government and would have supported her in it. If the Texans could have gained assurance of freedom from the menace of Mexican invasion and frontier depredations, they might have welcomed such an arrangement, particularly after the first refusal of Washington to admit them into the Union. Thus would have been established a comparatively harmless buffer state between Mexico and her dangerous neighbor. It might have been wise for Mexico to have followed this line of action—wise, but not Mexican and hardly human. The Mexicans considered the Anglo-Saxons in Texas the unscrupulous agents of a malevolent and land-greedy neighbor which had been conspiring from the start to obtain possession of the region. They believed that the revolution had been hatched and supported by the United States government in clever connivance with its frontier citizens, that Mexico probably confronted the dilemma of the reconquest of Texas or its absorption by the Yankees; and they did not like to admit defeat. Although the procedure of General Edmund P. Gaines on the Texas-Louisiana frontier, the failure of the United States to restrain its filibustering citizens, and the allegations of such men as Benjamin Lundy and John Quincy Adams, lent plausibility to this view of the matter, it was probably incorrect; and the refusal of the United States to take advantage of the first opportunity to annex the new republic should have counteracted these notions of Anglo-Saxon baseness and avarice. But the eagerness of the Tyler administration to secure California and the incontinent and imprudent haste with which Commodore Jones seized Monterey (1842) the moment he sensed the possibility of war between the United States and Mexico, destroyed the good effect of the refusal to incorporate Texas. Consequently, Mexico continued to harass the little state on the northern frontier, driving it for the second and the third time to seek protection under the North American flag; and European interference in Texas gave rise in the United States to apprehension and resentment which finally overcame much of the opposition to the annexation of the republic of the lone star.[19]

The passage of the joint resolution of annexation by the Congress of the United States and the favorable action of the Texas convention brought matters to a crisis. The Mexican government, long since convinced of the perfidy of the United States, had served notice that it would consider the act of annexation as tantamount to a declaration of war. The Mexican Minister accordingly asked for his passports and departed, and the Minister of the United States in Mexico was dismissed soon afterwards. Mexico then prepared to begin hostilities without an open declaration of war. Troops were ordered to the northern frontier, and Mexican diplomatic agents abroad were notified that Mexico must resort to the sword in defense of national honor and instructed to solicit aid from European governments.[20] In order to be prepared for action if it should become necessary, the United States dispatched troops to the southwest and ordered war vessels stationed in the Gulf of Mexico to hold themselves in readiness.

Meantime, President Polk determined to make a last attempt at

[19] On the whole Texas affair see Rives, *The United States and Mexico*, Vol. I; Eugene C. Barker, "President Jackson and the Texas Revolution," in *American Historical Review*, XII (1906–1907), 788–809; "Public Opinion in Texas Preceding the Revolution" in Amer. Hist. Assoc., *Annual Report*, (1911), pp. 219–228; Smith, *The Annexation of Texas*.

[20] Rives, "Mexican Diplomacy on the Eve of the War with the United States," in *Amer. Hist. Rev.*, XVIII (Jan. 1913), 275 ff.

pacific settlement. He sounded out the administration of President Herrera of Mexico and found it apparently disposed toward conciliation. He then sent John Slidell with instructions to negotiate for a readjustment of the boundary, offering Mexico, as compensation, what he considered a liberal sum of money, but on condition that a portion of the amount be retained for the satisfaction of long-standing claims of American citizens against the Mexican government. By the time Slidell arrived at Vera Cruz, Herrera found himself threatened by a serious revolution which denounced him, among other things, for his disposition to treat with the perfidious Yankees. This executive, therefore, timorously refused to open negotiations. A few weeks later he was overthrown by Peredes, whom Slidell approached early in March, 1846, in the interest of peace. But Paredes evinced marked hostility towards the United States and dismissed the American envoy in short order.

As soon as news of the probable failure of Slidell's mission reached Polk he ordered General Zachary Taylor, who had already been sent to defend Texas, to advance to the Rio Grande. Upon receipt of definite information that Peredes had refused to treat with the American envoy, Polk began to counsel with his Cabinet with reference to the preparation of a war message. All appeared to agree that "a message should be sent to Congress laying the whole subject before them and recommending that measures be adopted to take redress into our own hands for the aggravated wrongs done to our citizens in their persons and property by Mexico," but it was decided not to take this step until Slidell returned. At the end of the first week in May Slidell reached Washington and had a long interview with the President. On Saturday, May 9, the entire Cabinet, with the exception of George Bancroft, agreed that Polk should transmit his war message to Congress on the following Tuesday.

Four hours after the Cabinet adjourned a messenger arrived at the White House with the information that Mexican troops had fired on a detachment of Taylor's command in the region between the Nueces and the Rio Grande. This act may in a sense be taken as the formal opening of a war which Mexico had considered as existing ever since the annexation of Texas. Polk now planned his communication to Congress so as to play up this inflammatory incident and gain both congressional and popular support for the war. He could now say with considerable truth that war existed by Mexico's own act. But it is important to remember that he had determined upon hostilities before news of the shedding of American blood reached him, and that the alleged reason for the step was the maltreatment of American citizens residing in and having intercourse with Mexico. In other words, the executive departments of both governments were bent upon war. It was only a question of which would be first to begin hostilities, whether by formal proclamation or by an overt act without such a proclamation. To Mexico's announcement that the annexation of Texas would be considered as tantamount to war, she added the attack upon American troops in the Nueces-Rio Grande section. Mexico thus appears to have been the aggressor in the events immediately preceding the outbreak.[21]

If the Mexican army on the Rio Grande had not taken this fatal step at the time, it may be doubted whether Polk could have carried out his previous determination to resort to hostilities on account of injuries and outrages against American citizens. For several days prior to reaching its decision of May 9, the Cabinet and the President appeared to be waiting half in the hope that a clash might occur between the two armies which confronted each other along the Rio Grande. Had this clash not taken place it is possible that Congress would have refused to give its consent to a call to arms. It had declined to accept Jackson's recommendation of war over claims in 1837, and it had refused to advise a resort to hostilities later, when Van Buren had left the matter in its hands. Although numerous other grievances had accumulated, the Mexican government had agreed to a convention which had already imposed payment of more than two million dollars in satisfaction of American claimants, and some of the installments had been met.[22] It is true that liquidation of these awards had been suspended on account of the state of the Mexican treasury and irritation over the Texas question; it is likewise true that the growing expansion sentiment in the United States would have been cast into the balance in favor of war; but it may well be doubted, in view of the violent opposition subsequently manifested by the Whigs and the anti-slavery men, whether war would have been voted without the additional provocation of bloodshed on the southwestern frontier.

Once entered upon, the war necessarily became one of conquest. Americans had filed claims against Mexico to the amount of several millions and Polk had determined to force a settlement. These

---

[21] Polk, *Diary,* I, 319 ff.; Smith, *The War with Mexico,* I, 117–170. It should be remembered, however, that North American aggressiveness had been responsible for a war sentiment in Mexico which the Mexican government dared not defy. Some have argued, too, that the troops of the United States had no business in the Nueces-Rio Grande section.

[22] Kohl, *Claims as a Cause of the Mexican War,* gives a full treatment of this issue.

claims could be adjusted only by the acquisition of territory for the very simple reason that Mexico was bankrupt—had been for a quarter of a century; was likely to be indefinitely—and had nothing else with which to meet these obligations. It would be interesting to know, although it is impossible to determine, the relative importance of claims and territory in the train of reasoning and the rise of indignation which eventually led Polk to a war declaration. Slidell's secret instructions (November 10, 1845) show that the President, while anxious for California, was willing to settle the outstanding difficulties without demanding this region as a *sine qua non*.[23] But once having launched upon a war likely to entail considerable expense, he would necessarily be inclined to increase the territorial demands. Accordingly, Polk soon expressed in his diary the resolution to make the acquisition of Texas to the Rio Grande and of New Mexico and California indispensable conditions to the cessation of hostilities. At the same time, however, he evinced constant anxiety to bring the struggle to a speedy termination,[24] nor was he always scrupulous as to the methods he employed.

At first Polk based his hopes upon the return of Santa Anna to power in Mexico. Just before the outbreak of the war an agent of this wily schemer had approached Polk and informed him of Santa Anna's ardent desire to recover his lost authority and of his inclination, in case fortune smiled upon him, to effect arrangements which would probably prove mutually satisfactory. Polk appears to have been deeply impressed. Immediately after the declaration of war he dispatched a naval officer to Havana, Cuba, where Santa Anna was residing in exile, for the purpose of informing this fallen chief of the President's favorable disposition toward his restoration and of his willingness to issue an order that he be allowed to pass through the American blockade to Vera Cruz. Accordingly, in August, 1846, Santa Anna was permitted to return to Mexico, where he soon took command of the army and became president *ad interim* of the republic. One of the first diplomatic papers called to his notice was a peace proposal signed by Buchanan, the American Secretary of State. But peace negotiations were far from the mind of this soldier of fortune; and Polk had no recourse but the vigorous prosecution of the war.

In January and April, 1847, Polk made other vain efforts; and early in the following May Nicholas P. Trist, the peace commis-

---

[23] Buchanan, *Works* (Moore ed.), VI, 294 ff.
[24] Polk, *Diary,* June 30, 1846 and following, I, 495, *passim.*

sioner of the Washington government, was sent to Mexico. But it was not until the occupation of Mexico City had been effected, Santa Anna's army scattered, and this clever and treacherous schemer forced to abdicate, that negotiations could be entered upon with any probability of a favorable issue. And by this time the unprecedented conduct of the American commissioner had provoked Polk into authorizing his recall. Trist refused to take notice of a small matter like this, however, and proceeded to negotiate a treaty in accordance with the instructions which he had received almost a year before. This pact was completed and signed by the American and Mexican commissioners on February 2, 1848. It was reluctantly received by an embarrassed administration and soon accepted by the government of both countries. At last the war had ended. American claimants were now provided for, the Texas boundary was settled so far as Mexico was concerned, and the United States had acquired Spanish New Mexico and California.[25]

[25] Reeves, *American Diplomacy Under Tyler and Polk*, pp. 308–329; Smith, *The War with Mexico*, II, 233 ff.; McCormac, *Polk*, p. 373 ff.

CHAPTER II

THE UNFINISHED MISSION

THE territorial acquisitions of the Trist treaty by no means satisfied a large group in the United States. The sentiment of manifest
destiny which had already begun to show itself before the war
opened, increased under the stimulation of the victories won by the
American army in the fields of Mexico until an outcry was raised in
all parts of the country for the annexation of the entire republic.
The view of the Illinois *State Register,* that the struggle, once begun,
should not "close until the empire of Mexico, as well as Texas, is
[was] added to the territory of the Union," [1] gradually became the
conviction of an increasing number. In a short time "the whole
West seemed committed to the policy of a complete dismemberment
of Mexico." [2] The prominent papers of New York and the Washington *Union* soon fell into line. The New York *Sun* declared that
"providence had willed this war to unite and exalt both nations,
which result we now believe is as certain and inevitable as any event
in human history." [3] The *Post* violently protested against the withdrawal of the American troops and the resignation of "this beautiful
country to the custody of the ignorant cowards and profligate ruffians who have ruled it the last twenty-five years." [4] The *Union*
published with apparent approval the solemn address of the Hunker
Democrats of New York which urged the retention of all Mexico in
the following ruthless fashion: "The title of the Mexican government is a title by conquest from those who held it by conquest. If
we took it and held it by the same title, they could not complain.
Their title is legal and our title would also be legal." [5] Even an
anti-slavery organ like the *National Era* was in favor of the absorption of Mexico state by state as rapidly as, with free constitutions,
they should apply for admission into the Union. Calhoun, who

[1] December 27, 1844. As quoted by Dodd, "The West and the War with
Mexico," in The Illinois State Historical Society, *Transactions* (1912), p. 17.
[2] *Ibid.,* p. 18.
[3] Quoted in *ibid., loc. cit.*
[4] As paraphrased by *Niles' Register,* LXXII, 334.
[5] *Ibid.,* LXXIII, 391.

scanned the press with a critical and alarmed eye, exclaimed near the close of 1847: "Why you can hardly read a newspaper without finding it filled with speculation upon this subject." [6]

This desire for all of Mexico was entertained by many of the officers of the United States Army, whose return during the course of the war furnished occasion for loud proclamations of manifest destiny. In Calhoun's address, from which a quotation has just been given, he referred to a reception in honor of one of these officials. "The proceedings that took place in Ohio at a dinner given to one of the volunteer officers of the army returned from Mexico show conclusively," said Calhoun, "that the impression entertained by the persons present was, that our troops would never leave Mexico until they had conquered the whole country. This was the sentiment advanced by the officer and it was applauded by the assembly, and endorsed by the official paper of that State." General John A. Quitman came to Washington in December, 1847, and presented a plan for the permanent occupation of Mexico. He urged that it could be done without expense to the United States and without serious opposition on the part of the Mexican people.[7] At a great dinner given in Commodore Stockton's honor in Philadelphia on the last day of December, Stockton said: "Mexico . . . is prostrate at our feet,—we can afford to be magnanimous . . . I would with a magnanimous and kindly hand gather these wretched people within the fold of republicanism." And this sentiment received the applause not only of the banqueters, but also of a large part of the press throughout the country.[8]

Civilian addresses to many public gatherings contained the same views. The leading speaker at a New York Jackson dinner offered a toast to "A more perfect Union, embracing the whole of the North American continent." [9] Vice-President George M. Dallas, regretfully declaring his inability to attend a mass meeting of the New York Democratic electors, felt constrained to comment at length upon the Mexican War—with the view, of course, of having his comments published. Dallas declared, among other things, that he could "discover in our noble constitution of government nothing not perfectly equal to the vast task which may be assigned to it by the resistless force of events—the guardianship of a crowded and confederated continent." [10] Ashbel Smith told a Galveston audience

[6] Remarks of December 20, 1847, *Cong Globe*, 30 Cong., I Sess. p. 54.
[7] Clairborne's *Quitman*, II, 79.
[8] *Niles' Register*, LXXIII, 335.
[9] *Ibid.*, LXXIII, 336.
[10] *Ibid.*, LXXIII, 392.

that the war was "a part of the mission, of the destiny, allotted to the Anglo-Saxon race on this continent." "It is our destiny," said he, "to Americanize this continent. . . . Nor will there be a stay or hindrance until our institutions shall have extended to the Pacific Ocean on the West and the Isthmus of Darien on the South." [11] Elsewhere speakers drank to "Our Destiny—we may as well begin with Mexico," or to the more rhythmic sentiment:

> No pent up Utica contracts our powers,
> The whole boundless continent is ours.[12]

The opening of Congress in December, 1847, was expected to give rise to impassioned discussions of the war then in progress. Polk had pondered long over the territorial question in that part of his annual message which related to the continuance of hostilities. In April, 1847, Trist had been authorized to demand as an ultimatum the Rio Grande boundary and the cession of New Mexico and California. But Mexico's refusal of these terms had made a more vigorous prosecution of hostilities necessary and suggested the advisability of modifying the original instructions. On September 4, Polk informed his cabinet that "if Mexico continued obstinately to refuse to treat" he "was decidedly in favor of insisting on more territory than the provinces named." Three days later the President, Secretary Walker, and Attorney-General Clifford expressed themselves as desiring to acquire Tamaulipas in addition to the territory Trist had been authorized to procure. Secretary Buchanan, Postmaster-General Cave Johnson, and Secretary John Y. Mason opposed this proposal. It was suggested at the time that Trist should be recalled, but Polk would not consent to this step as yet. By October 5, Polk had changed his mind, however, and Trist's recall was ordered. The following month brought about at least one important change in the attitude of the cabinet. Buchanan, presumably having sensed the trend of the popular mind, began to advocate the seizure of a much larger portion of Mexican territory, embracing not only Tamaulipas, but all the region east of the Sierra Madre Mountains.[13]

As the time for the annual message (1847) approached, Polk requested Buchanan to prepare a paragraph setting forth the proposed course of the United States in case Mexico still persisted in her refusal to negotiate. The Cabinet agreed that Polk should say "that, failing to obtain a peace, we should continue to occupy

[11] As quoted by Kohl, *Claims as a Cause of the Mexican War*, p. 75.
[12] *Cong. Globe*, 30 Cong., 1 Sess., p. 362.
[13] Polk, *Diary*, September 4 and 7, October 5, November 9, 1847, III, 159-166, 185, 215-218.

Mexico with our troops & encourage and protect the friends of peace in Mexico to establish & maintain a Republican Government able and willing to make peace." But if peace could not be had in this way, still another step would have to be taken. What should the President advise? Buchanan stated in his draft that, in that event, "we must fulfill that destiny which Providence may have in store for both countries." To this expression Polk objected on the ground that it "would be too indefinite & that it would be avoiding my [his] constitutional responsibility," but his entire Cabinet, with the exception of Clifford, favored this expression. Walker persisted in his preference for Buchanan's draft, "avowing as a reason that he was for taking the whole of Mexico, if necessary, and he thought the construction placed on Mr. B.'s draft by a large majority of the people would be that it looked to that object." Thereupon, Polk responded with firmness that he was "not prepared to go to that extent," and furthermore that he desired to avoid all obscure expressions in this portion of his message.[13a] As finally revised, the crucial paragraph read: "If . . . we shall ultimately fail, then we shall have exhausted all honorable means in pursuit of peace, and must continue to occupy her country with our troops, taking the full measure of indemnity into our own hands, and must enforce the terms which our honor demands."[14] But in a previous passage Polk renounced the "all-of-Mexico" idea in very explicit terms. "It has never been contemplated by me," said Polk, "to make a permanent conquest of the republic of Mexico, or to annihilate her separate existence as an independent nation."[15]

The congressional session inaugurated by this message was destined to make frequent revelations of expansionist sentiment. Senator Cass professed to hope that it would not be necessary for Uncle Sam to devour the whole of Mexico, but he made it clear that he did not think such a repast would seriously injure the digestive organs of this tall and hungry gentleman.[16] Hannegan of Indiana resolved "That it may become necessary and proper, as it is within the constitutional capacity of this Government, for the United States to hold Mexico as a territorial appendage."[17] Representative F. P. Stanton of Tennessee believed that the "tendency of things was toward the subjugation of the whole of Mexico." This he

[13a] Ibid., November 9, 18, 20, and 23, 1847, III, 215–218, 225–230.
[14] Richardson, Messages and Papers, IV, 545.
[15] Ibid., IV, 544.
[16] Cong. Globe, 30 Cong., 1 Sess., p. 215. Speech of Jan. 20, 1848.
[17] Ibid., p. 136. Jan. 10, 1848.

considered "unavoidable" and indeed "desirable." [18] Dickinson of
New York said he feared no evil consequences from the acquisition
of northern Mexico and that the day was not far off when "all this
and much more" would be "realized." "New territory is spread out
for us to subdue and fertilize," said he; "new races are presented for
us to civilize, educate, and absorb; new triumphs for us to achieve
in the cause of freedom." [19] These and other similar expressions
were not unusual, but the new House and some of the members of
the Senate had been chosen when opposition to the war was at its
height and, consequently, the majority now appeared to be opposed
to the all-of-Mexico idea.

While Polk narrowly watched the flow of sentiment in Congress
the Trist treaty arrived in Washington. He was somewhat embarrassed and puzzled to know what should be done with the document. Two members of his Cabinet—Buchanan and Walker
—counseled its rejection; Mason, Marcy, Johnson, and Clifford
advised its acceptance. At length Polk decided to transmit the agreement to the Senate with the advice that they ratify it without modification of its territorial provisions. Polk was governed in his
action by expediency and a desire to avoid inconsistency. On more
than one occasion he had publicly declared against the total dismemberment of Mexico; he realized the immense value of the region
acquired by the treaty; and he feared that an attempt to secure more
under the conditions prevailing both in Mexico and in the United
States might result in the loss of everything gained thus far. It
was plain, however, that "this resolute Augustus, enlarger of empire," [20] was somewhat disappointed. If he had had his way, he
would perhaps have demanded the Sierra Madre as a boundary.
He submitted to stern necessity and awaited the action of the
Senate. [21]

[18] *Ibid.*, p. 135. Address of Jan. 10, 1848.
[19] *Ibid.*, p. 157 ff. Address of Jan. 12, 1848.
[20] Bourne, "The United States and Mexico, 1847–1848", in *The American
Historical Review* (1900), V, 501.
[21] Polk assigned the following reasons for submitting the Trist treaty:
". . . The treaty conformed on the main question of limits & boundary to the
instructions given to Mr. Trist in April last; and . . . though, if the treaty
was now to be made, I should demand more territory, perhaps to make the
Sierra Madre the line, yet it was doubtful whether this could be ever obtained
by the consent of Mexico. I looked, too, to the consequences of its rejection.
A majority of one branch of Congress is opposed to my administration; they
have falsely charged that the war was brought on and is continued by me with
a view to the conquest of Mexico; and if I were now to reject a Treaty made

The attitude of this body caused him no little uneasiness. For a time it looked as if the no-territory and the all-of-Mexico-or-none men would combine and defeat the treaty. At length, however, on March 10, the Senate, after having made several alterations, agreed to ratification by a vote of 38 to 14. Their action had been determined by territorial, slavery, and party issues. It now remained to secure the acceptance of the revised draft by the Mexican Congress and effect the final formalities necessary to give the document legal force.[22]

Meanwhile, Polk was offered an opportunity partially to satisfy the unappeased appetite for domain. The offer was presented by the agent of the state of Yucatán in Washington. Since the days of the war for Mexican independence this peninsula had experienced many vicissitudes. It had been a part of the empire of Iturbide until the dissolution of the latter, whereupon it had asserted its independence while awaiting developments. Eventually it had decided to cast its lot with the Mexican confederation, of which it continued a member until driven to revolt in 1840. It had soon regained its independence, along with Tabasco, however, and had entered into friendly relations with the Texas republic. In 1843 it had recognized the central government which was on the point of being established in Mexico and agreed, while maintaining local autonomy, to send delegates to the national congress. Three years later the peninsula had once more declared its independence and sent a representative to the United States. During the war between the United States and Mexico then drawing to a close, it had assumed, as far as possible, a neutral position.[23] But while this war was in progress a formidable Indian uprising had occurred and the government had been forced, in order to save the whites from extermination, to call for outside assistance. Accordingly, on March 7, Justo Sierra, the Yucatecan agent, had appealed to the United States.

Polk immediately took up the matter with his Cabinet. Buchanan

upon my own terms, as authorized in April last, . . . the probability is that Congress would not grant either men or money to prosecute the war. Should this be the result, the army now in Mexico would be constantly wasting and diminishing in numbers, and I might at last be compelled to withdraw them, and thus lose the two Provinces of New Mexico & Upper California. . . . Should the opponents of my administration succeed in carrying the next Presidential election, the great probability is that the country would lose all the advantages secured by this Treaty. . . . If I were now to reject my own terms, as offered in April last, I did not see how it was possible for my administration to be sustained." Polk, *Diary*, February 21, 1848, III, 347–348.

[22] Smith, *The War with Mexico*, II, 246–247.
[23] Rives, *The United States and Mexico*, I, 451, 462, II, 225.

and Walker were in favor of compliance with Yucatán's request and the President himself, after some hesitation, consented to authorize Commodore Perry to supply the white inhabitants with ammunition, provided he could be assured that it would not pass through Yucatán to other parts of Mexico.[24]

While the chief executive was meditating what course to take, Sierra was reiterating his importunities. At length, on April 25, he presented a formal communication from the governor of Yucatán with a resolution of the Yucatecan congress giving the governor discretionary power to act in the crisis. The communication offered "dominion and sovereignty" over the peninsula in return for military aid in saving the whites from extermination, and stated, also, that a similar offer had been made to Great Britain and to Spain.[25] Aroused by this prospect of foreign interference, Polk insisted in a cabinet council that the United States "could never agree to see Yucatan pass into the hands of a foreign monarchy to be possessed and colonized by them." Rather than permit this to take place, he thought the government should furnish the aid and protection asked. He believed, however, that such a step could be taken only with the consent of Congress.[26]

Accordingly, the President immediately began the preparation of a message on the subject. He took great pains to frame the communication in such manner as to obtain the support of his party, and as submitted to Congress on April 29, 1848, it probably had the approval of his cabinet as well as of various members of the House and the Senate.[27] After calling attention to the deplorable condition in Yucatán, and stating that the Yucatecan government had offered, in return for the succor requested, to transfer the "dominion and sovereignty of the peninsula" to the United States, the message pointed out the fact that similar offers had been made to England and Spain. Polk declared that while he did not propose "to recommend the adoption of any measure with a view to the acquisition of the 'dominion and sovereignty' over Yucatan," he was of the opinion that it would be contrary to the established policy of the United States to permit a "transfer of this 'dominion and sovereignty' either to Spain, Great Britain, or any other European power."[28] The President made no specific recommendations, but left the matter to the judgment of Congress. From his diary, one may nevertheless learn that

---

[24] Polk, *Diary*, III, 374, March 7, 1848.
[25] *Sen. Ex. Doc.* No. 40, 30 Cong., 1 Sess., pp. 16–19.
[26] Polk, *Diary*, III, 433, 434.
[27] *Ibid.*, III, 436–438.
[28] Richardson, *Messages*, IV, 581 ff.

he was in favor of annexing the region rather than see it become a British possession.[29]

The message occasioned a long debate in the Senate. It was referred to the Committee on Foreign Relations, from which, on May 4, Hannegan of Indiana reported a bill enabling the President to "take temporary military occupation of Yucatan." The supporters of the measure usually employed the humanitarian argument, but they put most stress upon the contention that such an act was expedient in order to prevent a violation of the Monroe Doctrine. Great Britain was, of course, the power mainly feared, and much attention was given to the encroachments of the English lion. The dispute over the Maine boundary, the Oregon question, British interference in Texas and California, British aggressions in Central and South America, British designs upon Cuba—all were reviewed. Hannegan declared that England "cherished the design to secure the most practicable route for an artificial means of communication between the two oceans," and in order to effect that object was "rapidly absorbing the entire isthmus." The seizure of Yucatán by Great Britain would, he thought, be inevitably followed by the seizure of Cuba. "Cuba," said he, "has been called the key of the Gulf. Yucatán and Cuba combined are the lock and the key. Place them in the hands of England, and she controls the mouth of the Mississippi, as absolutely as she controls the mouth of the Thames!"[30] Foote of Mississippi saw the matter in the same light, and he went a step further in sounding the British alarm. He expected that country to follow up the occupation of Yucatán by the immediate seizure of Cuba.

Long has England been sighing for this prize; and nothing has deterred her from seizing upon it but the declaration of Mr. Monroe and the well-founded belief which she entertained that that declaration would be maintained by arms, if necessary. Let her ascertain once that our government has resolved to cower before her, and to permit her to colonize again on this continent, and she will own Cuba and Mexico up to the Rio Grande, in less than ten years from the present time.[31]

As to what should be done with Yucatán, those who supported the bill appeared not to be in perfect agreement. Some of them seemed to favor the permanent retention of the peninsula. For instance, Hannegan, who, let it be noted, was chairman of the Com-

[29] "Mr. Walker was in favor of its ultimate annexation to the United States, & Mr. Buchanan opposed it. I concurred with Mr. Walker rather than see it fall into the hands of England." *Diary*, May 6, III, 444-445.

[30] *Cong. Globe*, 30 Cong., 1 Sess., App., p. 596.

[31] *Ibid.*, p. 602.

mittee on Foreign Relations, said there were motives which might lead to permanent occupation, and, personally, he meant to make no promises. Davis of Mississippi, while supporting the bill mainly on the ground that it was a necessary part of the President's war policy, said in regard to Cuba and Yucatán: "Whenever the question arises whether the United States shall seize these gates of entrance from the south and east, or allow them to pass into the possession of any maritime Power, I am . . . ready to declare that my step will be forward, and that the cape of Yucatan and the island of Cuba must be ours." [32]   Foote was in favor of purchasing Cuba, and, apparently, of permanently retaining Yucatán. [33]   Bagby of Alabama rejoiced in the opportunity of obtaining permanent hold of the peninsula, and he was confident that manifest destiny would soon lead to the annexation of all Mexico. He was certain that if the United States did not act in the matter, some other nation would, simply because of the inability of the Mexican people to rule themselves. "If there be a man alive [he said] who believes that Mexico ever has had, or ever will have, a well-regulated, . . . established Government, [he] must have some testimony on the subject that I have not." [34]

On the other hand, the message of the President and the wording of the bill expressly designated "temporary military occupation," and such expansionists as Dix of New York and Cass of Michigan denied any intention of permanently holding Yucatán. The former thought that the occupation of a country in order to ward off European designs would be unwise except in "very extraordinary circumstances," and for this reason he proposed to amend the bill so as to make it call for the aid of the United States given in concurrence with the "State of Yucatan." [35]   The latter declared that the United States government was to go there not for conquest but for protection; after the fulfillment of this duty it could "retire with safety and with honor." [36]   Houston of Texas apparently agreed with Cass, but he thought the United States should be remunerated for its trouble by "commercial concessions." [37]

The chief arguments introduced by the opponents of the bill were that it would be a violation of the policies of neutrality and non-intervention, and that it would interfere with the negotiations pend-

[32] *Ibid.*, p. 599.
[33] *Ibid.*, p. 592.
[34] *Ibid.*, p. 636.
[35] *Ibid.*, p. 637.
[36] *Ibid.*, p. 613 ff.
[37] *Ibid.*, p. 604.

ing with the Mexican republic. Moreover, mild interpretations of the Monroe Doctrine were set forth. As construed by Calhoun, the sole survivor of the cabinet of the president for whom the policy was named, it became a harmless declamation—a simple and friendly declaration of the desires of the United States, with "not a word . . . in reference to resistance." With this construction Niles of Connecticut was virtually in agreement. According to his understanding of the matter, Monroe meant by the European "system" not monarchy, but the combination of powers known as the Holy Alliance "which divided and disposed of the small states of Europe according to their pleasure." Monroe had been opposed to the extension of the operations of this system to the western hemisphere. This did not mean, however, that the United States should assume the duty of controlling the destiny of the nations here, or of defending them from all European interference.

Both Calhoun and Niles considered the fear of British encroachments groundless. In line with this idea, also, Miller of New Jersey said that the "cry of England's interference with the nations on this continent" had "lost its effect on" him. This fear, "real or affected," had been expressed constantly for the last six years, and it had done much, he said, to acquire foreign territory. It commenced with the annexation of Texas, it had been raised in reference to Oregon, it served as an excuse for revolutionizing and annexing California and detaining the army of the United States in Mexico, and now it was used to justify the occupation of Yucatán! If it were so necessary to keep England out of this hemisphere, the proper method of obtaining this end would be an open, direct warning. Busy with her own affairs as she was, England would not risk a war with the United States over a difficulty arising on this side of the Atlantic.[38]

Was there really an ulterior and far-reaching design concealed in this movement for sending troops into Yucatán? Professor Dodd, in a brilliant article, suggests that this is probable.[39] He contends that the expansionists who had accepted with reluctance the—what appeared to them to be—inadequate acquisitions of the Guadalupe Hidalgo treaty, had received news that the European nations hitherto so eager to block the expansion of the United States were now so absorbed in their own difficulties that they were powerless to intervene, and that these expansionists had accordingly resolved to re-open the Mexican war with the view of absorbing the entire

[38] *Ibid.*, pp. 625–630, *passim.*
[39] Dodd, "The West and the War with Mexico," *loc. cit.*

country. There are indications that this may have been true. Hannegan, whom Polk knew to be "bent on holding all Mexico," was given charge of the Senate bill making provision for carrying out the President's recommendation. Senator Cass's remark to the effect that "Providence has placed us, in some measure, at the head of the republic of this continent and there never has [had] been a better opportunity offered to any nation to fulfill the high duty confided to it than the present," [40] appears to be significant. Somewhat suspicious, too, are the words of Sam Houston, who certainly was not ignorant of European jealousy of the United States. This veteran inquired of the Senate: "When again will the state of Europe be found so auspicious to the upbuilding of free institutions on this continent?" "Europe is convulsed," he added; "England has to guard her own position . . . We are left to the accomplishment of the great object of our mission here." [41] It may be noted also that those who opposed the bill expressed the fear that it would lead to the renewal of hostilities and the absorption of all Mexico. But the whole affair remains purely a matter for speculation, for news of an armistice between the opposing forces in Yucatán reached the United States before the bill came to a vote and while Senators were still indulging in their oratory. And moreover, there is a further incident that Dodd failed to consider, which renders his theory of premeditated aggression a very doubtful one, so far as President Polk was concerned. Early in August, 1848 (just three months after Polk's Yucatán move and while Europe was still "convulsed"), the Mexican government sent an agent to Washington for the purpose of urging the United States to dispatch a thousand troops to assist Mexico in the maintenance of order, and Polk declined to consider the step. [42]

The Yucatán episode is nevertheless not without its importance for the historian. Aside from giving rise to new pronouncements on the Monroe Doctrine, it had revealed most of the forces which were to shape the Mexican policy of the United States for the next decade. This policy was to be characterized by an eagerness to annex a part or the whole of Mexico, an eagerness created by land hunger, sincere or alleged fear of European designs upon the region, and real or pretended sympathy for the Mexicans themselves—a strange mixture of greed, benevolence, and apprehension.

[40] Globe, 30 Cong., 1 Sess., App., p. 591.
[41] Ibid., p. 604.
[42] The debate on Yucatán consumed a good portion of the time of the Senate from May 4 to May 17, 1848. See Globe, as cited, pp. 712, passim, and App., 591, passim; Clifford, Nathan Clifford, p. 197 ff.

Mexico had been saved from annihilation by a very narrow margin—saved, it may well be, only by the Trist treaty, the choice of members of the United States Congress more than a year before the beginning of their actual service, the uncompromising stand of Polk, and the timely patching up of difficulties by the belligerents in Yucatán. The expansionists "retired chagrined from the field nearly won but lost by a fumble." [43]

Not for this reason, however, did their ardor for territory abate. The most radical of the group soon adopted the name "Young America." Those who were unwilling to go their full length in imperialistic enterprises were called "Old Fogies." Newspapers, periodicals, and political orators continued to expatiate upon the greatness and destiny of their country. The bitter dispute over the disposition of the soil acquired by the recent war and the possibility that more territory might lead to the disruption of the Union were powerless to silence them. In June, 1852, *The Democratic Review*, the chief organ of Young America, interpreted one of the planks in the Democratic platform to mean the acquisition of "Cuba and all the islands on the main Gulf; . . . Canada and all North at the proper time; . . . the re-assertion, vigorously and practically, of the Monroe Doctrine in Central America and on the Isthmus, both of Tehuantepec and Granada; . . . full expansion, North, South, West, and moreover East. . . ." [44] Equally extravagant in their expressions were the *Herald* and the *Sun* of New York. The former, commenting upon the tripartite agreement alleged to have been proposed by France and England in respect to Mexico, asked if it would be advisable for the United States to enter into an alliance which might prevent the extension of its territory "from the Arctic Ocean to the isthmus of Darien." The editor then expressed his confident anticipation that before the end of the century "every sea that laves the shores of North America will [would] mirror the stars and stripes." [45] Other publications which gave utterance to similar sentiments were the *United States Review*, *De Bow's Review*, the New York *Times*, the Washington *Republic*, the *Delta*, the *Crescent*, and the *Picayune* of New Orleans, some of the most important of the California papers, and, in fact, a large part of the Democratic press in general.

Indeed, some of the journals which pretended to look upon expansion with a certain amount of disfavor considered it inevitable.

[43] Dodd, *op. et loc. cit.*, p. 23.
[44] XXXI, 492.
[45] Sept. 9, 1852. Quoted in *El Universal*, 12 de octubre de 1852.

One of these was the *Commercial Advertiser*, a Whig paper of New York. This journal declared that although such an eventuality was desirable neither on the part of Mexico nor of the United States, the annihilation of the former as an independent power and its annexation to the latter was inevitable.[46] The *Post* of the same city, which now professed to have given up its expansionist tendency, ventured the opinion that the greater part of Mexico would fall into the hands of the Union, however unwise such an augmentation of the territory of the United States might be.[47]

The halls of Congress continued to resound with just as exaggerated expressions of destiny as could be found in the periodicals of the time. In 1853, Douglas of Illinois, while opposing the Clayton-Bulwer Treaty, exclaimed that "you may make as many treaties as you please to fetter the limits of this giant Republic, and she will burst them all from her, and her course will be onward to a limit which I will not venture to prescribe. . ."[48] In 1855 Boyce of South Carolina told the House that "a feverish impatience" seemed to him to be seizing upon the people of the United States: "In some quarters the cry is for the Canadas . . ."; in others, for the "Sandwich Islands; some are looking to another partition of Mexico; others are looking to the regions watered by the mighty Amazon; more are bent upon the acquisition of Cuba, and some have such inordinate stomachs that they are willing to swallow up the entire continent [hemisphere?]."[49] At about the same time Weller of California expressed the firm belief that "our destiny is to cover this continent, and although the intrigues of foreign Governments and the action of our own may *impede,* they cannot prevent its ultimate accomplishment."[50] Three years later President Buchanan declared in a message to Congress: "It is, beyond question, the destiny of our race to spread themselves over the continent of North America, and this at no distant day. . . . The tide of emigrants will [then] flow south, and nothing can eventually arrest its progress."[51] In discussing this communication Douglas showed that he was still desirous of seeing the boundaries of his country "extended gradually and steadily," as rapidly as the countries acquired could be Americanized,[52] while Hawkins of Florida declared

[46] Quoted in *El Universal,* 10 de agosto de 1851.
[47] Quoted in *El Omnibus,* 23 de deciembre de 1853.
[48] *Cong. Globe,* 32 Cong., 2 Sess., App., p. 262.
[49] *Ibid.,* 33 Cong., 2 Sess., App., p. 91 ff.
[50] *Ibid.,* 34 Cong., 1 Sess., p. 110.
[51] Buchanan, *Works,* X, 174.
[52] *Cong. Globe,* 35 Cong., 1 Sess., p. 223.

that the territorial expansion of the United States would be "inevitably southward" and it was no more possible to stop it than to prevent the "expansion of steam or powder in a state of ignition." [53]

It must be noted, however, that the slavery issue often added zest to these outbursts. For instance, Representative Lamar of Mississippi said that he desired, if it could be done consistent with the honor of his country, "to plant American liberty with southern institutions upon every inch of American soil"; [54] and Thayer of Massachusetts had the expanding free population of the North in mind when he said: "Necessity knows no law. We must go somewhere. . . . The bounding billows of the western tide of our immigration are dashing fiercely against the base of the Rocky Mountains. . . . [It cannot be checked.] This progress must be onward, and we *must* have territory. . . . I have no doubt we will have Central America in this Government, and all between this and Central America also." [55]

The sectional factor became even more prominent in two bombastic speeches delivered in 1859. Representative Cox of Ohio declared: "We have become a Colossus on this continent, with a strength and stride that will and must be heeded. With our domestic policy as to local governments established, we can go and Americanize this continent and make it what providence intends it shall become. . . ." [56] Speaking in similar but even more exaggerated strain, Reuben Davis of Mississippi burst forth: "Our vessel of State rides upon a tide swollen and even enraged by mighty events, and no anchor can stay it . . . If we will leave all the subjects in which the people are directly interested to the States, then we may expand so as to include the whole world. Mexico, Central America, South America, Cuba, the West India Islands, and even England and France [we] might annex without inconvenience or prejudice, allowing them with their local Legislatures to regulate their local affairs in their own way. And this, Sir, is the mission of the Republic and its ultimate destiny." [57]

These illustrations will be sufficient to indicate the prevalence of the spirit of expansion during the decade preceding the Civil War. It did not, of course, pervade the entire nation; the growing desire to prevent the extension of slavery cooled the ardor of some of the

[53] *Ibid.*, App., pp. 461–463.
[54] *Ibid.*, App., p. 50.
[55] *Ibid.*, p. 228.
[56] *Ibid.*, 35 Cong., 2 Sess., p. 430 ff.
[57] *Ibid.*, p. 704.

northern expansionists for territory south of Mason and Dixon's line, while the possibility that the acquisition of more territory might disrupt the Union may have made others cautious; but it was especially strong in the Democratic party, and this party had charge of the foreign affairs of the country during most of the manifest destiny period. In fact, it would perhaps not be an exaggeration to assert that the emotion of manifest destiny underlay, and in a measure shaped, the entire foreign policy of the years between 1837 and 1861.

But this is not to say that the government of the United States, as likewise the people in general, did not prefer to obtain territory by peaceful purchase if possible; that, failing in this, they would have resorted to violence without provocation in order to gain their object; or that, in the case of Mexico, violent methods would have been threatened and actually employed had the country been the scene of a vigorous civilization and a stable government equal to the fulfillment of its obligations, domestic and foreign. So far as the Mexican republic was concerned, manifest destiny was an ever-present force tending to magnify the injuries which were inflicted upon the citizens of the United States, to arouse in Mexico a bitterness and suspicion which did much to prevent a calm and fair settlement of the questions at issue, and to intensify the fear, on the part of the United States, that European powers might intervene in the neighboring republic.

Moreover, the possibility of European intrusion in the western hemisphere appears to have continued to exert considerable influence upon the policy of the United States for more than a decade subsequent to the Mexican War. Of course it may often have been used for political purposes or as a cloak to cover expansionist designs: manifest destiny never pointed to the acquisition of a region so unmistakably as when undemocratic, conservative Europe revealed an inclination to interfere or to absorb; but one who is familiar with the political literature of the time cannot escape the feeling that the fear of Europe may have been real to some of the statesmen and publicists of the United States. And what more effective means of keeping Europe out of Mexico was there than the seizure of the country for themselves?

The threat of foreign intervention in the new world which had called forth the Monroe Doctrine had almost ceased to attract attention for a decade after 1826; but it will be recalled that in the early forties the whole question was suddenly renewed; and it continued to be a source of great disturbance for more than a quarter of a century, ending at last in the worst infringement the doctrine

has ever suffered. During this time the ubiquitous British lion
made his appearance on the borders of Maine; in Texas, Oregon,
and California; in Hawaii, Cuba, and Santo Domingo; in Central
and South America. During this time, likewise, the French seemed
to reveal a desire to take a hand in the affairs of the western world;
and the suspicions regarding the colonial designs of Louis Napoleon
on this side of the Atlantic were confirmed by the proposed
tripartite agreement regarding Cuba, as well as by reports of his
interference in Santo Domingo, Hawaii, Central America, and elsewhere. The *rapprochement* between England and France (1854)
regarding the Near Eastern Question created apprehension in the
United States where it was feared that these two powers might now
endeavor jointly to control the destiny of America as well as of Europe. Should they decide upon such a step, of course the aid of
Spain, whose American possessions were thought to be threatened
by the United States, could be counted upon.[58]

European intervention in Mexico did not actually occur until near
the close of 1861, but uneasiness had been felt in the United States
regarding the possibility of such a step for a long time. Political
disorders in Mexico with resulting violence to foreign subjects residing there and consequent inability to meet financial obligations,
furnished in European countries a perennial excuse; and it was
feared that a majority of the people of Mexico would eventually
despair of their capacity for self-government and call in aid from
Europe. Early in 1845 William R. King had written from Paris
that England and France were in concert to prevent the annexation
of Texas,[59] Slidell had reported from Mexico in 1846 that there were
possibly designs on the part of several European powers to establish
a monarchy there, and Buchanan thought he had received information which corroborated the statement. In regard to the prospective attitude of the political elements in Mexico with reference to a
monarch, Buchanan said: "It is supposed that the clergy would
generally favor such a project and that a considerable party already
exists among the people which would give it their countenance and
support. It is believed by many that this party will continue to

[58] For general discussions of the foreign relations of the period see Hart,
The Monroe Doctrine; Smith, *Parties and Slavery;* Fish, *American Diplomacy;*
Johnson, *America's Foreign Relations.* An adequate idea of this apprehen-
siveness may be obtained perhaps in no better way than by consulting Buchanan,
Works (Moore ed.), index under Great Britain, France, Spain; and *Cong.
Globe,* 1848–1860, index under Cuba, Central America, Clayton-Bulwer
Treaty, etc.

[59] Buchanan, *Works,* VI, 127.

increase in consequence of the several revolutions which may afflict that country, until at length a majority of the people will be willing to throw themselves into the arms of a monarch for security and protection." [60]

Polk was of the opinion that Great Britain had interfered to prevent Mexico from receiving Slidell (in 1846) and that it was her purpose to seize California.[61] Moreover, after the outbreak of the Mexican War, many American statesmen felt that both England and France were friendly to Mexico.[62] In case the victory of the United States should be incomplete or long delayed, they expected interference from these powers. The Senators from New York were especially apprehensive. On January 12, 1848, Dickinson declared that the natural resources of Mexico presented a "tempting occasion for European rapacity to revive upon this continent their execrable proposal to regulate the balance of power." If the army of the United States should be withdrawn before victory was complete, gentlemen might "expect to see some supernumerary of the House of Bourbon placed" at the head of the Mexican government "to play automaton to the British Cabinet." [63] Two weeks later Senator Dix went fully into the whole question. He spoke of a book written by an *attaché* of the French legation in Mexico, and published under the "auspices" of Marshal Soult, President of the French Council, and of M. Guizot, Minister of Foreign Affairs. The topics the work was supposed to treat were Oregon and California, but it had much to say about European policy in the Western Hemisphere, and made reference to the establishment of a European monarchy in Mexico as a project calculated to "put an end to the divisions and annihilate the factions which desolated that beautiful country." Dix also referred at length to the balance of power idea suggested by Guizot in the French Chamber of Deputies in 1845; and he presented in a note to his published speech documents indicating that Spain had recently spent large sums of money in the interest of monarchy in Mexico.[64] During the year 1848, likewise, Senator Foote of Mississippi gave utterance, as has been noted, to the foreboding that unless the United States presented a bold front, England would own,

[60] *Ibid.*, VI, 405.
[61] *Diary*, I, 337.
[62] Buchanan, *op. et loc. cit.*
[63] *Cong. Globe*, 30 Cong., 1 Sess., pp. 157–160.
[64] *Ibid.*, App., p. 176 ff. The publication to which Dix referred was an account of the travels of Duflot de Morfras in Oregon and California. Guizot thought it was the duty of France to preserve the balance of power between the United States, British America, and Spanish America.

within ten years, not only Cuba, but Mexico "all the way up to the Rio Grande." [65]

Such apprehensions continued to be expressed right down to the time when European intervention became a reality. Omitting the constant alarms sounded by such publications as the New York *Herald* and *Sun*, the *Alta California*, the *Picayune* and *Delta* of New Orleans, and the *Democratic Review*, it will be sufficient for present purposes to confine attention to statements of a more or less official nature. In 1852 and 1853 three Senators, at least, scented French designs in Mexico, the occasion for the suspicion being the filibustering schemes of the French element in California. W. M. Gwin, one of the Senators from that state, was disturbed by the report that these Frenchmen had taken possession of Sonora with the intention of holding it "as a province of the French Empire." [66] Douglas of Illinois declared that, in view of the recent events in northern Mexico, he was unwilling to commit himself to any policy which would tie his hands in advance.[67] Cass of Michigan seemed to be most perturbed of all. He quoted from French sources evidence which he thought confirmed the opinion that the filibusters had the backing of the French government, and declared that had their attempt in Sonora succeeded, that region would soon have passed into the hands of the French. Since it failed, its true history would probably not be known until read "in another attempt, and perhaps a successful one." Cass was of the opinion, moreover, that if Louis Napoleon desired to find employment for his army and navy in the New World, he would have the "aid of Europe provided he takes [took] steps which promise [d] to result in curbing the spirit, or crippling the resources and setting bounds to the extension of the United States." [68] In 1856 Senator Bell of Tennessee declared that a group in the United States was expecting the "better class of Mexican inhabitants" to appeal to some foreign power to assume the task of governing the country, Spain with the backing of England and France being a possibility; [69] while in 1858 a congressman declared with regard to England, that "any day, no man in the republic would be astonished to learn that she had treated for Yucatan, for Vera Cruz,

[65] *Ibid.*, p. 172. For further instances of this apprehension, see *Ibid.*, 29 Cong. 1 Sess., App., pp. 385-395, 681-695, 950-955; 30 Cong. 1 Sess., App., pp. 137-146.

[66] *Cong. Globe*, 30 Cong., 2 Sess., p. 146.

[67] *Ibid.*, p. 172.

[68] *Ibid.*, pp. 158-159, App., pp. 91-95.

[69] *Cong. Globe*, 34 Cong., 1 Sess., App., pp. 114-115.

or half of the Mexican Republic." [70] Lastly, the despatches from
the diplomatic agents of the United States in Mexico during the
period contained frequent references to "anticipated, projected, or
impending intervention." [71]

Political disorders in Mexico constitute another factor which, as
already suggested, should not be overlooked in this connection. Indeed, this factor must be emphasized if a correct view of the matter
is to be had. The achievement of Mexican independence was followed by forty years of almost constant revolution. From 1822 to
1867 the form of government changed nine times and the country
was ruled by thirty-nine different administrations, which, for the
most part, gained their power by violence and retained it only so
long as they had superior physical force at their command. It is
not necessary here to attempt an explanation of the causes of these
convulsions. In the main the struggle was one between the Conservatives, who, aided and dominated by the clergy, sought to establish a highly centralized government—or even a monarchy
—and the Liberals, who desired federal republican institutions.
Moreover, the situation was complicated by selfishness and greed for
power on the part of the leaders of both factions. Whatever the
causes, the struggle was long and bitter, and prospects of stability
were never more unpromising than during the middle of the nineteenth century.[72]

This chaotic condition tended to influence American policy toward
Mexico by giving plausibility to the contention, in the United States,
that the annexation of a part or even the whole of the country would
be a benevolent act. In 1848, before the Mexican War had been
completed, Stanton of Tennessee predicted that the Mexican people
would in their souls regret the hour when the troops of the United
States were withdrawn.[73] Three years later the New York *Sun*
declared that until Mexico "is completely absorbed by the United
States, and its . . . inhabitants placed under our truly republican
institutions, it will enjoy neither peace nor prosperity." It then
dwelt at length upon the greatness and progress of the American
people, and concluded with the remark that this "army of free

[70] *Ibid.*, 35 Cong., 1 Sess., App., p. 461.
[71] J. M. Callahan, "Evolution of Seward's Mexican Policy," in West Virginia University, *Studies in American History*, Series I, Nos. 4, 5, and 6, p. 1.
See also *post*, Ch. XI.
[72] M. Romero, *The United States and Mexico*, p. 339 ff.; H. H. Bancroft,
History of Mexico, V., 557 ff.
[73] *Cong. Globe*, 30 Cong., 1 Sess., p. 135.

men" could not afford to "permit Mexico long to remain in the condition of a poor, miserable, and abandoned state"; for Mexico stood
first in the path which destiny had marked out for them.[74] Similar
sentiments were expressed by the New York *Herald*, the *Delta* and
Picayune of New Orleans, and the *Alta California*. The *Herald*
remarked that a period of thirty years was very ample time to
determine whether the Mexicans were capable of self-government.
The experiment had proceeded from bad to worse until the country
had reached a condition which excited the pity and impelled the
"intervention of its more fortunate neighbors, to the end of furnishing some alleviation." [75] The *Alta California* declared that the
disturbances in Mexico furnished almost conclusive proof that its
people were "totally incapable of self-government," and urged that
the proper solution of the situation would be complete subjugation
to American laws and American rule.[76]

Similar opinions were expressed by statesmen after the close of
the Mexican War. In 1853 Representative Lane of Oregon declared
that the sooner the Mexican states came into the American Union
the better "for them and for the rest of mankind." [77] At about the
same time Douglas gave notice in the Senate that he would not be
surprised to see Mexican affairs come to such a state as to demand
intervention from motives of humanity as well as of national security.[78] In the following year Gerritt Smith of New York exclaimed:
"Poor Mexico needs to be brought under radically transforming
influences. Indeed, she is perishing for the lack of them. It is
for her life that she cease to be an independent nation, and not
only so, but . . . that she become a part of our nation. For say
what we will of its faults and its crimes, . . . our nation is the
mightiest of all civilizing and renovating agencies . . ." [79] John
Forsyth, who served as minister of the United States to Mexico in
the late fifties, thought that the only hope for Mexico's stability lay
in an alliance with the republic to the north whereby there would be
made possible "the infusion of Americans into the Mexican army." [80]
In February, 1858, Houston of Texas dwelt at some length upon
the incapacity and poverty of the Spanish American people, declar-

---

[74] June 9, 1851, as quoted in *El Universal*, 19 de julio de 1851.
[75] Quoted in *El Universal*, 8 de deciembre de 1852.
[76] February 6 and 7, 1853.
[77] Speech of January 4, 1853, *Cong. Globe*, 32 Cong., 2 Sess., p. 211.
[78] Speech of February 14, 1853, *Ibid.*, p. 172.
[79] Speech of June 27, 1854, *Cong. Globe*, 33 Cong., 1 Sess., p. 1016.
[80] Callahan, "The Mexican Policy of Southern Leaders under Buchanan's
Administration," Am. Hist. Assoc., *Ann. Rept.* (1910), p. 137.

ing in the course of his remarks that "the day is coming when an influence which is now in the East, must pass off to the West and the South, and control and enlighten these people." [81] Lastly, President Buchanan based his proposed intervention in 1859 and 1860 partially upon humanitarian motives, [82] while Senator Toombs of Georgia put the matter upon the high plane of justice, to Mexico when he said, in 1859, that the Mexicans "had a right" to the institution of the United States at the close of the Mexican War, and that if these institutions had been given them then, subsequent years of suffering and misfortune would have been avoided. [83]

The political disorders of Mexico thus furnished the expansionists a benevolent argument for their designs. Indeed, they did more. They continued to give rise to irritating exactions from and injuries to American citizens residing in and having intercourse with Mexico; citizens of other countries suffered in a similar way; and the Mexican treasury became bankrupt, while the Mexican highways and frontiers remained unprotected. Injuries to Europeans residing in Mexico and the inability of the Mexican government to pay off European debts caused especial uneasiness in the United States; for it was feared that if European intervention ever took place such complaints would be one justification for this step. And the injuries to American citizens as well as the possibility of European interference furnished motives for such aggressive proposals as that of Polk regarding Yucatán in 1848 and that of Buchanan a decade later.

The reaction of the Mexican government and public to these proclamations of manifest destiny and discussions of the debility and probable fate of Mexico is a topic which has been too little considered. It has already been noted that the first Mexican agents at Washington expressed suspicion that the United States entertained designs upon Texas—a suspicion aroused by the claims which certain statesmen had made to that province as a part of Louisiana, as well as by assertions of a former Spanish minister at Washington to the effect that the North Americans believed their dominion was to extend to the isthmus of Panama at an early day, and ultimately to all the regions of the New World. [84] It should also be noted that by 1830 the Mexican Secretary of Foreign Affairs had become convinced that the government and the people

[81] *Cong. Globe,* 35 Cong. 1 Sess., pp. 736–737.
[82] Buchanan, *Works,* X, 357.
[83] Speech of January 24, 1859, *Cong. Globe,* 35 Cong., 2 Sess., pp. 541–542.
[84] W. R. Manning, *Early Diplomatic Relations between the United States and Mexico,* p. 1 ff.

of the United States had entered into a sort of conspiracy whereby the latter, as traders and colonists, were to serve as an entering wedge for territorial aggrandizement. In this manner, it was alleged, the Floridas had been obtained and in this fashion Texas was to be seized.[85] From such a conviction proceeded most of those restrictive measures which brought about the Texas revolution. The events connected with that revolution and the later annexation of the newly formed republic served as further confirmation of the suspicions already entertained and virtually rendered the Mexican war of 1846–1848 inevitable.

It was contended that the magnanimity shown during the Mexican War and the brief reign of order which the American occupation gave Mexico, won the friendship of the country to such an extent that many Mexicans were desirous that American control should continue. Nicholas P. Trist, while negotiating a treaty which should put an end to that war, thought that the *Puros,* or radical party, in Mexico opposed the interruption of hostilities because it was hoped that annexation to the United States might eventually be accomplished.[86] Much also was made of the fact that a committee of prominent Mexicans had offered General Scott a large sum of money to remain in Mexico and organize a government with the view of ultimate annexation to the Anglo-American Union.[87] It was likewise asserted that when General Quitman, who had won the friendship of the Mexicans by his excellent administration of Mexico City during the American occupation, was raising his Cuban expedition, "many persons in Mexico" urged him to direct his forces towards their country.[88] In October, 1851, the Minister of the United States in Mexico, writing in regard to pending negotiations relating to Tehuantepec, said that a "very large number" from all political parties in Mexico opposed a treaty with reference to the subject "under the confident expectation that its rejection may [might] lead to a rupture between the two countries, and in that event, it is [was] hoped, the annexation of Mexico to the United States would follow." [89] In 1853, the *Alta California* made the dis-

---

[85] As expressed in a quotation given by C. R. Fish, *American Diplomacy,* pp. 243–244.

[86] Trist to Buchanan, Dec. 29, 1847, *Senate Ex. Doc.* No. 52, 30 Cong., 1 Sess. (Ser. 509), pp. 274–80; Rives, *The United States and Mexico, 1821–48,* II, pp. 643–644.

[87] Scott refers to the matter in his *Memoirs,* II, 581–582.

[88] The N. Y. *Herald* reviewed the whole affair in 1857, and the editorial was quoted in *La Nación,* 27 de februar de 1857.

[89] Letcher to Webster, Oct. 29, 1851. *Sen. Ex. Doc.* No. 97, 32 Cong., 1 Sess. (Ser. 621), p. 102.

covery from Mexican newspapers that many of the "business men and land owners" were in favor of annexation, though they did not "say so openly"; [90] and about the same time the *Herald* of New York published a letter purporting to have been written by ex-President Arista, in which he asserted that Mexico would find in the American Union not only an escape from its political ills, but an "inexhaustible fountain of riches and prosperity." [91] Consul John Black, who had lived in Mexico City many years, wrote to Buchanan in 1857 that "many of the people of property and standing" in Mexico, "worn out and tired by these continual revolutions . . . and fully satisfied that they are not capable of governing themselves, . . . would willingly throw themselves and country into the arms of the United States." [92] Lastly, Sam Houston declared in 1860 that an invasion of Mexico led by himself at any time during the past three years for the purpose of establishing a protectorate, would have been welcomed and supported by a "large portion of the Mexican population." [93]

Houston probably had the northern frontier of Mexico in mind, for it was in respect to the states of this region that the annexationists were most hopeful. W. H. Seward expressed the opinion on one occasion (1853) that just as fast as these states were "severed from the Mexican stock," they would seek annexation to the United States. [94] Forsyth wrote from Mexico in 1857 that nothing but the distrust aroused by the filibustering raids of the Anglo-Americans had "prevented the Mexican states bordering upon the United States—especially like those of Sonora and Chihuahua, overrun by the savages and receiving no protection from the Mexican government—from . . . seeking in annexation with us that security of life and property of which they are now wholly destitute." [95] Three years later, A. Navarro of Texas, who had been sent as a commissioner to investigate disturbances along the Mexican border, reported that "many of the most intelligent men of Tamaulipas regarded a protectorate as the only means by which Mexico can [could] be redeemed from the reign of outlaws and petty tyrants." [96]

[90] June 21, 1853.
[91] Genaro García, *Documentos . . . para la historia de México,* XXVI, 65.
[92] Black to Buchanan, Nov. 16, 1857, Consular Letters, Mexico, Vol. 10.
[93] Houston to Floyd, March 12, 1860, *House Ex. Doc.* No. 52, 36 Cong., 1 Sess. (Ser. 1050), pp. 140–142.
[94] *Cong. Globe,* 32 Cong., 2 Sess., p. 126.
[95] Forsyth to Cass, April 24, 1857, *House Ex. Doc.* No. 34, 35 Cong., 1 Sess. (Ser. 955), pp. 2–3.
[96] Navarro to Houston, Jan. 31, 1860, *ibid.,* No. 52, 36 Cong. 1 Sess., pp. 17–18.

Contemporaneously, Simeon Hart wrote from Chihuahua in joyful anticipation that this state would, "by her congress, ask . . . for annexation to us." [97]

What, in fact, was the attitude of this prospective victim of the redemptive absorption of the Anglo-Saxon? All these rumors seem to indicate that the United States must have had some friends in Mexico at the time, but since the reports of Mexican desire for incorporation in the American Union came mainly from the expansionists, one is inclined to feel that the wish may have been father to the thought. Attitude toward the United States was indeed an element in Mexican politics, but discussions of the matter consisted mainly of reciprocal charges and mutual denials of desire for annexation. So far as has been ascertained no candidate, state or national, ever sought support on the ground that he favored such a step. As a matter of fact, one of the severest arraignments of political enemies was the accusation that they harbored such a design. The Conservatives called the Liberals "annexationists," and the latter could find no better retort than to deny the charge and hurl it back at their opponents.

In 1851 El Universal, the leading Conservative newspaper, used this weapon against General Arista,[98] and two years later this general, who had then lost his power, complained that his opponents had forged a letter in which he had been represented as declaring in favor of joining the North American Union.[99] The accusation that they were intending to annex Mexico to the United States was made in 1855, against the group who were fighting under the Plan of Auytla. A document was circulated which purported to be a treaty between the insurgents and the United States providing for the establishment of a protectorate over Mexico; and the state of Mexican public opinion is revealed by the fact that these leaders requested James Gadsden, the American Minister, to publish a statement denying that such an arrangement had been made.[100] The opponents of this revolution even went so far as to accuse its champions of undue friendship for the United States merely because they happened to begin the discussion of their proposed reforms on July 4.[101] The governments which held temporary sway over Mexico from 1857

[97] Hart to Representative Phelps, ibid., p. 99 ff.
[98] See the number of 15 de agosto de 1851.
[99] Arista to Doblado, June 28, 1853, in García, op. cit. XXVI, 61-63.
[100] Ibid., XXVI, 214-15; Vicente Riva Palacio, Méjico á través de los siglos. V, 72-73.
[101] Manuel Rivera, Historia de Jalapa, IV, 680.

to 1861 gave evidence of much fear of the possible accusation that they were inclined to permit the interference of the United States in Mexican affairs.[102] It may be that during this latter period, if such a dilemma had presented itself, the Liberal party would have chosen the "athletic embrace" of the United States in preference to European domination; and of course that party was willing, after the intervention of Europe became a certainty, to grasp at almost any straw in order to avoid submergence; but annexation to the United States, if ever contemplated at all, was considered only as a choice between evils.[103]

The Mexicans in general observed the attitude of the North Americans towards their country with much care and uneasiness. A file of the leading newspapers of Mexico during the twelve years subsequent to 1848 furnishes a relatively complete index to the expansionist publications and utterances in the United States; and the importance of these expressions was magnified rather than discounted. Most of the difficulties which the neighboring republics confronted, such as, for instance, the raids of the Anglo-American filibusters, proposed American operations on the Isthmus of Tehuantepec, and the dispute regarding the southern boundary of New Mexico, served as occasions for the Mexican orators and journalists to denounce the United States and call attention to the Yankee menace.

And these agencies for the moulding of public opinion received the able assistance of Spanish newspapers designed to defend the interests of Spain in America. Among these journals were three founded in Mexico City alone—the *Eco de España,* the *Correo de España,* and *El Español.* The nature of their propaganda may be gathered from three illustrations. On January 7, 1852, *El Español* declared that all the Hispanic republics of America excited the avarice of the United States, and that the most sensible policy would be to form an alliance among themselves and with Spain for the purpose of mutual defence; on July 30, 1853, the *Eco de España* contained a violent editorial which called attention to the United States

[102] H. L. Wilson, "Buchanan's Proposed Intervention in Mexico" in *The American Historical Review,* V (July 1900), 687 ff.; Callahan, "The Mexican Policy of Southern Leaders under Buchanan's Administration," Am. Hist. Assoc., *Annual Report* (1910), p. 137 ff.

[103] On April 29, 1853, Santa Anna issued a decree providing for the arrest and military trial of any person expressing a desire that Mexico should be annexed to the United States. This may indicate little more than a scheme on the part of a would-be dictator to promote his absolutism. See *El Universal,* 9 de mayo, and *El Siglo XIX,* 10 de mayo de 1853.

as a source of imminent danger to the Spanish race in America; in the month of September, 1854, the *Correo de España* contained several tirades against the colossal invader of the North which was likened to a Russia unrestrained by the balance of power, and it suggested a Pan-Hispanic alliance as the best method of obtaining an equilibrium.[104]

Some such alliance seems actually to have been seriously considered. Early in 1856 the Spanish Minister at Washington held conferences with the agents of the Hispanic-American countries for the purpose of discussing plans of union. A project was drawn up which proposed to bind the contracting parties to resent the abridgment of the independence or the infringement of the territorial integrity of any of the signatory powers and to treat the invader or offender of any member of the prospective confederation as a common enemy. No provision was inserted at the time which would include Spain in the union, but the action of the minister was approved and the Spanish Secretary of State considered the matter of sufficient importance to be communicated to the Captain General of Cuba.[105]

The Mexican Minister happened not to be in Washington when the conference was held, but the assembled diplomats entertained little doubt as to what his disposition with reference to the matter would be. In November, 1856, the agents of several of these countries, including Mexico, actually signed some such pact as that described above.[106] Mexican diplomats who sensed the danger of Anglo-American aggression did not mean to linger in supine inaction.

Indeed, they made overtures not only to their neighbors in the New World, but they looked to Europe as well. The monarchical sentiment which had been suspected by the United States in 1846 gathered strength in the years that followed. It was particularly strong among the conservatives. Riva Palacio says that in the summer of 1853 the Liberal newspaper, *El Siglo XIX*, "contended alone and unaided against all the conservative periodicals, partisans without exception of a protectorate and monarchy."[107] From 1854 to the time when intervention actually occurred, an agent seems constantly to have been kept by this party in Europe in search of a monarch willing to accept Mexico as a kingdom,[108] and it is cer-

---

[104] Files of these papers are in Bancroft Library, University of California.

[105] *The American Historical Review*, XII (January, 1906), 94 ff.

[106] Francisco José Urrutia, *La Evolución del principio de arbitraje en América*, p. 57; New York *Herald*, March 30, 1857.

[107] Riva Palacio, *op. cit.*, IV, 815.

[108] Arrangoiz y Berzábal, *Mexico desde 1808 hasta 1867*, II, 353; and see also an anonymous pamphlet published in New York in 1868 under the title

tain that Europe was appealed to more than once for protection from apprehended aggression by the United States.[109]

Such was the background of United States-Mexican relations from 1848 to 1861, and such the atmosphere in which the diplomatic difficulties of the two countries were confronted. Surprise need not be occasioned, therefore, that two crises arose and Mexico's national integrity was exposed to serious peril.

Mexico and the United States (copy in the Bancroft Collection, University of California).

[109] H. E. Bolton, *Guide to . . . the Principal Archives of Mexico,* pp. 229–230.

CHAPTER III

AMERICAN COMPLAINTS, 1848–1853

THE most important subjects which forced themselves upon the attention of the United States and Mexico during the months following the ratification of the Treaty of Guadalupe Hidalgo were: (1) claims of citizens of the United States arising from injuries and outrages suffered in Mexico, (2) depredations committed upon the frontiers of Mexico by Indians residing for the most part in the United States and roaming along the international border, (3) raids of filibusters from the United States into Mexico, and (4) disagreements regarding certain portions of the boundary between the two countries. These issues emerged almost simultaneously and, continuing unsettled, rapidly increased in importance until they reached a critical stage in the summer of 1853. A chapter will now be devoted to each of them.

The treaty of Guadalupe Hidalgo had provided for the assumption by the United States of all claims of its citizens against Mexico originating prior to 1848, thus removing for a time this source of trouble. But the settlement proved only temporary. Hardly a year had passed before new complaints began to arise and citizens of the United States began to call for the interposition of their government. No contemporary list of these claims has been published, but from a report submitted to the Senate on January 19, 1859, and from the published abstract of cases presented to the Joint Commission which sat under the claims convention of July 4, 1868, something of their number and nature may be ascertained. According to these reports some seventy or eighty claims, amounting to several millions of dollars had arisen prior to the negotiation of the Gadsden Treaty [1] (1853).

Among the first from the standpoint of time were those growing out of commercial relations. Soon after Taylor's invasion of Mexico in 1846, the government of the United States issued circulars establishing its own tariff and inviting American merchants to intro-

---

[1] *Sen. Ex. Doc.* No. 18, 35 Cong., 2 Sess. (Ser. 981), p. 82 ff.; *ibid.*, No. 31, 44 Cong., 2 Sess. (Ser. 1720), p. 18 ff.

duce their goods.[2] The tobacco dealers seem to have been most inclined to take advantage of this opportunity. When hostilities came to a close many of the commodities introduced under this special tariff remained unsold. The treaty of peace accordingly made provisions for their protection. Article XIX of the agreement stipulated that goods brought into the ports and interior points of Mexico during their occupation by the forces of the United States should not be subject to import or sale duties, or to confiscation after the withdrawal of the troops.[3] In spite of this provision, however, the Mexican authorities proceeded to levy duties upon them, refused to grant permits for their entrance into the interior, and in some instances seized them outright. Prior to 1853, eighteen claims amounting to almost a million dollars, arose from this source, and of these fourteen had to do with tobacco.[4]

The general nature of these tobacco claims may be conveyed by a brief sketch of two of them which were closely connected. Turner and Renshaw of New Orleans had imported during the American occupation 565 bales of tobacco which remained unsold when the treaty of peace was signed. The Mexican government delayed from time to time the granting of permits to proceed to the interior. As a result, the tobacco was injured and Turner and Renshaw were at length forced to sell it at a reduced price, obtaining an average of $13 instead of a possible $25 per hundred. Samuel A. Belden and Company of Matamoras, taking advantage of what appeared to be an opportunity to reap handsome profits, purchased 300 bales. After having obtained proper permits, agents of this latter company set out toward the south (October, 1850). When they arrived at Saltillo the tobacco was seized by order of the federal judge, condemned, and sold. Moreover, Belden and Company were subjected to a fine of $26,000, their store and stock at Matamoras were seized as security, and Belden himself was forced to flee to Texas to avoid arrest.[5]

Besides the complaints on account of the violation of Article XIX of the Treaty of Guadalupe Hidalgo, there were numerous others resulting from commercial irregularities, such as the collection of excessive duties, the granting of privileges which discriminated against American merchants, the seizure and destruction of cargoes and vessels. There were also several instances of robbery of stores,

---

[2] *Ibid.,* No. 80, 32 Cong., 1 Sess. (Ser. 620), p. 57.

[3] Malloy, *Treaties,* etc., I, 1115–1116.

[4] *Sen. Ex. Doc.* No. 18, 35 Cong., 2 Sess. (Ser. 981), p. 82 ff.; *ibid.,* 44 Cong., 2 Sess. (Ser. 1720), p. 18 ff.

[5] *Sen. Ex. Doc.* No. 80, 32 Cong., 1 Sess. (Ser. 620), p. 1 ff.

haciendas, mines, ranches, and other kinds of property, and a few instances of breach of contract on the part of the Mexican government, the most important case in the last category being the annulment of the privileges held by the assignees of Garay.

But the most urgent and numerous complaints arose from personal injuries and outrages perpetrated against citizens of the United States. There were several cases of insults, slight injuries, and expulsions, and a few cases of murder, but the most important were those of imprisonment. The suspicion aroused in Mexico by the filibusters was a frequent cause of this sort of maltreatment. The bold expression of expansionist sentiment in the United States, and the numerous raids into Mexico, Central America, and Cuba, caused the authorities and populace of Mexico to look upon every American as a potential filibuster.

Even the sanctity of the officials of the United States seems not always to have been respected. There were four complaints of this nature prior to 1854. These arose at Guaymas, Acapulco, and Fontera de Tabasco. In October, 1848, Buchanan wrote the United States Minister in Mexico that he approved of his attempts to obtain satisfaction for the insults suffered by R. Porter, Consul at Tabasco, and he hoped that they would meet with a successful issue.[6] S. V. R. Ryan claimed to have been illegally arrested on February 23, 1852, while Consul *pro tem.* at the same place.[7] But most important instances of this sort of grievance were those of John A. Robinson at Guaymas, and of Francis W. Rice at Acapulco.

The injuries suffered by Robinson resulted from his supposed connection with William Walker's filibustering enterprise of 1853–54.[8] It happened that he was the owner of the Brig *Caroline* which had conveyed Walker's original party to Lower California. Since his captain had disobeyed orders in taking on the party, Robinson thought he should have been entitled to some clemency. So great was the bitterness aroused in Mexico, however, that magnanimity and discrimination were not always employed. Robinson and his family soon became the subjects of vilification and outrage. Writing from Guaymas to the *Stockton Post,* on November 18, 1853, he declared that he had been obliged to pay a fine of $3,000 dollars for the abuse of the Mexican flag which the *Caroline* floated, and that he and his family were in actual danger.[9] In the

---

[6] Buchanan to Clifford, October 10, 1848, Buchanan, *Works,* VIII, 216.

[7] *Sen. Ex. Doc.* No. 18, 35 Cong., 2 Sess. (Ser. 981), p. 84; *ibid.,* No. 31, 44 Cong., 2 Sess., Case No. 10.

[8] *Post,* p. 93 ff.

[9] Quoted in *Alta California,* January 4, 1854.

spring of the following year the persecution of the populace and the authorities finally forced him to abandon his home and business.[10]

In the summer of 1852, Francis W. Rice, Consul of the United States at Acapulco, became involved with the Mexican authorities there in a dispute over the sale of an American vessel for sailor's wages and expenses. The vessel was sold to Mr. Snyder, the chief engineer, for $11,500, but when a deposit of $3,000 was required, the engineer was unable to raise it. Rice thereupon proceeded to sell the vessel for only $4,500 to Ralph S. Fretz of New Orleans. For this he was accused of disposing of the vessel illegally and at a ridiculously low price to a personal friend. Snyder, in behalf of himself and the crew, appealed to the Mexican admiralty court at Acapulco. This court issued an order of attachment, declared the second sale void, and posted notices for another sale of the ship. Rice responded by posting counter-notices warning all persons against buying. The Mexican judge ordered the counter-notices torn down and commissioned Snyder as agent to execute the mandate. When Snyder came to the door of the consulate to remove one of these notices, Rice ordered him away with a pistol. On the ground that this action constituted contempt of court, the judge commanded the American Consul to appear before him. Rice refused and a squad of soldiers was dispatched for his arrest. On June 11, he was taken into custody and confined to prison. Although released soon afterwards, he was ordered to consider and conduct himself as a prisoner in his own house. On two other occasions previous to his retirement from office near the close of the year 1852, he claimed that the sanctity of his office had been violated.[11]

Some attempt had been made to obtain a general settlement of these claims prior to the summer of 1853. Buchanan had made "strong demands" based upon the violation of Article XIX,[12] and R. P. Letcher, American Minister to Mexico, had been instructed to negotiate for a mutual settlement of claims;[13] but only in regard to a few isolated cases had pressure been exerted. The most prominent of these were the complaints of Rice and of the Louisiana Tehuantepec Company.

[10] Sen. Ex. Doc. No. 31, 44 Cong., 2 Sess. (Ser. 1720), Case No. 25.

[11] Sen. Ex. Doc. No. 106, 32 Cong., 1 Sess. (Ser. 621), p. 3 ff.; ibid., 32 Cong., 2 Sess. (Ser. 660), p. 18 ff.; Sen. Misc. Doc. No. 33, 32 Cong., 2 Sess. (Ser. 670), pp. 1–4.

[12] Buchanan to Consul Slemons, January 6, 1849, Works, VIII, 272–274.

[13] Webster to Letcher, August 19, 1851, Webster, Works, (National ed.), XIV, 443 ff.

Immediately after his imprisonment, in 1852, Rice had written both to Webster and to Letcher, declaring that he and his wife had been compelled to listen to vile and insulting language from the soldiers who came to arrest him; and that, without any charge having been preferred, he had been confined in a felon's cell with drunkards, criminals, and negroes.[14] Upon receiving Rice's note, Letcher had immediately visited the Minister of Justice, as well as the Minister of Foreign Relations, and protested against the action of the authorities. He had demanded that Rice be removed from the felon's dungeon at once and treated with proper consideration. In reporting the result of these interviews to Webster, Letcher said that both ministers evinced deep concern, and promised to have a full investigation made and the judge at Acapulco punished if circumstances should warrant such action.[15]

A few days later, Ramírez (Mexican Minister of Relations) wrote Letcher that although the official details of the affair had not been received at that time, he thought the accounts which had reached Letcher had been somewhat exaggerated. The Consul had been arrested, but there seemed to be no proof of any severity of treatment. He assured Letcher that the President had issued orders for an investigation and for prompt and impartial administration of justice.[16] In keeping with this view Letcher later informed Webster that a personal visit from Rice had convinced him that he had been "egregiously misled" by Rice's letter; for the Consul had never been confined in a felon's cell, but only ordered there. Letcher said in the same note that the Mexican authorities continued to manifest great concern, and assured him that they were determined upon a rigid inquiry and an impartial trial; but that they "repeatedly and in a delicate way intimated a wish for Mr. Rice's removal." Letcher refused to advise compliance with the latter suggestions at the time, as he thought that such action would be unjust to Rice and considered his treatment an indignity meriting the particular attention of his government.[17]

The Senate of the United States soon became interested in the matter and called upon the President for the correspondence (July 20, 1852). When the request was complied with, documents were revealed which tended to cast a shadow upon Rice's integrity and

[14] Rice to Webster, June 11, and to Letcher, June 14, 1852, *Sen. Ex. Doc.* No. 106, 32 Cong., 1 Sess. (Ser. 621), pp. 5–9.
[15] Letcher to Webster, June 21, 1852, *ibid.*, pp. 13–14.
[16] *Sen. Ex. Doc.* No. 17, 32 Cong., 2 Sess. (Ser. 660), p. 4.
[17] Note of July 27, 1852, *ibid.*, pp. 12–13.

to envelop the whole affair in uncertainty.[18] Therefore, when the question of Rice's reappointment was pending before the Senate, Gwin of California, acting upon representations made by seemingly responsible parties, made verbal complaint to President Fillmore. Rice was soon removed from office.[19] But the Senate, apparently not yet satisfied, called for additional correspondence on December 13.[20] On February 4, following, a memorial from Rice was submitted, wherein he complained not only of outrages committed against him, but also of those perpetrated against other citizens of the United States at Acapulco.[21] This was referred to the Committee on Foreign Relations and ordered to be printed, but no further action was taken.

Soon after Pierce's inauguration the whole affair was placed before him by James W. Simonton,[22] one of Rice's friends, and Rice, who was now at Boston, addressed to the President a letter asking that the United States, in exacting satisfaction for the violation of its flag, should also demand such personal indemnity for him as seemed proper.[23] This letter was dated June 1, 1853. In the following October, Rice appealed to Secretary of State Marcy.[24] The latter transmitted Rice's letter to the Minister of the United States in Mexico and instructed him to lay the matter before the Mexican Minister of Relations with a request that an investigation be made and indemnity granted.[25] At this point all special consideration of this claim appears to have ceased.

Far more important and irritating than the case of Rice was that of the Louisiana Tehuantepec Company. Its complaints related to a projected enterprise which was thought at that time to be of vital concern to the future of the United States. The idea of trans-isthmian communication was much cherished during the five years subsequent to the treaty of 1848, the more so because many feared that a railroad across the mountains to the west of the Mississippi would be difficult to construct or, if constructed, still more difficult to operate. One of these proposed routes, the Isthmus of Tehuantepec, lay within Mexican domain.

[18] See statements of Snyder and Wilson, for instance, *Sen. Ex. Doc.* No. 106, 32 Cong., 1 Sess. (Ser. 621), pp. 16-22.

[19] *Ibid.*, 33 Cong., 2 Sess. (Ser. 752), pp. 37-39.

[20] *Sen. Ex. Doc.* No. 17, 32 Cong., 1 Sess. (Ser. 660), p. 1.

[21] *Sen. Misc. Doc.* No. 33, 32 Cong., 2 Sess., pp. 1-4.

[22] Simonton to Marcy, July 11, 1853, *Sen. Ex. Doc.* No. 38, 33 Cong., 2 Sess. (Ser. 752), p. 7.

[23] *Ibid.*, pp. 7-9.

[24] *Ibid.*, pp. 12-17.

[25] *Ibid.*, p. 17.

The interest of the United States in this route was awakened during the Mexican War when the acquisition of Pacific possessions became assured. Vice-President Dallas considered it of sufficient importance to merit the publication of a statement setting forth its peculiar value.[26] Polk's entire Cabinet agreed that the sum of five million dollars was not too much to pay for it. Secretary Walker even went so far as to declare that he deemed it of more importance than Upper California and New Mexico combined and to urge that its sale be made a *sine qua non* of peace.[27] Lewis Cass later declared that the "proximity" of the isthmus to the United States, "the salubrity of the climate, the adaptedness of the ground for the construction of a railroad, and the great diminution of distance in comparison with other southern routes . . ." all pointed Tehuantepec out as "far preferable to any . . . route outside" of the domain of his government.[28] The South and West [29] were particularly interested in the route, the attention of the former being called to the matter at the Memphis commercial convention of 1849, and during four subsequent southern conventions.[30] In brief, the Isthmus of Tehuantepec was deemed of great importance during the period under consideration. Any difficulties placed in the way of its construction, or any infringements of the concessions held by American citizens there, would be sure to occasion deep concern on the part of the government of the United States.

Tehuantepec first entered the field of United States and Mexican diplomacy during the negotiations which terminated the Mexican War of 1846–1848. On April 15, 1847, Nicholas P. Trist, who had charge of those negotiations, was authorized to pay thirty, instead of fifteen, million dollars for Upper and Lower California and New Mexico, provided he could obtain also the right of passage and transit over the Isthmus of Tehuantepec. The project for a treaty enclosed with these instructions made provision for the grant and guaranty of such a right.[31] But the Mexican commissioners refused the proposal outright, giving the following explanation with reference to the stand taken by their government:

[26] *De Bow's Review,* July, 1849, p. 11.
[27] Polk, *Diary,* III, 471 ff.
[28] *Sen. Ex. Doc.* No. 72, 34 Cong., 1 Sess. (Ser. 930), pp. 40–41.
[29] Webster wrote Letcher on March 16, 1852, that there were "excited and anxious feelings, especially at the south and west" regarding the Tehuantepec situation. *Ibid.,* No. 97, 32 Cong., 1 Sess. (Ser. 621), p. 127.
[30] Alabama Historical Society, *Transactions* (1904), p. 153 ff.
[31] *Sen. Ex. Doc.* No. 52, 30 Cong., 1 Sess. (Ser. 509), pp. 82–88.

... In the eighth article of your Excellency's draft, the grant of a free passage across the Isthmus of Tehuantepec to the South Sea is sought in favor of North American citizens. We have orally explained to your excellency that some years since, the government of the republic granted to a private contractor a privilege, with reference to this object, which was soon transferred, with the sanction of the same government, to English subjects, of whose rights Mexico cannot dispose.[32]

The concession referred to by the Mexican commissioners has become rather widely known as the Garay Grant. By a decree of March 1, 1842, and a contract made the following day, Santa Anna, who was at that time virtually a dictator, had granted José de Garay the privilege of constructing a communication across the Isthmus of Tehuantepec and had given him in fee simple all the unoccupied land for ten leagues on each side of the proposed route. An important provision of the decree required the making of surveys within eighteen months and the commencement of actual work on the communications by July 1, 1844. On February 9, 1843, Garay had reported to the government that he had completed the first obligations, and asked to be placed in possession of his lands. This request had been granted by a decree of the same day. On October 4, three hundred convicts had been provided for the work, but in the following December the period for the commencement of operations had been extended for another year. Moreover, the numerous revolutions which disturbed Mexico at the time had forced Garay to ask yet another extension. Two more years had accordingly been granted by another dictator, Mariano Salas. Then a series of contracts running through 1847 and 1848 transferred all the privileges of Garay, "without any limitations whatever," to Messrs. Manning and Mackintosh. These gentlemen were the "English subjects" to whom the Mexican commissioners had referred.

But in February, 1849, Manning and Mackintosh transferred their concession to the Hargous Brothers of New York. Thus citizens of the United States—though not the American government—had at last acquired the coveted Tehuantepec grant. And three days after acquiring it they presented to the Senate a memorial inviting attention to their project and setting forth its merits.[33]

Soon afterwards these American assignees evinced uneasiness with respect to Mexico's attitude toward them. Nor was it long before

[32] *Ibid.*, p. 337.
[33] *Sen. Ex. Doc.* No. 97, 32 Cong. 1 Sess. (Ser. 621), pp. 132–133; Dublán y Lozano, *Legislación mexicana*, IV, 120–123, 705, V, 187; *Sen. Misc. Doc.* No. 50, 30 Cong., 2 Sess. (Ser. 533).

this anxiety was transmitted through them to the government which had manifested such interest in the Tehuantepec route. On June 20, 1849, Nathan Clifford, Minister of the United States in Mexico, in obedience to instructions which he had received from the American Secretary of State, addressed a note to the Mexican Minister of Relations, informing him that some apprehension had arisen lest Mexico should annul the Garay privilege largely because citizens of the United States had acquired an interest in it. "If such should be the fact," Clifford wrote, "the measure could not fail to be regarded by the President of the United States as proof of a disposition wholly at variance with the existing pacific relations between the two countries, and with the spirit and even the letter" of the treaty of 1831.[34]

In reply, the Mexican Minister assured Clifford that the privilege in question had not been annulled, and that the supreme authorities of Mexico would never be influenced in the matter by "any feeling of dislike to the national character of the citizens of the United States." At the same time, however, Clifford was politely informed that the question as to the validity of the grant or its forfeiture for non-compliance with the obligations it imposed was exclusively a Mexican affair, "to be discussed, decided and determined according to the laws and by the constitutionally competent authorities of Mexico, to the exclusion of those of any other power." [35] Such language was not likely to remove American apprehension.

On September 18, 1849, Secretary of State Clayton instructed Robert P. Letcher, now United States Minister to Mexico, to arrange a convention with that country providing for the protection of the rights and property of the parties who desired to construct the communication. This step was essential, Clayton maintained, in order that the capitalists who were then, or who might thereafter, become interested in the contract, might be able to proceed in good faith with an enterprise so important to the United States, to Mexico, and to the world at large. He further stated that while his government had no desire to acquire Tehuantepec, it would not guarantee Mexico's sovereignty over the isthmus, and that such a guaranty in the case of New Granada was not to be cited as a precedent, for that treaty had been concluded without instructions from the department, reluctantly submitted to the Senate, and hastily approved at the close of the session in 1848.

[34] *Sen. Ex. Doc.* No. 97, 32 Cong., 1 Sess. (Ser. 621), pp. 7–8. Reference is made to the most favored nation clause.
[35] *Ibid.,* pp. 9–10.

That the Secretary of State gave the American company an important place in his thoughts is shown by the following suggestions:

It is deemed advisable, however, before any attempt shall be made to conclude the convention with the Mexican government, that, in the name and on behalf of this government, you should enter into a contract with the holders of the grant in favor of Don José de Garay, with a view to fix the amount of tolls to be levied by that company on citizens or officers of the United States who may be passengers, and on goods transported across the isthmus on the road, railroad or canal which the company may construct.[36]

Indeed, from the very outset the object of the United States government seems to have been not so much to insure the neutrality of the communication and its free use for all nations, as to furnish protection to its subjects who held the privilege. And the determination to protect its citizens and to accomplish the enterprise by their efforts was mainly responsible for the difficulties which were to bring the two countries to the verge of war.

Along with the letter of September 18, Clayton sent a draft of such a convention as he desired Letcher to sign. Since this served as a basis for the negotiations of the next three years, it will be necessary to present its main points.

Art. I. Individuals upon whom the Mexican government may have bestowed or may bestow the privilege of constructing a road, railroad or canal across the Isthmus of Tehuantepec, and those employed by them, shall be protected in their rights of person and property from the inception to the completion of the work.

Art. II. For this purpose either party shall be at liberty to employ such military or naval force as may be deemed necessary, which shall be hospitably received in the harbors of the isthmus, or allowed to occupy the line of the work and so much of the region adjacent thereto as may be indispensable.

Art. III. The same protection, by the same means, shall be extended to the work when it shall have been completed.

Art. IV. In entering into this compact, the United States hereby solemnly disavow any intention to acquire rights of sovereignty over the Isthmus of Tehuantepec.

Art. V. Decision as to non-compliance with the terms of the grant shall be left to an arbiter. In case the decision should result in forfeiture, the property of the grantees in the work shall be sold at auction to the highest bidder.

Art. VI. No foreign government or corporation shall be allowed to purchase the property mentioned in Article V. The right to purchase the same shall accrue to individuals only, and shall be accompanied by an obligation on the part of the purchasers to prosecute the enterprise to its completion . . .

Art. VII. When the privileges of the grantees shall have been forfeited pursuant to the fifth article of this convention, the obligation of the contract-

[36] *Ibid.,* pp. 11–13.

ing parties to continue the protection stipulated by the first and second articles shall be suspended, but shall be resumed when the work shall again be prosecuted, pursuant to the sixth article.

Art. VIII.   No higher rates shall at any time be charged for the transportation of passengers, being citizens or officers of the United States, or freight for goods belonging to them or to the government of the United States, on the road, railroad or canal referred to in this convention, than may be charged on the transportation of Mexican citizens or officers of the Mexican government, or on the property belonging to them or to that government.[37]

Letcher entered upon negotiations early in March, 1850, when, after a long interview with Señor Lacunza, Mexican Minister of Relations, he submitted a rough draft. During the conference Lacunza insisted on a discrimination in favor of Mexican vessels, but Letcher refused to consider such a concession. The Mexican Minister of Relations then submitted the draft confidentially to the British Minister in Mexico, remarking to him that he would insist upon this discrimination with the view of making the treaty popular in Mexico but that he would not make it a *sine qua non*.

The British Minister was so interested in the proposed convention that he called on Letcher, related the substance of his interview with Lacunza, and intimated that England desired to join in a guaranty of the integrity of the Isthmus. He remarked, too, that he felt sure that France and Spain "would like to do the same thing." To these suggestions regarding the desires of the European powers Letcher answered that he was afraid of "too many cooks over a small dish." He then applied to his government for instructions regarding the matter.[38]

Clayton authorized him, by letter of April 23, to allow and invite other nations to join in the treaty guaranteeing the neutrality of the proposed communication. Before this despatch reached Mexico, however, Letcher, perceiving that the forces working in opposition to a favorable settlement were "quite formidable," had already agreed to a treaty.[39]

This treaty, which, on account of its negotiators, may be called the Letcher-Pedraza Convention, had been signed on June 22, 1850. Important additions and revisions had been made in the original draft submitted by Clayton: (1) The United States was to lend assistance in the protection of the route only in case Mexico required it, and then only "in the manner and on the terms, and . . . for the period" which Mexico should designate; and in no case was this as-

[37] *Ibid.*, pp. 13-14.
[38] Letcher to Clayton, March 16, 1850, *ibid.*, p. 16.
[39] *Ibid.*, pp. 19-20.

sistance to be employed against the functionaries of the Mexican government. (2) The productions of the soil or industry of Mexico were to be charged one-fifth less toll than those of the same class belonging to the United States. (3) The United States was to join Mexico in maintaining the neutrality of the route and of the country for a distance of ten leagues on each side of it. (4) Other nations were to be granted the same privileges enjoyed by the United States in return for joining in this guaranty.

In transmitting the document to Clayton, Letcher said that it fell short of what he had desired in some particulars, but that it was the "best that could be obtained." [40] Three weeks later, he declared that it was doubtful whether the Mexican Congress would ratify the treaty even as it stood, since some of the leading prints of the city "were violently opposed" to it. [41]

While discussions of the Convention were in progress Peter A. Hargous was approaching the council chambers of his government and taking American business men into his project. On February 16, 1850, he requested that passports be obtained from Mexico for engineers who were about to be sent to survey the route. By the early part of April Letcher had procured them. Before the close of the month Hargous wrote Clayton again, notifying him that a company of citizens of the United States residing in New Orleans was about to be formed for the purpose of obtaining the Tehuantepec privileges. He expected that these citizens would prosecute the work with "intelligence and vigor," and he hoped, therefore, that he would be pardoned the suggestion that it would be advisable for Letcher to be "officially informed of these movements . . . and instructed to lose no time . . . in bringing his negotiations to a speedy and satisfactory close." [42]

That Hargous's influence upon his government was not without weight may be inferred from the fact that the convention of June 22, 1850, provided that the holder of the Garay privilege should give his consent to it in writing. This document was submitted to Hargous for his perusal and criticism, and on August 12, he presented a full statement of his objections. They centered mainly around the desire for greater protection from his government. The fourth article of the convention stipulated that in no case was the assistance of the United States to be carried so far as to be directed against a functionary of the Mexican government. This would

---

[40] Letcher to Clayton, June 24, 1850, and enclosure, *ibid.*, pp. 20–23.
[41] Letcher to Clayton, July 13, 1850, *ibid.*, p. 23.
[42] Hargous to Clayton, April 22, 1850, *ibid.*, p. 15. See also p. 15.

prevent the United States from restraining or repelling these functionaries, even though they should be acting contrary to the wishes
and orders of the Mexican national authorities themselves. An
American commissioner should be permitted to reside on the line
of the work along with the Mexican commissioner provided in the
Convention. The United States should have an equal voice with
Mexico in fixing and modifying rates charged for transportation.
Lastly, Hargous begged for "some assurance" that his company's
property would be "protected from unjust confiscation and violence"
whatever happened to the proposed convention.[43]

On the following day Webster, now Secretary of State, gave
Hargous a very definite promise of official support for his "vested"
interests in Mexico. He assured him that citizens of the United
States who had put their money into the enterprise could confidently
rely upon their government to remonstrate against the invasion of
their rights, and that should this remonstrance prove insufficient,
"any other means" necessary to their protection would be "authorized and employed." [44]

Replying to this letter Hargous gave his reluctant consent to
the Convention, but at the same time he entreated Webster to notify
the Mexican government that the United States was relying upon
it to give security to the property of those engaged in the enterprise, and that if this just expectation should not be realized, the
government of the United States would deem itself bound to "take
the protection thereof in its own hands." [45]

Before this reply of Hargous arrived Webster had instructed
Letcher to obtain the following important modifications in the convention: (1) Citizens of the United States were to be expressly
mentioned as holders of the Tehuantepec grant; (2) the protection
provided by the convention was to be extended not only to those
engaged in constructing the communications, but to "all persons
and interests concerned therein"; (3) in the same manner, the
force sent in for purposes of security was to be permitted to occupy
"any point whatever" within the "limits of the grant"; (4) a commissioner of the United States residing on the line of the work was
to have authority in certain contingencies to call upon the Mexican
government for protection of all the privileges enumerated in the
grant and, in case of Mexico's failure to comply within sixty days,
"to make application therefor to his own government."

[43] Ibid., pp. 23–26.
[44] Ibid., pp. 27–28.
[45] Hargous to Webster, Aug. 26, 1850, ibid., pp. 28–29.

These were truly amazing modifications. Assuming by implication that Mexico was unable to keep order in a very important area of her territory, Webster proposed a protectorate not only over the line of the projected communication but also over a zone twenty leagues wide extending across the entire isthmus and perhaps soon to be occupied by immigrants from the United States. Blaine in his palmiest days was never more aggressive. Nor is this all. Webster went on to make certain statements to the effect that the United States would take the affair into its own hands if Mexico rejected these overtures, and hinted that the Mexican government might be influenced to acquiesce by a threat of withholding some of the money due under the Treaty of Guadalupe Hidalgo.[46]

Upon receiving the draft Letcher immediately called the attention of the Minister of Relations to the desired alterations, but this official persistently refused to accept them. Thereupon, Letcher, at his own request, was given an interview with the President and Cabinet. These officials likewise remained steadfast, maintaining that the proposed amendments infringed upon "the sovereignty, and honor, the dignity and the national pride" of Mexico; that to "adopt them would be at once to paralyze, to disgrace, and in short to overthrow the present administration"; that a treaty embodying these provisions would be unanimously rejected by the Mexican Congress. When at length Letcher suggested that the United States was determined to take the affair into its own hands in case a satisfactory treaty could not be arranged, substantially the following reply was made: "Your government is strong; ours is weak. You have the power to take the whole or any portion of our territory you may think fit; we have not the *faculty* to resist. We have done all we could do to satisfy your country and to gratify you personally. We can do no more." [47]

When he received news of the vigorous Mexican opposition to his proposed draft, Webster instructed the United States Minister to effect a compromise as favorable to his government as possible, and Letcher, following out his orders, succeeded in completing the negotiations for a new treaty by January 25, 1851.[48]

But very little had been accomplished by the efforts of Letcher, for the treaty was virtually the same as that of June 22, 1850. The United States was permitted to furnish protection to the work only in case Mexico requested it, and Letcher had been forced to give over

---

[46] Webster to Letcher, Aug. 24, 1850, and enclosed draft, *ibid.*, pp. 29–35.
[47] Letcher to Webster, October 22, 1850, *ibid.*, pp. 36–38.
[48] *Ibid.*, pp. 41, 44.

both in regard to permission for a commissioner to reside on the line of the work, and with reference to the express designation of American citizens as holders of the privilege.[49]   This treaty, unsatisfactory as it was, received the approval of Hargous and the ratification of the United States Senate.

By this time, however, it had become evident that the Mexican Congress was not likely to approve any treaty which would enable Americans to carry out the stipulations of the Garay grant.   As early as January 17, 1851, Letcher had reported that opposition to the treaty in any form was "violent from almost every quarter." The clergy, the interests connected with rival routes, prominent men of state, and foreign influences—all were hostile.   Only the new President, Arista, manifested a friendliness toward it, and he was accused of desiring to cede a portion of the country to the United States.   During the following month, Buckingham Smith, United States *chargé ad interim,* reported that the people of Mexico had become no more favorably inclined toward the convention, and on April 1, he said that, according to current opinion, the treaty could in no way or shape receive the ratification of the Mexican Congress. There was not a member of the Cabinet who favored it, and all agreed that "the experiment with Texas should be enough."   If their neighbors were given "a foothold in Tehuantepec" they would seize "one-half of the remaining territory of the republic." [50]

It is not surprising, therefore, that when Webster transmitted Hargous's letter of approval to the Mexican Legation at Washington, De la Rosa, the Mexican Minister, declared he had no instructions regarding the matter and consequently would probably not communicate the letter to his government.   Pursuant to advices he received later, however, De la Rosa sent Webster a rather lengthy note in which he sought to draw a clear distinction between what he considered two entirely different and independent subjects; namely,

the treaty concluded with the government of the United States for the purpose of facilitating an inter-oceanic communication through the Isthmus of Tehuantepec, and the grants . . . in favor of Don José de Garay. . . . Whether the aforesaid contractor still preserves any right by the grants which the Mexican government has made in his favor, . . . or whether he has forfeited such rights, is a point which will have to be decided by the supreme government of Mexico, to which tribunal . . . this matter has been referred.

As for the communication itself, De la Rosa said that he was anxious to see the enterprise brought to a successful conclusion, and he

[49] *Ibid.,* pp. 43, 47–50.
[50] *Ibid.,* pp. 41–42, 43, 45.

hoped no question concerning private interests would frustrate or delay "one of the most magnificent undertakings that ever was devised on the face of the earth." [51]

This stand on the part of the Mexican Minister aroused the ire of Webster, and he responded with a long and vigorous note. He began by expressing surprise at the attitude of the Mexican government, and then launched into an argument in favor of the American holders of the grant:

> Citizens of the United States have embarked their fortunes upon their reliance on the good faith of both governments. They have trusted to the decrees and plighted faith of Mexico . . . They have already expanded great sums of money in commencing the undertaking. More than fifty surveyors and attendants are now on the route of survey, who went thither with the express permission and under express sanction of the Mexican government. More than a hundred thousand dollars have already been advanced by the company associated with the holders of the grant.

He concluded his note by referring to the "serious embarrassments" which failure to ratify the treaty might cause and expressed the hope that the "calamity" of its rejection might be avoided.[52]

Meanwhile, the whole affair was being complicated and Mexican opposition further stimulated by the activities of the assignees of the Garay privilege. During the year 1850 Hargous had succeeded in interesting several residents of New Orleans in his grant, and they had chosen a "Permanent Committee" to take the enterprise in hand. This committee had agreed to form a company with a capital of nine million dollars, one-third of which was to be issued to Hargous in payment for his concession. But when they appealed to the Governor of Louisiana for a special session of the legislature to incorporate the concern, he declined to assist them. Undaunted, however, they had formed a temporary organization, opened an office for the issuance of stock, dispatched a company of engineers to the isthmus, and prepared to finance the enterprise, in part, by the sale of lands in the twenty-league strip adjacent to the communication.[53]

The engineers of the company had arrived at the isthmus in December, 1850, and the sale of the land had probably begun as early as March of the following year; for on the 7th of that month De la Rosa spoke of men who were "projecting enterprises in

[51] De la Rosa to Webster, February 25 and March 7, 1851, *ibid.*, pp. 44, 54-58.

[52] Webster to Le la Rosa, April 30, 1851, *ibid.*, 60-66.

[53] *De Bow's Review* (January, 1851), Old Series, X, 94; Butler, *Judah P. Benjamin*, p. 125.

Tehauntepec" when they had no right whatever to dispose of the lands on the isthmus, or its rivers, or its forests; and gave notice that any individuals or families who should go to settle, or who had already gone to settle there as colonists or proprietors of lands, would be treated as "trespassers upon the national domain." [54] On July 3, he declared that those who pretended to have succeeded Garay in his rights had contemptuously and almost derisively disposed of the lands, rivers, and woods on the isthmus. Moreover, "some of the Newspapers in New Orleans, and from other points of the United States . . . dwelt continuously on this undertaking, and almost invariably spoke of it, not as a legal enterprise, undertaken with the consent of the Mexican government, but rather as an acquisition which ought to be made of a portion of Mexican territory," [55]

De la Rosa asserted that the conduct of the so-called American grantees had led the Mexican Congress to a resolution to consider the matter thoroughly, and to adopt means for preventing a repetition of the Texas event. This is hardly a fair statement of the matter. Reference has already been made to Letcher's note of July 13, 1850, stating that there was opposition to the first Letcher-Pedraza convention. Even before this date, and before the Garay privilege had fallen into the hands of Hargous, a prominent Mexican statesman had expressed fear lest the United States should acquire the grant, while in February and March, 1851, steps had been taken which would interfere with the operation of the vessels of the New Orleans company.[56]

As a matter of fact, the Mexican government watched with great uneasiness every action of the United States and its citizens. In the recent war it had lost half of its territory, and yet the despoiler appeared to be unsatisfied. Every movement which could be considered at all aggressive on the part of its neighbors was therefore interpreted as the beginning of the last act in the drama of Mexico's absorption. The New Orleans company thus proceeded in an atmosphere charged with suspicion and every step it took was likely to be misinterpreted.

In the early spring of 1851, United States chargé, Buckingham Smith, had been informed that the Mexican government would not allow foreign vessels to enter the ports of the isthmus "under any circumstances," and the Mexican Vice-Consul at New Orleans had

[54] *Sen. Ex. Doc.*, No. 97, 32 Cong., 1 Sess. (Ser. 621), p. 57.
[55] *Ibid.*, p. 81.
[56] *Dictamen de la Comisión especial de Tehuantepec del Senado*, March 22, 1851, pp. 22, 31.

been directed to deny the American company all communication with the region. But the company had insisted on its right to proceed with operations. Accordingly, the steamer *Gold Hunter* had been dispatched from San Francisco for Ventosa, in the State of Oaxaca. After it had arrived there (April 6, 1851), the cargo and passengers had been detained several days and eventually forbidden a landing. In consequence, the captain declared that he had been subjected to heavy and unnecessary expenses and demanded damages from the Mexican government.[57]

Soon afterwards, the schooner *Sears* had proceeded without clearance papers from New Orleans. Touching at Vera Cruz on May 2, it had asked permission to continue the voyage to the Coatzacoalcos River with supplies for the surveying party. "After several denials" she was at length "allowed to proceed, paying duties on her articles; but it was not until after some delay" and much trouble to the United States *chargé.*[58]

The Mexican Senate had by this time reviewed the entire Tehuantepec affair, and had reported in favor of declaring null and void the Salas decree (of November 5, 1846) which had allowed Garay an additional two years for beginning operations, alleging in justification of this step that the provisional government at that time did not have the power to dictate it. These activities of the company served to precipitate matters, so that the report was almost unanimously adopted and the decree in question nullified on May 22, 1851.[59]

On the same day, the Minister of Relations instructed the Governor of Oaxaca to suspend the survey of the isthmus and to expel, if necessary, the laborers of the company. Notice of these orders was served on the surveyors, and steps were immediately taken to put an end to all operations.

When news of the affair reached Webster, he protested against the action of the Mexican Congress as unconstitutional, and expressed the hope that Mexico would reconsider and reverse this law which she had passed with haste and under "an entire misapprehension" of the consequences which might result. At the same time, and perhaps still hoping that Mexico would change her mind, Webster instructed Letcher, who was returning to his post, to use all his efforts to effect the ratification of the Tehuantepec agreement.[60] The New Orleans com-

---

[57] *Ibid.,* pp. 22, 31.

[58] *Sen. Ex. Doc.,* No. 97, 32 Cong., 1 Sess. (Ser. 621), pp. 52-54, 75.

[59] *Sen. Ex. Doc.,* No. 97, 32 Cong., 1 Sess. (Ser. 621), 85; *Dictamen de la Comisión especial de Tehuantepec del Senado,* March 22, 1851, p. 51.

[60] Webster to Letcher, No. 71, Aug. 18, 1851, Mex. Inst., Vol. 16.

pany, insisting likewise upon its rights, continued to dispatch vessels to the isthmus, and rumors spread abroad to the effect that five hundred laborers were being raised for the purpose of taking possession by force.[61]

The Mexican press gave much space to the affair, quoting from the United States expansionists, writing editorials on the "threatening absorption of the Spanish race by the Anglo-American," and keeping the Mexican people in a state of general alarm while exhorting them to unity in order to resist the onslaught of the Colossus of the North which recognized no law except that of superior force.[62] The Mexican government, backed by popular feeling, remained firm. When news of the threats of the New Orleans company reached President Arista, he sent to the American *chargé* asking for a conference. The desired interview took place on August 1, and on the following day Smith reported the result to his government.

> I found him [Arista] quite calm, and he said directly that things appeared to be very threatening in the North. . . . I told him that I had received no despatches from Washington, and that I had in no way understood that the United States had any part in these movements to which he referred . . . During the interview I asked him if the bill for the military colonies at Tehuantepec had been signed, and he said that it had . . . The president added that he must obey the law and the judgment of Congress on the Garay grant. I asked if there were troops at the Goatzacoalcos River, and he said there were twelve hundred under orders to march to that point.[63]

Besides the establishment of military colonies referred to in this interview, other preparations were made. "The headquarters of the comandancia general of Vera Cruz were moved to Acayucan . . . ; the national guard of the adjoining states was enlisted and ordered to be in readiness; arms were distributed and four vessels stationed off the Goatzacoalco."[64] Furthermore, in order that there should be left no pretext for Americans to visit the isthmus, the *exequaturs* of the United States consuls at Ventosa and Minititlán were taken away.[65]

The Carvajal revolt on the Rio Grande frontier, attributed as it was to citizens of the United States, of course added fuel to the

---

[61] *Sen. Ex. Doc.* No. 97, 32 Cong., 1 Sess. (Ser. 621), pp. 80–88, 93–95; *El Universal,* 30 y 31 de julio de 1851.

[62] *El Universal,* 9 de julio y 10 de agosto de 1851; *El Siglo XIX,* 6 de octubre de 1851; *El Omnibus,* 17 de julio de 1852.

[63] *Sen Ex. Doc.* No. 97, 32 Cong., 1 Sess. (Ser. 621), p. 89.

[64] Bancroft, *History of Mexico,* V, 590.

[65] *Sen. Reports,* No. 355, 32 Cong., 1 Sess. (Ser. 631), p. 11; *Sen. Ex. Doc.* No. 97, 32 Cong., 1 Sess., pp. 95–96.

flame of Mexican suspicion and indignation. Letcher was finally compelled to yield to the request of the Mexican Minister of Relations for the negotiation of a new treaty and, a few weeks later, to sign a protocol proroguing the date for the ratification of the treaty of January 25, until April 8, 1852.[66]

It soon became evident, however, that nothing would come of these new attempts. At first Ramírez, the Mexican Minister of Relations, showed a disposition to recognize the New Orleans Company to the extent of giving it a preference in the bids for the enterprise, and submitted a draft embracing this proposal; [67] but he soon suffered a change of mind. On February 14, 1852, Letcher reported that he was satisfied he could neither negotiate an acceptable new treaty, nor obtain satisfactory changes in the old; that he believed it was the "deliberate aim of the government and of Congress to reject the treaty"; but that he was determined Mexico should "have a full view of the dangerous precipice over which" she stood.[68]

The danger to which Letcher referred was the state of public opinion in the United States and the determination of his government to uphold the claims of its citizens. News that Mexico intended to transfer to England the right to construct the proposed communication had arrived and occasioned considerable excitement. On December 22 and 23, 1851, Webster had instructed Letcher to make known to the Minister of Relations that the United States "could not see with indifference that isthmus or any part of it possessed under the sway of any European state; or that the railroad or canal should be controlled by the government of such state." He authorized him to notify the Mexican government that failure to ratify the treaty before the expiration of the time limit would lead to serious consequences: "The temper of the people and the disposition of Congress are [were] both assuming a very decided tone . . . , especially since the proposition in the Mexican Senate to transfer the right to England." [69]

The tensity of the situation led President Fillmore to "waive," as he said, "the ceremony of diplomatic intercourse" and address the Mexican President an unofficial note regarding the difficulties between the two countries. In this despatch Fillmore called attention to the importance of the Tehuantepec communication to the United

---

[66] *Sen. Ex. Doc.* No. 97, 32 Cong., 1 Sess., pp. 95-96. For this revolt see *Post*, p. 89 ff.

[67] *Sen. Ex. Doc.* No. 97, 32 Cong., 1 Sess. (Ser. 621), p. 121.

[68] Letcher to Webster, *ibid.*, pp. 112-114.

[69] Webster, *Works*, National ed., XVI, 633; *Sen. Ex. Doc.* No. 97, 32 Cong., 1 Sess. (Ser. 621), pp. 109-111.

States and to Mexico, but he laid most weight upon the rights of the holders of the Garay grant.

> I beg leave, [he said] most earnestly to call the attention of your Excellency to the probable difficulties that may grow up between the two nations, should Mexico break her plighted faith in the grant to Garay. Our citizens, relying upon her good faith, have become interested in that grant; they have advanced large sums of money for the purpose of carrying out its object; they have surveyed a route for a railroad, and demonstrated the practicability of constructing it; and it is not possible that they should now be deprived of privileges guaranteed by that grant, and sustain the heavy losses that must ensue, without appealing to their own government for the enforcement of their rights. My anxious desire is to avoid the too probable consequences that must result from such an appeal. We cannot if we would, be indifferent to it . . . I have but a few months to remain at the head of this government, when my responsibility will cease, and this difficult and complicated matter will devolve upon some other agent. I can assure you that my love for my country, as well as my sincere desire to promote the prosperity of yours, induces me most earnestly to urge upon your Excellency to leave nothing undone to adjust the controversy upon this subject . . .[70]

But Fillmore's letter arrived at the Mexican capital too late to influence the deliberations which were taking place. Ramírez's open declaration of his intention to oppose the ratification of the treaty, and his publication of a memorial defending the action of Mexico in refusing to recognize the Garay grant, so exasperated Letcher that he addressed a long and vigorous note to the Minister, censuring the publication and distribution of the memorial as unprecedented in the "annals of negotiation," reiterating the determination of the United States to stand by its citizens, and requesting that the treaty in question be submitted to Congress.[71] This request was immediately complied with, and, as expected, the convention was almost unanimously rejected.[72]

Fillmore's letter reached Arista on April 14, 1852, and in order to forestall the disagreeable impression which the news of the rejection of the treaty might produce in the United States, the Mexican President replied immediately. He assured Fillmore that the ques-

---

[70] Fillmore to Arista, March 19, 1852, *ibid.*, pp. 157–158. Fillmore had first submitted this letter to Webster for criticism and revision, Webster, *Works*, XVIII, 517.

This note represents the utmost effort which Fillmore was willing to put forth in the interest of the grantees. He was opposed to a war with Mexico "to gratify the wishes or cupidity of any private company." (See his letter to Webster of July 19, 1851, in Webster Papers, Vol. 10; see also his letter of May 20, 1852, in Van Tyne, *The Letters of Daniel Webster*, p. 528.)

[71] Letcher to Ramírez, April 2, 1852; *ibid.*, pp. 129–139.

[72] *Ibid.*, p. 128.

tion of a communication through Tehuantepec certainly should not produce any friction between the two countries, since Mexico had always desired to see the enterprise consummated. The real difficulty, as it appeared to him, lay in the obstinacy with which the New Orleans company insisted upon the validity of the Garay grant. It had been proposed to Letcher that these pretensions be abandoned, and that the company apply directly to Mexico for another concession. At first the United States Minister had seemed disposed to accept this method of settlement, but soon afterwards, "to the astonishment and regret of all," he had demanded that the treaty of January 25 be submitted as it stood to the Mexican Congress. Such a course of action seemed to warrant the conclusion that the "object particularly aimed at was an occasion to bring the two countries into a conflict." Moreover, Mr. Letcher had recently given offence to the Minister of Relations.

For all these reasons Arista said he had determined to refer the matter directly to Fillmore. With this in view he had already dispatched Don Manuel Larrainzar to Washington with a full account of the recent occurrences. He was also enclosing a copy of the Ramírez memorial which would set forth the "true history of the [Tehuantepec] affair, traced from the fountain head and supported by authentic documents." He hoped that his Excellency the President would carefully peruse it and bear in mind that he was "accountable to God and to the world" for the use of the "power entrusted to his hands." [73]

To all appearances a deadlock had now been reached. The government of the United States, apparently convinced that it had a just complaint against Mexico, seemed to be prepared to support the claims of its citizens by force if necessary. Mexico was just as determined to resist what she considered an encroachment upon her territory. Larrainzar was not authorized to recede one step from the position of non-recognition of the assignees of the Garay grant.[74]

In July, 1852, the Congress of the United States decided to take a hand in the dispute. Mason of Virginia brought forward a resolution calling upon the President for the correspondence relating

---

[73] Arista to Fillmore, April 15, 1852, *ibid.*, pp. 159–162. For the correspondence between Letcher and Ramírez, see *Sen. Rep.* No. 355, 32 Cong., 1 Sess. (Ser. 631), pp. 14–19.

[74] Larrainzar to Webster, July 10, 1852, Notes from Mex. Leg., Vol. 6. On May 19 Webster had written Fillmore that he feared Mexico would provoke the U. S. into taking "another slice of territory, and paying for it, for the benefit of persons concerned in the government." (*Works*, XVIII, 531–533.)

to the Tehuantepec negotiations and it was immediately given unanimous approval. President Fillmore soon complied, and the correspondence was hurried to the Committee on Foreign Affairs. On August 30 this committee submitted along with their report, three resolutions declaring: (1) That it was not "compatible with the dignity" of the United States government to "prosecute the subject further by negotiation"; (2) that any renewal of negotiations should only be acceded to in case the proposition from Mexico was not inconsistent with the demands of the United States in regard to the Garay grant; and (3) that the United States stood committed to the protection of the rights of its citizens, and "should Mexico within a reasonable time, fail to reconsider her position concerning said grant" it would become necessary for the United States to take remedial action.

Senator Brooke of Mississippi introduced at the same time an informal resolution proposing that Mexico be given only until March 1, to put the American holders in possession of their property and franchises.[75]

As this session of Congress closed on August 31, no action was taken except to table the resolutions, but the matter was given considerable attention during the early part of the next session, Seward of New York and Hale of New Hampshire opposing the resolutions, while Mason of Virginia, Downs of Louisiana, and Brooke of Mississippi spoke in their defence. These discussions revealed the fact that war with Mexico was by no means as imminent as it had seemed. Not only were those who favored rival routes jealous of the Tehuantepec interests, but even the supporters of the resolutions, with no idea that war would result, apparently urged the matter as a sort of bluff. If this method should fail to accomplish results, they were of the opinion that the American company could still obtain possession of its rights.[76]

Though a portion of the Mexican press continued to utter forebodings of an Anglo-American invasion of the isthmus and the government itself showed uneasiness as late as August, 1852, it is probable that Mexican statesmen had already conceived a plan whereby they confidently expected to achieve a pacific settlement of the issue. Private interests in the United States had been largely responsible for the critical situation; might they not also be made to furnish a way of escape? As early as August, 1851, the editor of

---

[75] *Globe*, 32 Cong., 1 Sess., p. 2485 ff.

[76] *Cong. Globe*, 32 Cong. 2 Sess., pp. 365, 458, 469, 537, 628, App., pp. 134–147, 160–170.

El Universal had descried a "ray of hope" in the fact that such an expansionist journal as the New York *Herald* had begun to champion the Vanderbilt projects in Nicaragua.[77] Soon afterwards there began to arrive in the Mexican capital letters from "citizens of New York, Washington City, and other places," as well as "publications in large numbers," all advising the Arista administration of the dangers which lurked in the ratification of the Tehuantepec treaty, and perhaps leading it to conclude that the rejection of the pact might not, after all, be attended by serious consequences.[78] Even before the Mexican Congress refused to ratify the treaty, A. G. Sloo of New York had been introduced to prominent Mexican politicians.[79] Articles written by B. E. Green to the New York *Herald* in the fall of 1852 and violently opposing the New Orleans company had found their way into the Mexican archives, as had also a letter addressed by Thomas H. Benton to his constituents.[80] It is not unlikely therefore that these factors influenced Mexico to seek to give further impulse to this rivalry and incidentally to replenish her needy treasury by bestowing a new concession upon *Sloo and Associates.*[81]

This new grant was free from most of the dangerous provisions of the Garay concession. No lands for colonization were included, rigorous provisions regarding the introduction of armed forces were made, the holders were forbidden recourse to any except Mexican courts, one-third of the company's stock was placed for six months at the disposal of Mexican purchasers, and the Mexican government was to be a shareholder. In return for the cession the company was to pay Mexico six hundred thousand dollars,[82] and by a secret

[77] Rich to Webster, No. 20, Aug. 31, 1852, Mex. Desp. Vol. 15; *El Universal,* 23 y 24 de agosto de 1851.

[78] Letcher to Webster, No. 101, Dec. 14, 1851, Mex. Desp. Vol. 15. In order to illustrate this propaganda against the Tehuantepec grant Letcher enclosed a copy of a letter written by Jonas P. Levy to President Arista. Levy was interested in a projected line of steamers between the United States and Mexico. He warned Arista of the "pending danger" of the "loss of territory" which the Tehuantepec scheme involved.

[79] *El Siglo XIX,* 13 de enero de 1853. On April 24, 1854, *El Universal* contained an article advocating a mixed company.

[80] *Archivo Mexicano. Actas de las Sesiones de las Camaras,* I, 109-132, 275-303.

[81] Consult *El Universal,* 29 de noviembre de 1852, 13 y 14 de enero y 7 de febrero 1853; *El Siglo XIX,* 11 de enero de 1853. See also Letcher to Webster, No. 11, June 20, 1852, Mex. Desp. Vol. 15, and Conkling to Secretary of State, No. 1, Nov. 23, 1832, *ibid.,* Vol. 16, where reference is made to accusations of bribery on the part of the rivals for the cession.

[82] *Sen. Ex. Doc.* No. 72, 35 Cong., 1 Sess. (Ser. 930), pp. 21-26.

arrangement it obligated itself to stand between the Mexican government and the New Orleans company.[83]

The death of Webster, moreover, seemed to remove another difficulty. His term as secretary of state had been characterized by vigor, and the New Orleans company had found in him a faithful and able champion; but no sooner had Conrad, who succeeded to Webster's duties during his last illness, taken up the pen, than he addressed a letter to Conkling, who had been appointed in Letcher's place as Mexican minister, showing a disposition to give over to Mexico. Conkling was told not to reopen negotiations, but to ascertain if possible what were the objections of Mexico to the Garay grant, and to persuade the New Orleans company to dispense with or modify the obnoxious clauses. If Mexico's pride should not permit her to recognize the Garay privilege in any form, he was cautiously to sound the government upon the question of ceding the right of way to the United States government.[84] These instructions clearly indicated a spirit of moderation. Conkling, upon arriving in Mexico, manifested a friendly disposition, and, on March 21, 1853, signed a convention recognizing the Sloo grant.

The attitude which the Democratic administration would assume when it entered upon its duties now became an important consideration. Although the Mexican press had seen in the Sloo grant what was termed a "way of escape," there was still considerable uneasiness in regard to the "loco-focos." It was quite the fashion of this group while parading under the name of Young America to denounce the foreign policy of the Whigs as lacking in force and decision, and to declare the absorption of the entire continent as the destiny of their nation. Of such a tenor were the articles contained in the *Democratic Review* for January and June, 1852. The first of these ridiculed the foreign policy of the Whig administration, censuring it, among other things, for allowing American citizens in "defiance of public contract and private purchase" to be driven from Tehuantepec. The other, in commenting upon the expansionist plank in the Democratic platform, declared that it meant full expansion and a vigorous policy in regard both to the Isthmus of Tehuantepec and to Panama.[85] Other exponents of this expansionist sentiment were the Washington *Republic* and the New York *Herald,* and it often received vigorous expression in the halls of Congress and at banquets given in honor of Democratic statesmen. *El Universal,* the leading Mexican conservative paper of the time,

[83] *Ibid.,* pp. 5, 39.
[84] Conrad to Conkling, October 14, 1852, *ibid.,* pp. 12–14.
[85] Vol. XXXI, 2, 492.

took upon itself the special task of keeping watch over the movements of the Democrats. On November 26, 1852, the editor of this publication declared that the dangers from the North had increased since the "demagogical party" had come into power and expressed the fear that Pierce, like Polk, would take advantage of Mexico's dissensions to rob the nation of its territory. On March 30, 1853, a letter taken from the New Orleans *Picayune* and asserting that the Tehuantepec affair would be one of the first considerations of the new administration, was quoted.[86] These and similar articles served to keep up a state of uneasiness in Mexico which, if it should have been somewhat allayed by the failure of the vigorous resolutions of the Senate of the United States to come up for further consideration, could not have been expected to vanish when it became known that the Pierce administration did not approve the Conkling convention.[87]

[86] For further notice of this expansionist sentiment in the contemporaneous Mexican press, see files of *El Universal,* 1852–1853; *Eco de España,* 15 y 19 de octubre de 1853; *El Siglo XIX,* abril to deciembre, 1853.

[87] *Sen. Ex. Jour.,* IX, 247–248.

CHAPTER IV

MEXICAN GRIEVANCES, 1848–1853: THE INDIAN PROBLEM

WHENEVER and wherever the white race and the red have come into contact with each other conflicts have usually occurred. When the Indians have dwelt in an intermediate position between two nations of white men occasions for trouble have been multiplied. This has been particularly true in the case of virile and warlike Indians roaming over inaccessible frontier regions. Since Mexico had often felt the savage strength and cruelty of Apache, Comanche, and other tribes living on its northern borders, it was only natural that the Mexican government should evince great anxiety with reference to their disposition in the treaty which brought the war with the United States to an end.

The eleventh article of this treaty placed upon the United States responsibility for the control of such of these Indians as lived along the northern side of the new boundary. The main provisions of the article were the following: (1) The United States was bound to restrain the Indians residing within the acquired territory from incursions into Mexico and to *exact satisfaction* for such as should unavoidably occur. (2) It was to be made unlawful for any inhabitant of the United States to acquire captives or property taken from Mexico by the Indians inhabiting either country. (3) The United States was to rescue and deliver to Mexican agents all captives brought into its territory from Mexico. (4) The United States agreed to pass without delay such laws as the fulfillment of these obligations required and, in removing the Indians, to bear in mind the security of the Mexican frontier.[1]

Merely a cursory notice of these terms will impress one with the magnitude of the task imposed upon the United States government. What considerations led to the assumption of such a responsibility?

In his message of December 7, 1847, President Polk advanced a benevolent argument to justify the annexation of New Mexico. He suggested that since the Mexican government was too weak to restrain the wild Indians from their depredations upon the province

---

[1] Malloy, *Treaties,* I, 1112–1113.

and upon other portions of the northern frontier, it might desire to place this region under the United States. "If New Mexico were held and governed by the United States," Polk argued, "we could prevent these tribes from committing such outrages and compel them to release the captives and to restore them to their families and friends."[2]

It was necessity more than altruism, however, that eventually moved the United States to accept the Indian burden. While the negotiation of the pact of 1848 was in progress, the legislature of Chihuahua recommended "that no treaty be concluded . . . which shall [should] not establish a sufficient security that neither the government of the United States, nor the citizens of that nation, shall [should] buy from the savages the plunder obtained by robberies committed within the Mexican territory; nor furnish them . . . with means for making war; nor drive them upon our territory by purchasing from them their lands; nor favor their incursions directly or indirectly."[3] In commenting upon Article XI, Trist had declared that the assumption of responsibility for the Indians was "indispensable to make the treaty acceptable to the Northern States [of Mexico], or to any who take the proper interest in their security; in a word, to anyone who has [had] the feelings of a Mexican citizen, or at least respect for the obligations which a federal union imposes."[4]

Trist seems to have anticipated opposition to the article on the part of his government; and with the view of forestalling it, he had suggested that the obligation did not differ essentially from that assumed by the 33d article of the treaty of amity, commerce, and navigation, of 1831. In the new treaty, he argued, it had "the character of a practical law, agreed upon and established upon serious consideration of its requirements, and in the bona fide intention that these shall be fulfilled."[5] When the article came up in the Senate, it did occasion considerable debate, and attempts were made to strike out one paragraph after another until virtually the whole was embraced. Excepting the clause which made it unlawful for any inhabitant of the United States to furnish the Indians with fire-arms or ammunition, however, all these attempts failed.[6]

Secretary of State Buchanan, in a letter to the Mexican Minister of Relations, also assigned a humanitarian motive for the Senate's

[2] *Sen. Ex. Doc.* No. 1, 30 Cong., 1 Sess. (Ser. 503), p. 11.
[3] *Sen. Ex. Doc.* No. 52, 30 Cong., 1 Sess. (Ser. 509), p. 176.
[4] *Ibid.,* p. 293.
[5] *Ibid., loc. cit.*
[6] *Ibid.,* pp. 11–13.

action in regard to this clause. "This amendment was adopted on a principle of humanity. These Indians must live by the chase; and without fire-arms they cannot secure the means of subsistence. Indeed, for the want of such arms the extremity of hunger and suffering might drive them to commit the very depredations which the treaty seeks to avoid, and to make incursions for food either upon the Mexican or American settlements." [7]

In the same paragraph Buchanan asserted that his government possessed "both the ability and the will to restrain the Indians within the extended limits of the United States from making incursions into Mexican territories as well as to execute all the other stipulations of the eleventh article." During the next few years Mexican officials were to question the "will" and the United States was to have its eyes opened as to the "ability" required to restrain the Indians in question.

There were in the territory acquired by the annexation of Texas and the treaty of 1848 some 160,000 to 180,000 Indians.[8] By no means all of them were within reach of the Mexican border and a great number were semi-civilized or docile, but the wildest and most cruel habitually lived upon the chase and upon plunder taken from the inhabitants of northern Mexico. The Apaches and Comanches especially, and to a lesser degree the Utahs, Navajos, Kiowas, and Yumas, had been since Spanish times the terror of the frontier.[9] These tribes, moreover, were often at war with each other and with the semi-civilized Indians, so that by the acquisition of the new territory the government of the United States assumed the three-fold task of keeping them at peace with each other, protecting its own citizens from their outrages, and restraining the wild tribes from their accustomed depredations upon Mexico. This task was to be complicated and rendered more difficult by mountain, desert, and summer's heat, by somewhat unscrupulous traders and "land sharks," and by numerous other obstacles.[10]

The United States had perhaps never confronted an Indian prob-

[7] *Cong. Globe*, 30 Cong., 2 Sess., p. 494.

[8] "Report of Commissioner of Indian Affairs," November 26, 1853, *House Ex. Doc.* No. 1, part 1, 33 Cong., 1 Sess. (Ser. 710), p. 243.

[9] Bancroft, *North Mexican States and Texas*, II, 593 ff.; *El Universal*, 3 de junio and 22 de julio de 1849.

[10] *The Official Correspondence of James S. Calhoun*, pp. 50–51, 250, 260, 379, 421–422, 438, 445–455, *passim*, hereafter cited as Calhoun, *Correspondence; Sen. Ex. Doc* No. 1, 31 Cong., 2 Sess. (Ser. 587), p. 43; *El Universal*, 13 de enero de 1853. The Indians of California, excepting those living near Yuma Junction, appear not to have made incursions into Mexico.

lem of such magnitude and it was slow to formulate a definite and consistent policy. The proper course would have been the establishment of numerous reservations, distant from the frontier, under the direction of an efficient corps of agents and the surveillance of a large army. In this manner both the American and the Mexican frontiers might have been protected from Indian outrages. But such a policy was not seriously considered until long after 1848.[11] The War Department and the Commissioner of Indian Affairs were forced to deal with the Indians in their native haunts.

The heads of these bureaus were dependent upon Congress for funds, supplies, and equipment. But during this period the national legislature was busy discussing the slavery issue, responsibility for the Mexican War, and other partisan or sectional questions. Moreover, it had no adequate appreciation of the new problem of frontier defence and, frightened by the expenses of 1846–1848, had now determined to pursue a policy of rigid economy. As a result, it failed to give sufficient support either to the army or to the Indian department. Some three or four thousand soldiers were provided where ten thousand were needed. Infantry and artillery were assigned the work of cavalry. Five or six Indian agents were expected to accomplish the task of twenty.—If the nation failed to live up to its international duty during these years the blame rests largely upon Congress.[12]

The Indian department diligently applied what means it could obtain and kept the treaty obligations to Mexico constantly in mind. On April 7, 1849, James S. Calhoun was made Indian agent for New Mexico and instructed, among other things, to "determine the number of prisoners held by the Indians in that territory, whether they were Americans or Mexicans and, if Mexicans, whether they were taken prior to the termination of the war and treaty with Mexico, or subsequently." [13] Calhoun arrived at his post on July 22, and for the next three years, first as Indian agent, and then as Governor and Superintendent of Indian Affairs, he labored arduously and conscientiously, but was always greatly handicapped by lack of means and equipment. In the spring of 1849, J. C. Hays had been sent to the Gila Apaches, but in January of the following year he had

[11] The reservation policy was not adopted until 1854.

[12] For a fuller discussion of this phase of the question, see Rippy, "Indians of the Southwest," etc., in *The Hispanic American Historical Review*, II (August, 1919), p. 366 ff.

[13] Commissioner of Indian Affairs to Calhoun, April 7, 1849, Calhoun, *Correspondence*, pp. 3–5.

resigned his post declaring his "inability to be of any service whatever with the means furnished." [14]   Early in 1850 Calhoun took the liberty of sending Cyrus Choice as agent to the Utahs, with the hope of obtaining means for paying him by a later appropriation.[15] Other than the services of these Calhoun seems to have had no assistance until the four agents appointed by the law of February 27, 1851, arrived.

It does not fall within the scope of this work to follow in detail the labors of these Indian agents. The primary interest here is in their attempts to carry out the provisions of Article XI. An examination of their work will reveal considerable effort to meet this responsibility.   During the period of their service prior to December 30, 1853, when negotiations for the Gadsden Treaty were completed, four important Indian treaties were made, three of which were ratified by Congress.   Each contained the stipulation that the Indians should deliver up Mexican prisoners.   The treaty with the Gila Apaches (July 1, 1852) went a step further and pledged the Indians to desist from making incursions of a hostile or predatory character into the territory of Mexico and to refrain from taking captives therefrom.[16]

Moreover, on at least three occasions Calhoun reported that prisoners taken from the Indians of New Mexico had been handed over to the Mexican authorities.   On June 27, 1850, thirteen Mexican captives were given to José N. Prieto, at El Paso.[17]   On August 5, 1851, five more were delivered at the same place, and later in the month Calhoun reported that three others were being held awaiting the advice of the Mexican government.[18]   As it was well known that the Gila Apaches had numerous Mexican prisoners,[19] it is not unlikely that after the treaty of July, 1852, these captives also were sent to their homes.   This much at least was accomplished by the Indian agents of New Mexico—a not inconsiderable task when the difficulties under which they labored are borne in mind.

The efforts of the Indian agents in Texas were perhaps not so fruitful in tangible results.   This was probably due to the lack of coöperation caused by the fact that there was no superintendent of Indian affairs in Texas, as well as to the great difficulties arising

---

[14] *Ibid.*, p. 34, note.
[15] *Ibid.*, pp. 122, 142–143, 187.
[16] Kappler, *Laws and Treaties,* II, 585–586, 598–600; Calhoun, *Correspondence,* pp. 314–316.
[17] Calhoun, *Correspondence,* p. 227.
[18] *Ibid.*, pp. 390, 401.
[19] *Ibid.*, p. 401.

from the absence of a definite policy. The time of the agents was chiefly occupied in distributing rations from the various posts on the frontier and in pacifying the Indians in regard to their lands.[20] By the treaty of 1846 the leading tribes of Texas agreed to surrender "all white persons and negroes" whom they captured.[21] Lieutenant Colonel Hardee reported in August, 1851, that the Comanches and Lipans had handed over seventeen Mexican captives to Judge Robbins [Rollins], one of the special Indian agents of Texas, and that they had been restored to their families. Hardee stated that these were the "only Mexican prisoners delivered up by the Indians" since the establishment of the eighth military department.[22] No further instances of the return of prisoners by the Texan agents has been found.

Finally, on July 27, 1853, Special Agent Thomas Fitzpatrick negotiated at Fort Atkinson a treaty with the Comanches, Kiowas, and Apaches, the fifth article of which bound these tribes to refrain from warlike incursions into the Mexican provinces and, not only to restore all captives which might be taken by "any bands, war-parties or individuals of said several tribes," but to make restitution for all wrongs inflicted upon Mexicans.[23]

In general, however, these treaties were not adhered to with any degree of faithfulness; and to the conciliatory negotiations of the agents it was necessary to add the chastisements of the army.

In the distribution of troops on the Southwestern frontier fulfillment of treaty obligations to Mexico seems to have been kept in mind. The Secretary of War, when informing General Brooke of his appointment as Commander of the Eighth Military Department (Texas), urged him to make earnest efforts to reclaim and restore all captives who had been taken and carried away by the Indians. "This duty," he continued, "has been assumed in behalf of the Mexican people by a treaty with Mexico, which is considered as superadding only a specified obligation to the general claim which humanity imposes on all civilized nations."[24] On February 3, 1849, Lieutenant-Colonel Washington of New Mexico had written Adjutant-General Jones that he had neglected nothing to effect a

[20] *House Ex. Doc.* No. 5, Part II, 31 Cong., 1 Sess. (Ser. 570, pp. 963–965; ibid., No. 2, Part III, 32 Cong., 1 Sess. (Ser. 636), pp. 515–526; *Sen. Ex. Doc.*, No. 1, Part I, 32 Cong., 2 Sess. (Ser. 658), pp. 431–436.

[21] Kappler, *Laws and Treaties,* II, 554.

[22] Hardee to Deas, August 29, 1851, *House Ex. Doc.* No. 2, 32 Cong., 1 Sess. (Ser. 634), pp. 121–122.

[23] Kappler, *op. cit.,* II, 600–602.

[24] Crawford to Brooke, June 4, 1849, *House Ex. Doc.* No. 5, 31 Cong., 1 Sess. (Ser. 569), pp. 138–139.

speedy release of prisoners in accordance with the treaty of 1848. Many had been restored to their homes in New Mexico, and others were awaiting instructions from the Mexican republic.[25] In his annual report of 1849 the Secretary of War stated that military operations in Texas and New Mexico had resulted in the recovery of numerous captives, several of whom had been returned to their homes.[26] Thus it will be seen that the War Department had been alert from the outset. Again, in the spring of 1851, when new commanders were sent to Texas, California, and New Mexico, respectively, each of them was given specific instructions regarding the organization of his department. In establishing military posts they were told to be governed by three principles, one of which was the protection of Mexico from the raids of hostile savages. The letters contained a complete statement of the Secretary's views in regard to the matter. He ordered those officers to "bear in mind that the Mexican territory is as much entitled as our own to the protection of our troops against Indian tribes within our limits." [27]

The great need of the frontier was efficient soldiers. The Adjutant-General's report of December 2, 1848 showed a total of 616 troops, rank and file, at the New Mexican posts while 322 more were *en route*. According to the same report Texas had 787 rank and file present, with 575 *en route*. At the close of the next year there were only 708 rank and file present in New Mexico, while there were 1074 in Texas. These troops were gradually increased until in 1853 there were 1,407, including officers, in New Mexico, and 2,649 in Texas. Adding to these the 114 stationed at Fort Yuma, there would have been a total of some 4,100, rank and file, stationed within reach of the Mexican frontier in 1853, though by no means all of them were sufficiently near for immediate service. The only portion of this force which could be considered really effective against Indians, who were usually well-mounted and always excellent horsemen, was the cavalry. In this respect, however, the frontier force was weakest. From the mouth of the Rio Grande to El Paso no cavalry was stationed upon the immediate border prior to 1854. Beginning with 1849 dragoons were posted some distance back of the line, about forty or fifty having been stationed in that year along with the infantry at Fort Inge and Fort Martin Scott. They re-

---

[25] *Ibid.*, p. 105.

[26] *Ibid.*, p. 94.

[27] Secretary of War to Smith, April 30, 1851, *House Ex. Doc.* No. 2, 32 Cong., 1 Sess. (Ser. 634), p. 117; *ibid.* to Sumner, April 1, 1851, *ibid.*, p. 125; *ibid.* to Hitchcock, May 3, 1851, *ibid.*, p. 143.

mained at the latter post till 1851 and at the former till 1852. Beginning with 1852, more than two hundred mounted riflemen were posted at Forts Inge, Ewell, and Merrill, a number increased to 324 in 1853; and in the latter year some fifty dragoons were stationed at Fort Territt. Above El Paso, at Socorro, New Mexico, there were some thirty-five or forty dragoons stationed during 1848, 1849, and 1850, and probably a few more than this number at Doña Ana during the latter two years. Beginning with 1851 an average of about eighty dragoons was stationed at Fort Fillmore, New Mexico, while almost an equal number was at Fort Webster in 1852 and 1853. It will thus be noted that there were within immediate reach of the frontier from 1848 to 1852 not more than 180 mounted men at any one time, and never more than 600 at any time during the entire period.[28]

The regulars were often supplemented by volunteer companies. Following a severe raid on Corpus Christi in the late summer of 1849, three companies of mounted militia were called into service. In March of the following year the Governor of Texas was called upon for another company. These four were retained in service until fall.[29] During the spring and summer of 1851 volunteer companies under McCullock, Wallace, Connor, and Ford were kept in the field.[30] In response to a call issued by Governor Washington of New Mexico on March 20, 1849, four companies, one of infantry and three of cavalry, were mustered into service.[31] Among the force which proceeded against the Apaches from Rayado, New Mexico, in July, 1850, were ninety Mexican volunteers, citizens of New Mexico.[32] Probably there were other instances when militia was used, but there was always the expense objection, and early in 1852, considerable suffering resulted in that region because the poverty of the territorial government would not permit the purchase of arms and ammunition and the Governor neither had power to call out

[28] See reports of Adjutant-General, 1848-1853, in *House Ex. Doc.* No. 1, 30 Cong., 2 Sess. (Ser. 537), p. 184; *Sen. Ex. Doc.* No. 1, Part I, 31 Cong., 1 Sess. (Ser. 549), p. 188; *ibid.,* No. 1, Part II, 31 Cong., 2 Sess. (Ser. 587), p. 116; *House Ex. Doc.* No. 2, Part I, 32 Cong., 1 Sess. (Ser. 634), pp. 200-206; *Sen. Ex. Doc.* No. 1, Part II, 32 Cong., 2 Sess. (Ser. 659), pp. 58-60; *ibid.,* No. 1, Part II, 33 Cong., 1 Sess. (Ser. 691), pp. 118-121.

[29] *House Ex. Doc.* No. 5, 31 Cong., 1 Sess. (Ser. 569), pp. 146-150; *Sen. Ex. Doc.* No. 1, Part II, 31 Cong., 2 Sess. (Ser. 587), p. 31; *House Ex. Doc.* No. 1, Part II, 32 Cong., 2 Sess. (Ser. 674), p. 16.

[30] *Cong. Globe,* 32 Cong., 2 Sess., pp. 1906-1915.

[31] *House Ex. Doc.,* No. 5, Part I, 31 Cong., 1 Sess. (Ser. 569), pp. 107-110.

[32] *Sen. Ex. Doc.* No. 1, Part II, 31 Cong., 1 Sess. (Ser. 587), p. 74.

the militia nor the ability to persuade the commander of the ninth
department (New Mexico) to furnish army supplies.[33]   The President had authority after 1850 to mount the infantry when occasion
demanded, but such improvised cavalry was necessarily inefficient.
The military forces, assisted by the Indian department, when the
two could work in harmony, were admittedly and decidedly unable to
cope with the Indian problems.   Citizens of Texas and New Mexico
frequently sent in memorials and the Secretaries of War and Interior
constantly complained of the inadequacy of the resources placed in
their hands.[34]   A joint resolution of the Texan legislature (January 28, 1850), urging their representatives to lay the matter before
Congress, declared that "vast numbers" of citizens had been captured
and killed, and property, "to a vast amount," had been stolen and
carried away by the Indians.[35]   A petition dated at Santa Fé, on
February 27, 1850, and signed by fifty-two citizens, asserted that although some of the petitioners had lived in New Mexico from five to
fifty years, they had never known Indian troubles to be as terrible
and alarming.[36]   Petitions of a similar nature were presented in the
summer of the following year.[37]   General Brooke of Texas said in
1851 that he needed three thousand cavalry for his department,
while McCall of New Mexico asked for fourteen hundred.[38]   So far
as the Texans and New Mexicans were concerned, the Indians were
reported quiet in 1852,[39] but during this very time their raids upon
Mexico were particularly destructive.[40]

Officials of the United States were inclined at times to accuse
the Mexican government of failing to coöperate with them in the
pursuit of Indians and of making little attempt to defend its frontier.[41]   The facts, however, will hardly bear out this view.   Indeed, Mexico made a special effort during this period to provide for

[33] Calhoun, *Correspondence*, pp. 366, 473, 480, 507.

[34] See reports of 1850, 1851, in *Sen. Ex. Doc.* No. I, 31 Cong. 2 Sess.
(Ser. 587), p. 19; *ibid.*, Part II (Ser. 587), p. 3; *House Ex. Doc.* No. 2, 32
Cong. 1 Sess. (Ser. 634), p. 105; *ibid.*, Part II (Ser. 635), p. 489.

[35] Gammel, *Laws of Texas*, III, 85.

[36] Calhoun, *Correspondence*, p. 157.

[37] *Ibid.*, pp. 366–386.

[38] *Globe*, 31 Cong., 2 Sess. p. 722.

[39] Calhoun, *Correspondence*, 529, 540; "Report of the Secretary of War,"
House Ex. Doc. No. 1, Part II, 32 Cong., 2 Sess. (Ser. 674), p. 3.

[40] Mexican Border Commission of 1873, *Report*, pp. 292, 332; John Bartlett,
Personal Narrative, II, 385; *El Universal*, 18 de agosto y 17 de noviembre de
1852; Pinart Transcripts, Sonora, V, 1–135.

[41] Report of the Secretary of War, *House Ex. Doc.* No. 2, 32 Cong., 1 Sess.
(Ser. 634), p. 106; Fillmore's annual message, *House Ex. Doc.* No. 2, 32 Cong.,
1 Sess. (Ser. 634), pp. 18–19; Globe, 33 Cong., 1 Sess., pp. 1534–1548.

the protection of the northern frontier, and she failed from lack of means and on account of internal disturbances and filibuster raids rather than from indifference.

By special law of December 4, 1845, designed to direct colonization, a provision had been made for establishing "military colonies, composed of Mexicans or foreigners, or of one of both, along the coasts and frontiers as the government shall [should] designate, especially in order to restrain the inroads of the savages." [42]   A decree dated June 19, 1848, called attention to the fact that the frontier line as marked by the late treaty with the United States demanded urgent attention in order to conserve the integrity of the nation's territory and "to defend the frontier states from the frequent and cruel incursions of savages," and proceeded to provide for the establishment of military colonies. The northern frontier was marked out into three divisions, designated as the Frontier of the East, the Frontier of Chihuahua, and the Frontier of the West, and eighteen colonies were distributed among them. Seven were allotted to the East, which included Tamaulipas and Coahuila, five to Chihuahua, another five to Sonora, and one to Lower California. The land around each colony, after being divided into lots and improved at government expense, was to be assigned to the soldiers for cultivation. Voluntary enlistment for a term of six years was provided, at the end of which time each soldier was to receive a bounty of ten *pesos* and the allotment of land which he had been cultivating. During his term of service he was to share the fruits of the soil. Provision was made for civilian settlers around each colony and, upon reaching a certain population, the settlement was to be given a civil government. In the eighteen colonies troops to the number of 2,426 were to be stationed, consisting of 1,715 cavalry and the rest infantry, and each cavalryman was to be equipped with two horses. [43]   This last stipulation is of especial interest when the proportion of cavalry which the United States provided for the frontier is borne in mind.

In the course of the next three years these colonies were laid out either at the points designated or provisionally in places as near as the Indian situation would permit. The report of the Minister of War and Marine for 1850 states that in Chihuahua the colonies of Del Norte and El Paso del Norte were established in May and June, 1849, while those of San Carlos and Pilares were planted in May and July of the following year. Janos had not been established in the place determined, but preparations for it were being made.

[42] Maza, *Código de colonización*, p. 356.
[43] *Ibid.*, pp. 400–406, Doc. 2.

On the frontier of the East the colonies of Rio Grande, Guerrero, Monclova-Viejo and Monterey had been set up, but Camargo was yet unfounded and the colony of San Vicente had been left provisionally at Santa Rosa. None of the colonies of the West had been established in their ultimate destinations, although 225 troops and 200 civilians were at the ancient presidio of Fronteras and other soldiers intended for the colonies were campaigning against the Indians. During the following year, however, all the colonies were set up either permanently or temporarily.[44]

At the close of 1850 there had been recruited for the Colonies of the East 434 troops and 972 horses, for those of Chihuahua, 296 troops and 220 horses, for those of the West, 340 troops and 306 horses. By the end of the next year, the troops had increased to 502, 334, and 445 respectively, but there had been a falling off of almost 200 in the number of horses, while the report of December, 1851, showed a decrease in both stock and men, there being in all the colonies at that time 1,093 troops and 689 horses and mules.[45]

Moreover, by treaties of October, 1850, and July, 1852, peaceful Seminoles and Muskogees had been permitted to settle in the vicinity of the colonies of the East and of Chihuahua.[46] In 1851, reduced Sierra Gorda Indians were sent to augment the frontier forces. In

[44] The situation of the military colonies in 1851 is given as follows:
  1. Camargo, in the town of that name.
  2. El Pán, at Lampazos.
  3. Monterey, at Paso de Piedra.
  4. Rio Grande, at Misión Neuva.
  5. Guerrero, at Piedras Negras.
  6. Monclova-Viejo, at Moral.
  7. San Vicente, in the old presidio of Agua Verde.
  8. San Carlos, in the old presidio of that name.
  9. Del Norte, at Presidio del Norte.
  10. Pilares, in Vado de Piedra.
  11. Paso, about fourteen leagues down the Rio Grande from El Paso.
  12. Janos, near the village of Janos.
13–17. The five colonies of Sonora, at the presidios of Bavispe, Fronteras, Santa Cruz, Tucsón, and Altar.
  18. Rosario, at Mision Santo Tomás in Lower California.
  (See Manero, *Documentos sobre colonización,* pp. 28–36.)
[45] Ministerio de Guerra y Marina, *Memoria,* enero de 1850, Doc. No. 4, enero de 1851, Doc. No. 1, and deciembre de 1851.
[46] Mexican Border Commission of 1873, *Report,* p. 304; Ministerio de Guerra y Marina, *Memoria,* 31 de deciembre de 1851, in Manero, *Documentos sobre colonización,* p. 30. A. M. Jauregui, Inspector of the Colonies of the East, had written in regard to the matter in July, 1850, and a decree of November 18, 1850, had stated the conditions under which they were to be received. (Maza, *Código de colonización,* pp. 474–475.)

March, 1853, General Blanco, the new inspector, arrived in Sonora with resources sufficient to place 1,500 men under arms, and during the same year a French colony, accepting privileges extended in accordance with Article 45 of the decree of 1846, settled at Cocóspera.[47]

Besides these colonies a considerable number of regular troops was stationed in the frontier states; and, in 1849, following out the recommendation of a *Junta* of the federal Congress formed for the purpose of considering means of frontier protection, an appropriation was made for raising 4,000 national guards.[48] Moreover, the towns of the afflicted sections formed leagues for common defence; private individuals contributed to war and ransom funds; Durango, Chihuahua, and Sonora offered bounties for scalps and prisoners; and, finally, the frontier states of Neuva León, Chihuahua, Coahuila, Zacatecas, Tamaulipas, and San Luis Potosí began after 1851 to consider plans for union to resist the common peril.[49]

Most of these measures were rendered ineffective, however, by internal disturbances and the chaotic state of the national funds, by the poverty of the frontier states, by epidemics of cholera and fever, by the quest for gold which drew a large number of Sonorans annually to California, and lastly, by the filibusters who, beginning their raids in 1851, kept the whole northern border in almost constant agitation.[50] Taking such difficulties as these into consideration, one will not be surprised to learn that the number of troops of all classes on the northern frontier was only 2,136 at the close of 1849, and 3,189 in January, 1851.[51]

Yet these Mexican troops carried on frequent campaigns against the Indians. Tables compiled by the Mexican Commission sent to the border in 1873 show that the forces in Nuevo León had thirty-three encounters with the savages from 1848 to 1853 inclusive, while

---

[47] Pinart Transcripts, Sonora, V, 2, 8, 11. By decree of May 20, 1853, Santa Anna seems to have incorporated the military colonies with the *milicia activa*. Dublán y Lozano, *Legislación mexicana*, VI, 407, 412.

[48] *Legislación mexicana*, VI, 551–552.

[49] Mexican Border Commission of 1873, *Report*, pp. 273, 298, 340; Pinart Transcripts, Sonora, IV, 188, 215–216; Bancroft, *History of Mexico*, V, 579–580.

[50] Mexico, *Documentos relativos a la reunión en esta capital de los cobernadores de los estados convocados para proveer a las exigencias del Erario Federal*, pp. 2–52; Bancroft, *History of.Mexico*, V, 603–605, 685–686; Pinart Transcripts, Sonora, IV, 86–87, 264, 273, 283; Ministerio de Guerra ÿ Marina, *Memoria* (1850), pp. 14–15; *Sen. Ex. Doc.* No. 97, 32 Cong., 1 Sess. (Ser. 621), pp. 89, 113.

[51] Ministerio de Guerra y Marina, *Memoria*, 24 de enero de 1850, Doc. No. 4; *ibid.*, 3 de enero de 1851, Doc. No. 1.

these of Coahuila had more than forty. Files of *El Sonoriense* mention some thirty or forty in Sonora from 1848 to the beginning of the filibuster raids in September, 1851. Data as to the exact number of campaigns and skirmishes in the other states have not been available, but it is safe to say that they were proportionately numerous.[52] Indeed the federal government had adopted the policy of war to the death and favored an arrangement whereby the boundary of the United States could be crossed in pursuit of the depredating bands.[53]

An attempt to ascertain the effectiveness of these encounters would be uninteresting and perhaps meagre in results. It is not necessary, however, to go into this matter, for the purpose of the writer is merely to determine whether the Mexican government in good faith *endeavored* to defend itself. The best proof of the failure of both the United States and Mexico to cope with the Indian problem is found in the losses sustained by the latter country during the five years subsequently to 1848. The Indian incursions were destructive and frequent as far down the Mexican border as Reynoso, in Tamaulipas. They increased in numbers and severity further north and west, assuming horrifying proportions in Sonora. Commenting upon the news of the frontier press, one of the Mexican journals of the period remarked: "The first thing that meets our eyes is always something about savage Indians. Agriculture, industry and commerce relapse into insignificance, the revenues cease, tranquillity is lost in the constant fear of the peril which threatens life, honor, and family interests; all in short present the most doleful picture of misfortune and desolation." Three hundred and sixty-six claims arising from the depredations of this period and amounting to almost thirty-two million dollars were presented to the joint claims commission which was created in 1868. One may of course readily admit that press reports and demands of the claimants alike were exaggerated and still hold the conviction that the Mexican border states were in a lamentable condition. Indeed, this was never denied by officials of the United States serving on the southwestern frontier at the time, nor was it ever successfully refuted by American diplomatists who were called upon to defend the United States against the charge of non-fulfillment of treaty obligations.[54]

[52] See Mexican Border Commission of 1873, *Report*, pp. 253–281; files of *El Universal*, 1850–1853; Comisión Pesquisidora de la Frontera del nordeste Informe, Apéndice, I–XLI; Pinart Transcripts, Sonora, vols. IV–V.

[53] Ministerio de Guerra y Marina, *Memoria* (1850), p. 14.

[54] For a more elaborate treatment of this phase of the question, see Rippy, "The Indians of the Southwest in the Diplomacy of the United States and

Mexican complaints against the United States for failure to comply with the eleventh article of the treaty of 1848 were numerous and widespread. A *Junta* of the Federal Congress, organized in 1849 for the supervision of matters pertaining to the defence of the frontier, declared that the Indian wars could be terminated if the United States would do its duty and called upon the government for a report upon Article XI, "as a basis upon which to predicate the action most expedient for the welfare" of the frontier states.[55] The *Inspector* of the frontier, in his report to the *Junta*, dated July 8, 1849, said that defence of northern Mexico would be impossible until the United States lived up to its obligations. In 1851 the Sub-Inspector of the Chihuahua section said that Mexico might as well cease to expect the United States to restrain the Indians and proceed to take matters into its own hands, the Sub-Inspector of the East requested permission to cross the Rio Grande in pursuit of the savages, and complaint after complaint was raised in Sonora.[56] Lastly, the plan of defence drawn up by an association of frontier states and published in February, 1852, contained the following article:

The government of the coalition will earnestly urge the supreme national authorities to obtain from the government at Washington permission for the Mexican forces to cross the Rio Grande, and attack the nomadic tribes which reside in that territory; without omitting to demand constantly and vigorously the fulfillment of Article 11th of the treaty of Guadalupe, and an indemnification for the losses which the frontier has heretofore suffered from the non-fulfillment of that article.[57]

On March 20, 1850, De la Rosa, Mexican Minister at Washington, began to complain of the failure of the United States to "restrain and repress the Indians" on the Mexican frontier. He declared that the only advantage which could accrue to Mexico from the late treaty, the only advantage which could "compensate her for the many sacrifices" it "rendered necessary," was the exact fulfillment of the stipulation with respect to these Indians. To obtain this the Minister considered his chief duty. In conclusion, he declared that Mexico would "continue . . . to use all her efforts for the re-pression of the tribes of those frontiers."[58]

Four more times during the course of the year De la Rosa

Mexico, 1848–1853," in *Hispanic American Historical Review*, II (August, 1919), 363 ff., and authorities therein cited.

[55] Mexican Border Commission of 1873, *Report*, p. 298.
[56] Pinart Transcripts, Sonora, IV, 113, 244–245.
[57] Mexican Border Commission of 1873, *Report*, p. 340.
[58] *Sen. Ex. Doc.* No. 44, 31 Cong., 1 Sess. (Ser. 558).

complained to the Secretary of State with reference to the matter, his most persistent note bearing the date of December 5. In this document he reminded Webster that it was "daily becoming more and more indispensable that the government of the United States should adopt the promptest and most active measures in order to prevent . . . the incursions of the Indian savages of the United States upon the population of the Mexican frontier." He expressed the anxious hope that Congress, in accordance with the President's recommendations, would give the matter "all the attention which its importance" required. He was especially concerned because of the season of the year and the weakened condition of the frontier population which had been caused by the failure of their crops.[59]

On March 17, of the following year, the Mexican Minister again made urgent inquiries as to what the last session of Congress had done to furnish more adequate protection to the frontier. He said that he had been persistently instructed to address Webster in reference to the matter, but that he had refrained from doing so because each day during the recent session of Congress he had hoped to hear that their body had taken some action in regard to the Indians. He now asked what his government might expect with reference to the fulfillment of this important obligation.[60] This inquiry Webster promptly answered by mailing De la Rosa a report of the Secretary of War on measures which had been taken to defend the frontier.[61]

At about the same time the Indian question began to be pressed upon the Minister of the United States in Mexico. In February, 1851, President Arista requested Buckingham Smith, American *chargé* at Mexico City, to notify his government of the fact that "the Indians severely ravage the country along the northern frontier of the Republic, in some instances as many as fifty persons having been destroyed at a time." In reporting this request Smith stated that Arista was inclined to "propose an union of troops with ours on both sides of the line." [62] In the following July a tentative proposal for reciprocal crossing of the border was actually made by the Mexican government and referred to Washington for advice.[63]

[59] De la Rosa to Webster, May 6 and 15, Sept. 4, 1850, Notes from the Mex. Leg., Vol. 5. The letter of Dec. 5 is printed in *House Ex. Doc.,* No. 4, 31 Cong., 2 Sess. (Ser. 596).
[60] Notes from the Mex. Leg., Vol. 5.
[61] Note of April 3, 1851, Notes to Mex. Leg., Vol. 6.
[62] Smith to Webster, No. 45, Feb. 16, 1851, Mex. Desp., Vol. 14.
[63] *Id.,* No. 74, July 12, 1851, *loc. cit.*

Such a suggestion was destined under somewhat different circumstances and three decades later to be followed with great advantage to both countries, but Webster was not interested in it now. He had other plans in view. He instructed Letcher, who was returning to the Mexican post after a brief leave of absence, to obtain release not only from the eleventh article of the Treaty of Guadalupe Hidalgo, but also from the thirty-third article of the treaty of 1831. Webster declared that the President deemed this a matter of "utmost importance." If the articles in question should remain in force the government of the United States would be "constantly liable to imputations of bad faith. Exaggerated and fraudulent claims for indemnification will [would] be preferred against it, and there will [would] be no hope of preserving harmonious relations with the government of Mexico." While admitting that the inhabitants of the northern states of Mexico had suffered severely from Indian depredations, he maintained that the United States had given equal care to the protection of Mexico and of the United States and that the treaty did not promise individual reparation. Nevertheless, he declared that his government was willing to give a pecuniary consideration for release from the article, provided that portions of the sum could be applied to the liquidation of unpaid installments under the claims convention of 1843 and to the satisfaction of claims of citizens of the United States which had arisen against Mexico since 1848; and he authorized Letcher to make some such proposal.[64]

But negotiations for release from the Indian obligation proceeded slowly. The meddling of speculators and busybodies and the inopportune severity of Indian invasions rendered Letcher's task very difficult. "Kind-hearted . . . letter writers, feeling a deep interest in the welfare of Mexico, . . . warned her, in the most solemn manner, against making any agreement to change the 11th Article . . ."[65] A certain Señor Escandón, a wealthy Mexican intriguer interested in buying up Indian claims, returned from Washington in the fall of 1851 and advised that the United States would give ten million dollars for release.[66] At about the same time Indians from the United States hurled themselves with savage fury against the Mexican frontier.[67] On January 24, 1852, Letcher declared that "this Indian question" was "becoming more and more important every hour of

[64] No. 72, Aug. 19, 1851, Mex. Ins., Vol. 16; Webster, *Works*, XVIII, 462.
[65] Letcher to Webster, No. 101, Dec. 14, 1851, Mex. Desp., Vol. 15., printed in *Sen. Ex. Doc.* No. 97, 32 Cong., 1 Sess. (Ser. 621), p. 105.
[66] Private of Jan. 19, 1852, Mex. Desp., Vol. 15.
[67] *Ibid.*

the day." "If the treaty be not made now," he said, "G—d only knows the consequences which our country may suffer hereafter." [68]

In the letter of January 24, Letcher asked for authority to augment the sum he had originally been instructed to give for the abrogation of the article in question. In reply, Webster instructed him to offer an additional two millions. But to Letcher's proposal to abrogate Article XI, the Mexican Minister countered with a demand for twelve millions, after having informed Letcher that the Secretary of War had estimated that the claims arising from Indian depredations at eight millions, that Mexico had already spent three millions in a defence which the United States should have provided, and that it would require another eight millions to put Mexico in a position to protect herself. [69] Letcher feigned great irritation, and informed Ramírez that the negotiation might be considered at an end.

Although Letcher still hoped that a treaty could be secured, nothing was accomplished with reference to the matter prior to his recall. His successor, Alfred Conkling, was not authorized to make so favorable an offer to Mexico. The same sum that Letcher had been instructed to propose as a maximum was placed at his disposal, but Mexico was not to be freed from the claims of American citizens against her. [70]

Conkling had been at his post almost a year before he found opportunity to enter into negotiations with reference to the subject. On June 16 and 20, 1853, he conferred with the Mexican Minister of Foreign Relations, who declared that the Mexican government was of the opinion that it might reasonably expect thirty-five or forty millions for the abrogation of the article, and that it would not think of considering less than ten millions. Conkling thereupon informed him that it would be useless to continue the discussions, and thus the matter stood when Gadsden proceeded to Mexico City two months later. [71]

[68] Private, *loc. cit.*
[69] No. 2.
[70] Webster to Conkling, No. 4, Oct. 14, 1852, Mex. Ins., Vol. 16.
[71] Conkling to Webster, No. 47, June 20, 1853, Mex. Desp., Vol. 17.

CHAPTER V

MEXICAN GRIEVANCES, 1848–1853: FILIBUSTER RAIDS

RAIDS of bands of filibusters from the United States caused great uneasiness and bitterness in Mexico for some time subsequent to the treaty of 1848. The decade following the Mexican War may be accurately described as the Golden Age of Anglo-American filibustering. The advance guard of manifest destiny, these adventurers not only made incursions into Cuba, Mexico, Central America, and the Sandwich Islands; but they even talked of giving more than mere sympathy to Ireland and the oppressed peoples of Europe.[1]

Between 1848 and 1853 Cuba and Mexico were the main centers of attraction. With reference to many of the expeditions it was often uncertain which of these regions was the goal, the conquest of one always being a possible preliminary step in the occupation of the other. The Mexican government and the Mexican public were therefore almost as much disturbed by expeditions designed for Cuba as by plans for the actual invasion of Mexico.

Threats of invading Mexico began to be made soon after the Treaty of Guadalupe Hidalgo was signed. On May 30, 1848, at midnight, a party of eighteen armed Americans entered the pueblo of Nuri, in the district of Alamos, Sonora, robbed and burned the homes of the leading inhabitants, seized a number of stock; and then fled. Upon being pursued, they were forced to abandon their plunder, but as they retreated by the *rancho* of Tarahumares they carried off eleven animals, three saddles, and forty dollars in money.[2]

This, of course, was merely a band of robbers. Before the close of the year, however, rumors of a filibustering expedition of an important nature became current. On August 30, Buchanan, then Secretary of State, sent circulars to the District Attorneys of St. Louis, Little Rock, Jackson (Tennessee), Natchez, Galveston, and Mobile, instructing them to guard against an apprehended attempt on the part of

---

[1] *D .10cratic Review,* Old Series, XXXI (Feb. and May, 1852), 97–128, 401–424, XXXII (July, 1852), 4 ff. Recall in this connection the visit of Kossuth and cf. Scroggs, *Filibusters and Financiers,* and Callahan, *Cuba and International Relations.*

[2] Comisión Pesquisidora de la Frontera del Noroeste (1872), *Informe,* 7–8.

citizens of the United States to invade the northern states of Mexico. This design, if it ever existed, was soon thwarted, however.[3]

Then came the year 1849 with swarms of emigrant gold-seekers passing along the southern routes to California.[4] On June 1, a band of forty of these fortune-hunters attacked and pillaged the undefended *mineral* of Cieneguita, in Sonora, maltreated its citizens, and then escaped across the Gila before an organized pursuit could be made. This, too, was perhaps no more than a band of ruffians out for adventure, but such adventurers were later to give Mexico trouble from their new home in California.[5]

In the following August more formidable plans were set on foot. A certain Colonel White who had fought in the race war of Yucatán collected a group of some 540 men on Round Island, near New Orleans. He was said to be expecting reinforcements from New York, Boston, and Baltimore. Although the purpose of the filibusters could not be ascertained, reports indicated that they were destined either for Yucatán, for Cuba, or for the Sierra Madre states where an independent republic had recently been proclaimed.[6] This expedition also was soon broken up.[7]

Next, in May, 1850, and in August, 1851, occurred the López expedition against Cuba. The first of these went by way of Yucatán and left a portion of its forces on the Mexican island of Contoy.[8] The second occurred at the time the Louisiana Tehuantepec Company was threatening to invade Mexico, and this coincidence probably gave rise to the report, by the correspondent of *El Universal* at New Orleans, that 50,000 filibusters were preparing to attack Tehuantepec.[9] At any rate, the destiny of Mexico was conceived to be so closely linked with that of Cuba that it could not look with indifference upon Cuba's fight with the "pirates."[10]

Before the second expedition of López left the United States imultaneous preparations for invasions of Mexico were begun in California and in Texas.

The organization of the former enterprise seems to have been loosely planned. Indeed, there may have been in progress at the same time

---

[3] Buchanan, *Works*, VIII, 192–195.

[4] Audubon, *Journal of Western Travels;* Eppard, The Southern Emigrant Trails to California, University of California Library, MS.

[5] Comisión Pesquisidora de la Frontera del Noroeste, (1872), *op. cit.*, p. 8.

[6] *Sen. Ex. Doc.* No. 57, 31 Cong., 1 Sess. (Ser. 561) p. 4 ff. Taylor in his proclamation was uncertain whither the expedition was bound.

[7] Caldwell, *The López Expeditions to Cuba*, pp. 43–56.

[8] *Ibid.*, p. 70 ff.

[9] *El Universal*, 10 de agosto de 1851.

[10] *Ibid.*, 30 de agosto, 2 y 6 de setiembre, 1853.

preparations for more than one raid, but the chief promoter of the schemes seems to have been Joseph C. Moorehead, Quartermaster-General of California.

In March, 1851, news came from Los Angeles to the effect that a party of men armed with rifles and six-shooters had passed through that town. They were said to be a portion of a band of three hundred who were ostensibly on a prospecting tour to the Gila, but really intending to make a descent upon Sonora.[11] It was further rumored that during March and April several parties numbering from twenty-five to one hundred had departed with the avowed purpose of revolutionizing the same state.[12]

It is possible that these belonged to the Moorehead enterprise. On April 20, after having disposed of a considerable portion of the arms and munitions under his charge and appropriated the proceeds, Moorehead purchased the bark *Josephine* and left for Mazatlán. With him he carried only about forty-five men, but there seem to have been two other divisions, one of which was to proceed *via* Los Angeles, and the other by sea to La Paz.[13] Before the close of the month the *Josephine* landed at San Diego, where most of the adventurers deserted their bankrupt leader and set out on their return to San Francisco.[14] Moorehead himself, fearing arrest for misappropriation of state property, spent some time in Lower California.[15] At length, about May 8, he set sail for Mazatlán.[16] No other information regarding him has been found.

On July 2, the *Prefect* of Guaymas reported that American adventurers whom he supposed to be filibusters had landed at La Paz.[17] What steps were taken against them has not been ascertained. They may have received rough treatment, as Mexican soldiers and artillery had been ordered by the central government to that territory in the previous May.[18]

The division which went by land reached Sonora in July. On the 6th of that month, the commander of the military colony at Santa

---

[11] *Alta California*, April 5, 1851; Pinart Transcripts, Sonora, IV, 312–313.
[12] Los Angeles *Star*, May 26, 1851. Quoted in *El Universal*, 11 de julio de 1851.
[13] Bancroft, *History of California*, VI, 584.
[14] *Alta California*, May 17, 1851.
[15] On April 25, the Governor had asked the Legislature to make provision for Moorehead's apprehension by a suitable reward, or by sending some person with authority for his arrest, but the request was not granted. *Journals of the California Legislature*, 2d Sess., pp. 452, 479, 496, 1716, 1717, 1720.
[16] *Alta California*, May 17, 1851.
[17] *El Universal*, 18 de julio de 1851.
[18] *Ibid.*, 22 de mayo de 1851.

Cruz reported that he had found an encampment of North Americans near San Javier. Three days later four of the party arrived at Arispe, whither they said they had come to ask permission of the state government to work the mines.[19] During the same month two others of the same party came to San Ignacio to purchase tea and coffee.[20] Preparations for the expulsion of the filibusters proceeded slowly, however, for on August 10 the original party, now increased to sixty-seven, had been allowed to take up its quarters in a ranch house; and it was not until November that they were expelled from the state.[21]

The disturbances in Texas were of greater magnitude, and they resulted in greater injury to Mexico. During the war of 1846–1848, the United States government promulgated a tariff system of its own and invited Anglo-American merchants to introduce their goods.[22] This was the signal for a considerable rush for the lower Rio Grande. When the war closed these merchants soon found themselves involved in difficulty. Their goods were subjected to vexatious delays before being permitted to proceed to the interior, or were confiscated outright,[23] and their chances for future profits were virtually cut off by high tariffs and prohibitions.[24] This was disappointing and exasperating, and they were made to feel the situation more keenly by the belief that British interests had dictated the Mexican tariff system.[25] Having once got a taste of the profits of Mexican trade, they did not easily give up, however. The practice of smuggling was soon begun, and, judging from the amount that went on, the returns must have been large. Practically every Anglo-American along the line chose the pursuit of a merchant rather than that of stock-raising or agriculture, and smuggling, ceasing to be blameworthy, soon became meritorious.[26]

But this pursuit was by no means free from difficulty. The

[19] Flores to Governor of Sonora, July 9, 1851, in Pinart Transcripts. Sonora, IV, 329–330.
[20] Prefect of San Ignacio to Governor of Sonora, August 14, 1851; Ibid., IV, 333.
[21] Prefect of Guadalupe to id., August 20, and El Sonoriense, 7 de noviembre de 1851, Ibid., IV, 342.
[22] Sen. Ex. Doc. No. 80, 32 Cong., I Sess. (Ser. 620), p. 57.
[23] Supra. pp. 56–58.
[24] Dublán y Lozano, Legislación mexicana, V, 42–44, 62–63, 545–546, VI, 42–43; Sen. Ex. Doc., No. 52, 32 Cong., 2 Sess. (Ser. 665), pp. 227–229.
[25] Sen. Ex. Doc. No. 80, 32 Cong., 1 Sess. (Ser. 620), p. 4; Em. Domenech, Missionary Adventures, p. 327.
[26] Emory, "Report," House Ex. Doc. No. 135, 34 Cong., 1 Sess. (Ser. 861), pp. 63–64.

customs-house guards of Mexico seemed to show considerable energy. In November, 1849, they seized a contraband, and in January, February, and March, 1850, other cargoes were taken.[27] On July 20, the federal government made provision for a special guard for the northern frontier.[27a] This attempt to give the revenue system rigorous enforcement made the merchants even more desperate. They now began to organize bands for the recovery of cargoes seized by the Mexican officials, and their efforts sometimes met with success.[28]

Just at this juncture there occurred a revolution in Tamaulipas which furnished an opportunity for operations on a larger scale.[29] Prominent among the insurgents was José María Carvajal, who had been educated in the United States and was fairly well known on both sides of the international line.[30] The merchants accordingly decided to support this leader, at least until they could introduce large quantities of their goods virtually free of duties. Backed by their contributions, Carvajal was able by the offer of attractive pay to induce several Americans to enlist. Others were perhaps moved by the filibustering spirit of the times, while still others saw in the enterprise an opportunity to profit by the seizure of runaway slaves.[31]

On September 19, Carvajal, at the head of one hundred Mexicans and seventy Americans, attacked Camargo. Darkness came before the battle was decided, but during the night sixty more Americans crossed over from Davis's Ranch, and on the following morning the defenders of the town were forced to capitulate.[32] The insurgents held Camargo until October 9, when they began to move upon Matamoras.[33] Meantime their forces had received considerable recruits—possibly including a few deserters from the United States army—and Ávalos, the commander of the Mexican troops at Matamoras, had experienced much excitement. The merchants, too, had probably

[27] Mexican Border Commission of 1873, *Report*, pp. 179–180; *Sen. Ex. Doc.* No. 31, 44 Cong., 2 Sess. (Ser. 1720), U. S. Claims No. 200 and 363.

[27a] Dublán y Lozano, *op. cit.*, V, 729–730.

[28] Mexican Border Commission of 1873, *op. et loc. cit.*

[29] For the plan of *La Loba* under which the revolutionists were operating, see *El Siglo XIX*, 30 de setiembre de 1851. The fact that this plan provided for the reduction of the tariff, the moderation of the punishment for smuggling, and the removal of the federal troops from the state, indicated that the Anglo-American merchants may have had something to do with it.

[30] Domenech, *Missionary Adventures*, pp. 327–328.

[31] Smith to the Adjutant-General, July 18, 1852, in *Sen. Ex. Doc.* No. 1, 32 Cong., 2 Sess. (Ser. 659), pp. 15–20.

[32] Vicente Comacho to the Comandante General of the State of Neuvo León, September 24, 1851, *El Siglo XIX*, 14 de octubre de 1851.

[33] Ávalos to the Minister of War, October 11, 1851, *ibid.*, octubre de 1851.

decided that it was not to their interest to allow the revolution to assume too great proportions, and had suggested to Avalos a method of counteracting it.[34] Accordingly, the latter had on September 30, issued a tariff of his own which removed the prohibitions and greatly reduced the duties.[35]

On October 20, the siege of Matamoras began. A series of what might almost be termed sham battles ensued; and at length, "after eleven days of attacking, sacking, and burning, the filibusters retired demoralized and with great losses." [36] Carvajal took refuge in the United States where he collected the remnants of his scattered forces and recrossed the Rio Grande only to be severely chastised, after a four days' attack upon Cerralvo, and compelled again to seek refuge on the other side of the river.[37] On February 21, 1852, he made a third attempt near Camargo, having with him on this occasion more than four hundred Anglo-Americans, but the opposition of the authorities of the United States had precipitated and crippled his movements so that his defeat was easily accomplished. His forces suffered considerable losses and he was compelled once more to flee into Texas.[38] Even these defeats did not put an end to his efforts, however, for in the spring of 1853 he and his filibusters made another sally, and in 1855 rumors of still another invasion were current.[39]

By this desultory fighting the Mexican treasury was deprived of much needed revenue, the Rio Grande frontier was kept in a state of almost constant excitement, and race bitterness was intensified. The Americans along the border were chagrined by the defeat of their comrades and by the execution of several who were taken prisoners. Avalos was burned in effigy at New Orleans, and hanged in effigy, after much celebration, on the banks of the Rio Grande opposite Matamoras; [40] an officer of the filibusters crossed the river one evening at twilight, surprised and dispersed a Mexican guard of ten persons, and seized their horses; and a party of Anglo-Americans from Laredo, Texas, several times menaced the Mexican town of Monterey-

[34] Domenech, op. cit., p. 329.

[35] El Siglo XIX, 29 de octubre de 1851.

[36] Bolton, Guide to . . . the Principal Archives of Mexico, p. 299.

[37] Comandante of Nuevo León to the Minister of War and Marine, December 9, 1851, El Siglo XIX, 26 de deciembre de 1851.

[38] Antonio Canales to Comandante of Nuevo León, 10 de februar and 9 de marzo de 1852; Smith to Adjutant-General, July 18, 1852, Sen. Ex. Doc. No. 1, Part II, 32 Cong., 2 Sess. (Ser. 659), pp. 15–20; Letcher to Webster, March 8, 1852, ibid., No. 87, 32 Cong., 1 Sess. (Ser. 621), p. 125.

[39] Bolton, op. cit., pp. 299–300. An interesting British account of this raid is enclosed in Smith to the Secy. of State, Nov. 20, 1851. Mex. Desp., Vol. 15.

[40] Domenech, op. cit., pp. 347–348.

Laredo on the opposite bank of the river.[41] The Mexicans, on the other hand, were encouraged by the success of their arms to make excursions into Texas. Members of a party which destroyed the ranch of A. V. Edmundson some forty miles above Brownsville declared that they intended to rob and kill all the Americans living along the river.[42] Avalos, who naturally was not pleased with the attitude assumed by the Anglo-Americans toward him, retaliated by instigating a widespread Indian invasion of Texas.[43]

While Carvajal and his followers were disturbing the tranquillity of the lower Rio Grande, French adventurers, very numerous at this time in California, were attempting to get possession of the mines of Sonora. The first two of their schemes, led by Charles de Pindrey and Lepine de Sigondis respectively, simply responded to an offer of lands on the part of Mexico in return for fighting the Apaches on the frontier, and were therefore devoid of filibustering intent.[44] The third seems to have been in its inception merely a mining and colonization enterprise, but it later developed into something quite different.

Gaston Raousset de Boulbon, a French nobleman and soldier of fortune, had become deeply interested in the mines of Sonora. He soon evolved a mining and colonization scheme so attractive that it enlisted the interest of the French consul at San Francisco and of the French Minister in Mexico.[45] In the early spring of 1852 he effected the organization of a company which styled itself *La Restauradora*, obtained the approval of the Mexican government, and secured the Swiss bankers Jecker, Torre and Company as underwriters for the enterprise.[46] On May 19, 1852, with a company of 150 Frenchmen, he set sail for Guaymas. Soon after his arrival at that port, he found he had rivals in the field whose influence upon the government tended greatly to embarrass his movements.[47] He was forced to remain here a month before he was able to start for his destination, and after his departure he was subjected to one limitation after another by Señor Blanco, the military commander of the Mexican frontier. At length

---

[41] Emory, "Report," *loc. cit.,* pp. 61–62; Mexican Border Commission of 1873, *Report,* pp. 188–189.

[42] *Alta California,* June 16, 1852.

[43] Domenech, *op. cit.* pp. 347–348.

[44] *Alta California,* October 18, 1852; Scroggs, *Filibusters and Financiers,* 20–23 and authorities cited; Juda, "California Filibusters," *Grizzly Bear,* February, 1919, pp. 3–4.

[45] Scroggs, *op. cit.,* pp. 24–25.

[46] *Alta California,* November 25, 1852, Scroggs, *op. cit.,* pp. 25–26.

[47] A banking house of San Francisco had enlisted the interest of prominent officials in Sonora in the same mines which Raousset had set out to procure. *Alta California,* October 25, and November 22, 1852; Scroggs, *op. cit.,* p. 25.

his exasperation became uncontrollable, and he determined upon open rebellion. He posed as the champion and protector of an independent Sonora, and began hostilities by an attack upon Hermosillo, which he stormed and took on October 14. This victory, however, brought little advantage. The population did not respond to Raousset's appeal, several of the company had received wounds, and Raousset and a number of his officers were ill. The Frenchmen accordingly became anxious to withdraw. They soon patched up an agreement with the Mexican authorities by which they were to be allowed to proceed unmolested to Guaymas in consideration for the evacuation of Hermosillo. Setting out thither, they were met on the outskirts of the town by Blanco, who induced them to disband and submit to the laws and authorities of the country. Most of them soon found their way back to San Francisco. The count himself, who had gone to Mazatlán, did not return to California until the following spring.[48]

When he finally reached San Francisco, Raousset was met with an ovation which left no doubt as to the sentiments of the Californians towards filibustering; and, enthused by this reception, he immediately set about to plan an invasion of Sonora. News of these preparations soon alarmed the Mexican government. The members of the foreign diplomatic corps in Mexico were notified of the affair and of the attitude which the government was to assume toward it.[49] At the same time the executives of Sonora, Chihuahua, Sinaloa, and Lower California were ordered to prepare for the defense.[50] But Santa Anna, who had just come to power, was apparently pondering whether it would not be wise to use the French as a buffer against the Indians and the expansionists of the United States. Levasseur, French Minister in Mexico, learned of Santa Anna's state of mind and wrote the Consul of his government at San Francisco. The month of June accordingly found Raousset again in Mexico, not as an invader, but as a promoter seeking a contract for the peaceful introduction of a French colony. For some reason, however, he not only failed in his efforts, but so aroused the enmity of Santa Anna that he proclaimed the Count an outlaw and forced him to flee for his life.[51]

[48] Scroggs, op. cit., pp. 27–28; Juda, op. cit., p. 4. It was reported that the merchants of Guaymas, in order to avoid the injury which an open conflict would occasion to their business, paid the Frenchman to disband and leave in peace. See Alta California, December 18 and 23, 1852.

[49] Circular al Cuerpo Diplomático estranjero, 17 de mayo de 1853, Bolton Transcripts.

[50] Pinart Transcripts, Sonora, IV, 173.

[51] Scroggs, op. cit., p. 29.

When Raousset arrived at San Francisco once more he found that the Americans in California had almost completed plans for an expedition against Mexico. This strengthened his determination to secure a foothold in Sonora, and he now began to solicit funds for a new enterprise. But his scheme progressed very slowly on account of the great popularity of the American project.[52]

The proposed American expedition was none other than that of the famous filibuster, William Walker. With the details of this enterprise *per se* the writer is not so much concerned as with its international aspects and its general place in the series of raids against Mexico. The incidents of this raid will therefore be narrated very briefly.

Walker, who was living at the time in California, became interested in the founding of a colony in Sonora sometime during the year 1852,[53] and in June, 1853, he and his former law partner, Henry P. Watkins, went as agents of the enterprise to Guaymas. Here they asked permits to proceed to the interior, where they intended to have an interview with the Governor of Sonora; but the Mexican authorities, suspicious of their intentions, refused to grant the request and suggested that it would be wise for them to get out of the country.[54] They acted upon the suggestion, but Walker had remained at Guaymas long enough to convince himself that a small body of Americans could hold the frontier of Sonora and protect its inhabitants from the Indians;[55] and, accordingly, his failure to gain a semblance of legality for the enterprise was in no way discouraging.

When the agents returned to California they found preparations well under way, and on October 17, at one o'clock in the morning, after having experienced considerable vexation from the federal authorities, a party of forty-five under the leadership of Walker set sail in the brig *Caroline*.[56] Although Walker's ultimate destination was Sonora, he deemed it wise first to occupy Lower California as a base.[57] Proceeding down the coast, he put in for the first time at

---

[52] *Ibid., op. et loc. cit.;* Juda, *op. cit.,* pp. 4–5. For the correspondence exchanged between Raousset and the Mexican military authorities, see Pinart Transcripts, Sonora, V, *passim.*

[53] Walker, *The War in Nicaragua,* p. 19.

[54] Antonio Campuzano to the Governor of Sonora, July 3, 1853, and accompanying documents, Bolton Transcripts.

[55] Walker, *op. cit.,* p. 21. The protection of the Sonorans from the Indians was a favorite plea of Walker.

[56] Scroggs, *Filibusters and Financiers,* p. 36, says they set sail on the 16th, but this is evidently an error. See *Alta California,* October 18, and the Statement of F. Duclaud, a passenger on the *Caroline,* in Bolton Transcripts.

[57] Walker, *op. cit.,* p. 6.

Cape San Lucas. In the vicinity of this port the filibusters spent several days awaiting reënforcements which they expected to arrive at any time. Concluding at length that the auxiliaries had passed them, they set out for La Paz, the designated point of reunion. They landed here on November 3, and had little trouble in making prisoner of Governor Principal Espinosa and seizing the town. One of the first things they did was to tear down the Mexican flag and hoist one of their own, proclaiming the republic of Lower California. Then for the next few days they seem to have engaged in pillage and destruction, not only sacking the customs-house and the home of the Governor Principal, carrying off the archives of both, and setting fire to the buildings, but also plundering whatever other houses suited their fancy.

When they were on the point of leaving La Paz, a new executive, Rebolledo, who had been sent out to supersede Espinosa, put in his appearance. He was just in time to fall into the hands of the filibusters, and they accordingly confined him along with their other prisoners. The procedure occasioned some delay, and, during the interval, it was learned that Mexican troops were coming up. This emboldened the citizens of La Paz to attack the filibusters while they were embarking. In the encounter which followed three of the Walker party were killed and others were wounded. The Mexicans also suffered some casualties.[59]

From La Paz Walker returned to Cape San Lucas. Landing here two days later, he prepared to set up his government, but for some reason changed his mind. Magdalena was next spoken of as a possible capital, and again Walker changed his mind. Ensenada was then decided upon, and the filibusters reached here on November 29. The President immediately organized his government, and issued an address to the people of the United States giving his reasons for the course he had taken.[60]

At the same time he sent out a detachment to a neighboring ranch to secure horses for mounting his troops. These having been obtained, he dispatched a force of improvised cavalry to take the village and military colony of Santa Tomás. Negrete, the commander of the colony, was notified of their intention, however, and he succeeded in

[59] Testimony of Duclaud, *loc cit.* The filibusters claimed that a party of six who were sent ashore to gather wood were fired upon, and that Walker and a company of thirty came to their rescue, administering a sound defeat. For both reports as they reached Upper California, see *Alta California,* December 8, 1853, and January 3, 1854.

[60] *Alta California,* December 8, 1853.

repulsing the filibusters and forcing them to retire. Moreover, the Mexican leader harassed them during their retreat, pursuing them to the filibuster encampment to which he laid seige. On the morning of December 14, the filibusters made a sortie and drove the besiegers away. But the captive Mexican executives in the meantime had induced the Quartermaster of the *Caroline* to sail away with the arms and supplies which remained on board.[61]

This left the filibusters in desperate straits, but re-enforcements arrived a few days later, and the party, now numbering more than two hundred, began to forage off the country and to prepare for the advance into Sonora. While the filibusters seized horses to mount their men, and confiscated and slaughtered cattle in order to obtain dried beef for the march, their leader proclaimed the Republic of Sonora and annexed to it the state of Lower California.[62]

On February 13, they set out to occupy their new republic, marching *via* Santo Tomás and San Vicente. While at the latter village, Walker summoned the natives to a convention. The delegates were received with military honors, and forced both to take the oath of allegiance and to subscribe to a declaration which Walker presented to them.[63] Having thus obtained useful evidence of the adhesion of the natives, the adventurers, now considerably reduced in number by sickness and desertion, left a small garrison at San Vicente and set out for their destination.

Two weeks later a party of ragged, half-starved filibusters were said to have crossed over the Colorado. Fifty of them immediately deserted and went to Fort Yuma. Walker, with the remainder, stayed in Sonora only three days. The little band then recrossed the Colorado and retraced their steps to San Vicente. Arriving there, they found that the garrison had been annihilated by the band of the famous robber, Meléndrez. This chieftain now began to threaten and annoy Walker and his company until they decided it was time for them to effect their escape into the United States. Meléndrez, though constantly encircling them in bantering fashion, did not risk an encounter. At length, early in May, 1854, thirty-three of the filibusters

---

[61] Samuel Ruland to the San Diego *Herald*, December 16, 1853, quoted in *Alta California*, December 27, 1853; Espinosa to the Minister of War and Marine, December 18, 1853, Bolton Transcripts.

[62] *Alta California*, January 30 and 31, 1854.

[63] *Ibid.*, March 15, 1854; Marcy to Almonte, June 12, 1854, Bolton Transcripts, and Notes to the Mex. Leg., Vol. 6. See also Almonte to Marcy, May 31, 1854, Notes from the Mex. Leg., Vol. 7.

crossed over the line near Tía Juana where they surrendered themselves to the officers of the United States army.[64] From this sketch of the filibustering raids it will be seen that between 1848 and 1853 Mexico was rarely free from their threats. Moreover, the situation was rendered more serious by the fact that the government of the United States was either unwilling or unable to restrain its lawless, adventurous subjects. While it is probable that Mexico clung to the former view, there seems nevertheless to have been a great deal of truth in the latter. On the whole, it may be asserted that during this period (1848–1853), as during the Texas revolution, the federal administration was not *unwilling*, but *unable* to restrain them. In taking this view, it is not necessary to maintain that the motives of the government were entirely unselfish. What it desired at the time was transit and communication privileges, commercial concessions, and probably more land; and the saner statesmen realized that these filibuster raids constituted one of the main obstacles preventing the achievement of these ends. If the administration had the disposition to prevent such raids, why then was it unable to do so? In order to answer this question it will be necessary to consider briefly the origin and development of the neutrality laws of the United States, as well as some of the attempts to enforce them.

It will be recalled that the question of neutrality was first brought to the attention of the United States government by the European war which resulted from the French Revolution. Washington's stand in regard to the attitude which his nation should assume toward this struggle is well known. On April 22, 1793, he issued his famous proclamation of neutrality, and circular letters were immediately dispatched to the executive authorities of the several states requiring their coöperation, with force if necessary, in order to obtain its observance. But French sympathy was strong; the proclamation was not supported by an undivided public opinion; and the question, moreover, assumed a sort of political aspect. The states either had no laws reaching the subject, or felt little disposition to enforce the laws they had, and those indicted by the federal government had recourse to that palladium of English liberty, the jury trial. The outcome may be illustrated by the case of Gideon Henfield who was prosecuted for taking service on a French privateer in 1793. A sym-

---

[64] *Alta California*, April 26, and May 16, 1854. The best account of this expedition is found in Scroggs, *Filibusters and Financiers*, p. 31 ff. The writer, as will appear from the citations, has not only had access to most of his sources, but he has used transcripts of Mexican official documents and other Mexican sources, as well as the archives of the State Department of the United States, none of which Scroggs used.

pathetic jury brought in a verdict of not guilty, and his acquittal was hailed with applause by a large number of American citizens.[65]

Washington at length called a special session of Congress to consider means of enforcing his policy, and one of the results was the neutrality law of June 5, 1794. This act contained a provision for its expiration within a little more than two years, but it was extended for a limited time in 1797 and perpetuated by act of April 24, 1800. The revolt of the Spanish colonies led to an attempt to revise the law, and on April 20, 1818, an act superseding all previous legislation was approved; but except for the addition of the phrase, "colony, district, or people," so as to make it applicable to the Spanish American insurgents, it was virtually identical with the act of 1794. The Canadian insurrection gave occasion for another attempt to modify the regulations regarding neutrality, which resulted, however, only in the temporary measure of March 10, 1838. The law of 1818 was therefore in operation during the period under consideration; and, in order to understand the procedure of the United States in regard to the filibuster raids which have been recounted in this chapter, it will be necessary to quote the portion of this act which was applicable to them.

And be it further enacted, That if any person shall, within the territory or jurisdiction of the United States, begin or set on foot, or provide or prepare the means for, any military expedition or enterprise, to be carried on from thence against the territory or dominion of any foreign prince or state, colony, district, or people with whom the United States are at peace, every such person so offending, shall be declared guilty of a high misdemeanor and shall be fined not exceeding three thousand dollars, and imprisoned not more than three years.[66]

In the application of these provisions several difficulties were confronted. In the first place, the language is indefinite. In speaking of the portion of the law which has been quoted, John Marshall said there was "want of precision in the description of the offence, which might produce some difficulty in deciding what cases should come within it." [67] The act made it a misdemeanor to set on foot an expedition, or to prepare means for an expedition against a country at peace with the United States; but was it a violation of the law to

---

[65] Marshall, *Life of Washington,* V, 418 ff.; U. S. v. Henfield, 11 *Federal Cases,* 1099, and U. S. v. O'Sullivan et al., 27 *ibid.,* p. 368 ff.

[66] 3 *U. S. Stat. at L.,* 449, Sec. 6. For the provisions of the other acts see *U. S. Stat. at L.* under dates mentioned. A concise history of the laws is given in U. S. v. O'Sullivan, 27 *Fed. Cases,* 377 ff.

[67] *Democratic Review,* Old Series, XXXI (April, 1852), p. 310.

hold meetings and appoint committees to provide means and make collections for the purpose of aiding a revolution in such country? [68] It was to be a penal offense to set on foot a military expedition; what was meant by the term "military expedition"? Would the act apply to emigrants who were leaving with their arms for protection, but with no apparent military formation? [69] What, moreover, was meant by the phrase, "to be carried on from thence"? If a leader who had determined to engage in hostilities against a country friendly to the United States should decide upon a certain rendezvous outside of the jurisdiction of the United States, would citizens who proceeded as individuals to the rendezvous in response to an informal invitation to join the enterprise expose themselves to the penalties of the law? [70]

In the second place, the law was penal rather than preventive, and therefore did not provide sufficient precautionary means to enable the government to arrest persons entering upon such enterprises before the crime was consummated.[71]   In so far as it related to the acts of armed ships, this defect was remedied by a measure passed on March 3, 1817, which provided that the owners of vessels must give bond for their orderly conduct while upon the high seas. But this was repealed in the following year. Again, on March 10, 1838, the crisis in British relations led to the passage of a law adapted to the peculiar conditions of the northern frontier. By this act, a new rule of evidence was introduced, founded on probable cause alone as sufficient authority to seize and stop, without a warrant, the incursions into Canada; and a new set of officers,—collectors, surveyors, inspectors of customs, naval officers, marshals, etc.—was charged with the duty of enforcing its provisions. But this law expired by its own limitation, and no similar provision was enacted thereafter.[72]

Lastly, the regulations regarding neutrality were not backed by public opinion, without which any law is impotent. It was sometimes difficult to get the federal officials in the regions where the infractions occurred to run counter to public sentiment and enforce the laws; [73] and when indictments were obtained, it was virtually impossible to

[68] *House Ex. Doc.* No. 74, 25 Cong., 2 Sess. (Ser. 325), pp. 392–393; U. S. v. O'Sullivan, *loc. cit.*

[69] *House Doc.* No. 2, 24 Cong., 2 Sess. (Ser. 301), pp. 52, *passim.*

[70] *Democratic Review,* XXXI (April and June, 1852), 310–311.

[71] U. S. v. O'Sullivan, *loc. cit.; House Doc.* No. 35, 25 Cong., 3 Sess. (Ser. 346), p. 340.

[72] 5 *U. S. Stat. at L.,* 212.

[73] This was especially true in regard to the Texas Revolution. See *House Doc.* No. 2, 24 Cong., 2 Sess. (Ser. 301), pp. 38–41, 52, 64, and House Doc. No. 74, 25 Cong., 2 Sess. (Ser. 325), pp. 389–390.

find a jury that would convict. In fact, it was asserted in 1851 that there had not been a single conviction under the sixth article of the act of 1818.[74]

The assistance given by citizens of the United States to the Texans had revealed to Mexico the inefficiency of the attempts of the government at Washington to maintain complete neutrality. The results of the attempts to suppress the filibustering enterprises from 1848 to 1853 were hardly more assuring. The Round Island scheme of 1849 was completely shattered by a vigorous presidential proclamation and by the efforts of seven war vessels which cut off all supplies from the adventurers and made their departure impossible. Warrants were then issued for the arrest of five of the leaders; but owing to the fact that the enterprise seemed discredited, and on account of the state of public opinion, no further action was taken.[75]

The failure of the Round Island enterprise caused the filibusters to move with great caution. The vigilance of the authorities in New York had led López early in 1850 to shift his main base to New Orleans. Here the filibusters found legal advisers who counseled them how to operate within the law.[76] And when after the invasion of Cuba had been consummated, the remnant of the expedition was chased into Key West by a Spanish man-of-war, no attempt was made to arrest them, although their vessel was seized.[77] Soon afterwards, however, the Grand Jury of New Orleans found true bills against sixteen of the leaders. The Secretary of the Interior urged upon the District Attorney there the importance of the case, declaring that the filibusters had brought the laws of the country into disrepute and disturbed its relations with a foreign power, and that therefore it was the President's "earnest" desire that they should be "brought to trial and punishment." [78] In regard to the first trial that came up, that of Henderson, the charge of the judge was, moreover, somewhat unfavorable to the defendant. Nevertheless, three successive juries were divided and failed to convict, and then the other fifteen filibusters were discharged.[79]

The federal authorities also made considerable effort to break up the López expedition planned in 1851. There was another proclama-

[74] U. S. v. O'Sullivan *et al.*
[75] Caldwell, *The López Expeditions to Cuba*, pp. 54–55.
[76] *Ibid.*, p. 57; District Attorney Hunton to Clayton, May 1, 1850, *Sen. Ex. Doc.* No. 57, 31 Cong., 1 Sess. (Ser. 561), p. 25; Caldwell, *op. cit.*, p. 57 ff.
[77] Caldwell, *op. cit.*, p. 74.
[78] Ewing to Hunton, June 10, 1850, quoted in *ibid.*, pp. 77–78.
[79] Caldwell, *op. cit.*, pp. 78–79.

tion even more vigorous than that of 1849.[80] Contingents in Ohio and New York were arrested and brought to trial, and once more there was an earnest, though vain, attempt on the part of the federal judge to obtain a verdict of guilty from a too sympathetic jury.[81] But, due either to uncertainty regarding the application of the law or to willful neglect, the officer of the customs house at New Orleans allowed the preparations of the main division of the expedition to go on virtually unmolested, and made no attempt to prevent its departure. The good intentions of the federal government were evinced, however, by the severe censure and ultimate dismissal of this official.[82]

With reference to the proposed expeditions against Mexico the federal authorities seem likewise to have exercised some little precaution. So far as has been ascertained, no action was taken in regard to the Moorehead expedition. The readiness with which it fell to pieces of its own accord may have been taken as an indication that none was needed. Preparations for an invasion of the Sandwich Islands from California had given occasion for the instruction of Hitchcock, the commander of the Pacific Division, to obstruct the projected expedition or any other movement there in violation of neutrality.[83] For the first Raousset enterprise, which in its inception was free from filibustering intent, the government of the United States would of course not be responsible. The Count's plans in the spring of 1853 had led the Mexican Minister of Relations to address Conkling, the United States Minister, upon the subject; and the latter, in reply, said that he was sure his government had taken no action only because the necessary positive proof was lacking.[84] News of the plans of Walker occasioned another exchange of notes. Conkling notified the Mexican government that he would transmit information of the expedition to his government in "full assurance" that it would "exert," if necessary, all the "powers with which it is [was] in-

---

[80] In this proclamation Fillmore declared that those apprehended in their invasion of Cuba by the Spanish government need expect no intercession from the United States, no matter how desperate the straits to which they should be reduced. See *Sen. Ex. Doc.*, No. 1, part 1, 32 Cong., 1 Sess. (Ser. 611), pp. 82–83.

[81] U. S. v. O'Sullivan et al., *loc. cit.; Democratic Review*, XXXI (April, 1852), 307 ff.

[82] Caldwell, *op. cit.*, p. 90, and note.

[83] Evidence submitted by U. S. District Attorney Inge to the California Superior Court, *Alta California*, Oct. 11, 1854.

[84] Conkling to Alamán, May 18, 1853, Bolton Transcripts; also enclosed with No. 40, Mex. Desp., Vol. 17.

vested by the constitution and laws of the Union, to cause its neutral obligations to be faithfully fulfilled." He declined, however, to address a letter to the Governor of California relative to his duties in regard to the matter, because he felt that the public functionaries of that state and in that state were already aware of these duties, and because he was shortly to be superseded.[85] Gadsden had arrived at his Mexican post before the ability of those functionaries to prevent an invasion of Mexico from California had been tested. The attitude of the government of the United States towards proposed filibuster incursions into Mexican territory during the period under consideration had to be judged, therefore, largely by the measures taken to suppress the Carvajal enterprises.

These measures were legion but somewhat ineffective. As soon as news of the movements of filibusters under Carvajal reached Washington, the federal government began to act. On September 22, 1851, President Fillmore instructed Twiggs and Smith, commanders of the military forces in Louisiana and Texas, to restrain the proposed expeditions.[86] One month later he issued a proclamation warning citizens of the United States of the penalties of the law regarding such enterprises and, as in the case of Cuba, declaring that all participants would place themselves beyond the pale of American protection.[87] Pursuant to his orders, the commander in Texas seems to have made considerable exertions to break up the filibuster plans. All the troops in the department were ordered to join in carrying out the instructions of the President, and between the officers at Fort Brown and General Ávalos at Matamoras there was apparently perfect harmony. In speaking of the raids of 1851, Webster declared that his government could "reproach itself with no dereliction of duty," though the efforts of the military authorities had been in a measure paralyzed by the desertion of troops to join the standard of Carvajal,[88] while Smith reported that the final suppression of the raid of 1852 was, "in a great measure, due to the personal efforts of General Harney, which so embarrassed and precipitated the final revolutionary movements, that all precautions for certain success could not be taken."[89] In the spring of that year, Harney arrested Carvajal

[85] Same to Bonilla, August 8, 1853, *ibid.;* see also No. 62, Mex. Desp., Vol. 17.

[86] Instructions are quoted in *El Siglo XIX,* 30 de octubre de 1851.

[87] *Sen. Ex. Doc.,* No. 1, part 1, 32 Cong., 1 Sess. (Ser. 611), pp. 82–83.

[88] Webster to Letcher, December 22, 1851, *Sen. Ex. Doc.* No. 97, 32 Cong., 1 Sess. (Ser. 621), pp. 109–111.

[89] Smith to Adjutant-General, July 18, 1852, *Sen. Ex. Doc.* No. 1, 32 Cong., 2 Sess. (Ser. 659), pp. 15–20.

and turned him over to the civil authorities, but he was immediately released on bond and began preparations for another invasion.[90] It was possibly these preparations that led Webster to suggest to Fillmore the advisability of recommending to Congress the reenactment of a measure similar to that of 1838, but even more stringent. Fillmore followed Webster's suggestion, but Congress failed to take any action.[91] Early in 1853, therefore, Carvajal, as has been seen, was able to make other incursions into Mexico. In the spring of that year, however, he and some of his associates were again apprehended by the military authorities of the United States.[92] On this occasion they were prosecuted, and acquitted as usual; [93] but the Mexican government probably did not learn the result of the trial until after the Gadsden treaty had been signed.

The significance of these expeditions can not be fully appreciated unless one considers the impression they made in Mexico. None of them was important from a military standpoint, and under normal conditions they need have occasioned no great alarm; but the memory of the Texan affair was still fresh in the Mexican mind, and the war of 1846–1848 had left its legacy of bitterness and suspicion which the loud expression of expansionist sentiment in the United States would not allow to subside. It was easy, therefore, for exaggerated rumors to gain a certain amount of credence. In October, 1850, the editor of *El Siglo XIX*, who was usually not an alarmist, expressed his conviction that the "turbulent waters of the Rio Bravo" opposed a very weak barrier to the "audacious marauders of the opposite bank." [94] The editor of *El Universal* had likewise expressed alarm regarding the northern states of Mexico; and when news arrived of Clingman's prediction (made in Congress, February 15, 1851) that the Californians would soon move upon the adjacent provinces of Mexico, this journalist seized upon the speech as evidence confirming his view of the matter.[95]

Then came the report of the departure of the Moorehead expedition. On July 9, *El Universal* printed an article which had been sent from New Orleans by some friend of Mexico. The correspondent declared that the greed of the American people was increasing, and that if they once obtained a foothold in Sonora they would receive such

[90] Zamacois, *Historia de Méjico*, XIII, 530.
[91] *House Ex. Doc.* No. 112, 32 Cong., 1 Sess. (Ser. 648), pp. 1–2.
[92] Zamacois, *op. cit.*, XIII, 482, *passim*.
[93] *The Texas Monument*, January 25, 1854.
[94] 21 y 28 de octubre de 1850.
[95] 15 y 29 de abril de 1851.

constant reënforcements that it would be very difficult to dislodge them. As proof of this growing sentiment for expansion, he cited an article from the New York *Sun* of June 9, which contended that Mexico could never enjoy peace and prosperity until it was completely absorbed by the United States and its inhabitants placed under their truly republican institutions. When the sub-Inspector of the military colonies in Sonora reported that a party of forty-eight Americans—presumably a portion of the Moorehead expedition—had crossed the line, he said he expected six hundred to follow soon.[96] Similar fears were expressed by *La Voz del Pueblo* of Ures.[97] Probably the climax of alarm regarding this enterprise was voiced by the editor of *El Universal* on July 20. A quotation from the *Herald* of New York praising the vigorous and progressive population of the Pacific who were already in search of other territory where they might exercise their skill and industry, furnished the theme for an editorial entitled: "Watch, therefore, for Ye Know not the Day nor the Hour"!

The Carvajal raids excited even more alarm, because they tended to confirm the doubt which had previously been entertained regarding the loyalty of some of the North Mexican states. As early as 1849 a faction on this frontier had proclaimed the Sierra Madre Republic.[98] When the plan of *La Loba,* under which Carvajal was fighting, was promulgated it was probably natural that it should at once be connected with this movement. On October 12, 1851, *El Siglo* printed a letter from Saltillo declaring that the scheme had for its object the formation of a republic of the Sierra Madre States. The *Bandera Mexicana* of Matamoras reported that it was designed not only to set up such a republic, but ultimately to seek annexation to the United States.[99] On October 15, *El Siglo* quoted from the *Rio Bravo* of Brownsville, Texas, a journal which was squarely back of the enterprise. This paper declared that if foreign gold and Arista should attempt to suppress the movement, ten thousand Americans would be ready to hold aloft the flag of Sierra Madre; but, at the same time, it maintained that there was no desire for annexation to the United States. The editor of *El Siglo* believed that this disclaimer was false, and in confirmation of this opinion, reported two weeks later that Carvajal and his followers had laid aside all pre-

[96] Sub-Inspector of Military Colonies to the Governor of Sonora, July 9, 1851, Pinart Transcripts, Sonora, IV, 329–330.
[97] Quoted in *El Siglo XIX,* 29 de agosto de 1851.
[98] Bolton, *Guide to . . . the Principal Archives of Mexico,* p. 298.
[99] *El Siglo XIX,* 15 de octubre de 1851.

tense and boldly proclaimed the Sierra Madre Republic and annexation.[100]

Excitement seemed to be just as intense in Mexican official circles as among journalists. On October 28, Tornel made a speech regarding the situation in the Senate. He said that he believed the purpose of the enterprise was to "despoil the nation of three states immediately, of others later, and of its sovereign and independent existence," ultimately. His opinion was based, in part, upon the reports of the newspapers of Texas, Louisiana, Florida, and New York.[101] Letcher, who was Minister of the United States to Mexico at the time, complained in October, 1851, that the movement embarrassed all his negotiations exceedingly. "Why grant privileges," it is said, "to a people whose object it is to rob us of the whole of our country whenever it may suit their convenience or gratify their cupidity?" [102] Again, in 1852, he wrote that the "third invasion against Mexico by Carvajal . . . has [had] awakened a feeling of intense prejudice against everything connected with American interests." [103]

There was similar excitement in regard to the proposed new scheme of Raousset de Boulbon and that of Walker and associates. The Mexican officials on the Pacific coast grasped with avidity every bit of information which could possibly be had. A favorite method was to take the sworn statements of the captains and passengers who put in at the ports of this section. Such statements taken from a British vessel which entered the port of Mazatlán in the spring of 1853 indicated that Raousset had a force of fifteen hundred adventurers.[104] Of a more alarming nature was the testimony taken from some of the Mexican passengers of the *R. Adams* which anchored at Guaymas in December, 1853. They estimated the number of filibusters already on their way to Mexico at from fifteen hundred to two thousand, while they believed some four or five thousand would follow in case the first detachment met with success. The meetings of the adventurers in San Francisco were quite open, and the enterprises had the support of several wealthy firms of that city. The officials there were ostensibly opposed to, but in reality in favor of, the schemes. Moreover, the filibusters were in communication with certain individuals of Sonora, which state, together with

[100] *Ibid.*, 28 de octubre.

[101] Quoted in *El Universal*, 30 de octubre.

[102] Letcher to Webster, October 29, 1851, *Sen. Ex. Doc.* No. 97, 32 Cong., 1 Sess. (Ser. 621), pp. 100–102.

[103] *Ibid.*, p. 125.

[104] *El Siglo XIX*, 8 de abril de 1853.

Lower California, they intended to annex within a year. Having accomplished this, they then contemplated the annexation of the remainder of Mexico—an achievement which they expected to realize by the end of three years.[105]

How was the crisis to be met? That the Mexican government was in no condition to repulse a formidable invasion seemed obvious. Santa Anna's picture of the situation when he came to power in the spring of 1853 was probably little exaggerated. He said the fortresses were dismantled, the frontiers abandoned, the treasury empty and credit exhausted, the army disorganized and poorly equipped.[106] It will not be surprising, therefore, if Mexico under the circumstances should demand, as a *quid pro quo* of any negotiations with the United States, an agreement on the part of the latter more vigorously to prosecute such piratical attempts.

[105] Bolton Transcripts.
[106] Santa Anna, *A Sus Compatriotes,* p. 8 ff.

CHAPTER VI

THE BOUNDARY DISPUTE

In order to proceed with proper understanding to the topic of this chapter, it will be necessary to quote a considerable portion of the fifth article of the Treaty of Guadalupe Hidalgo. This article reads as follows:

The boundary line between the two Republics shall commence in the Gulf of Mexico, three leagues from land, opposite the mouth of the Rio Grande, otherwise called Rio Bravo del Norte, or opposite the mouth of its deepest branch, if it should have more than one branch emptying directly into the sea; from thence up the middle of that river, following the deepest channel, where it has more than one, to the point where it strikes the southern boundary of New Mexico; thence, westwardly, along the whole southern boundary of New Mexico (which runs north of the town called Paso) to its western termination; thence, northward, along the western line of New Mexico, until it intersects the first branch of the river Gila; (or if it should not intersect any branch of that river, then to the point on the said line nearest to such branch, and thence in a direct line to the same;) thence down the middle of said branch and of the said river, until it empties into the Rio Colorado; thence across the Rio Colorado, following the division line between Upper and Lower California, to the Pacific Ocean.

The southern and western limits of New Mexico, mentioned in this article, are those laid down in the map entitled *"Map of the United Mexican States. as organized and defined by various acts of the congress of said republic, and constructed according to the best authorities. Revised edition. Published at New York, in 1847, by J. Disturnell . . ."*

In order to designate the boundary line with due precision, upon authoritative maps, and to establish upon the ground land-marks which shall show the limits of both republics, as described in the present article, the two Governments shall each appoint a commissioner and a surveyor, who, before the expiration of one year from the date of the exchange of ratifications of this treaty, shall meet at the port of San Diego, and proceed to run and mark the said boundary in its whole course to the mouth of the Rio Bravo del Norte . . .[1]

The progress of the survey of the boundary here described was hampered from the beginning by partisan politics in the United States. On July 6, 1848, two days after the proclamation of the Treaty of Guadalupe Hidalgo, Polk sent a special explanatory message to the House and asked for appropriations. In this message he

[1] Malloy, *Treaties,* I, 1109–1111.

referred to the stipulation in the fifth article which required both countries to appoint a commissioner and a surveyor who should meet at San Diego within a year from the date of the ratification of the treaty. He said it was necessary that *"provision be made by law"* for the appointment of a commissioner and surveyor on the part of the United States.[2] The Senate promptly passed a bill making such provision,[3] but it was introduced into the House just three days before the close of the session and died in the hands of the Committee on Foreign Affairs.[4]

The general appropriation bill passed by this session of Congress provided, however, for $50,000 to be expended in defraying the expenses of the boundary commission.[5] Polk thereupon proceeded to make the necessary appointments. This he did either because he thought the stipulation in the appropriation bill warranted such action, or because he was anxious to fill the positions on the commission before the expiration of his term of office. The Senate, which contained a membership of thirty-six Democrats and twenty-two Whigs, of course confirmed Polk's nominations.[6]

When the Senate bill providing for the organization of the commission was taken up in the House during the next session of Congress, the Whigs, who held a majority in this body, attempted to nullify the action of Polk. They introduced amendments confining appointments to the boundary commission to members of the Topographical Corps, and providing that no part of the money appropriated then or thereafter should be used to pay the salaries of any officers or persons connected with the boundary survey, whose appointment had been made without authority of law. Both of these amendments passed the House, and their partisan nature is shown by the yeas and nays on the latter. Eighty-one Whigs and two Democrats voted for the measure, while forty-four Democrats and one lone Whig voted against it.[7] The Senate refused to accept the bill as amended by the House,[8] and, consequently, the boundary commission was forced to proceed with limited funds and with uncertainty as to the amount of salary each member was to receive.

The joint commission from Mexico and the United States met at San Diego on July 6, 1849, only a few days after the time stipu-

---

[2] *Cong. Globe,* 30 Cong., 1 Sess., pp. 901–902.
[3] *Ibid.,* pp. 1043–1052.
[4] *Ibid.,* p. 1064.
[5] *9 U. S. Stat. at L.,* 301.
[6] *Sen. Ex. Journal,* VIII, 24.
[7] *Cong. Globe,* 30 Cong., 2 Sess., pp. 617–624.
[8] *Ibid.,* pp. 667–668.

lated by the treaty. The American group was composed of John B. Weller, commissioner; Andrew B. Gray of Texas, surveyor; William H. Emory, astronomer; and John C. Cremony, interpreter. The Mexican government was represented by Pedro García Condé as commissioner, and José Salazar y Larregui as surveyor and astronomer.[9] Besides these, there were several assistants and a military escort for the Commission of each government.[10]

On October 10, 1849, the initial point of the boundary was ascertained. A written statement in English and Spanish was placed in a bottle which, after being hermetically sealed, was deposited in the ground, and a temporary monument was erected upon the spot. The commission then proceeded to determine the point of junction of the Gila and the Colorado. In the following January this point was agreed upon. All that now remained to be done, so far as this portion of the boundary was concerned, was to survey a straight line from the junction of these two rivers to the initial point on the Pacific coast. Accordingly, engineers were appointed for this task, and the commission adjourned on February 15, 1850, to meet in El Paso on the first Monday in the following November.[11]

But long before this part of the task had been completed, the Whigs had determined to force Weller out of office. Even prior to his arrival at San Diego, where he was to take up his work, his successor had been appointed. Weller reached San Diego on July 1, 1849,[12] but on June 26, John C. Frémont had been chosen to supersede him and had been given a letter from the Secretary of State to Weller informing him of his dismissal.[13] Frémont at first accepted the appointment, but he later changed his mind, having in the meantime decided to run for United States Senator from California.[14] The letter of June 26 apparently never reached Weller.[15] Soon afterwards the oversight of the boundary commission was transferred from the Department of State to that of Interior. On December 19, the secretary of the latter department addressed another letter of dismissal to Weller.[16] This despatch the commissioner received, and he proceeded according to instructions to turn over

[9] *Sen. Ex. Doc.* No. 119, 32 Cong., 1 Sess., (Ser. 626) pp. 59, 67, *passim.*

[10] *Ibid., loc. cit.*

[11] *Sen. Ex. Doc.* No. 119, 32 Cong., 1 Sess., (Ser. 626), pp. 60, 65; *ibid.,* No. 34, 31 Cong., 1 Sess., (Ser. 558), pp. 31–38.

[12] *Cong. Globe,* 31 Cong., 2 Sess., pp. 78–79.

[13] *Ibid.,* pp. 78–84; *Sen. Ex. Doc.,* No. 34, 31 Cong., 1 Sess., (Ser. 558) pp. 9–10.

[14] Emory, "Report," *House Ex. Doc.* No. 135, 34 Cong., 1 Sess., (Ser. 861), p. 5.

[15] *Cong. Globe,* 31 Cong., 2 Sess., p. 80.

[16] *Sen. Ex. Doc.,* No. 34, 31 Cong., 1 Sess., (Ser. 558) p. 15.

the books, papers, and other paraphernalia to Major Emory. The letter of the Secretary of Interior accused Weller of carelessness in the management of the commission, and this secretary later declared that Weller had maltreated subordinate officials; but as all this occurred, if at all, after the decision to remove Weller had already been made, there is strong suspicion that the whole affair was a political move.[17]

At any rate Weller was removed and John Russell Bartlett was at length appointed in his stead (June 19, 1850).[18] A virtual reorganization of the commission then took place. Gray was retained as surveyor, but John McClellan was appointed as chief astronomer instead of Emory who had resigned.[19] Neither the American nor the Mexican group reached El Paso by the appointed time. The former, with the exception of Gray, arrived on November 13, and the latter put in their appearance on December 1.[20]

The first question to be decided regarding this portion of the line was the initial point on the Rio Grande. According to Article V of the treaty of 1848, as has been seen, the southern and western boundaries of New Mexico were to be those laid down in Disturnell's map, and the boundary of the United States was to extend up the middle of the Rio Grande "to the point where it strikes the southern boundary of New Mexico (which runs south of the town called Paso)." But it was soon found that there were errors in the Disturnell map. El Paso was not only located thirty minutes too far north, but both it and the Rio Grande were placed more than two degrees too far to the east. Again, according to this map the southern boundary of New Mexico was three degrees (175.28 English miles) long and seven minutes north of El Paso. A dispute therefore arose as to whether the actual position of El Paso and of the Rio Grande should be made the starting point and a line beginning seven minutes north of El Paso run westward for three degrees, or 175.28 miles, or whether the points should be located by parallels and meridians as laid down on Disturnell's map. The Mexican commissioner contended that the initial point should be fixed on the Rio Grande as actually situated, but at the parallel of thirty-two degrees and twenty-two minutes as it appeared on the Disturnell map; and that, moreover, in determining the length of the southern boundary of New Mexico, the distance between the Rio Grande as actually situated and as it

[17] *Cong. Globe,* 31 Cong., 2 Sess., pp. 80 ff.
[18] *Sen. Ex. Doc.,* No. 119, 32 Cong., 1 Sess. (Ser. 626), p. 87.
[19] *Sen. Ex. Doc.,* No. 34, 3 Cong., 1 Sess. (Ser. 558), pp. 12–13.
[20] Bartlett, *Personal Narrative,* II, 145, 150.

appeared upon this map should be subtracted from the 175.28 miles, thus leaving this portion of the line less than one-third its length as shown on the Disturnell map.[21]

The commissioner for the United States dissented from this view and after a number of meetings a compromise was reached by the terms of which the southern boundary of New Mexico was to extend three degrees west of the Rio Grande as the river was actually situated and run along the parallel of thirty-two degrees and twenty-two minutes, or seven minutes north of El Paso as that city appeared upon the Disturnell map.[22] With this compromise Bartlett was well pleased, for he believed that Condé would never have consented to the extension of the boundary three degrees west of the Rio Grande had the American commissioner refused to fix the initial point thirty minutes further north than it would have fallen according to the relative actual positions of the southern boundary of New Mexico and the town of El Paso. He felt, also, that in consenting to such a compromise he had yielded land of no great value while gaining territory rich in gold and silver mines.[23] Moreover, both the Secretary of the Interior and the Secretary of State approved Bartlett's action.

The agreement regarding the initial point was reached on December 25, 1850,[24] before Surveyor Gray put in his appearance. When he arrived late in July, 1851, he found the corner stone marking the spot already laid and a portion of the southern boundary of New Mexico already run.[25] He refused, however, to sign the agreement reached by Bartlett and Condé, and recalling Lieutenant Whipple, who had been acting as surveyor *ad interim,* from his work on this line, he sent him with two parties to the Gila.[26] Colonel Graham, who was now the astronomer of the commission, likewise disapproved, as did Whipple and, later, Major Emory.[27] Owing to

---

[21] Bartlett, *Personal Narrative,* I, 201–203; *Sen. Ex. Doc.* No. 119, 32 Cong., 1 Sess. (Ser. 626), pp. 289, *passim.*

[22] *Sen. Ex. Doc.* No. 119, 32 Cong., 1 Sess. (Ser. 626), pp. 391–394, 406–409, and accompanying maps. See also Bancroft, *History of Arizona and New Mexico,* p. 451.

[23] *Sen. Ex. Doc.* No. 119, 32 Cong., 1 Sess. (Ser. 626), pp. 145–148; *ibid.,* No. 131 (Ser. 627), pp. 1–3.

[24] *Ibid.,* p. 391.

[25] Bartlett, *Personal Narrative,* I, 206–207; *Sen. Ex. Doc.* No. 119, 32 Cong., 1 Sess. (Ser. 626), p. 298.

[26] The best statement of Gray's views is found in *Sen. Ex. Doc.* No. 55, 33 Cong., 2 Sess., (Ser. 453).

[27] For a statement of Graham's contentions, see *ibid.,* No. 121, 32 Cong., 1 Sess. (Ser. 627). The most concise presentation of Bartlett's reasons for his

quarrels between the American astronomer and surveyor, as well as between the commissioner and his subordinates, operations proceeded slowly on the Gila,[28] and both Gray and Graham were recalled before the end of the year.[29] Their combined functions were then conferred upon Emory and better results were achieved. By the fall of 1852 the survey was completed, so far as the United States commission was concerned, from San Diego to the head waters of the Gila, and from El Paso to Eagle Pass.[30] Notwithstanding the death of General Condé the Mexican commission had completed by that time the entire survey west of the Rio Grande, and had begun operations on that river.[31] Bartlett now decided to send Whipple back to the boundary of New Mexico to take up the work where he had left off, while he and most of his men prepared to join Emory at Eagle Pass.[32] But while *en route* he received a communication from Washington which convinced him that further operations of the commission would be impossible.[33] It was accordingly disbanded, and Bartlett and Emory set out for the capital.[34]

Congress had in fact legislated the commission out of existence. It will be recalled how slow that body had been in taking the action necessary for its organization. In April, 1850, a bill had at length been passed fixing the salaries of the commissioner, the surveyor, and the astronomer and providing for the termination of the commission three years from January, 1850. In May and in September of the same year appropriations were made amounting to $185,000, while the general appropriation bill for the following year set apart another $100,000 for the boundary survey.[35]

But signs of an approaching storm were already visible. When

course of action is contained in *Sen. Ex. Doc.* No. 41, 32 Cong., 2 Sess. (Ser. 665).

It would obviously not be pertinent to the main interest of this chapter to go into the arguments for and against the line agreed upon by the commissioners. They maintained that the boundary should have been established on a parallel thirty minutes further south than had been done by the compromise line.

[28] *Sen. Ex. Doc.* No. 119, 32 Cong., 1 Sess. (Ser. 626), p. 172 *passim.*
[29] *Ibid.,* pp. 442–443, also *ibid.,* No. 121, 32 Cong., 1 Sess. (Ser. 627), p. 49.
[30] *Ibid.,* No. 6, 33 Cong., Special Sess. (Ser. 688), pp. 18, 61–68, 117–119.
[31] *Sen. Ex. Doc.* No. 6, 33 Cong., Special Sess. (Ser. 688), pp. 18, 61–68, 117–119.
[32] *Ibid.,* pp. 71–74, 161.
[33] Bartlett, *Personal Narrative,* II, 514.
[34] *Ibid.,* 517 ff.
[35] Emory, "Report," *House Ex. Doc.* No. 135, 34 Cong., 1 Sess., (Ser. 861), p. 21; *Globe,* 31 Cong., 1 Sess., pp. 744, 745.

news of Weller's dismissal reached Washington early in 1851, it occasioned vigorous protests on the part of the Democratic element in the Senate.[36] Upon being released from the commission, Weller had remained in California where he had made a successful race for the United States Senate. As soon as he obtained his seat in that body, he began to take active interest in the boundary survey. In March, 1852, he introduced a long resolution calling upon the Secretary of Interior to submit copies of all instructions given the commission, all correspondence relating to it, the number and names of persons employed, the amount of money spent, the manner of its disbursal, and an estimate of the amount necessary to complete the work. Weller also brought in a resolution asking information as to whether any charges had been filed in the War Department against the commission.[37]

The latter resolution had reference to charges preferred against Bartlett by Colonel McClellan whom he had discharged from the commission for drunkenness, efforts to destroy the authority of the commission, and conduct unbecoming a gentleman and an officer.[38] The chief complaints against Bartlett were the private use of transportation provided by the government for the boundary commission, unpardonable mismanagement of the public interest and of funds entrusted to him, and neglect of the health, comfort, and lives of individuals connected with the commission.[39] Into the details regarding the charges it is not necessary to go. They are mentioned here because they tended to discredit the commission and to delay the appropriations necessary to carry out its work, while, at the same time, they have some bearing upon the complaints of the Mexican government to be considered later.

More important than these charges, was the contention that Bartlett had departed from the treaty of 1848 in establishing the initial point on the Rio Grande. Senator Rusk of Texas was the principal champion of this view. In May, 1852, he proposed, along with an amendment to the deficiency bill appropriating $80,000 for running the boundary, a proviso that nothing in the amendment should be construed so as to sanction a departure from the point on the Rio Grande north of the town called Paso designated in the treaty of Guadalupe Hidalgo.[40] In the following July, while speaking of the charges preferred against Bartlett, Rusk declared that he

---

[36] *Cong. Globe,* 31 Cong., 2 Sess., pp. 78–84.
[37] *Ibid.,* 32 Cong., 1 Sess., p. 814.
[38] *Sen. Ex. Doc.* No. 60, 32 Cong., 1 Sess. (Ser. 620), pp. 10–17, 46–63.
[39] *Sen. Ex. Doc.* No. 60, 32 Cong., 1 Sess. (Ser. 620), pp. 2–5, 23–46.
[40] *Cong. Globe,* 32 Cong., 1 Sess., p. 1404.

would do everything in his power to resist the appropriation of money until there was assurance that this treaty and not the agreement of the commissioners should settle the question of the initial point on the Rio Grande.[41] The $80,000 eventually appropriated for the boundary contained Rusk's proviso.[42]

Prominent among those who sided with Rusk was Mason of Virginia. In the latter part of August, 1852, when the expenses for running the boundary were being considered as an item in the general appropriation bill, he proposed "that no part of the appropriation should be used until it should be made to appear to the President of the United States that the southern boundary of New Mexico had not been established further north of El Paso than is laid down in the Disternell Map." [43] Before the close of the month the bill with the amendment received the approval of both houses and became a law.[44] Fillmore, in accordance with the provision, examined all the reports of the boundary commission, and, concluding that the money could not be used, ordered the Secretary of the Interior to discontinue operations.[45] It was the news of this procedure that had reached Bartlett while he was on his way to Eagle Pass.

In the following March that part of the appropriation bill which applied to the Mexican boundary was so amended as to permit the use of the funds necessary to complete the survey of the Rio Grande.[46] Work on the southern boundary of New Mexico was not to be resumed, however, and the dispute was left over for the incoming administration.

There were two factors which tended to lend gravity to the question. In the first place, it was believed that the settlement agreed upon by the commissioners involved the loss of the only practicable southern route for a Pacific railway. This was deemed a matter of considerable importance. Major Emory had brought the subject to Buchanan's notice while negotiations which resulted in the Guadalupe Hidalgo treaty were in progress.[47] A provision relating to the matter was embodied in that treaty as finally drafted, Article VI being made to provide for a joint agreement between the contracting parties with reference to the construction of a road,

---

[41] *Ibid.,* p. 1660.
[42] *Ibid.,* p. 1404.
[43] *Ibid.,* pp. 2270–2271.
[44] *Ibid.,* p. 2407.
[45] *Ibid.,* 32 Cong., 2 Sess., p. 10.
[46] *Ibid.,* pp. 881, 1045, app. p. 331.
[47] Emory "Report," *House Ex. Doc.* No. 135, 34 Cong., 1 Sess. (Ser. 861), pp. 50–51.

canal, or railway running "along the river Gila, or upon its right or its left bank, within the space of one marine league from either margin of the river." In his instructions to Weller, Buchanan had suggested that the "selection of individuals" for the boundary commission might be "made with reference to the incidental collection of information relative to the construction" of the proposed communication.[48] In the following February, the Secretary of State again called the subject to Weller's attention, declaring that the inquiry regarding the route was one of "great importance to the country." [49] The instructions of Commissioner Bartlett made the investigations regarding a railway of more than "incidental" importance. Referring to Article VI of the treaty of Guadalupe Hidalgo, Secretary of the Interior wrote:

> As the examinations to be made and the information to be collected, agreeably to this article, are of very great importance, you will make such organization of parties, and assign to them such duties, as will be productive of the desired results.[50]

At least one member of the commission, Major Emory, was intensely interested in the matter. Writing from San Diego, California, on April 2, 1849, he said:

> By pushing the survey eastward, and looking for a branch of the Gila which shall fulfill the conditions of the treaty—the first to intersect the boundary of New Mexico—you will inevitably be made to strike that boundary far north of the parallel of the copper mines; because all the streams south of that parallel, having their sources in the Sierra Madre, running towards the Gila, disappear in the sands before they reach Gila, except in cases of unusual freshets. Working eastward their almost trackless beds must escape the notice of the keenest explorer. Working from the "Paso del Norte" northward and westward, you strike the sources of the streams themselves; and although they may disappear many leagues before reaching the Gila, they may nevertheless be affluents of that river, and fulfil the condition of the treaty.
> Another view of the case may also be taken. The inaccuracy of the map upon which the treaty was made, and which thereby became a part of the treaty, is notorious. It is also known to all who have been much in the frontier States of Mexico, that the boundaries of those States have never been defined on the ground, and are unknown. This is particularly the case of the boundary betwixt New Mexico and Chihuahua. In this condition of things the commission must negotiate, and they may adopt the 32d parallel of latitude, until it strikes the San Pedro, or even a more southern parallel of latitude.

[48] Buchanan to Weller, Jan. 24, 1849, *ibid.*, No. 34, 31 Cong., 1 Sess. (Ser. 558), pp. 2–3.
[49] Letter of, Feb. 13, 1849, *ibid.*, 3–6.
[50] Secretary of Interior to Bartlett, Aug. 1, 1850, Bartlett, *Personal Narrative*, II, 589.

This would give what good authority, combined with my own observations, authorizes me to say is a practicable route for a railroad—I believe the only one from ocean to ocean within our territory.[51]

Speaking of this letter at a later date, Emory asserted that he had written it "in the hope that the United States commissioner might succeed in torturing the treaty of Guadalupe Hidalgo to embrace a practicable route" for the proposed road.[52] But Bartlett had agreed to the parallel of thirty-two degrees and twenty-two minutes, and had thus, as some believed, surrendered the line best adapted to the purpose.[53]

The second factor which tended to render the situation dangerous was the attitude of the inhabitants and the officials living in and near the territory in dispute. Of the area of some 5950 square miles in question,—that is to say, the territory between the compromise line and that claimed by Gray—all except a narrow strip along the Rio Grande was considered barren and worthless. This strip, called *La Mesilla,* was known to be very fertile.[54] As to the motives leading to its settlement, and the political sentiments of the inhabitants, the authorities differ. Bartlett says the Mexican element of Doña Ana, which had been exasperated by the encroachments of the Anglo-Americans, sought new homes there in the belief that it would fall within the limits of Mexico, and that the Mexican government later encouraged Mexicans from New Mexico to make homes in the disputed area.[55] Reports sent to the governors of New Mexico and forwarded by them to Washington indicated that the settlers came there with the clear understanding that it was to be within the jurisdiction of the United States.[56] At any rate, the settlement of the valley began about 1849 or 1850, the region was in a flourishing condition,[57] and there was difference of opinion in regard to the political desires of the settlers. The Mexican officials contended that virtually all of them were desirous of being annexed to Chihuahua,[58] and with this view Bartlett was apparently

[51] Emory, "Report," *House Ex. Doc.* No. 135, 34 Cong., 1 Sess. (Ser. 861), pp. 20–21.

[52] *Ibid.,* p. 51.

[53] *Cong. Globe,* 32 Cong., 1 Sess., pp. 2402–2404, App., p. 776 ff.

[54] Bartlett, *Personal Narrative,* I, 188, 212.

[55] *Ibid.,* I, 213, II, 391. See also Bancroft, *Arizona and New Mexico,* p. 652.

[56] Houghton to Lane, September 1, 1853, and inclosures; Mansfield to Merriwether, October 25, 1853; Marcy to Merriwether, May 28, 1853, State Department, B. I. A., Misc. Let.

[57] Bartlett, *op. et loc. cit.*

[58] Commissioners of Chihuahua to Lane, March 19, and Trias to Lane, March 28, 1853, State Department, B. I. A., Misc. Let.

in agreement, though he admitted that they may have been inveigled by wily land speculators to petition for annexation to New Mexico.[59] That a group of its inhabitants sent in a petition expressing vigorous opposition to annexation to Chihuahua is certain;[60] and Judge Hyde of El Paso declared that the American population and "many of the Mexicans" had organized to resist any authorities Mexico might send, and were preparing to petition the governor of New Mexico to order elections for the civil officials of the district.[61] There was probably some truth in both statements, the Anglo-Saxon portion of the heterogeneous population being, in general, partial to New Mexico, while the majority of the Mexican element gave preference to Chihuahua.

A population thus divided served to render the situation more critical. Soon after the boundary commission reached the compromise regarding the southern boundary of New Mexico, the chief executive of Chihuahua responded to the supposed desire of the people of the region for the protecting arm of his government, and apparently showed little regard for the persons and property of those who refused to accept his benevolence. The Americans, and those "favorable to American rights and privileges" naturally objected, not only petitioning the Governor of New Mexico, but also asking that their complaints be laid before the federal government for redress.[62]

So far as the Governor of New Mexico was concerned, their efforts resulted in little more than calling forth from a dying man a wail because one more vexation had been added to a situation already difficult.[63] Before the new governor, William Carr Lane, left the East, he was urged by the territorial delegates to Congress from New Mexico to occupy the disputed ground by force.[64] Lane took no action, however, until he learned that Congress had repudiated Bartlett's line. He then set out toward the disputed territory. When he arrived at Doña Ana, he issued a proclamation laying claim to jurisdiction over the contested region,[65] justifying the step on the ground (1) that the section had been under the acknowl-

[59] Bartlet, op. cit. II, 391–392.

[60] Citizens of Mesilla to Calhoun, August 25, 1851, Calhoun, Correspondence, pp. 404–405.

[61] Sen. Ex. Doc., No. 41, 32 Cong., 2 Sess. (Ser. 665), p. 13.

[62] Calhoun, Correspondence, pp. 404–405.

[63] Ibid., pp. 424–425.

[64] Lane to Taylor, January 23, 1854, House Rep. No. 81, 33 Cong., 1 Sess. (Ser. 742), pp. 1–2.

[65] Ibid., pp. 3–4.

edged jurisdiction of New Mexico from 1825 to 1851; (2) that the forcible annexation of the territory by Chihuahua at the latter date was illegal because the agreement of the commissioners did not constitute a final settlement; (3) that Chihuahua had signally failed not only to secure the inhabitants of the region in their rights of person, property, and conscience, but also to protect them from the depredations of the Indians; (4) that the revolutionary condition of Mexico precluded the hope of such protection being furnished in the future; (5) that a large portion of the inhabitants were claiming the protection of the United States and soliciting the re-annexation of that territory to New Mexico; (6) that during the year 1852 the United States had virtually asserted sovereignty over the region, and therefore that it was his duty now to reassert it.[66]

Lane mailed a copy of his proclamation to Angel Trias, the Governor of Chihuahua, who responded with a counter declaration and prepared to resist Lane's claim by military force. Trias declared that the limits of Chihuahua had extended not only over the territory in question, but even further northward; that, in regard to the disputed region, Mexico had in her favor (1) the possession of the territory from time immemorial, (2) its *pacific* occupation under the sight of the officials of the United States who were not accustomed to remain silent in cases where their rights were in doubt, (3) its inclusion within the limits of Mexico by the joint boundary commission, and (5) the establishment of the immigrants who had chosen to leave the United States within it. Trias maintained, furthermore, that the inhabitants of the disputed section did not desire annexation to the United States, and that even if they did, this would not justify annexation; that in resorting to force the Governor of New Mexico would violate the 21st article of the Treaty of Guadalupe Hidalgo; and that it was not the prerogative of this Governor to maintain the rights of the United States in a purely federal matter. In bringing his communication to a conclusion Trias sounded a note of warning regarding Lane's proposed occupation of the territory in dispute: "I shall use the means unquestionably necessary for its defence and conservation, in case it is attacked, and upon Your Excellency alone shall rest the responsibility for the consequences to which the procedure may give place." [67]

Prior to the arrival of this despatch Lane had received a long com-

[66] Proclamation of March 13, 1853, State Department, B. I. A., Misc. Let. A copy was printed in Spanish in *El Siglo XIX*, 10 de abril de 1853.

[67] Trias to Lane, March 28, 1853, *El Siglo XIX*, 10 de abril de 1853; also in *El Universal*, 11 de abril de 1853 and in State Department, B. I. A., *loc. cit.*

munication from the so-called Commissioners of Chihuahua who, endowed also with certain federal functions, were at that time upon the frontier. They set forth a line of argument similar to that of Trias, and the conclusion of their despatch was no less bellicose: "Your Excellency will pardon my recommending that, in the interest of peace and neighborliness . . . you will maturely reflect and abandon your present resolution; because, if you do not, it becomes my duty as a commissioner of the Mexican Government not to permit any occupation of territory which would be prejudicial to the national honor." [68]

To the commissioners Lane replied immediately, giving evidence designed to support the contentions of his proclamation, and declaring that neither he nor the people of the United States coveted any portion of Mexican territory. The tone of his reply, however, was by no means pacifying. He said:

> They [the American people] do not covet any territory that justly belongs to you; and if they did, you well know how easy would be the acquisition . . . I came here in the spirit of peace, to perform a rightful and imperious duty, and had hoped to have found the authorities of Chihuahua reasonable and law-abiding; but instead thereof, I have been met with demonstrations of absurd and impotent hostility . . .[69]

Before Lane found time to frame an answer to Trias, events transpired which modified the situation. In the first place, Colonel Sumner, Commander of the Department of New Mexico, refused to respond to his call for assistance in enforcing his proclamation; and although Texan and New Mexican volunteers offered to help him occupy the territory, he deemed it inadvisable under the circumstances to do so. Accordingly, he decided to lay the whole matter before the President.[70] Secondly, he received, on May 12, a letter from Alfred Conkling, Minister of the United States in Mexico, and another from Governor Trias. The Mexican Minister of Relations had transmitted to Conkling both the proclamation of Lane and the reply of the Commissioners of Chihuahua. Conkling's official duty would have been sufficiently discharged by forwarding the documents to Washington, but in view of the "extreme gravity" of the

---

[68] Despatch dated March 19, 1853, *El Siglo XIX,* 10 de abril de 1853; also English translation published in *Santa Fé Gazette,* a clipping of which is in the State Department, B. I. A., *loc. cit.*

[69] Despatch of March 23, 1853, State Department, B. I. A., *loc. cit.,* also Spanish translation in *El Universal* 15 de mayo de 1853.

[70] Lane to Taylor, January 23, 1854, *House Rep.* No. 81, 33 Cong., 1 Sess. (Ser. 742), pp. 1–2.

situation he decided to caution Lane that, in his opinion, nothing short of indubitable right and necessity could justify the occupation of the territory, and to advise him "gracefully" to change the attitude he had assumed.[71] The letter from Governor Trias informed Lane that he had received a copy of the letter of Conkling to the Governor of New Mexico, and expressed the confident hope that, in view of the advice of the Minister of the United States, Lane would do nothing to interrupt the amicable relations of the two countries.[72]

Lane's reply to Trias was therefore more conciliatory. He declared that the authorities of Chihuahua had erred in attributing to him warlike measures. He had brought the subject to the attention of the Cabinet in Washington and he did not propose to move further until he received advices from that source, "unless some unexpected contingency made further action indispensably necessary." [73]

Instead of instructing Lane as to further procedure in the matter, the federal government, in apparent disapproval of his action, sent out David Meriwether to supersede him. Meriwether was given full information regarding the state of the boundary dispute. He was told that an "unaccountable blunder" had been made in the survey. The American commissioner had given his consent to "an initial point on the Rio Grande about thirty-two miles further north than indicated by the map annexed to and made a part of the Treaty. In consequence of this mistake the line proposed to be established, would exclude a large and valuable tract of country, heretofore regarded as a part of New Mexico. . . . This error in the yet unfinished labor of the boundary commission has [had] furnished a pretext to Mexico to assert a claim to this extensive tract." For numerous reasons the United States could not admit this claim. What the Mexican government or the State of Chihuahua had done in relation to the occupancy of the country was not definitely known, but Meriwether was instructed to "abstain from taking forcible possession of the tract, even if on your [his] arrival in New Mexico you find [he found] it held adversely to the claim of the U. S. by Mexico or the authorities of Chihuahua." [74]

Colonel Sumner was likewise superseded .by Brevet Brigadier-General John Garland. The new commander was given a copy of Meriwether's instructions, and informed that they contained

[71] Despatch of April 8, 1853, State Department, B. I. A., *loc. cit.*
[72] Despatch of April 30, 1853, *ibid.*
[73] Despatch of May 15, 1853, *ibid.*
[74] Marcy to Meriwether, May 28, 1853, State Department, B. I. A., Dom. Let.

the views of the government in regard to the New Mexican boundary.

> Your tried patriotism and known discretion [said the Secretary of War] give all needful assurance that you will, on every occasion, promptly and properly maintain the rights of your country and the honor of its flag; and in doing so, it is expected that you will avoid, as far as you consistently can, any collision with the troops or civil authorities of the Republic of Mexico or State of Chihuahua.[75]

At the same time Secretary of State Marcy wrote Conkling that the administration had no intention of departing from the path marked out by international law in such disagreements. He said:

> Where a dispute as to territorial limits arises between two nations, the ordinary course is to leave the territory claimed by them, respectively, in the same condition in which it was when the difficulty first occurred, until an arrangement can be made . . . It has not been the intention of the United States to deviate from this course, nor has any notice been given by Mexico that she proposed to assume jurisdiction over it . . .
> Governor Lane is justified in claiming the disputed territory as part of New Mexico and in denying that the acts of the boundary commission had in any manner effected a transfer of the territory from New Mexico to Chihuahua, but his proceeding to enter the territory and hold it by force of arms [!] is not approved and will not be, unless it shall appear that the authorities of Chihuahua had changed or were attempting to change the state of things in the disputed territory from the condition in which they were before the action of the boundary commission on that part of the line. The successor of Governor Lane will proceed without delay to New Mexico with instructions to pursue a course fair towards Mexico and usual in such cases.[76]

Such of this correspondence as came to light, however, could hardly be calculated to allay the uneasiness and suspicion in Mexico. The Mexicans were especially apprehensive because of the aggressive attitude of the Anglo-Americans which was being revealed by the actions of the Tehuantepec company and of the filibusters, as well as in the United States press. The Mexican commissioner had shown certain uneasiness almost from the beginning. On April 20, 1850, De la Rosa complained to Webster of delay in the execution of the survey, concluding his note with the significant remark that he had called the matter to the attention of the United States government "in order that if in the future the unsettled state of the boundary between the two republics should unfortunately give rise

[75] Davis to Garland, June 2, 1853, War Department, MS.
[76] Moore, *Digest of International Law*, I, 754. Instructions of May 18, 1853.

to any unpleasant differences between them, no blame whatever may [might] be imputed to the government of Mexico." [77] In the following year, after the reorganization of the commission of the United States, he objected to the multiplicity of duties thrust upon the new body. He complained that it would require five years to finish the work at the previous rate of progress, and went on to call attention to the importance of the completion of the boundary survey in the preservation of the relations of friendship and good understanding between the two countries.[78] Again in 1852, La Vega lodged with the Secretary of State a somewhat lengthy protest. He reminded Webster that notwithstanding the fact that the joint commission had long since reached an agreement concerning the initial point of the boundary, its survey had been constantly delayed by the absence of the American surveyor, by numerous changes in the personnel of the United States commission, and by lack of harmony among its members. He implored the United States to organize the commission in permanent form, and declared that if the same method of confusion should be continued, Mexico would not be responsible for the consequences.[79]

The news of Lane's proclamation not only caused the State of Chihuahua to take immediate action, but it led to some preparations on the part of the Mexican federal government. On April 2, Trias was granted leave of absence for the purpose of proceeding to the frontier. He levied a forced loan,[80] collected troops and supplies, and before the close of the month, arrived at El Paso with some 800 men.[81] He dispatched to Mexico City a commissioner who was to present the claims of Chihuahua to the supreme government.[82] The action of Trias seems to have been approved. On April 1, the national government sent out circulars to the *jefes-politicos* instructing them to make effective the national guard. According to reports, the central government likewise ordered to Chihuahua two companies of the Battalion of the Line, the *cuerpos activos* of Aguas Calientes and Guanajuato, and three pieces of artillery.[83] At the same time

[77] *Sen. Ex. Doc.* No. 119, 32 Cong., 1 Sess. (Ser. 626), pp. 2–4.

[78] De la Rosa to Webster, *Sen. Ex. Doc.* No. 120, 32 Cong., 1 Sess. (Ser. 627), pp. 1–2.

[79] De la Vega to Webster, January 1852, *ibid.*, pp. 2–4.

[80] *El Siglo XIX*, 23 de abril y 17 de mayo de 1853; *El Universal*, 20 de abril de 1853.

[81] Trias wrote Lane from El Paso on April 30. See B. I. A., Misc. Let.

[82] *El Universal*, 11 de mayo de 1853.

[83] *El Siglo XIX*, 23 de abril y 17 de mayo de 1853; *El Universal*, 2 to 30 de abril de 1853.

the Governor of Durango was ordered to the aid of Chihuahua. The
chief executive of Zacatecas apparently had already dispatched 200
troops of the national guard to the frontier.[84]
The Mexican press showed considerable interest and uneasiness
regarding the matter. The two leading papers of Mexico City
sought to arouse the patriotism of their countrymen. On May 15,
the editor of *El Universal* exhorted his readers to recall the "infinite
offences" which their country had suffered with shameful resignation
from the neighboring republic. Seeking to stimulate confidence, he
contended that Mexico's seven millions were not defeated in 1847
by Scott, but rather by the vicious federal political system which
had created a perennial source of internal strife by placing the divided
power into the hands of the selfish and ignorant. Under such a
system good men had been made the victims of unjust contumelies
and atrocious persecutions, and had consequently lost all spirit and
hope. But all this had changed now. The present government,
based as it was upon fixed and sound principles, was capable of giving encouragement and creating patriotism. If Governor Lane was
judging Mexico in 1853 by Mexico in 1847 he was destined to have
his eyes opened. Mexico now had "magnificent prospects; *y un
pueblo con estas esperanzas no las abandona fácilmente, no se
deja subyugar.*" On May 24, the same periodical reported the
news that Lane's conduct had been disapproved by the Cabinet at
Washington. But the editor was still uneasy. This disapproval,
if indeed it had occurred, might indicate that Pierce would respect
Mexican rights, but his term would soon be over, and even during
his administration "unexpected contingencies" might arise. On
June 5, he came forth with an editorial urging the organization of
a strong army, pointing out as the chief reason for this action the
fact that the reported attitude of the Pierce government regarding
Mesilla could not be taken as unfailing evidence that the United
States would always be able to restrain the sentiment for unlimited
expansion.

Statements coming from an organ which, like *El Universal,* was
supporting Santa Anna and his centralist system, probably must be
somewhat discounted. The threat of foreign invasion may have
had something to do with his recall from exile,[85] and it could certainly
be used to consolidate his power. But even *El Siglo XIX* gave
evidence of considerable feeling and alarm. On June 5, the editor

[84] *El Siglo XIX,* 26 de abril de 1853.
[85] *El Universal,* 30 de marzo de 1853, and following; Bancroft, *History of
Mexico,* V, 634.

stated that indications pointed to the conclusion that the United States had not been responsible for Lane's action. It might be that war would not result. He hoped not. The Mexican people did not desire war, but they could not afford to allow their rights to be infringed upon. "If just because Mexico is weaker than the United States, we should submit to the most exaggerated pretensions, our country would be unworthy of the name of nation."

News that the disapproval of Lane's action was probably the cause of his removal, and that the commander of the federal forces in New Mexico had refused to support the territorial executive, should have served to allay the disturbed state of mind at last temporarily, but certain factors tended to nullify the effect of these actions. Lane had been replaced, but what instructions had been given to Meriwether who superseded him? Sumner had refused to assist Lane in his proposed occupation of *Mesilla,* but he had now been transferred elsewhere, and the instructions and attitude of Garland who had been placed in command of the New Mexican department were matters for uneasy conjecture. Conkling had assumed a conservative and friendly attitude regarding the dispute, but what instructions would be given to Gadsden who was soon to succeed to Conkling's post?

In the absence of definite knowledge the Mexican public turned to the American newspapers. On June 22, *El Universal* reported that the latest periodicals from the United States indicated the most interesting topic of discussion to be *La Mesilla.* It then proceeded to quote and summarize articles from these journals. The New Orleans *Picayune* had announced that the affair had taken on new complications. A number of troops had already received orders to proceed from Texas to New Mexico, among which were six companies of the eighth regiment of infantry. The two companies of light artillery already stationed in New Mexico were to receive fresh horses. Three hundred recruits were to leave Ft. Leavenworth on June 20th for Santa Fé. Under the command of Garland, they were to form a sort of escort for Governor Meriwether. Although the administration did not think war would result, it had resolved to have forces in readiness upon the frontier. The *True Delta* of New Orleans had declared that the United States meant to repel any Mexican force that appeared in the disputed region. The *Delta* did not believe a serious break would occur, however, for Mexico surely must know that such a step would mean "the disappearance forever of its nationality." At the same time these periodicals, together with the Washington *Union* which was supposed to be the official organ, had asserted that Gadsden was to proceed to Mexico with authority to purchase the Mesilla Valley and whatever other territory the government "desired" or was "compelled to have" for the purpose of a Pacific railway.

On June 29, the entire front page of *El Universal* was covered by an editorial treating of the recent news from the United States, and giving special attention to an article contained in a recent number of the *Union*. The editor remarked that although the first news from Washington had been gratifying, it now appeared that there had been a change. He was inclined to this opinion all the more because the news had been conveyed by official and semi-official channels. Moreover, Mexico need not be surprised to learn of the changed attitude, because the nation had already had occasion for grief because of the iniquitous genius of the Republic of the North for advancing its material interests. The *Union* had produced arguments in support of the contention that *La Mesilla* belonged to the United States; but to a nation whose politics were based upon the brutal law of force only one argument, that of self-interest, was necessary. Why not renounce the treaty of Guadalupe Hidalgo, renew the fight which it terminated, and require more territory as the price of peace?

President Polk invaded us because his country desired . . . more territory. To-day there exists the same desire . . . Why does not Mr. Pierce satisfy the democrats? Why does he not extend, as they say, the *area of liberty* so as to force to participate in its benefits the people which they consider slaves? Ah! it would be worthy of the Model republic to *emancipate* the new world by the same system which it had employed in Texas, California, and New Mexico.

Finally, while the same organ, on July 25, denied the statement that hostilities had opened between the Mexican and American forces in the neighborhood of *Mesilla*, it reported in its number of September 8, news purporting to come from a reliable source that the United States had 10,000 troops on the Rio Grande and that a skirmish had occurred between Trias and an American detachment.

Once more it must be borne in mind that *El Universal* was a supporter of Santa Anna whose interest such alarm would serve. Nevertheless, these reports must have kept the public in a state of anxiety. Moreover, *El Siglo* continued to give alarming excerpts from the news of the United States relating to the dispute. The *Chronicle* of New York, for instance, was quoted as reporting that Meriwether had orders to resist the occupation of Mesilla by Mexican troops, while a clipping from the *Times* declared that Trias and Garland could not carry out their respective orders without a "clash and bloodshed," and that the arms and munitions sent to the frontier were more than had been at the disposal of General Zachary Taylor during his campaign.[86] In the United States there was considerable uneasiness regarding the course which Santa Anna might take. Exciting rumors appeared to reach a climax in August. The *Alta California*, one of the best authorities on Mexican matters, declared that it was by no means certain that the boundary difficulty would be settled without a resort to arms. The sending of General Garland to the *Mesilla* Valley with troops was "entirely without meaning" if he did not intend to take possession, and if he took possession war would be "inevitable."[87] At the same time, the publications of New York, New Orleans, and Baltimore reported that Mexico was throwing a large body of troops on the Rio Grande with hostile intent. Such statements at length led the Mexican Legation in the United States to send to the papers of Washington a communication explaining that the movement of the Mexican troops had for its purpose the maintenance of order on the northern border and the defense of the frontier against the Indians.[88]

[86] *El Siglo XIX,* 11 y 13 de julio de 1853.
[87] *Alta California,* Aug. 22, 1853.
[88] *Harper's Monthly,* VIII (November, 1853), 835; *El Siglo XIX,* 11 de noviembre de 1853.

CHAPTER VII

THE NEGOTIATION OF THE GADSDEN TREATY

THE relations of the United States and Mexico thus appeared to be approaching another crisis in the spring and summer of 1853. Raids of Indians from the northern side of the international boundary were daily growing more destructive and Mexico was persistently clamoring for the fulfillment of treaty obligations and indemnity for the depredations which the savages were committing, while the government of the United States was urging that its inability to cope adequately with the Indian difficulty was largely due to Mexico's failure to furnish effective frontier defense, and maintaining that it was not bound by the treaty of 1848 to pay indemnity for the spoliations of these Indians. The old question of claims, which had been a source of difficulty since the administration of Andrew Jackson and constituted one of the causes of the recent war, was coming once more into prominence. Difficulties confronted in surveying the boundary laid down by the treaty of Guadalupe Hidalgo had culminated in a grave dispute regarding the southern limits of New Mexico—a dispute rendered critical on account of the attitude of the settlers and the authorities on the frontier and of the possibility that the loss of the contested area by the United States would mean the loss of a feasible route for a southern Pacific railway. Control of another route for interoceanic communication was being interfered with and the construction of the communication apparently delayed by Mexico's nullification of the Garay grant in Tehuantepec, now in the possession of American citizens who were clamorously demanding the protection of their alleged rights. That party which had fought the war of 1846–1848, but had not been fully satisfied with the territorial gains it had brought, was once more in power with a two-thirds majority in the House and thirty-seven out of sixty Senators. Noisy proclamations of manifest destiny were to be heard on every hand, and the more impetuous of the expansionists, filibusters on a far flung battle line, were girding their loins and putting on their armor in Texas and California. Mexican troops were advancing along the northern frontier, the United States was reënforcing its army in the southwest, and the newspapers of both countries were discussing the possibility of another war. The situation was extremely critical. Would war actually occur?

There were several factors which tended to induce both countries at least to attempt a peaceful settlement of the points at issue. The officials at the head of the Mexican government, no matter how much they talked of going to war, must have known that they were without funds and without equipment, and possibly with no better prospects for European allies than they had in 1846.[1] Moreover, the storm of protest and opposition in the United States to the recent war with Mexico surely had not been entirely forgotten by American statesmen. The Pierce administration and the editors of the expansionist organs of Democracy, even if they had been in favor of a resort to arms, must have known that another conflict with Mexico, the expenses of which could only be collected in territory, would not only endanger the solidarity of their party, but even imperil the Union itself. Undoubtedly, a pacific settlement could be calculated to commend itself both to Mexico and to the United States.

Moreover, why should the Pierce administration go to war when there was a reasonable prospect of obtaining everything it desired by purchase? Was not purchase good democratic procedure, and was not Santa Anna, that unscrupulous soldier of fortune, now at the helm in Mexico and much in need of funds to sustain his government? If he could be convinced that a treaty would serve to strengthen his position, might he not be expected to assume dictatorial powers in order to consummate it?

With the view of pursuing this line of action the administration sent James Gadsden to Mexico in July, 1853. Gadsden was perhaps not a bad choice for the mission. True, he had graduated from Yale without imbibing the first principles of diction or style and he persistently employed high-sounding and redundant phrases whose meaning he did not fully comprehend; but he had gained some little practical experience as a land speculator and a promoter of southern railways; he had been a Nullifier in 1829 and a Secessionist in 1850; and he was a friend of Jefferson Davis, sharing all this great Southerner's eagerness for a southern Pacific railway and the southward flight of the American eagle. Moreover, he was a man of considerable energy and persistency, with a fair amount

[1] It will be recalled that in the summer of 1853 the question of the Near East was threatening to convulse Europe.

of acumen and with few scruples as to the means of attaining the particular ends he had in view.[2]

Gadsden's instructions were much more moderate than might have been expected under the circumstances. After assuring the newly appointed envoy that his government earnestly desired a pacific settlement of the outstanding difficulties with Mexico, Secretary of State W. L. Marcy dwelt upon the rights of the citizens of the United States in Tehuantepec; the southern boundary of New Mexico and the acquisition of a practicable route for a Pacific railroad; release from responsibility for Indian depredations; mutual claims; and means of improving the commercial intercourse of the two countries.

The main portion of the instructions was devoted to the boundary difficulty, the railway, and release from Article XI of the treaty of 1848. With reference to the boundary, Marcy maintained that the line surveyed and agreed upon by the commissioners of the governments concerned was not final because it did not have the concurrence of the surveyor of the United States. Lieutenant Whipple who had acted as surveyor *ad interim* while the line was being run had been appointed without authority by the American commissioner. The fact that the survey had received the approval of the Secretaries of State and Interior in no way affected the matter. If the line had been run in accordance with the stipulations of the treaty of 1848, their approval would not be necessary to its validity. In case it had been erroneously surveyed, no amount of approval could serve to correct the error. Gadsden was therefore to take the stand that the southern boundary of New Mexico had not been established in accordance with the treaty, and to inform Mexico that the United States expected each party to "abstain from taking possession of the district in question or doing any act which indicates [would indicate] an exclusive appropriation thereof to itself." Although the former governor of New Mexico had apparently contemplated the occupation of the region and announced his purpose in a proclamation, he had acted without authority from the federal government. "His intention was never executed, his purpose was disapproved," and Mexico had already been notified that the United States would not attempt to take possession of the disputed area. The latter government expected, therefore, that Mexico would "take the same course," and it was Gadsden's duty to urge upon Mexico the "propriety and reasonableness" of the proposal.

Marcy declared that the Government of the United States was

more interested in acquiring a new boundary embracing territory adapted to the construction of a railroad than in establishing its claim to the territory in dispute. He hoped and expected that the most expedient mode of settling the question would be the merging of the boundary issue in the "negotiation for the alteration of the boundary," with the view of acquiring the contemplated route. In consideration of the many advantages which Mexico would secure from the construction of a railway along the international frontier Marcy presumed that "she would readily accept of a proposition to alter the boundary along that part of the line," ceding to the United States the strip of territory necessary for the proposed improvement.

While admitting that it would be difficult to ascertain without actual survey "the extent of alteration required for such a purpose," Marcy ventured two suggestions:

It would be important particularly to the interests of Mexico that such a railroad should connect with the navigable waters of the Gulf of California. For this purpose it is desirable that the true line—as we contend—the line commencing along the Rio Grande a few miles north of El Paso—should be continued for a considerable distance west beyond the treaty line, then run south about 30′ and then again west to the Gulf. Should Mexico be unwilling to make such a large cession of country as such a line would require she might agree to have the line on the southern border of New Mexico continued until it shall strike the River San Pedro and thence down that river to its junction with the Gila.

With the negotiations for the alteration of the boundary Marcy suggested that it might be proper to embrace a settlement of mutual claims. In regard to Mexican claims for indemnity under the eleventh article of the treaty of 1848, however, Marcy contended that the government of the United States could not admit of any responsibility. It had fulfilled its obligations to restrain the Indian incursions "in the same way, and with equal diligence and energy, as if the same incursions" had been "committed within its own territory, against its own citizens." Since 1848 the United States had kept a large portion of its military forces stationed in the vicinity of the international boundary for the purpose of "keeping the Indians in order and restraining incursions into Mexican territory." Better results had not attended their efforts largely because Mexico had left her border in an almost unprotected state. "It would be singular indeed," said Marcy, "if the United States could be held liable to indemnify Mexico or her citizens for injuries which she invited or at least might have prevented, and in virtue of being a government was bound to her citizens to prevent." Nevertheless, while denying the justice of these claims, Marcy realized that the offer on previous occasions of several millions for release from the obligations stipulated by the article in question put his government in a somewhat embarrassing position, from which he admitted that he would like to find a way of escape.

Marcy assured Gadsden that the government of the United States was willing to "pay liberally" for these three important considerations, but he did not state definite figures. Moreover, he left the subject of the concessions of citizens of the United States in Tehuantepec open for further instructions, and promised later advice concerning the subject of claims in general.

The concluding paragraph of Gadsden's instructions dealt with the commercial relations of the neighboring republics, describing the situation in a few brief sentences:

> The unsettled condition of affairs in Mexico for many years past has very much diminished our trade with the country. The constantly occurring political revolutions there rendered commercial intercourse unsafe; the frequent changes in her tariff and the severe penalties for the non-compliance with it,—even when imperfectly promulgated—were vexatious and often ruinous to our merchants . . . You will make known to Mexico the desire of the United States to establish with her intimate commercial relations on liberal terms. Such relations would in every respect, be advantageous to both countries.[3]

Whether the moderate views set forth in these instructions constituted a true representation of Marcy's attitude in midsummer, 1853, it is difficult to say. They certainly did not satisfy the ambitions of the agent to whom they were addressed, and who, perhaps more disposed to conform to the desires of the Secretary of War, appears to have had little notion of confining himself to the modest aims set forth therein.[4] On two occasions before leaving the United States Gadsden urged that A. B. Gray, who had been connected with the boundary survey, be employed to explore not only the section in the vicinity of the disputed area, but also the

---

[3] Marcy to Gadsden, No. 3, July 15, 1853, Mex. Inst., Vol. 6. (Department of State, Bureau of Indexes and Archives.)

[4] Jefferson Davis appears to have been the dominating figure in Pierce's Cabinet. His views with reference to Mexico may be judged from the fact that he was not satisfied with the territory acquired in 1848, that he proposed a mountain and desert boundary far south of the Rio Grande, and that he was in favor of occupying Yucatán in the spring of 1848. He was the first to notify Gadsden of his appointment to the Mexican post, Gadsden corresponded with him while in Mexico, and the ideas expressed by the Minister with reference to a natural boundary lead one to suspect that Davis is speaking through him. On this point see Dodd, *Jefferson Davis,* chapter on the Cabinet, and "The West and the Mexican War," in Ill. State Historical Soc., *Trans.* (1912), pp. 19–23; Gadsden to Marcy, May 19, 1853; *Senate Ex. Journal,* VII, 322–323.

Gulf of California and adjacent regions; for, said Gadsden, "any settlement of the boundary question which may involve a change from that defined (or rather so undefined) in the Treaty of Guadaloupe; should be made so discreetly and advisably as to preclude the necessity of a revisal hereafter. We must settle on a *Zone* which will give satisfaction to both parties; preclude neighborhood feuds by securing to the State what she requires, and as you probably know she will have." [5]

By the beginning of September, after having been in Mexico City only three weeks, he had evolved a philosophy of Mexican revolutions, reached a definite conviction in regarding the motives which uniformly actuated Mexican statesmen, and begun a series of urgent appeals for more complete and liberal instructions with reference to the amount of territory to be acquired. The war of independence at the beginning of the century had not achieved liberty or democracy, he said; they had merely achieved independence from Spain by an alliance between the Church, the native Spaniards, and the Creoles, none of whom cared anything about freedom, equality, or popular government. They had been interested in the people solely as objects of plunder and exploitation, and they had soon fallen upon each other because the spoils had not been sufficient to satisfy the greed of all. Thus the army came to be employed as an instrument of tyranny; thus despotism, sustained by a military force which remained loyal only so long as it was well paid and well fed, sprang into existence. All of this had a very direct bearing upon Gadsden's mission; and the early days of September found him far from pessimistic as to the outcome. The Mexican treasury had shown a seventeen million dollar deficit during the last fiscal year; the people who possessed ready cash were shipping it out of the country; there was little prospect of borrowing on the credit of the Church; rents and internal revenues would come in too slowly to meet an emergency; and yet there were numerous signs of an approaching revolution, and Santa Anna's army must be paid or lost. Would not these factors appear to justify the acquisition of more territory than originally contemplated—the five frontier states, for instance? If Santa Anna's immediate necessities should become extremely pressing, would it not be wise to place a portion of the sum to be paid into the hands of the despot at once? How large was the contingent fund of President Pierce? How much money

[5] Despatches of July 12 and 19, Mex. Desp., Vol. 18. Unless otherwise indicated all of Gadsden's correspondence referred to in this chapter will be found in this volume, in the State Department.

would the United States be willing to offer for these frontier states? These were some of the questions propounded by the enthusiastic agent of manifest destiny.

Moreover, in his most sanguine moments Gadsden rejoiced at another possibility. Santa Anna might be overthrown by the Moderates, and this group would perhaps "tender . . . the whole Country, to be annexed hereafter under our Constitutional requirements as states of our Federation . . . At the Crisis how should your minister act? His instinct is to receive and protect." [6]

Such was the situation as Gadsden saw it soon after his arrival. In succeeding despatches he frequently reiterated most of the opinions expressed in this private memorandum and gradually unfolded his plans and the methods he proposed to pursue in order to consummate them. While confessing his repugnance to despotism, he was not averse to lending it financial support provided his ends could be gained thereby. He condemned bribery on general principles, but when it was clearly the only means of accomplishing a specific object he was willing to make use of such "appliances," to resort to the "Antient Franchise," to apply the "oil" to the "axel," covering the action of his government by working through the medium of the agents of Sloo or Garay (rivals in Tehuantepec), for instance. He believed also in the efficacy of intimidation, urging repeatedly that the troops of the United States on the frontier be augmented and that vessels of war be sent to the coasts of Mexico. But his stock argument was of course that of manifest destiny.

An adequate conception of the difficulties and vexations which this apostle of expansion confronted and of the methods which he employed can not be had without a somewhat detailed study of his despatches. These will show the philosophy of Young America at its most aggressive stage, while they will reveal, at the same time, some of the fundamental problems of the period.

On August 31, Gadsden complained that the exaggerations of the American consul at Acapulco with reference to alleged outrages committed upon the captain and crew of the Schooner, *B. I. Allen,* had involved him in an unnecessary correspondence with the Mexican government. He referred, at the same time, to the "increasing disposition on the part of lawless Trespassers to disturb the tranquillity" of the frontier, and concluded his despatch by deprecating the practice followed by his predecessors of interposing diplomatically in the interest of private claimants prior to the consideration of each case by a competent tribunal.

[6] Private, of September 5, 1853.

On September 2, while advising Marcy with reference to the choice of consuls for Mexican posts, he declared that it would be better for the commercial relations of the two countries to "dispense with all consular appointments unless Americans of . . . character and capacity; well informed on the obligations imposed by their commissions, can [could] be secured." He said that the high duties and prohibitions imposed by the Mexican government tended to foment smuggling and contraband trade, in which Americans frequently participated; and that when they became involved in difficulties with the Mexican authorities, they invariably sought the protection of their government. Unless American consuls exercised firmness and discretion in such cases, they were likely to commit their government against the law instead of in its own support.

Two weeks later Gadsden went still further and indicted the entire consular system of the United States as applied to Mexico. He charged many consuls with being ignorant of the Mexican code and of Mexican port regulations. He said that they "too often combine [d] with and become [became] the partisans of those who have [had] incurred responsibilities in the violations" of this code and these regulations, "more than nine tenths of the issues on private claims" arising from "palpable disrespect" of the law.[7]

The diplomatic contest in which Gadsden was for several months to be a not unwilling participant, began in the latter days of August, when a complaint from the Mexican Minister of Foreign Relations, Manuel Diez de Bonilla, with reference to excesses committed by Americans on the Chihuahuan frontier presented an opportunity, perhaps in line with his policy of intimidation, for conveying the information that the recently appointed governor of New Mexico had been accompanied to his post by a military force sufficient to cope with the problems in the region. This note and rumors to the effect that two thousand American troops had been sent to New Mexico led Bonilla to make an uneasy inquiry as to the significance of the movement. Whereupon Gadsden responded with the assertion that they had been dispatched for the purpose of assisting the Governor "to preserve order on the Frontier."[8]

Meantime, something of the tactics of Gadsden's protagonists may be gathered from the busy circulation of exaggerated reports of Indian depredations in Sonora and Chihuahua in such a fashion that they could not escape the notice of the American Minister, and

[7] No. 5, September 17, 1853.
[8] Bonilla to Gadsden August 20, 30, and 31, 1853; and Gadsden to Bonilla, August 22, and 31, and September 1, 1853.

as likewise from a note of Bonilla with reference to the fulfillment of Article XI of the treaty of 1848. In this communication the Mexican Minister said:

The incessant incursions of savage Indians which are daily becoming more destructive and of which those states of this Republic bordering upon the frontier of North America are the victim, have compelled the President to direct the undersigned . . . to address this note to Mr. Gadsden . . . in order to call his attention to this subject which so deeply concerns the welfare of this nation and the . . . good name of the American Union, pledged as the latter is to the most exact fulfillment of compacts which on account of their transcendent importance, are deemed sacred among nations . . . In the various periodicals that are published, and, among them, in the official journal, . . . Mr. Gadsden will have seen since he has been in Mexico, reference made to a part of these incursions, both more destructive and more numerous than any that have occurred subsequent to 1848. It can be proved by means of documents bearing evidence of the fact, that during the short period of time which has elapsed since the peace of Guadalupe these incursions have been attended with less risk to the savages and have been more frequent and destructive to the aforesaid frontier states than they were a century ago, in consequence of these savages not having been restrained in American territory, as they should have been, and the facility with which they obtain shelter in American territory as soon as they are pursued by Mexico. . . . The natural and unavoidable result of this state of things is the increased energy with which the savages repeat their serious depredations, having on some occasions penetrated into the very heart of the Republic; the assassination or captivity of all who have the misfortune of falling into their hands, without distinction of age or sex; the robbery and pillage of cattle and whatever property they come upon; the prostration of villages and valuable plantations now laid waste and deserted; and the continuous decay of said states, once so flourishing[!], but now hardly able to sustain themselves because of their rapid depopulation and the consequent abandonment of their agriculture, commerce, and other sources of prosperity . . . Such deplorable events, which affect private individuals at the same time that they undermine the foundations of power and public wealth, are the result, and the undersigned is very sorry to say it, of the non-fulfillment of those engagements which the United States contracted with Mexico by the eleventh article of the Treaty of Guadalupe, and they proceed from the fact that the frontier has not been provided with a sufficient number of troops and that all other measures to which it is pledged for the purpose of restraining, pursuing, and chastizing the savages have not been adopted. Therefore, Mexico has preferred her complaints to the government of the United States, both . . . through the American legation here and through her own at Washington . . . General Almonte has been especially instructed to . . . present several of the many and numerous claims which have been submitted to this department by citizens who have sustained the disasters herein deplored, and those of other citizens will be forwarded from time to time . . . for the same object, as well as those which it behoves the nation to prefer on its own account . . . But in as much as . . . those devastating incursions are being repeated without intermission and as nothing can compensate for the loss of good and peaceful citizens and the desolation and extermination of families, the undersigned . . . has the honor of addressing himself to . . . the Envoy of the United States, begging that he will be pleased to communicate the contents of this note, together with the public and notorious facts which have been the cause of it, to his government, in order that, fully appreciating the immense importance of this subject, it may be pleased to render effective the stipulations of the Treaty of Guadalupe in regard to it by adopting all such measures as may be necessary for affording complete redress for all the injuries that have been incurred and for punishing and restraining the savages as the sacred obligations . . . of said treaty and the equally sacred rights of Humanity demand.[9]

Gadsden feigned great surprise at this stand on the part of the Mexican Minister. He declared he had supposed that the ghost of Indian indemnities had already been slain by his predecessors; quoted such so-called maxims of international law as: every interpretation of a treaty which deduces from it obligations morally and physically impossible is absurd and may be rejected, every agreement imposing burdens which are not mutual is odious, equality in international contracts can alone justify respect for the obligations incurred; and maintained that the United States government had done everything within its power to protect the inhabitants of Mexico from the incursions of the Indians. It had in fact defended Mexican citizens as diligently and as effectively as its own—which accorded exactly with the obligations imposed by Article XI. Since it was not accustomed to indemnify its own citizens for losses occasioned by Indian raids, Mexico and its frontier inhabitants need not expect indemnity. The government of Mexico had in large measure prevented the effective management of this whole Indian problem by disarming its frontier population, insisting on a preposterous boundary, and objecting both to the pursuit of the savages across the international line, and to the movement of American troops across, or stationing them within, the disputed area. He did not deem it appropriate for the government of the United States which had not originated these difficulties, which, in fact, had uniformly manifested a desire to avoid and terminate them, to suggest a mode of settlement, but he would nevertheless entertain any propositions looking to this end which Bonilla cared to submit.[10]

On September 18, in an official despatch to Marcy, Gadsden expressed the belief that Bonilla was on the point of presenting such proposals as would lead to the settlement of all outstanding difficulties. He felt sure that territory could be acquired, though the price demanded might be extravagant; and he asserted emphatically that no latitude north of 31° would be at all satisfactory, while he urged

[9] Note of August 30, 1853.
[10] Note of September 9.

that a natural line further south would "better subserve the objects of *restraining Indian incursions* . . . and promoting the *harmony of border neighborhood*."

In a private communication of the same date he called attention to the sensitiveness manifested in Mexico on account of the increase of the forces of the United States on the southwestern frontier and dwelt upon his favorite idea of intimidation. He was convinced, he said, that the augmentation of the "rank and file on the whole line of the Rio Bravo will [would] operate advantageously—so on the ocean." "We should show on all occasions the sword, however covered by the Olive." This policy was urged again on October 3, when he suggested that in case his mission had not attained a successful issue by the end of the year, a trip to Washington "for a private and confidential conference with the President," and simultaneous "preparations on the frontier" would have "the most decided influence" on the adjustment of outstanding difficulties; and likewise on the 18th of the same month, when he advocated stationing war vessels in both the Gulf and the Pacific and advancing an increased military force to the very banks of the Rio Grande, although in the latter despatch protection of American interests in Mexico was given as one motive for such procedure.

Preliminary conferences were held with the Mexican president on September 25, and on October 2. At last the negotiations seemed to be fully under way. During the course of these conferences Gadsden had recourse to his favorite argument of manifest destiny (or should one say geographical predestination?). Urging the sale of a much larger strip of territory than the boundary adjustment and the Pacific railway would require, he declared:

No power can prevent in time the whole valley of the Rio Grande from being under the same Government. All the sympathies of the Mexican States west of that river must and will be with the State or States east. And either Western Texas must come back to the Mexican Government or the States of Tamaulipas, New Leon; Coahula [sic] and Chihuahua, will by successive revolutions or purchases become united with Texas. These are solemn political truths—which no one can be blind to. It is for the consideration therefore of the two Powers claiming opposing jurisdiction to determine (where fate seems to have decreed) whether it is not in harmony with good neighborhood to the advantage of both Republics to sell and to purchase; and thus anticipate a union of States naturally bound to each other . . .

During these interviews it was agreed that the territory in dispute should remain in *status quo,* the military commanders of both governments on the frontier immediately to be informed of this fact; and, although Santa Anna refused to consent to the alienation of more territory than the amount absolutely indispensable to the proposed railroad and the settlement of the boundary dispute, Gadsden still hoped for a larger concession as he awaited the supplementary instructions promised him when he set out on his mission.[11]

Several busy and somewhat anxious weeks intervened, however, before these arrived. In the meantime, he occupied himself with the composition of extensive confidential speculations regarding the character and the fate of the Santa Anna régime, with the complaints of American citizens, the conjuration of Mexican suspicions, the appeasing of Mexican wrath, and the defeat of corrupt schemers who sought to convert the negotiations into a bag of gold for themselves. On October 12, he sought to allay the apprehensions of Bonilla with reference to the dangers lurking in a permit for American engineers to explore the region immediately south of the international boundary in search of the most practicable route for a Pacific railway. In a confidential note of October 18, he made a sweeping charge of universal corruption among the high official circles in Mexico and accused some of his own countrymen of an incontinent desire to share in the graft. On October 30, apparently for the purpose of continuing his policy of intimidation, he felt called upon to answer Bonilla's note safeguarding the *status quo* agreement against a construction unfavorable to the claims of Mexico, by the not altogether reassuring declaration that, since the Mexican government felt indisposed to acknowledge the understanding, the United States "must feel relieved from any recognition of a similar obligation, and at liberty to be governed as necessity or policy may [might] impose." During the next two weeks his time was mainly occupied with the refutation of Bonilla's extensive arguments in support of the right to demand indemnity for Indian depredations and with an earnest effort to convince Mexico that the federal authorities of the United States were acting in good faith with reference to the California filibusters.

At length, about the middle of November, the long-expected supplementary instructions arrived. Although bearing the date of October 22, and apparently written after Marcy had received Gadsden's report of the conferences of September 25 and October 2,[12] they seem to have been based upon the sanguine confidential despatches of September 5 and October 3. They were brought with great secrecy by Christopher L. Ward, a Pennsylvania lawyer ap-

[11] See Gadsden to Marcy, No. 6, October 3, 1853, and accompanying "memoranda."

[12] Carlos Butterfield left Mexico with despatches from Gadsden on October 3, and he presented these to Marcy on October 19. See Butterfield to Marcy, October 20, 1853, Marcy Papers, Vol. 43.

parently interested in the Garay grant, who had been solemnly enjoined not to enter Mexico with written instructions, but to communicate their contents orally to the Minister. Marcy later gave the following explanation for the procedure:

It was thought that there was at the time he [Ward] was sent out a very critical state of things in regard to the ruling power in that country, and that immediate pecuniary means would be indispensable for its maintenance; and to provide these means in the apprehended emergency a liberal concession of territory might be readily made. But at the same time it was suggested that should it in any way become publicly known that such a cession was contemplated that fact would not only defeat the object but overturn the existing government . . . It was also apprehended . . . that the very unlimited power of General Santa Anna might soon be circumscribed and he would not at a future period be able to do what his necessities would then incline him to do in order to get the means to strengthen his doubtful rule.[13]

Thus the government of the American Democracy which had wept over the oppression of the Greeks, received Kossuth with open arms, contemplated striking the chains from Canada, and posed as the mighty champion of liberalism everywhere, admitted its disposition to prolong the rule of a tyrant over a neighboring people, for it offered him what amounted, in effect, to a liberal bribe, in order to induce him to dispose of a portion of the birthright of the Mexican nation. There was sympathy for the submerged masses elsewhere, but none for those in Mexico!

Through Ward, Gadsden was instructed to direct his negotiations toward the achievement of three objects—(1) release from the eleventh article of the treaty of 1848, (2) the settlement of reciprocal claims, (3) the acquisition of a new boundary—all of which were to be embraced in one treaty. With reference to the boundary, the center and heart of the negotiations, five possibilities were suggested. The most southern boundary secured a mountain-desert barrier and involved the cession to the United States of a large portion of Tamaulipas, Nuevo León, Coahuila, Chihuahua, and Sonora, and all of Lower California. The most northern acquired only what was believed to be sufficient area for the contemplated Pacific railway route.[14] The maximum which Gadsden was authorized to

[13] Marcy to Gadsden, No. 20, Confidential, January 6, 1854, Mex. Inst., Vol. 6.

[14] For the southernmost boundary, see accompaning map. The five boundaries suggested were described as follows (see memorandum of instructions to Ward, Oct. 22, 1853, Mexico, Special Missions, Vol. 3):

No. 1

"From a point on the Gulf of Mexico midway between the Boquillas Cerradas and the Barra de Santander westward along the ridge dividing the waters

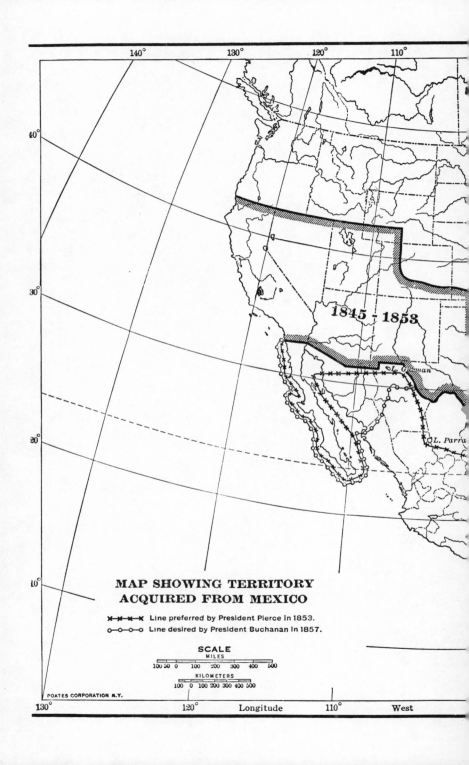

MAP SHOWING TERRITORY
ACQUIRED FROM MEXICO

✕—✕—✕ Line preferred by President Pierce in 1853.
o—o—o—o Line desired by President Buchanan in 1857.

SCALE
MILES
100 50 0   100   200   300   400   500

KILOMETERS
100 0 100 200 300 400 500

POATES CORPORATION N.Y.

1845 - 1853

L. Guzman

L. Parra

40°
30°
20°
10°

140°   130°   120°   110°

130°   120°   Longitude   110°   West

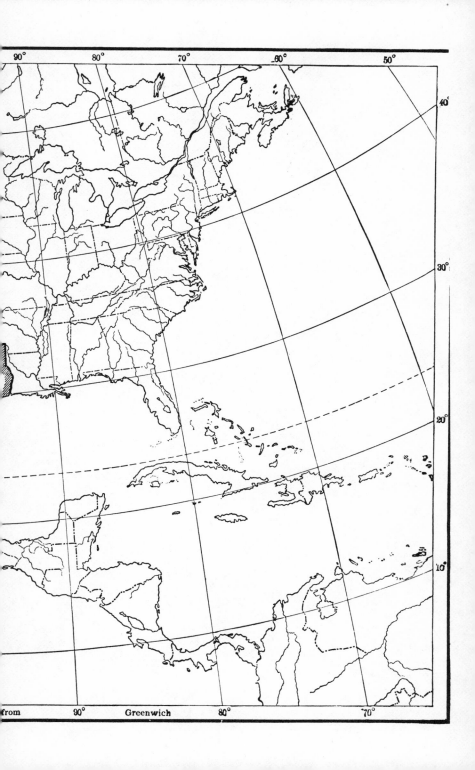

offer for the largest area was fifty million dollars; the maximum for the smallest area was fifteen million dollars, it being understood in all the proposals that the sums stipulated were to secure, also, the release of the United States from the obligations imposed by Article XI of the Treaty of Guadalupe Hidalgo and from all claims of the Mexican government and people against the United States. In each of the offers an attractive cash payment was provided, and

which flow into the river San Fernando from those which flow into the river Santander to the Coast range of mountains. Thence obliquely across that range on the South side of the Pass of Linares and along the heights which border the plains of Durango to a point South of the Lakes de Alamo and Parras. Thence along the highlands on the west side of the said Lakes following the principal ridge which divides the waters flowing into the Rio Conchos and Rio Sabinas up to the mountain ridge contiguous to the Rio Grande. Thence along said ridge and across the Conchos river up to the parallel of San Eliasario and thence westwardly passing on the South side of Lake Guzman along the highlands or the middle of the plains which divide the waters flowing into the Gulf of California from those flowing into the Rios Grande and Gila until the line so traced shall intersect the 111th degree of longitude west of Greenwich,—and thence in a direct course to the Gulf of California at the 31st degree of North latitude. Thence down the middle of said Gulf to its Southern extremity and around the Southernmost point of the Cape of Lower California and along its western coast including all adjacent islands to the termination of the U. S. Boundary on the Pacific."

No. 2

"From a point on the Gulf of Mexico midway between the Rio Grande, and the Rio San Fernando, westwardly through the middle of the plain, which divides the waters flowing into the Rio Grande and the Rio San Fernando, until the line so drawn shall reach the highlands and thence along said highlands, so as to include the waters flowing into the Rio Grande to the Pass of *Los Muertos,* thence northwestwardly along the highlands, including the waters of the Rio Grande, to a point on said river between the mouth of the Rio Pecos and the Presidio del Norte, where the highlands thus defined are intersected by the Rio Grande. Thence along said river to the 31st degree of North latitude—thence from the Cañon of the Rio Grande below San Eliasario, north latitude thirty one along the mountain ridge which is contiguous to the Rio Grande, up to the parallel of the Presidio San Eliasario . . . [Thence as in No. 1 to the middle of the Gulf of California.] Thence up the centre of Said Gulf and the channel of the Rio Colorado to the present boundary of the United States."

No. 3

"From the Cañon of the Rio Grande below San Eliasario . . . [as in No. 2 to the middle of the Gulf of California, thence as in No. 1 to the boundary of the United States on the Pacific.]"

No. 4

[Same as No. 3 to the middle of the Gulf of California, thence as No. 2.]

the remaining indebtedness was to be rapidly extinguished by large monthly installments. What better bribe could have been desired by a despot without disposition to distinguish between public and private funds? [15]

When Ward arrived in Mexico he evinced, as it appeared to Gadsden, undue concern with reference to the claims of the holders of the Garay grant. The Minister therefore refused to act upon his new instructions until Ward had reduced them to writing. Thus reduced, they coincided with the original, except for the confessed addition of a section urging the protection of the Garay concessionaires. In this portion of his communication Ward alleged that the President of the United States, far from any idea of abandoning the Garay group, "was determined [both] to support those claims in every proper form short of a declaration of war in regard to them alone" and to repudiate the Conkling treaty. The President's failure to give specific instructions on all the points at issue did not signify the intention on his part of precluding Gadsden from the "exercise of reasonable discretion." He had not given specific directions with reference to the Garay claimants because of haste and the fear that they might protract the negotiations; but if there should be a reasonable prospect of arranging this important affair, the President would be in favor of such a step. A treaty securing territory or a railway route which would be sure to have its rivals in the United States,

No. 5

"[(1)] Frontera on the Rio Grande is accurately ascertained to be in Latitude 31° 48' and some seconds. A line from that point of Latitude due West to the Gulf of California would throw within the limits of the United States a very good . . . route for . . . a rail road. [(2)] . . . A Line on the 32d parallel of latitude would give the United States a good route for a Rail Road from the Rio Grande to the Gulf, but neither a line from Frontera or on the 32d parallel would be a good boundary . . ."

[15] In reply to Gadsden's suggestion that bribery might be necessary to accomplish the objects of his mission, Marcy wrote:

"You intimate in your communications that possibly there may be money to a considerable amount which the president might use in order to facilitate a difficult negotiation, but it is not so. The secret service fund at the control of the President is small. The amount annually appropriated does not exceed $40,000, and the appropriation for the present fiscal year has been in part expended. Should the President make application for an immediate increase of it to a large amount, it would be necessary to explain to Congress the particular use to be made of it. The subject would of necessity go before both Houses and undergo much debate. It would be impossible to preserve secrecy as to the object to which it was intended to apply it. I cannot promise, therefore, that anything can be done in this way to facilitate your present negotiation." (Marcy to Gadsden, No. 19, December 22, 1853, Mex. Inst., Vol. 6.)

while leaving "unnoticed and unredressed . . . long-pending and real injuries of individuals," would reflect glory neither upon the American Minister in Mexico, nor upon the government which he represented. Ward therefore urged Gadsden to consider the wisdom of "arranging in one treaty, and at once, *all* the points of difference between the United States and the Mexican Republic, if the question of boundary should not thus be greatly delayed." [16]

This addendum to the original instructions does not seem to have been a very grave departure from the views and desires of Pierce, but the verbal advices, the extravagant claims, and the general attitude of Ward while in Mexico offended Gadsden, eliciting from him a long protest.[17] Nevertheless, he proceeded to include the Garay concessions in the project for a treaty which he submitted soon afterwards, and pressed them with no little pertinacity.

Soon after the arrival of his new instructions Gadsden had an extended and fervent interview with Santa Anna, at the close of which he was informed of the dictator's intention to appoint a commission to confer with him with reference to the settlement of all pending issues. Before formal announcement of the personnel of the commission had been made, however, Gadsden suspected that European interference had taken place "in the private parlors of the Palace." He accordingly proceeded, as he informed Marcy, to "read" Bonilla "a Chapter from President Monroe's Manifesto." What he did, in reality, was to sing a pæan to a type of manifest destiny very closely allied to the concept of geographical predetermination. He contended, in brief, that the inevitable result of the march of the age would be the absorption of a large part of northern Mexico—"a repetition of Texan history in the six border States including South [Lower] California"; that European meddling and appeals to Europe for support, such as he had reason to think that Mexico had recently made, would serve only to hasten this consummation; and that it would therefore be wise for the Mexican government to anticipate the inexorable by the sale of the region in question. By this simple process it would secure a "natural Territorial boundary, imposing in its Mountain and Desert outlines," check further desires for expansion on the part of citizens of the

---

[16] Ward to Gadsden, November 14, 1853, Mex. Special Agents.

[17] Gadsden urged that the Mexican government could hardly be expected to recognize a grant which it had repeatedly repudiated; that the deduction of five millions for the "Cormorant appetite of Ward and Co." and three millions for private claims would render the financial consideration inadequate to meet the needs of Santa Anna, and thus endanger the success of the negotiations. (Gadsden to Marcy, Private of Nov. 20.)

United States, remove the provocation for border feuds, lay aside the burden of protecting people who really preferred to be transferred to another jurisdiction, and, in a word, usher in the millennium in North America![18]

This preamble delivered, Gadsden was ready to settle down to the negotiations proper. These were brought to a conclusion after six sessions, extending from December 10 to 30, for each of which brief "protocols" were kept. These protocols, together with a despatch to Marcy, written while Gadsden was in the midst of his work, furnish a very satisfactory account of the difficulties Gadsden confronted and the contests he waged during the last days of his mission.

From Gadsden's letter to Marcy, dated December 16, it appears that after the close of the second formal conference, the American Minister was on the point of giving up in despair. The meddling of speculators interested in the Indian spoliation claims and in the Tehuantepec concessions, the presence of William Walker and his filibusters on Mexican soil, the attempt of the Mexican negotiators to transfer a portion of the issues to Almonte, the Mexican Minister at Washington, the extravagant demands of Mexico, "prompted me," said Gadsden, "to close all negotiations." When the diplomats of the Aztec nation observed his state of mind they asked for another conference, and Gadsden decided to make one more effort to accomplish the objects of his mission. Since, however, the American Minister persistently urged the cession of a large area of territory in spite of the refusal of the Mexican commissioners to consent to the alienation of more than the minimum required for the projected railway, one suspects that extravagant claims were not entirely confined to the agents of Mexico.

At length, after the greater part of four conferences had been consumed, Gadsden reluctantly consented to accept the contention of the Mexican commissioners with respect to the territorial feature. The negotiators then turned to the question of Indian indemnities, which evoked prolonged discussion. Bonilla demanded as a consideration for releasing the United States from Article XI, compensation both for the losses which the Mexican "Government and Citizens had suffered in the past, and for the responsibilities and obligations

---

[18] Gadsden to Bonilla, November 29, 1853. The commissioners appointed by the Mexican government were Bonilla himself, J. Mariano Monterde, and José Salazar y Larregui.

Gadsden's suspicions regarding European opposition to his negotiations were well founded. See Doyle (British Minister in Mexico) to British Secy. of State, No. 120, Dec. 18, 1853, F. O. 50, Vol. 261. For Santa Anna's appeal to Europe, see Bolton, *Guide to . . . the Principal Archives of Mexico*, p. 230.

of which the U. States in the future would be relieved," insisting
that eight million dollars be set aside in the proposed treaty specifically for this purpose. Gadsden refused either to admit the responsibility of his government for the Indian depredations or to item-
ize the compensation he proposed to offer for the various concessions
sought.

The fifth conference opened with an attempt on the part of Gadsden to secure recognition of the Garay grant. This the Mexican commissioners refused to concede on the ground that such a step would
permit an undue interference in what was purely a domestic and
administrative matter; and they persisted in this stand even when
Gadsden offered three million dollars for this consideration alone.
When Bonilla suggested that the only proper method of disposing
of the claims under the grant was to include it among the number
the United States proposed to assume, Gadsden objected that his
government was unwilling to expend more than five millions for
this purpose, but that the Garay claimants were demanding that
amount for themselves, and pressed the matter of the revalidation of
the concession until Bonilla finally informed him that further discussion was useless, as "he never would assent to anything that in
the slightest degree could affect the honor of his country or infringe
upon her sovereignty." Gadsden was finally convinced that further
efforts would prove unavailing and he once more gave over.

The commissioners then turned to the question of compensation
for the concessions which Mexico had signified her willingness to
grant. At first Gadsden offered seventeen millions, five millions to be
retained for the satisfaction of American claims against Mexico,
and twelve millions to be paid for the "other things agreed upon."
The Mexican commissioners insisted upon a larger amount, and
after considerable discussion, "it was finally decided that the U.
States should Pay $15,000,000 for all other concessions and $5,000,000
to be devoted for the satisfaction of private claims." [19] Of the
former sum, one-fifth was to be paid upon the exchange of ratifications and the remaining four-fifths in monthly installments of three
millions each—an arrangement which must have made the wily dictator chuckle! Nothing now remained but the signing of the completed document. This took place on December 30, and Gadsden
set out immediately for Washington.

The account of the Gadsden negotiations can not be considered
as complete, however, until Santa Anna's version of the matter has
been briefly examined. When news of his sale of the national do-

[19] The six protocols were inclosed with Gadsden to Marcy, March 20, 1854.

main aroused a storm of protest in Mexico, the dictator and his friends, profiting by the rumors of a threatened outbreak of hostilities with the United States which had arose in the summer and fall of 1853, endeavored to excuse his action by the allegation that the Yankees would have taken the territory by force had he not consented to its sale. This story was not sufficiently convincing to stem the tide of opposition which soon led to his overthrow, however, and on two subsequent occasions he referred to the affair, along with other matters, in attempt to restore himself to the good graces of the Mexican people. These two accounts, one contained in a *pronunciamento* issued from his place of exile in 1858, and the other in his memoirs written some ten years later, agree in essentials. In the first, he said, in substance, that the government of the United States, with the view of stirring up trouble, had dispatched a large force to threaten the department of Chihuahua; that the Mexicans "had nothing with which to oppose the invaders arrogantly appearing along the frontier but the sad spectacle . . . of exceeding weakness"; that, during the progress of the negotiations, Gadsden had given the Mexican officials to understand that the territory in question was absolutely essential to the development of the United States and that Mexico had better sell for a reasonable price what "imperious necessity" would sooner or later compel the Washington government to seize. In the second statement, Santa Anna asserted that the government of the United States, "with knife in hand, was attempting to cut another piece from the body it had just mutilated"; and that "an American division was already treading upon the State of Chihuahua." He then proceeded to describe the diplomatic conferences in detail. Although in the first account Santa Anna had said that Gadsden made proposals regarding "Baja California, part of Chihuahua and Sonora," in the later version he added Sinaloa and part of Durango. He remarked here, also, that Gadsden's threat to the effect that his government would resort to force in case Mexico should persist in refusing to part with territory, was made at a moment when the envoy was angry because of the pertinacity with which the Mexican negotiators supported their contentions.[20]

It will be noted that, according to this view, Gadsden is accused

[20] I have published a translation of Santa Anna's statements in *The Southwestern Historical Quarterly*, XXIV (January, 1921), 235 ff.

This version of the Gadsden Treaty has been accepted by the leading historians of Mexico. See, for instance, Vicente Riva Palacio, *México á través de los siglos*, IV, 812, 916; Niceto de Zamacois, *Historia de Méjico*, XIII, 663, 916; Francisco de Paula de Arrangois y Berzábal, *México desde 1808 hasta 1867*, II, 334; Ignacio Álvarez, *Estudios sobre la historia de México*, VI, 75–76.

of bluster and intimidation and the government of the United States is charged (1) with the occupation of the territory in dispute prior to Santa Anna's decision to sell it, and (2) with the concentration of troops on the Rio Grande for the purpose of intimidating Mexico into a territorial cession. The accusation against Gadsden, as has appeared from the foregoing analysis of his correspondence, is essentially true. The first charge preferred against the United States, however, is false. Reference had been made elsewhere [21] to the fact that, in the spring of 1853, Marcy notified the Mexican government that the United States had no idea of departing from the *status quo* principle usually observed in such disputes. It has been seen, also, that the region in question had not been occupied before Governor Lane's removal from office; that Governor Meriwether was instructed not to take any steps toward occupying the territory, even if upon his arrival he should find Mexican troops on the ground; and that General Garland, who superseded General Sumner as commander of the forces of the United States in the department of New Mexico, was given a copy of Meriwether's instructions for his guidance.[22] These facts seem to indicate the absence of any intention on the part of the United States immediately to occupy the disputed section; and apparently there was no change of purpose prior to the completion of the negotiations which resulted in the Gadsden Treaty. In the first letter written from his post of duty, Meriwether remarked that there were about thirty Mexican soldiers at *Mesilla* and that it was rumored that many more were on their way, but he made no reference whatever to United States troops being stationed there.[23] In his despatch of August 31, he confirmed his previous view of the situation, but maintained the same significant silence regarding the forces of the United States.[24] Gadsden's communication of October 8, to the military officer commanding in New Mexico, in which he informed him that an agreement to leave the area in *status quo* had been made but gave no direction as to removal of troops, appears to be conclusive evidence that no news regarding an occupation on the part of the army of the United States had reached the American Minister up to this time.[25] A letter from Meriwether to Marcy, dated November 14, indicates

[21] See "The Boundary of New Mexico and the Gadsden Treaty," in *The Hispanic American Historical Review*, IV (Nov., 1921), p. 732.
[22] *Ibid.*, pp. 728, *passim*. See also *ante*, p. 119 ff.
[23] Meriwether to Marcy, August 13, 1853, State Department, B. I. A., Misc. Let.
[24] *Ibid., loc. cit.*
[25] H. E. Bolton, Transcripts from the Archives of Mexico.

that such action had not yet been taken. Meriwether asked for instructions regarding a criminal who had escaped to the disputed region. He said he feared that if he asked the Governor of Chihuahua for the culprit, such request might be construed into an acknowledgment of the possession of the section by that state, while an attempt at forcible seizure might "precipitate matters more than it is [was] desirable to the government at Washington." [26]   Lastly, a very careful examination of the archives of the War Department at Washington has failed to reveal any evidence indicating the presence of troops of the United States in the disputed territory prior to December 30, 1853, when the Gadsden pact was signed. Therefore, the conclusion that the first charge preferred by Santa Anna against the United States is false seems warranted.

The second charge, however, apparently rests upon a firmer basis. During the summer and fall of 1853, some three hundred recruits were sent to New Mexico and preparations were made to establish a new post opposite El Paso.[27]   At the same time, recruits for the Fifth Infantry were dispatched to Texas, along with four additional companies of Artillery; and General Persifer F. Smith was ordered to concentrate the troops of the Eighth Department (Texas) on the Rio Grande and to erect "field works." [28]   It is quite possible that these preparations were represented by Gadsden as the expression of an intention on the part of the United States to accomplish its purposes by force in the event that negotiations proved unavailing. But so far as the Washington government itself is concerned, only three bits of evidence have been found which can possibly be construed as indicating that the concentration of troops on the frontier signified a determination to appeal to the sword when other measures failed to secure the coveted territory. These are as follows: In the concluding paragraph of his letter of November 14, 1853, Meriwether said, ". . . There is no military force

[26] Misc. Let.

[27] Adjutant-General to Brigadier-General Clark, April 23, 1853, Headquarters of the Army, Letter Book, Vol. 8; Garland to the Adjutant-General, August 3, 1853, War Department, Adjutant-General's Office, Old Files; Adjutant-General to Persifer F. Smith, September 15, 1853, Adjutant-General's Office, Letters Sent, Vol. 28; Garland to Adjutant-General, November 27, 1853, and January 24, 1854, Adjutant-General's Office, Old Files.

[28] Major-General Scott to the Chief of the Recruiting Service, April 15, 1853, and to Colonel Plympton, May 26, 1853, Headquarters of the Army, Letter Book, Vol. 8; Adjutant-General to Persifer F. Smith, July 30, 1853, Adjutant-General's Office, Letters Sent, Vol. 28. See also the returns from the military departments of Texas and New Mexico, Adjutant-General's Office, Returns Division.

in the disputed territory the Mexicans having removed their small force sometime since and should the general government desire to precipitate matters this will afford an opertunity [sic] of so doing." [29] On October 28, 1853, General Garland reported that there were "no troops at all at the Mesilla"; that there was "not much friendly feeling towards" the United States "on the other side [of the international boundary]"; and that he was "preparing to move down to that quarter at short notice." [30] On the 27th of the following December, this same commander wrote Gadsden that his "dispositions" were "so made" that he was "ready to *attack,* or repel, whichever may become necessary." [31] The fact that troops had been mobilized on the frontier, and that the governor of New Mexico and the commander of the federal troops in that department appeared to anticipate aggressive action, would not, however, necessarily imply the intention of the United States to resort to force if negotiations should fail. Moreover, mobilization may have been ordered as a precaution and counter move against the concentration of Mexican troops along the Rio Grande and the southern boundary of New Mexico, as well as for the purpose of dealing with Indian problems which were particularly grave at the time. A perusal of the correspondence of the War Department furnishes much to justify this view of the matter.[32]

[29] State Department, B. I. A., Misc. Let.

[30] Adjutant-General's Office, Old Files.

[31] The American Commanders of the military posts on the southwestern frontier kept the War Department fully informed regarding the apparently hostile movements of Mexico. See despatches of D. S. Miles (commanding at Ft. Fillmore, N. M.) dated March 20 and 22, 1853, and of P. F. Smith (commanding Eighth Department, Texas) dated July 2 and July 7, 1853, and enclosures, Adjutant-General's Office, Old Files.

[32] The Indian situation was critical in New Mexico. See General Garland's reports from August 9 to November 27, 1853, *loc. cit.*

In his instructions to Garland, Secretary Davis said: ". . . It is expected that you will avoid, as far as you consistently can, any collision with the troops or civil authorities of the Republic of Mexico or the State of Chihuahua." (Instructions of June 2, 1853, Office of the Secretary of War, Letters Sent, Vol. 34.) Ordering Smith to concentrate his forces on the Rio Grande, the Adjutant-General remarked: "While the Department is disposed to reply on the good faith of the authorities of Mexico . . . it considers that it would only be a measure of prudence, induced by the information communicated in your letters, to be prepared for any aggression which might be attempted from the quarter referred to."

CHAPTER VIII

THE STRUGGLE FOR RATIFICATION

The Gadsden Treaty was placed into the hands of the President on January 19, 1854.[1] Something of the contest over its ratification was forecast by the presence of the Hargous brothers among the passengers on board the vessel which brought Gadsden to New Orleans.[2] Through the agency of Ward they had written into the treaty a provision taking care of their claims under the Garay grant. They were now coming to the United States with the view of preventing any revision unfriendly to their interests.

For almost a month the pact proved an apple of discord in the Cabinet. The members of this body were divided on the question as to whether it should even be submitted to the Senate. Pierce himself, believing in a policy of aloofness with reference to private interests in foreign countries, was unwilling to favor either the Garay or the Sloo grant in the treaty.[3] He finally decided to transmit the document to the Senate, recommending three important changes therein. He advised that Article II be modified so as to make the obligation mutual with reference to the restraint of the Indians on the international frontier. He struck from Article III, which related to the mutual settlement of claims, the clause which expressly designated the Garay grantees as American claimants. He changed the eighth article from a formal agreement specifically stipulating the method by which the United States should co-operate in the suppression of filibuster raids to a general promise of cheerful co-operation in accomplishing this end.[4]

The pact was sent to the Senate on February 10, 1854. Few treaties have occasioned a more spirited contest. The absence of Senator Mason and debate on the Kansas-Nebraska bill caused considerable delay.[5] Consideration of the treaty did not begin until March 9. It then occupied much time in the Senate from March 13

---

[1] N. Y. *Herald*, Jan. 20, 1854.

[2] N. O. *Picayune*, Jan. 13, 1854; Washington *Union*, Jan. 17, 1854.

[3] N. Y. *Herald*, Feb. 9, 1854; Washington *Union*, April 9, 1854; N. Y. *Journal of Commerce*, Feb. 13, 1854.

[4] *Sen. Ex. Journal*, IX, 238–239.

[5] Washington *Union*, March 7, 1854.

until April 25, when, after every line of diplomatic correspondence even remotely connected with the negotiations had been demanded, it was finally accepted by that body. The senatorial discussions of the agreement were carried on in secret session and the confidential injunction has not been subsequently removed, but from the journal of the Senate and the information which leaked out to the contemporary press the careful student may ascertain the main features of an interesting contest.

Lines of cleavage in the Senate soon led to the formation of some five distinct groups. Strongest opposition to the treaty came from such anti-slavery irreconcilables as Foot, Seward, Sumner,[6] Fish, Chase, Wade, Walker, Hamlin, and Fessenden. Senator Mason of Virginia led a group of senators composed of Allen of Rhode Island, Hunter of Virginia, Adams of Mississippi, and Dodge of Wisconsin, who advocated the ratification of the pact in its original form. Directly opposed to these was a bloc under the leadership of Bell of Tennessee and including Bayard of Delaware, James of Rhode Island, and Geyer of Missouri, who demanded the recognition of the Sloo grant in the treaty. Rusk of Texas was the spokesman of a coterie which sought to center attention upon the acquisition of no more territory than merely what was necessary for a feasible railway route. Gwin and Weller of California, with the faithful assistance of Shields of Illinois, favored making a larger acquisition of Mexican territory and a port on the Gulf of Lower California a *sine qua non*.[7]

As finally ratified by the Senate the ten articles of the original agreement were reduced to nine. Since five of these nine were virtually identical with the provisions of the original treaty, they need not be considered at length here. Article V of the original (which became the fourth article of the final) treaty provided that the United States should have "free and uninterrupted passage through the Gulf of California, to and from their possessions situated north of the boundary line of the two countries," but that such a passage was to be used by land only with the express consent of

[6] It is possible that Seward and Sumner were influenced by Commodore Vanderbilt and other citizens of New York who were interested in rival projects for interoceanic communication.

[7] On January 19, 1854, Gwin remarked with reference to the Gadsden Treaty: "I hope that treaty embraces all the territory on our border which Mexico is not able to protect from .\. . [filibuster] incursions and Indian depredations, and that we shall have a mountain and desert boundary between the two Governments that can be defended by each." (*Cong. Globe*, 33 Cong. 1 Sess., p. 207 ff.)

the Mexican government; that the same "provisions, stipulations, and restrictions" were to be "observed and enforced . . . in reference to the Rio Colorado . . . for such distance as the middle of the river" constituted the common boundary between the two countries, as well as with respect to the Rio Grande below its intersection with the parallel of thirty-one degrees, forty-seven minutes, and thirty seconds. Article VI of the original (changed to Article V of the amended) treaty applied the stipulation of the eighth and ninth articles of the Treaty of Guadalupe Hidalgo to Mexican citizens and property in the newly acquired territory, recognized the right of each one of the contracting parties to fortify "whatever point within its territory" it judged proper and advisable, and provided that the terms of Article XVII of the same treaty (relating to commerce and navigation) should continue in force. Article VII of the original (changed to Article VI of the ratified) pact provided that no land grants within the acquired domain bearing date subsequent to September 25, 1853, should be considered valid, nor were any grants made previous to that date to be obligatory which had not been "located and duly recorded in the archives of Mexico." Article IX of the original (which became the seventh article of the amended) treaty provided for a procedure similar to that stipulated in Articles XXI and XXII of the treaty of 1848 in case of disagreements between the two countries. Lastly, the tenth article of the original document, which provided for a time limit of six months for exchange of ratifications, became Article IX of the final draft.[8]

These five articles having been disposed of in a rather summary fashion, consideration of the provisions which occasioned some deliberation, disagreement, and modification may now be entered upon. Article I, which described a new boundary, seems to have caused most difficulty. Some six or seven amendments were proposed to this one portion of the treaty. The important considerations appear to have been the desire for a port on the Gulf of California and for a route better adapted to a Pacific railroad. The boundary line as traced by the original article coincided with that of the treaty of 1848 from the Pacific coast to its intersection with the Colorado River; thence down the middle of the stream to a point two marine leagues north of the most northern portion of the Gulf of California; thence a right line to the intersection of the thirty-first parallel of latitude with the one hundred and eleventh of longitude, from which

[8] See Gadsden Treaty in Malloy, *Treaties*, I, 1121 ff. The original agreement appeared in the New York *Herald* on Feb. 15, and in the Washington *Union* on Feb. 18, 1854.

place it was to continue by another right line to the intersection of the parallel of thirty-one degrees, forty-seven minutes, and thirty seconds with the Rio Grande.

The first amendment to this article was offered by Shields of Illinois on April 4, and it retained to the United States more territory than any other amendment proposed. It described a boundary running down the middle of the Colorado and the Gulf of California to the thirty-first parallel, and thence out said parallel to the Rio Grande.[9] By reference to the map it will be seen that this line included a large portion of Sonora and Chihuahua.

Shields's amendment was rejected, and on April 5, Gwin proposed a boundary identical with that of Shields to the intersection of the thirty-first parallel of longitude with the 111th meridian; and continuing from here by direct line to the point where the parallel of thirty-one degrees, forty-seven minutes, and thirty seconds strikes the Rio Grande. This arrangement was likewise defeated. Then, on April 10, Rusk of Texas offered an amendment which described a line beginning on the Rio Grande at its intersection with the parallel of thirty-one degrees, forty-seven minutes, and continuing west one hundred and fifty miles; thence south thirty miles, and then by a right line to the Rio Colorado or the Gulf of California, as the case might be; and thence, as in the other proposals, to the Pacific. On the same day, likewise, Gwin proposed a boundary including considerably less territory than on the previous occasion. It began where the parallel of thirty-one degrees, forty-seven minutes and thirty seconds intersects the Rio Grande, ran west one hundred and fifty miles, and south thirty miles; thence by a right line to a point on the Gulf of California one marine league south of the southernmost point of the Gulf of Adair; thence to the middle of the Gulf of California; and thence up the middle of said gulf and the Colorado River to the boundary line of 1848. Gwin's amendment was not approved. That of Rusk passed; but two days later he carried through a motion to reconsider the vote, whereupon he proposed a line beginning at the intersection of the parallel of thirty-one degrees and forty-seven minutes with the Rio Grande, running west one hundred miles, south thirty miles, and, then west to the

[9] *Sen. Ex. Journal,* IX, 278. Gwin of California said in his memoirs (written in 1878) that he proposed at the time to extend the boundary of the United States to a line drawn from thirty miles south of Mazatlán to a point on the Gulf of Mexico thirty miles south of the mouth of the Rio Grande; but it is rather strange that no record of the proposal appears in the journal. Gwin's statement that Jefferson Davis was then in the Senate makes one even more distrustful of his memory. See Gwin's Memoirs, p. 96.

111th meridian; thence directly to a point on the Rio Grande twenty English miles south of the junction of the Gila with said river.[10] This amendment was likewise accepted; but on April 25, while the resolution for the ratification of the whole treaty was before the Senate, Mason of Virginia submitted an article defining the boundary as it was eventually fixed; namely, beginning at the intersection of the parallel of thirty-one degrees and forty-seven minutes with the Rio Grande; "thence due west one hundred miles; thence south to the parallel of thirty-one degrees twenty minutes; thence along the said parallel . . . to the 111th meridian of longitude west of Greenwich; thence in a straight line to a point on the Colorado River twenty English miles below the junction of the Gila and the Colorado Rivers; thence up the middle of the said Colorado until it intersects the present line between the United States and Mexico." [11]

Article II of the original pact dealt with the vexing question of Indian indemnities. As submitted to the Senate, it probably revealed some of the difficulties encountered by Gadsden in his attempt to obtain complete release from this obligation. According to its terms, the eleventh article of the treaty of 1848 was declared abolished and annulled, but, for the future, responsibility for the conduct of the Indians was made almost as exacting as formerly. It was agreed that the United States should pass the necessary laws relating to the subject, among other things, making it a penal offence for an inhabitant of the country to receive property of any kind known to have been stolen within Mexican territory by the Indians; that such property, when recovered, should be returned to its legitimate owners; that the government of the United States should use "every fair and reasonable means" to rescue and return to Mexico captives taken from that country by said Indians, requiring, so far as Mexico was concerned, simply the assumption of the expenses occasioned by such return; and that the United States in preparing for the removal of said Indians should take special care not to place them "under necessity of seeking new homes by means of incursions into the Mexican territory." [12]

On March 9, the Committee on Foreign Relations, following out the suggestion of the President, proposed that the thirty-third article of the treaty of amity of 1831, which likewise related to the Indians on the international border, should also be abrogated; and that there should be attached to the end of the proposed Article II, a clause

---

[10] *Sen. Ex. Journal*, IX, 280–281, 283–284, 289–290.
[11] *Ibid.*, IX, 309–310; Malloy, *Treaties*, I, 1121–1122.
[12] *Sen. Ex. Journal*, IX, 290.

making mutual the obligations it stipulated.[13] These amendments occasioned no action; and the opposition of the Senate to the assumption of any sort of responsibility relating to the matter was attested by the unanimous vote to strike out the article in question.[14] As finally amended and accepted, Article II contained simply the abrogation of Article XI of the treaty of 1848 and the 33d article of the treaty of 1831.[15]

Articles III and IV of the original treaty related to the subjects of compensation for the territory acquired by the first article and of mutual settlement of claims outstanding between the contracting parties. Originally, as has been noted, it was proposed to pay Mexico $20,000,000 for territory and for release from responsibility for the Indians of the Southwest, $5,000,000 of which were to be retained for the satisfaction of American claimants; but this sum was first reduced to $9,000,000, then to $7,000,000, and finally raised to half of the original figure.

The original pact, as has been noted, also contained the provision that the government of the United States should assume all claims of its citizens against Mexico and specifically mentioned among the number the claimants under the Garay concession. This feature was retained by the Committee on Foreign Relations, whose chairman, Mason of Virginia, had long since become the champion of Hargous and company. But the Senate rejected the proposal along with all arrangements for the settlement of mutual claims.[16]

Sloo and his associates, the rivals of the Garay group, fared somewhat better at the hands of the Senate. Under the able leadership of Bell of Tennessee, they succeeded in writing an article into the final treaty which must have given them no little satisfaction. Soon after the treaty was submitted to the Upper House, Senator Bell had called for the Conkling pact which had been signed with Mexico on March 21, 1853, as a sort of supplement to the Sloo concession. Subsequently he introduced an amendment confirming the contract of Sloo and associates and containing in substance the following provisions:

(1) Neither government was to interpose any obstacle to the transportation across the isthmus of persons and merchandise of both nations, persons and property of citizens of the United States having the benefit of the most favored nation clause. (2) Transportation by the company of the mails of the United States in closed

[13] *Ibid.*, IX, 238–239, 260–262.
[14] *Ibid.*, IX, 290. The vote was taken on April 12.
[15] *Ibid.*, IX, 304.
[16] *Ibid.*, IX., 238–239, 260–262, 291–292.

bags was to be permitted, and the effects of the government of the United States were to be transported free of duty. (3) Neither passports nor letters of security were to be required of persons crossing the isthmus and not remaining in the country. (4) After the Sloo Company had completed its proposed railway the Mexican government was to open a "port of entry, in addition to the port of Vera Cruz, at or near the mouth of the Coatzacoalcos River." (5) The governments were to enter into arrangements for the transport of troops and munitions of the United States which the latter country might "have occasion to send from one part of its territory to another lying on opposite sides of the continent. (6) The government of the United States was to be allowed to extend its protection to the company when it felt such action "sanctioned and warranted by the public or international law." [17]

Bell's amendment was likewise defeated; but Article VIII, of the treaty as finally ratified differed from the proposal of Bell only in that the Sloo Company was not expressly designated, and agents of the United States and not of the transit company were mentioned in connection with the transportation of United States mails.[18] The Sloo group had won at least a partial victory.

Article VIII of the original compact related to the subject of filibuster raids. It contained an agreement for reciprocal co-operation in the suppression of "unlawful invasions of any of the citizens or subjects of either power against the territory of the other" and prescribed the manner of co-operation in the following detailed fashion:

They mutually and especially obligate themselves in all cases of such lawless enterprises which may not have been prevented through the civil authorities before formation, to aid with the naval and military forces, on due notice being given by the aggrieved party of the aggressions of the citizens and subjects of the other, so that the lawless adventurers may be pursued and overtaken on the high seas, their elements of war destroyed, and the deluded captives held responsible in their persons and meet with the merited retribution inflicted by the laws of nations against all such disturbers of the peace and happiness of contiguous and friendly powers. It being understood that in all cases of successful pursuit and capture, the delinquents so captured shall be judged and punished by that nation to which the vessel capturing them may belong . . .[19]

When the President submitted the treaty to the Senate he advised striking out the paragraph just quoted, and the Committee

[17] *Ibid.*, IX, 299.
[18] Malloy, *Treaties*, I, 1124.
[19] *Sen. Ex. Journal*, IX, 292–293.

on Foreign Relations reiterated his recommendation. The Senators went a step further, however, and eliminated the entire article.[20]

On April 17 a vote on ratification of the entire treaty was taken and it was defeated by a count of 27 to 18. Twelve anti-slavery Senators, three of the friends of Sloo, and Gwin and Shields had voted against it. The champions of the treaty then accepted an amendment favorable to the Sloo grantees and, soon after making this concession, succeeded in pushing the pact through the Senate, the final ratification taking place on April 25.

Soon afterwards the much mutilated agreement was accepted by Santa Anna.[21] The House was then called upon for the appropriation necessary to carry out its terms.

The inaccessibility of the Senate discussions perhaps justifies a full report of the debates in the House. The treaty was submitted to this body on June 21, 1854, and referred immediately to the Ways and Means Committee. On the following day the chairman of this committee introduced a bill making the appropriation which it required. At the same time, something of the turn the discussion was to take was indicated by Benton's announcement of his intention to introduce the question of the privilege of the House in regard to such treaties.[22]

Four days later consideration of the bill began. Peckham of New York, who was one of the first to gain the floor, attempted to put before the body a resolution requesting the President to communicate all the correspondence relating to the treaty. He was ruled out of order, however, and the Speaker recognized Benton, who read his resolutions regarding the question of privilege. These sought to commit the House not to consider the proposed appropriation before it had decided whether its privileges had been infringed, nor until it had "obtained full information on the negotiation and conclusion of said Treaty," and declared the right and duty of that

[20] *Ibid.*, 299, 302, 310, 311.

[21] For an account of Santa Anna's attitude, see Gadsden to Marcy, May 21, June 1, June 9, and June 17, Mex. Desp. Vol. 18; Doyle to Clarendon June 2, 1854, F. O. Mex., Vol. 267 and July 3, *loc. cit.*, Vol. 268.

In an interview with Doyle, the British Minister in Mexico, Santa Anna hinted that he would not accept the treaty if he could be assured of European backing against the United States. Doyle replied somewhat ambiguously, but gave the dictator very little encouragement.

Gadsden was disgruntled because of the Senate's modifications. He thought more territory should have been acquired and objected to the protection of the Sloo enterprise and the failure to settle the claims.

[22] *Cong. Globe,* 33 Cong., 1 Sess., p. 1476.

body to deliberate upon the expediency of carrying the treaty into effect.[23]

The House then resolved itself into a Committe of the Whole and the bill providing for the appropriation was taken up. In putting the matter before the assembly, Houston of Alabama, the Chairman of the Ways and Means Committee, urged the necessity for hasty action.

Jones of Tennessee was the first speaker who expressed his sentiments regarding the treaty. He declared his purpose to vote for the bill, not because the action of the President and the Senate bound him to do so, nor in consideration of the land the treaty acquired, but rather because it obtained release from Article XI of the Treaty of Guadalupe Hidalgo.[24]

Jones was followed by Benton who made the leading speech of the opposition. He objected strenuously to the violation of the privilege of the House, declaring that whenever a treaty requiring an appropriation was to be made, that body should first be consulted. If it was not consulted before the Senate and the President took the people's money, there would be nothing left in the constitution worth preserving.

Benton then began a violent attack upon the provisions of the treaty itself. He most vigorously opposed the stipulation acquiring a route for a railway. This was a question to be decided by the representatives of the people who were better judges of what suited the people than the President, the Senate, and Santa Anna. Why pay $10,000,000 for a route when there was a good national route already within the territory of the United States along the parallels of thirty-eight and thirty-nine degrees, and a sectional one along the parallels of thirty-four and thirty-five? The route acquired was not even sectional: it was beyond the limits and latitudes of the southern states, a thousand miles out of the way to San Francisco, and through a country so *"desolate, desert, and God-forsaken,"* that Kit Carson said "a wolf could not make a living upon it." Even if such a route were desirable, it could have been bought for much less. Robert J. Walker, president of the Million Dollar Railroad Company, had been on the point of obtaining a railway concession in Chihuahua and Sonora for $6,500 and $500,000 worth of Texas railroad stock when news came of the Gadsden negotiations. When

[23] *Ibid.*, p. 1519.
[24] *Ibid.*, p. 1520. It will be recalled that this article released the United States from responsibility for Indians acquired with the territory ceded by this treaty.

it was proposed to pay $10,000,000 for what had previously been offered for a pittance, he suspected that there was graft somewhere. He believed that Walker and certain army officers who were speculating in New San Diego had exercised undue influence upon the administration.

This route for a railway, as undesirable as it was, constituted the only real acquisition of the treaty. The land adjacent to the proposed route was so worthless that the more the government obtained the poorer it would be. The question of claims arising from Article XI was all fancy. The United States was to give the same protection to Mexican citizens as to its own, and no more. The satisfaction to be exacted was to be from the Indians and not from the United States. The government had fulfilled the article; it had given Mexicans as ample protection as had been accorded its own citizens, and Mexico could not rightfully demand a cent.

Moreover, the eighth article of the treaty was more of a liability than an asset. It seemed that the administration had a passion for "outside roads" and speculators. Walker and associates had been given a road, the promoters of New San Diego had been favored, and Mr. Sloo had not failed to get his turn. He had drawn the United States and Mexico into an agreement by which both powers were to have the right of protecting the route across the Isthmus of Tehuantepec—"and of course the right of quarreling and fighting over it, or paying indemnities" for release from the obligation. In this connection, he desired his colleagues to remember how nearly the Garay grant had led the country to war a short time since.

Lastly, Benton dwelt upon the absurdity of the contention that the treaty settled the boundary dispute. There was in fact no boundary dispute; for the question had already been settled, and there was no legitimate ground for dispute, "unless a subject of foreign relations, settled under a whig administration, and become a part of a treaty, as much so as if inserted therein," could be repudiated two years later by a Democratic administration. In support of his contention he quoted Secretary Stuart's letter of July 24, 1852, in which the latter held the agreement of the commissioners to be final. This had been the view of the Fillmore administration, and in his conception it was right; but, right or wrong, it was the procedure of the government and could not be nullified by a subsequent administration. This administration might "nullify appointments—turn in and turn out officials—change them all—make the whole catalogue walk out and walk in, until a rigadoon dance is [was] performed between them," but never could it nullify a treaty in this fashion.[25] After Benton had finished, and considerable delay had been occasioned by an attempt on the part of Jones of Tennessee to limit debate upon the pending bill, Bayly of Virginia spoke at length in reply to Benton. He took some pains to show that the President and the Senate had not infringed upon the rights of the House and declared that Benton's real motive for opposing the treaty was his fear that the acquisition of a southern route to the Pacific would interfere with his own pet project.

Then, turning to the merits of the treaty, he placed special emphasis upon the release from the obligations of Article XI. He declared that the United States government had notoriously disregarded its pledges in this matter, and that it was, consequently, liable to claims for indemnity. He had reason to believe that these claims now amounted to more than $40,000,000. Of all the embarrassing agreements the United States had ever entered into, this was one of the worst; and he was willing to give "without any reference whatever to a right of way to the Pacific, a large sum of money to get rid of" it. Besides this important consideration, there was the *Mesilla* Valley, a fine route for a railroad to the Pacific, and the Tehuantepec right of way "for which Mr. Polk offered many millions of dollars." Would any member present surrender these valuable acquisitions by withholding the necessary appropriation under the fanciful idea of vindicating the privileges of the House? [26]

Bayly's address closed the consideration of the bill for the day. On June 27, the discussion was opened by J. Glancy Jones of Pennsylvania, who began by emphasizing the merits of the treaty. He explained that two constructions had been placed upon the eleventh article from the day of its ratification. According to one view, the United States government was to punish the Indians making incursions into Mexico by exacting from them the "same measure of satisfaction" which would be exacted for depredations upon its own soil. This was the proper construction, according to his conception of the matter. But the Mexican government construed the article differently. It maintained that whenever damage was done by Indian incursions into Mexico, the United States was to be held responsible for the damage and required to make compensation for it from the treasury. Every member of the House must know that

[25] *Ibid.*, pp. 1031–1036.
[26] *Ibid.*, pp. 1042–1044.

Mexico, acting upon this interpretation of the article, had already presented with vouchers claims amounting to $16,000,000. He had reliable information, also, that Fillmore had been willing to pay $6,000,000 to obtain release from the obligation. It had even been asserted that the Arista government had claimed $40,000,000 for damages. Whatever the amount, the matter had not been settled; and where such radically opposite views were maintained, the dispute must either be arranged by compromise, or else terminate in war.

Jones contended, moreover, that there existed a real boundary dispute. The inability of the American boundary commission to agree as to the initial point on the Rio Grande had led to a disagreement between the co-ordinate branches of the government, in which the Fillmore administration took one side and Congress the other; the work had been suspended, the situation was critical, and would remain so until the treaty under consideration was ratified. For this reason, therefore, the appropriation bill should appeal to those opposed to war; for the amount it stipulated would not "keep an army in active operation for three months."

The speaker next pointed to Polk's former offer of $15,000,000 for the Tehuantepec concessions as evidence of the importance of this route, and then, taking up the question of privilege raised by Benton, devoted the rest of his speech to the refutation of his argument.[27]

Jones was followed by Haven of New York, who took the stand that the United States government was bound by Article XI only to exact satisfaction from the Indians, not to pay it itself; and he assured the House that Fillmore and his Cabinet, whatever they would have been willing to see paid to Mexico to settle a controversy likely to arise between the two governments, did not consider Mexico's claim just and equitable. He then proceeded to express suspicion regarding the transactions connected with the treaty. Reports were being circulated to the effect that Gadsden had been sent out with instructions to offer Mexico $10,000,000 for certain concessions, but that later some "stock-jobbers and hungry politicians," who were interested in the Garay and Sloo grants, had made a successful descent upon the administration and placed their affairs in such a light before it as to persuade it to instruct Gadsden to pay an additional $10,000,000 for a settlement of their "pretended or prospective" losses under these grants. With this end in view, a Mr. Ward had been sent out as a kind of special agent with verbal instructions. Gadsden had refused, however,

[27] Ibid., App., pp. 1008-1009.

to negotiate outside of his written orders and the record; and when it became evident that the scheme must fail unless the instructions were written, the secret agent had proceeded to reduce them to writing. Thereupon, acting in conformity with the written instructions, Gadsden had inserted the article providing indemnity for the "jobbing companies of Garay and Sloo." Haven said that he meant to cast no reflection upon the administration, but, because of these rumors, he was unwilling to take a step in the dark and vote for the bill to carry out the treaty stipulations. Moreover, he thought it was due to the gentlemen connected with this affair that the correspondence be placed before the House in order that the administration might be absolved from slander in case the reports were false.[28]

Phillips of Alabama next obtained the floor. He replied at length to Benton's argument regarding the privileges of the House; pointed out the merits of the treaty, emphasizing especially the route for a railroad and the Tehuantepec concession; and concluded with a few words on the rumors of fraud connected with the negotiation of the treaty. In speaking of the route for a railway, he referred to the plans of Texas for the construction of a road across the state and pointed out the fact that the distance from the western boundary of this state to San Diego was only eight hundred miles. He declared that what had a few months before appeared as a delusion now seemed to him a reality. As for the allegations of corruption, two-thirds of the Senate, after having seen the correspondence, had voted in favor of the treaty; and this, in itself, ought to "create a presumption of fairness not to be overcome by the gossiping slanders of the hour."[29]

Keitt of South Carolina, the next speaker, arose mainly to defend Gadsden from an imaginary charge of violating his instructions. Before he resumed his seat, however, he took occasion, while asserting that he saw no sectional issue in the treaty, boldly to declare his southern bias. He also explained that he meant to vote for the treaty because it acquired territory, obtained the Tehuantepec route, the abrogated Article XI of the treaty of 1848.[50]

Keitt was followed by Gerritt Smith of New York, who gave evidence of considerable eccentricity. In regard to the question of privilege, he said that all the House had to do with the treaty was either to obey or to disobey the call for money. The moment the

28 *Ibid.*, pp. 1535–1539.
29 *Ibid.*, App., p. 1018 ff.
30 *Ibid.*, pp. 1540–1541.

treaty was accepted by competent Mexican authorities and the President and Senate of the United States, it would become a law of the land, regardless of the action of the House. The members of the latter body now had either to appropriate the sum necessary or to assume the responsibility of "law-breakers." With reference to the merits of the treaty, he said that, in his conception, there were only two: the acquisition of territory, and release from the obligations of Article XI. He was willing to take all the land he could get from Mexico by righteous means. "I would that the treaty gave us whole provinces; yes, and even all Mexico." He was not willing, however, to compensate the Mexican government for granting routes of communication across, or adjacent to its territory; for that government should be glad to do so without price so long as others undertook to build the roads. He thought that the sum of $10,000,000 was too much for the considerations obtained by the treaty, and he meant to become a law-breaker by voting against it.[31]

The next two speakers, Giddings of Ohio and Washburn of Maine, took essentially the same stand. The former declared that he saw no justice or propriety in the treaty in the present state of his knowledge. If the correspondence had been submitted so that he could have learned more about it, his opinion might have been different; but this had been refused, and he was therefore going to vote against the measure before the House. In keeping with this attitude, Washburn declared his absolute unwillingness to vote away the people's money in such a "sweeping and blindfold manner."[32]

Boyce of South Carolina declared that the House was free to exercise its discretion in regard to the treaty and took considerable pains to establish his point; but he maintained, at the same time, that there were numerous considerations in favor of the pact. In the first place, it had the approval of the President and the Senate, being in its present form virtually a product of their own hands. In the second place, it would settle a boundary dispute which was undoubtedly grave and thereby keep the country out of war. He had read the arguments relating to the boundary and had been convinced that the United States was in the right; but he had rather yield to Mexico's demands than go to war with a "weak, distracted, convulsed and tottering power." Moreover, he believed the eleventh article of the treaty of Guadalupe obligated the United States government in the strongest possible manner to protect the northern provinces of Mexico, and if that government had failed to do so, it

[31] *Ibid.*, App., pp. 1015–1017.
[32] *Ibid.*, p. 1540 ff.

was "bound to make indemnity." He was not in favor of taking the opposite stand just because Mexico happened to be weak. Finally, he contended that the treaty obtained the best, because it was the shortest, route to the Pacific. Texas had under way a road from the western border of Louisiana to El Paso; and from the latter point to the waters in the vicinity of the Gulf of California was only four hundred and fifty miles. Only the construction of this part of the road was needed to connect the Atlantic and the Pacific; thereafter, the line could be extended at leisure, probably with the aid of California, to San Diego and San Francisco.[33]

Peckham of New York, who had been so anxious to obtain the papers relating to the treaty, introduced his remarks by comment on the Kansas-Nebraska act. He then entered upon a somewhat bitter criticism of the administration. In his opinion, the correspondence had not been submitted because the administration realized it could only walk through the House in safety on the measure when it walked in utter darkness. If the instructions and the proceedings under them had been such as would reflect credit upon the government, the storms of heaven could not have kept them from being revealed.

Peckham declared in regard to the treaty itself, that it was of no moment. That the land obtained was worthless all admitted; and, personally, he did not believe a route suitable for a railway would be acquired by the boundary it defined. The argument that it would settle the boundary question scarcely deserved a grave rejoinder. "Must this Government . . . pay a large sum of money simply to settle a disputed line without gaining anything? If that be so we shall soon have to settle with Mexico again." He was willing to give Mexico the benefit of any doubt in regard to the matter of indemnity for Indian depredations; but in his mind there was no doubt. He did not believe that any party to the treaty of 1848 ever dreamed that the United States should pay Mexico for all the damages sustained by the incursions of the Indians. The government was bound to act impartially in the matter, giving inhabitants of both countries the same amount of protection. There was not, and never had been, any law requiring the United States to indemnify its own citizens for damages sustained by raids of the savages. Why the stipulation in this same Article XI, that the Mexican government should pay the expenses of returning captives taken by the Indians from its territory, if it was understood that the whole

[33] *Ibid.*, pp. 1544-1545.

burden of damage was to be shifted to the United States? Claims amounting to between twenty and forty million dollars presented by Mexican citizens did not frighten him. Mexican language readily became "magniloquent" and the Mexican exchequer was not over-flowing. Even if the claims were eighty millions, he would "give bond to settle them all before any impartial tribunal for a quarter of a million and take my [his] pay out of the surplus." Again, the stipulations regarding the Isthmus of Tehuantepec were worthless, since they conceded nothing which did not already rightfully belong to citizens of the United States.

Moreover, the treaty was "not without positive demerits": it failed to protect the just claim of citizens of the United States. The agreement, in the nineteenth article of the treaty of Guadalupe, which related to merchandise that American citizens had introduced during the war, had been notoriously violated by Mexico and these citizens had sustained losses amounting to millions. He had recently presented to the House claims of one firm amounting to some two hundred thousand dollars. Numerous other complaints had been made to the United States government; but they had been ignored, and now this treaty proposed utterly to disregard these rights and demands. If a portion of the $10,000,000 were going to indemnify its own citizens, the United States could better afford to expend the sum. Instead of this, however, it was being contributed to "pro-long the existence" of a despot.[34]

Perkins, one of Peckham's colleagues, then explained briefly why he meant to vote against the bill. He said he was bound to oppose the treaty until the administration and the Senate showed it was right. He considered as sufficient ground for its rejection, the statement of the Washington *Union,* supposedly the official organ of the administration, to the effect that the House was bound to make this appropriation. The *Union* had recently spoken of the ad-visability of either purchasing Cuba or of taking the island by force. There was probably some connection between these two utterances of this periodical; the granting of the sum now requested would fix a precedent which the House would soon be called upon to follow in respect to Cuba. Moreover, in regard to the objections to the treaty under consideration, he said he desired to add one other to those already mentioned: the United States would probably not acquire one foot of land by Article I, but only dominion over land. There was not a particle of evidence that every acre of territory in

[34] *Ibid.,* App., pp. 1028–1031.

the region to be acquired had not long since been granted away by the Mexican government.[85]

Perkins was followed by three Virginians in rapid succession. The first of these (Millson) made no particular contribution to the discussion; [36] the speeches of the other two are interesting because they deliberately brought in the sectional issue between the North and South. Bocock declared that the cries of infringed prerogatives had come either from men "distinguished for their hostility to the Southern States of the Union" or from those "bitterly hostile" to the administration. He then spent some time in pointing out the benefits which the treaty would confer. He considered the two rights-of-way important. He was glad, also, that the treaty offered a peaceful means of settlement with Mexico:

I am glad to be at peace with that nation. With an American railroad on her northern frontier, and another through her southern territory, acting like magnetic currents upon her social and political organization, American feeling, American energy, and American mind will be brought in contact with hers. Soothed by friendly intercourse, her opposition to us will relax. She will receive in her veins our healthy blood. She will catch our spirit, adopt our views, and become assimilated in character with us, and then the question of her future relations towards our Republic will be one of friendly calculation between us.

Bocock recurred, in conclusion, to the sectional issue. He declared that if those who were opposing the Pierce administration and the South

. . . should go on to override the laws and break the constitution; if they should build up, as they desire, a great anti-slavery party of the North to trample upon the rights, confiscate the property, and endanger the security of the South; if they should succeed in raising a mighty whirlwind of fanaticism and fury, which . . . they could neither control nor allay, their very success would prove their own sorest punishment . . . The tiger fresh from the jungle would be tame . . . compared with what the southern part of this Union would be under such dominion . . .[87]

Smith of Virginia pursued essentially the same line of argument as his colleague. In the course of his address he remarked that he had understood Perkins to say that he was going to vote against the proposed appropriation because he had become convinced that the South was contemplating an enlargement of its territory with the view of "dissolving the Union and establishing themselves as a great

[85] *Ibid.*, pp. 1545–1546.
[86] *Ibid.*, pp. 1546–1548.
[87] *Ibid.*, App., pp. 1045–1050.

southern Republic." Perkins admitted that he had made some such statement with reference to the South, but not in connection with the treaty before the House. The little strip of territory acquired by it was "too insignificant to be spoken of in such connection." [38]

Formal debate upon the measure closed on June 28. On the same day it was submitted to vote and passed by a majority of 103 to 62.[39] On June 29, the president placed his signature to the agreement. On June 30, ratifications were exchanged with the Mexican Legation at Washington, and on the next day Almonte, the Mexican Minister, was handed a draft for $7,000,000, the first installment under the treaty.[40]

It may be noted by way of summary that several factors influenced the vote upon the document and the appropriation to carry out its stipulations. Some objected to the methods pursued in negotiating it. Others joined in opposition because it was an administration measure or because it threatened to interfere with rival projects for interoceanic communication. Still others were influenced by their attitude towards the Sloo or the Garay grantees or by fear that the rejection of the treaty might be followed by war. The California Senators and Shields of Illinois opposed it because it did not acquire enough territory; some of the anti-slavery irreconcilables objected to an arrangement which gave to the South the double boon of territory and a railway route.

Although the most consistent support of the treaty came from the South, the sectional issue may not have been the decisive factor. The main consideration of the friends of the pact seems to have been the acquisition of a suitable route for a railroad. The vote on the Shields amendment to Article I, which included more territory than the original treaty or any other amendment offered, shows fifteen northern and six southern Senators among the yeas and six northern and fourteen southern Senators among the nays. Gwin's amendment of April 5, embraced the second largest amount of territory, yet it could marshal only three southern votes in its favor, while Rusk's proposal of April 12, which included the smallest amount of territory of any of the proposals and even less than the final treaty, was opposed by eleven northern but only two southern Senators, and approved by fifteen of each. Obviously the Southerners did not desire the question of territory to stand in the way of their Pacific railway line. Opponents of the treaty may have

[38] *Ibid.,* p. 1548.
[39] *Ibid.,* p. 1565.
[40] Malloy, *Treaties and Conventions,* I, 1107; Washington *Union,* July 1, 1854.

been seeking to defeat it by increasing the territorial acquisition, but this does not seem probable.

Nor does the vote on the treaty as a whole indicate a purely sectional alignment. It is true that the rejecting vote of April 17 showed fifteen southern and twelve northern men for the treaty and only one southern to seventeen northern men against it; and that the ratification line-up of April 26 did not number a single southern vote among the nays; but before accepting this evidence as conclusive, one must not lose sight of the fact that in the last-mentioned vote more northern men favored the treaty than opposed it (14 to 12, or 13),[41] nor must he permit himself to leave the Tehuantepec matter out of consideration. There is, in fact, good circumstantial evidence supporting the view that the fate of the treaty hinged upon the acceptance of the Sloo contract. The only important change in the treaty between the time of its rejection and its final ratification was the insertion of an article recognizing this contract, and seven of those who voted for the treaty on April 26, but did not vote for it on April 17, were strong supporters of this article. And since the vote on this new article was not sectional, one might with considerable justification urge that the Tehuantepec question and not sectionalism was the decisive factor.[42]

Further support of the view that sectionalism did not have decisive weight in the consideration of the treaty may be derived from a careful summary of the House discussions already given. A northern Representative was accused of opposing the treaty because it added territory to the southern portion of the Union, but he denied that any such motive had influenced him; a southern extremist alleged that opposition to the treaty came from the enemies of the administration and of the South; another southern Representative professed his partiality for the South, but declared that he saw no sectional issue in the subject under discussion. When it is remembered that some twenty-five Representatives expressed themselves upon the measure, this show of sectionalism will not be considered extraordinary. The House vote on the bill appropriating funds for carrying out the stipulations of the treaty included among the yeas forty-six northern and fifty-seven southern Representatives, and among the nays fifty-six northern and six southern Representatives. This might indicate considerable sectional bias were it not for the question of party affiliation. But the latter was an influential,

[41] For the data given above, see *Sen. Ex. Journal,* IX, 279 ff.

[42] The majority of the senators from Missouri, Iowa, Indiana, Illinois, and Wisconsin voted in favor of the treaty, thus indicating, apparently, that Benton's rival railway project had little influence on them.

if not a determining, factor. The affirmative vote showed ninety-three Democrats to ten Whigs, and the negative fourteen Democrats to forty-five Whigs, every southern man voting against the measure being a Whig, and every northern man voting for it, with one exception, being a Democrat.[43]

[43] *Cong. Globe,* 33 Cong., 1 Sess., p. 1565. For a fuller discussion of certain phases of this question, see Garber, *The Gadsden Treaty,* pp. 109–145.

CHAPTER IX

FILIBUSTERS AND FRONTIER DIFFICULTIES, 1854-1860

THE Gadsden Treaty, though one of the most important land-
marks in the relations of the United States and Mexico, left unsettled
several questions which were destined to furnish ample trouble.
In striking out Articles II and VIII of the agreement originally
negotiated by Gadsden, the government of the United States had
rejected an effective means of settling the claims of its citizens
against Mexico, and at the same time, had refused to take a
more decided stand against the filibusters. Moreover, the original
treaty had failed to acquire as much territory as the expansionists
had desired, and the Senate had cut down this amount to a bare
half.

It must be noted also that political affairs in Mexico continued
in the same disorderly fashion. Santa Anna's assumption of
dictatorial powers and his sale of Mexican territory aroused formidable opposition. On March 1, 1854, a group of Liberal leaders
proclaimed the "plan of Ayutla." After trying in vain to subdue
the insurrection which spread rapidly over the whole country, the
dictator abandoned his government and went into exile in August,
1855. The Liberals soon succeeded in establishing themselves in
power,[1] and for a time it appeared that the forces of order would
achieve a complete triumph. They called a constitutional convention which met first at Cuernavaca, and later in Mexico City. A
constitution was framed, a popular election held, and a President
chosen. But the new President, Ignacio Comonfort, hesitated,
sought to conciliate both parties, and, at length, turning traitor to
the Liberal cause, dissolved Congress, and set aside the constitution.
This action reopened the whole question. The Liberals immediately
forsook him and, early in 1858, installed Benito Juárez as President.
Thereafter, Mexico had two governments, one in Mexico City and
the other at Vera Cruz, in constant conflict with each other. Under
these circumstances it would obviously be difficult to secure redress

[1] Romero, *The United States and Mexico*, pp. 359-360; Bancroft, *History of
Mexico*, V, 646-665.

for old claims or to prevent new ones from arising; filibuster raids might be expected to continue; and the expansionists would be given additional proof of Mexico's incapacity and additional ground for the fear of European intervention.[2]

It will be recalled that with the view of ascertaining the strength of the filibustering spirit in California and the prospects of re-enforcements being sent to Walker, the officials of Mexico had taken sworn statements from travellers proceeding from the ports of that state. Most of this testimony indicated that hundreds and even thousands were preparing to set out, provided the Walker expedition revealed prospects of success. The promoters of enlistments sought to justify the undertaking by the arguments that the people of the northern frontier of Mexico would thus be protected from the Indians, and that the resulting development of the resources of the country would accrue to the benefit of the Mexicans who were living there. In order to destroy the basis of these arguments and to resist the filibusters, Santa Anna, who had been contemplating the step for some time,[3] at last decided to employ the Frenchmen of California. He accordingly authorized Luis del Valle, the Mexican Consul at San Francisco, to send three thousand of these adventurers to Guaymas at once. Del Valle straightway consulted Dillon, the French Consul, and the latter, perhaps without the knowledge of Del Valle, summoned Raousset, whose filibustering preparations had for a time been overshadowed by Walker's. Plans for the enterprise were hastily pushed forward, and by March, 1854, eight hundred of the desired number had been enlisted. A British ship, the *Challenge*, had been chartered, and the expedition would have put out immediately had the federal authorities in San Francisco not interfered. But their interposition, though occasioning delay, did not break up the enterprise, and on April 2, the *Challenge* departed with three hundred and fifty men.

Either for the purpose of promoting enlistments, or because he was not entirely in favor with Del Valle, Raousset remained behind. The federal officials soon made things too disagreeable for him, however, and on the night of May 23, with a good supply of ammunition and eight companions, he stole away to join the comrades who had preceded him in the *Challenge*. In the latter part of June, after having suffered many mishaps, he arrived at Guaymas, entering the town under cover of darkness. He immediately set about to persuade the Frenchmen to seize and fortify the place until re-

[2] Bancroft, *op. cit.*, V, 665 ff.
[3] Pinart Transcripts, Sonora, V, 204.

enforcements could arrive from California, but his efforts did not meet with a very enthusiastic response. He next tried to win over Yáñez, the commander of the Mexican garrison, to a joint revolt against Santa Anna. Once more he was unsuccessful, however, and desperate measures were determined upon. With a small number of Frenchmen who had joined his standard, he made an unsuccessful attempt to storm the barracks of Guaymas. His badly demoralized force then began to scatter, and soon a large number of them, the Count included, were placed under arrest. Raousset's followers were pardoned, but the Count himself was condemned by a military tribunal for exciting conspiracy and rebellion and shot. With his death, on August 12, 1854, apparently ended the era of French filibusters in California.[4]

The plan to counteract filibusters with filibusters had therefore failed, and worse than failed, because the people of the frontier of the United States were piqued by this manifestation of prejudice against the Anglo-Americans, while not a few thought they saw in the French attempts the hand and ambition of Louis Napoleon.

Nor could the treatment accorded the filibusters in California be calculated to serve as an effective warning against such undertakings. It is true, indeed, that the federal authorities had exercised considerable vigilance. As has been mentioned above, Gadsden had written the authorities in California regarding the matter in August, 1853. These officials seem to have been reasonably attentive to their duty. On September 30, a detachment of United States troops acting under the orders of General E. A. Hitchcock seized the brig *Arrow* which was preparing to convey the supplies of Walker and associates to Guaymas; but they were ordered by the local court to release the vessel. Again, on October 16, ammunition designed for the brig *Caroline* was seized by the federal officials, and the departure of that boat was so precipitated that many of the adventurers were left behind.[5]

Hitchcock's efforts seem to have met the approval of Jefferson Davis, the new Secretary of War; but for reasons of another nature he was relieved of his command by General John E. Wool, who arrived at San Francisco on February 14, 1854. In giving the latter his instructions Davis had pointed out that certain extraordinary duties would devolve upon him and remarked that among these would be the "duty of maintaining our international obligations,

[4] Scroggs, *Filibusters and Financiers*, p. 54 ff.
[5] *Ibid.*, pp. 35–36.

by preventing unlawful expeditions against the territories of foreign powers." "Confidence is felt [said Davis] that you will, to the utmost of your ability, use all proper means to detect the fitting out of armed expeditions against countries with which the United States are at peace, and will zealously co-operate with the civil authorities in maintaining the neutrality laws." [6]

Immediately after his arrival, Wool began a vigorous prosecution of the filibusters. On March 1, he reported that Colonel Watkins had been arrested at his request, and that notwithstanding the fact that the civil authorities did not seem eager to check the filibustering expeditions, he was determined to prevent such enterprises. He said he had already entered into communication with the naval officials of the United States on the Pacific, and that he intended immediately to confer with the district attorney and the marshal.[7] On March 15, he notified Davis of the arrest of Frederic Emory and of others belonging to the Walker party. Eight days later, at Wool's instance, the *Challenge,* which Del Valle had employed to convey the Frenchmen to Guaymas, was seized on the technical ground that it had on its list more passengers than the law allowed. As noted above, the vessel was later allowed to depart; but it was apparently because the French Consul had procured its release by pledging his personal honor as well as that of his nation that the passengers aboard were merely colonists.[8] The arrest, on May 8, of Walker and the thirty-three of his companions at the United States boundary near Tía Juana has already been noted.

Thus far the record of the United States had been commendable; and on June 12, Secretary Marcy, in answering the complaints of Almonte regarding the actions of the filibusters in Baja California, dwelt upon it with a certain amount of pride. He maintained that

the government of the United States has [had] given to Mexico indisputable proofs of its vehement and sincere desire to maintain the integrity of the laws regarding the violation of the rights of friendly nations. The greatest vigilance has [had] been enjoined upon the civil and military employees of the United States on the Pacific with the view of discovering and frustrating all the illegal expeditions; and although Walker [had] succeeded in avoiding being discovered when he left the coasts of California, his forces and provisions have [had] been detained by these respective authorities, his principal agent and his Secretary of State were [had been] apprehended on or near the field of

[6] Davis to Wool, Jan. 12, 1854, *House Ex. Doc.* No. 88, 35 Cong., 1 Sess. (Ser. 956), p. 6.

[7] *Ibid.,* pp. 10–11.

[8] *Ibid.,* p. 19; Scroggs, *op. cit.,* pp. 55, 56, note.

his operations by officials of the Portsmouth, a vessel of the United States on that coast; and the total result of these exertions has [had] been the complete destruction of the expedition of Walker.[9]

Such had been the fruits of the efforts of the federal officials; but the conduct of the juries summoned to try the cases tended to counteract all they had done. The jury disagreed in regard to the French consul Dillon, who was probably "the high-priest of the French filibusters," acquitted Walker, and brought in a verdict of guilty against Watkins and Emory, as well as against the Mexican Consul, who had likewise been haled into court under the pressure of public opinion. The cases against the minor filibusters were then dropped, and the penalties of the law were never exacted from those who had been convicted.[10]

Moreover, General Wool, who had been so faithful in the discharge of his duties, received from the Secretary of War a mild censure for exceeding his instructions and usurping the functions of the civil authorities by originating "arrests and prosecutions for civil misdemeanors"; [11] and both the Secretary of War [12] and the Washington Union,[13] the organ of the administration, criticized Wool for confining his attention to the port of San Francisco while neglecting his duty in regard to other portions of his command. These criticisms may have been conscientious; but the later recognition of Walker as President of Nicaragua, and the disapproval of the action of Commodore Paulding who arrested him, make one skeptical regarding the matter. At any rate, its effect upon Wool was paralyzing, so far as the pursuit and prosecution of filibusters was concerned. He sulked like Achilles in his tent, and "subsequent filibustering expeditions were allowed to depart unmolested." [14]

The last attempt of Raousset-Boulbon was followed by almost simultaneous, though unconnected, raids from California and from Texas. The former enterprise was promoted by agents of a Mexican revolutionary party in San Francisco; the latter was connected with frontier difficulties along the Rio Grande.

As the military forces of the United States crowded the Indians of the Southwest more and more, some of them sought refuge in Mexico. By agreements of 1850 and 1852, peaceful Seminoles and

[9] Notes to the Mex. Leg., Vol. 6. See also Almonte to Marcy, May 31, 1854, Notes from the Mex. Leg., Vol. 7.
[10] Scroggs, op. cit., pp. 52–66.
[11] House Ex. Doc., No. 88, 35 Cong., 1 Sess. (Ser. 956), p. 52.
[12] Ibid., p. 99.
[13] Quoted in Alta California, December 24, 1854.
[14] Scroggs, op. cit., p. 66.

Muskogees had been allowed to settle in the vicinity of the military colonies of the East and of Chihuahua.[15] Soon afterwards Chihuahua adopted for a time a general policy of pacification.[16] Wild Cat and his bands were living near Santa Rosa in 1853,[17] while in June of the following year Persifer F. Smith, commander of the military department of Texas, reported that a tribe of Lipans and three bands of Mescalero Apaches had established themselves in Mexico, the former opposite Laredo and Fort Duncan, and the latter in Chihuahua.[18] In due time complaints that these Indians were raiding into Texas began.

Moreover, the loss of slaves by their escape into Mexico was becoming large and irritating. Carvajal had enlisted the support of a group of men who were interested in the recovery of slaves, and the breaking up of his force had been complicated by the fact that the leader of a contingent held a permit from the Governor of Texas for the recovery from Mexico of negro fugitives. From time to time, also, masters of runaways had organized bands and pursued them into Mexico, without permission.[19]

Apparently both of these factors—Indian invasions and runaway slaves—combined with an ever present spirit of aggression in the Southwest to force a crisis in 1855. In the spring and fall of that year, Lipans, Kickapoos, and other tribes from Mexico made serious incursions into Texas.[20] In July, Captain W. R. Henry of Texas made some attempt to organize an army of volunteers with the view of assisting Mexico to establish a government more in line with the interests of Texas and, ultimately, of bringing Mexico under the protection of the American Union. This particular attempt failed,[21] but soon afterwards a group of citizens in San Antonio decided to make an effort to recover the slaves which, in large numbers, had taken refuge on the frontier of Coahuila. On August 25, they addressed a letter to Colonel Lanberg, who had command of the federal troops of Mexico on the frontier of that state, inquiring how many

[15] Mexican Border Commission of 1873, *Report,* p. 304; Ministerio de Guerra y Marina, *Memoria* (1851), p. 30.

[16] Emory, "Report," *House Ex. Doc.* No. 135, 34 Cong., 2 Sess. (Ser. 861), p. 86.

[17] *Ibid.,* 43.

[18] *House Ex. Doc.* No. 1, Part 11, 34 Cong., 1 Sess. (Ser. 841), pp. 53–54.

[19] *House Ex. Doc.* No. 1, Part II, 32 Cong., 2 Sess. (Ser. 674), p. 16; Mexican Border Commission of 1873, *Report,* pp. 178–179.

[20] Commissioner of Indian Affairs, *Report* (1855), p. 179; Gadsden to the Mexican Minister of Relations, Oct. 25, 1855, summarized in Bolton, *Guide to the principal Archives of Mexico,* p. 230.

[21] Almonte to Marcy, Aug. 14 and 15, and Oct. 18, 1855, and enclosures, Notes from the Mex. Leg., Vol. 8.

negroes could be recovered and under what conditions they would be delivered at the banks of the Bravo. Their letter closed with the scarcely concealed threat that they were "prepared to act promptly," and that "future measures and proceedings" would depend wholly upon the report made by Lanberg. This communication was sent to the Governor of Coahuila and Nuevo León, who replied that although he was aware of the losses suffered by the citizens of both countries in runaway servants, he was not in favor of taking the matter up with private individuals. Moreover, he answered the threat of the San Antonians by ordering Colonel Lanberg, in case of an invasion, to "resist force with force." [22]

By the first of October an American expedition consisting of three companies under the command of J. H. Callahan and W. R. Henry had reached the Rio Grande, near Fort Duncan. They claimed they were under orders of the Governor of Texas and in search of Indians. It is likely, however, that slave hunters were interested in the expedition, and there may have been a vague intention, also, of occupying a portion of northern Mexico.[23] Crossing the river apparently with the consent of the Mexican authorities, and proceeding southward, the expedition soon fell into an ambuscade of Mexicans and Indians. The Texans retreated to Piedras Negras, pillaging and burning the town before they finally recrossed the Rio Grande—under cover of the cannons of Fort Duncan, as it was later alleged.[24]

The defeat of Callahan and Henry caused indignation at San Antonio, where it was reported that the troops of their command had been treacherously attacked after having been invited across the Rio Bravo by the Mexican authorities. A public meeting was held, committees and officers were chosen, and preparations made for a much larger expedition into Mexico. On October 16, a call for volunteers was issued through the San Antonio *Sentinel* and the rendezvous and time of departure were designated. Commenting

---

[22] This correspondence is printed in *El Siglo XIX*, 12 de noviembre de 1855. See also Mexican Border Commission of 1873, *Report*, pp. 191–192.

[23] Vidaurri to Marcy, Oct. 18, 1855, printed in *El Siglo XIX*, 12 de noviembre; Olmstead, *Journey Through Texas*, p. 333; Mexican Border Commission of 1873, *Report*, pp. 191, 193; *State Gazette* (Austin, Texas), Oct. 13 and 20, 1855.

[24] The Texas side of the story is related in Callahan to Governor Pease, October 13, 1855, printed in *State Gazette* of Oct. 20. The Mexican version will be found in Vidaurri to Marcy, Oct. 18, 1855, and enclosures, printed in *El Siglo XIX*, 12 de noviembre de 1855. The account of the United States military officials is found in Persifer F. Smith to Adjutant-General, Oct. 10, 12, 14, 17, 21, 1855, Adjutant-General's Office, Old Files.

upon the affair, the *Sentinel* remarked that although Callahan's position might be considered a "somewhat peculiar one, and one out of which serious difficulties may [might] arise," it should be rer...mbered that there was at that time no government in Mexico.[25]

But the vigorous stand of General Persifer F. Smith [26] and the presence of Colonel Lanberg with a large number of Mexican troops on the Rio Grande probably cooled the ardor of the Texans. The expedition never materialized; and the total result of Callahan's procedure was the death of several Texans and Mexicans, the destruction of Mexican property, for which the United States was, in the future, to be called upon to pay heavy indemnity, and the increase of bitterness and suspicion not only along the frontier, but even in the government councils at Mexico City.

When the Mexican Minister at Washington complained of this invasion, he found Marcy ready to defend the action of the Rangers, as well as of the Governor of Texas and the officer of the United States army at Fort Duncan. The chief executive of Texas had not, it is true, authorized the expedition of state troops into Mexico, but he had subsequently justified it on grounds which seemed to Marcy entirely ample. If Callahan had been invited to enter Mexico and then treacherously attacked by Mexicans and Indians, the measures adopted by him and the federal officer at Fort Duncan in order to cover the retreat of the Texans, were "not only justifiable, but meritorious." Even if "there was no invitation to the Rangers from competent Mexican authority, their crossing the Rio Bravo under the circumstances may be considered as justifiable, by the law of nations, which authorizes the pursuit of an enemy into neutral territory." [27]

Marcy admitted that the obligation with reference to the frontier Indians was mutual, however. He said that "if Indians whom the United States are bound to restrain shall, under the same circumstances, make a hostile incursion into Mexico, this Government will [would] not complain if the Mexican forces who may be sent to repel them shall [should] cross to this side of the line for the purpose, provided that in so doing, they abstain [ed] from injuring the persons and property of citizens of the United States."

To be sure, the Callahan-Henry expedition had not "abstained from injuring the persons and property" of citizens of Mexico, but in this respect, too, Marcy was ready for a rejoinder. While he

[25] Quoted in Olmsted, *op. cit.*, pp. 506-507.
[26] Smith to Pease, Oct. 11 and 17, *loc. cit.*
[27] Marcy to Almonte, Jan. 23, 1856, Notes to the Mex. Leg., Vol. 7.

deplored any sufferings to which the inhabitants of Piedras Negras might have been subjected by the burning of the village, he declared that "in the judgment of the Undersigned . . . and, as is believed, in that of all impartial men, that will be considered a laudable, and not a blamable act of self defence." The Texans had fired the town in order to effect their retreat and to save themselves from Mexicans who had sought to lure them to their destruction.[28]

There is reason to doubt the filibustering intention of the expedition which sailed from the port of San Francisco a few days after the Callahan-Henry raid; but, since it was so considered by Mexico, it may be narrated under this heading. In the summer of 1855, the supporters of the plan of Ayutla sent an agent to California to obtain financial aid. Although he had great difficulty in securing funds, he found numerous adventurers anxious to volunteer their personal services. One of these, Jean Napoleon Zerman, a Frenchman of Italian extraction, communicated directly with General Álvarez, the Mexican insurgent leader, and succeeded, as he alleged, in securing a naval commission and authority to raise an expedition for the purpose of preying upon the commerce of Santa Anna and blockading the ports which remained under the control of the dictator. On October 10, Zerman set out with a party of some ninety persons on board the bark *Archibald Gracie*. Before the close of the month the party arrived at Cape San Lucas, where Zerman chartered the American vessel *Rebecca Adams*, employed her crew, and transferred to her a number of his men. With his party now augmented to one hundred and twenty-six, he proceeded to La Paz, the scene of the recent activities of William Walker, and attempted to get into touch with the authorities there. The Mexican military commander at this place had already declared for Álvarez, and the so-called filibusters, anticipating no trouble, were off guard. It was accordingly an easy matter for this official and his soldiers, spurred to vengeance and treachery by the remembrance of Walker's operations,[29] to make prisoners of the entire expedition. They were in fact captured without the least resistance and afterwards robbed and subjected to cruel and inhuman treatment, many of them being forced to languish in prison for many months.[30]

---

[28] *Id.*, Feb. 4, 1856, *loc. cit.*

[29] Ministerio de Guerra y Marina, *Memoria* (1857), p. 35.

[30] United States and Mexican Claims Commission, Opinions, Vol. B. This entire volume is given to the claims arising under this expedition.

Although doubt may be entertained in regard to the authenticity of the document establishing the official connection of Zerman's expedition with the insurgents fighting under the *plan* of Ayutla, the following considerations ren-

The year 1856 probably witnessed no important invasion of Mexican soil by an armed band from the United States, but there were threats and rumors of raids both from Texas and from California. In Texas they were connected with the schemes of Carvajal, Emilio Sánchez, and Francisco Vidaurri,[31] none of which materialized. In California they were related to the preparations of Henry A. Crabb, who, like Walker, was a Tennesseean, a lawyer, and a politician. He had met with some success in the local arena, having been a member of both houses of the California legislature, but when he aspired to the national field his hopes were quickly shattered.[32]

Crabb had been interested for some time in Sonora, in Nicaragua, and in filibustering, but his predominating inclination for politics had kept him in California. His recent political disappointment, news of Walker's success in Nicaragua, the desire to recover the property of his wife's family in Sonora, all combined in 1856 to turn his attention once more toward the south. During the early part of the year he set out with his wife and some of the members of her family and a company of about one hundred men, consisting for the most part of former Sonorans. Upon reaching Los Angeles, a number of the party became discouraged at the prospects of a journey through the desert and withdrew from the expedition; but the remainder continued. When they reached Sonora, they found a revolution against Governor Gándara in progress under the leadership of Ignacio Pesqueira. The insurgents appeared to be very desirous of Crabb's aid, and they offered him a number of inducements to bring a colony into the country, declaring, according to the report of the filibusters, that they contemplated the annexation of Sonora to the United States.[33]

Encouraged by the prospect, Crabb hastened back to California to perfect plans for his colonization scheme. Upon his arrival,

der such connection strongly probable: (1) Alleging that Álvarez had promised to have a house ready for him at Acapulco, Zerman carried with him on the expedition his son of nine years, his daughter of sixteen, and his pregnant wife, together with his household furniture, relics, and badges of honor; (2) he acted in an entirely unsuspicious and unguarded fashion at La Paz; and (3) the Mexican court found no charge against him and his party on the score of filibustering.

For the heated correspondence with reference to these prisoners, see Forsyth to Marcy, No. 6, Nov. 4, 1856, No. 11, Dec. 4, 1856, *passim*, Mex. Desp., Vol. 20. A list of the awards made to them will be found in *Sen. Ex. Doc. No. 31*, 44 Cong., 2 Sess. (Ser. 1720).

[31] Bolton, *op. cit.*, pp. 299, 302–303.

[32] Scroggs, *Filibusters and Financiers*, pp. 308–309; Rasey Biven to Forsyth, June 18, 1857, *House Ex. Doc. No. 64*, 35 Cong., 1 Sess. (Ser. 955), pp. 45–47.

[33] *House Ex. Doc. No. 64*, 35 Cong., 1 Sess., *loc. cit.*, and pp. 71–72.

however, he found that the presidential election had engrossed the attention of the people to such an extent that his enterprise would have to be temporarily postponed.[34] This delay proved to be unfortunate for Crabb; for in the meantime the rival factions of Sonora came to terms, so that when the "Arizona Colonizing Company" at length reached Sonora, they found not friends but traitors.

The company started from Sonora, Tuolumne County, California, on January 20, 1857, proceeded by land to San Francisco, thence by water to San Pedro, and then by land again to Sonora, Mexico, passing without molestation by Fort Yuma on their way thither.[35] Immediately after crossing the Mexican boundary near Sonoyta, Crabb received intimations that his expedition would meet opposition; but as the sequel was to prove, he failed to give the fact sufficient consideration. On March 26, he addressed a note to the *Prefect* of Altar informing him that he had under his direction one hundred men, merely the vanguard of nine hundred more to follow, that his intentions were entirely peaceful, and that he was surprised at signs of opposition. He concluded his despatch, however, with a warning that the punishment which the Mexicans contemplated inflicting upon his party might perchance fall upon their own heads.[36]

Opposition to the filibusters was clearly to be formidable. As early as March 11, Pesqueira, who was now the chief executive of the state as well as commander of the military forces on the frontier, had issued a rather bombastic address to the people and the soldiers of Sonora.[37] After the news of the arrival of the filibusters reached him, he became more indignant than ever, sending forth a proclamation calling the Sonorans to arms, and declaring that "no pity, no generous sentiments" would be shown the filibusters.[38]

But Crabb did not appreciate the strength of this opposition; for he moved toward Caborca on March 27, with his forces in careless formation; and five days later, just as he reached the outskirts of this village, he was surprised by an ambuscade. After severe suffering, his company succeeded in obtaining refuge in a row of adobe houses. Here they were besieged until April 6, when the party, now reduced to sixty-nine, surrendered unconditionally, ac-

[34] *Ibid.*, pp. 45–47.
[35] Mowry to Cooper, March 3, 1857, *ibid.*, pp. 82–83. After reporting rather fully in regard to their actions and statements, Mowry made the significant remark, "It is not in my line of duty to draw the very obvious conclusion suggested by the above facts."
[36] *Ibid.*, p. 31.
[37] Pinart Transcripts, Sonora, V, 4–5.
[38] *House Ex. Doc.* No. 64, 35 Cong., 1 Sess. (Ser. 955), pp. 32–33.

cording to the Mexican version, but under the promise that their lives should be spared and their wounded cared for, if the American account may be accepted.[39] Whatever the conditions of the capitulation, all of them save a boy of fourteen were shot on the following morning. Besides these, several other small parties were captured and subjected to the same fate, the total number of victims being augmented to ninety-three.[40]

The extermination of the ill-fated Crabb expedition probably ended the raids of the filibusters from the United States into Mexico during the period under consideration, but the filibustering spirit and the youthful energy and desire for expansion which lay back of it persisted, ever ready to express itself anew when suitable occasion presented. But more of this in another connection.

Two years later the situation was in a measure reversed, and the frontier of the United States suffered from the depredations of Mexican adventurers. The slavery difficulty, which had been a factor in the operations of Carvajal as well as in the invasion of Callahan, had grown very serious in Texas, and along with it hatred for the lower class of Mexicans had increased. A runaway slave whom Olmsted interviewed during his trip to Piedras Niegras in 1855 informed him that he knew of forty of his fellows who had made their escape to that section within the last few months, while a great many more were crossing over at places farther down the river.[41] A gang of them was found by the same traveler a few days' walk from Eagle Pass. The magnitude of their losses led the planters of central and western Texas to consider plans for putting an effectual stop to the evil.[42] It was felt, moreover, that the Mexicans living in the region were fraternizing with the negroes and aiding and abetting their escape. Accordingly, in September, 1856, when a slave plot was discovered in Columbus, Colorado County, the Mexicans in the community were arrested and ordered to leave. At about the same time, likewise, they were driven out of Matagorda County.[43] During the course of the next year residents of Uvalde County voted resolutions forbidding Mexicans from passing through without special permission and parties of Mexicans were driven out of San Antonio.[44]

[39] Ibid., pp. 47–48, 64–68.
[40] Smith to Forsyth, June 22, 1857, ibid., pp. 47–48. The best account of the expedition is found in Scroggs, op. cit., 308–316.
[41] Olmsted, Journey Through Texas, p. 323 ff.
[42] Ibid., passim.
[43] Ibid., p. 164.
[44] Mexican Border Commission of 1873, Report, pp. 129–131, and note.

It was in the region south of San Antonio, however, that the most severe treatment was reserved for the Mexican population. A colony of Mexicans had settled near the San Antonio River. They were apparently peaceful and innocent, but the Texans had two strong grievances against them: they were supposed to be the rendezvous of runaway slaves, and with their carts and oxen they were underbidding the Texan teamsters in the transportation trade between the coast and the inland towns. The teamsters soon formed a secret organization, and bands of masked men began to waylay the cart-drivers, killing them and plundering their cargoes. As their organization grew in efficiency, they ceased to confine their outrages to Mexicans alone and began a series of wholesale robberies. Their operations became so widespread that even the commander of the United States forces in Texas had to protect his supply trains with a military escort.

On October 14 and 19, (1856) respectively, the Mexican Legation at Washington addressed the government of the United States in regard to the matter and stated that seventy-five Mexicans had fallen victims already.[45] On November 11, the State Department communicated with Governor Pease, who immediately began an investigation and recommended that the State Legislature take some action. This body was slow to move, and the Governor seems to have called into service upon his own initiative a body of volunteers. By this time, moreover, the citizens of the disturbed section who had been suffering from the indiscriminate robberies of the secret bands began to employ Lynch law and the disorders were soon suppressed.[46]

It was out of this bitterness that the depredations of Cortina grew. Juan Nepomucina Cortina was a chieftain of Mexican extraction, but of uncertain citizenship.[47] A native of Camargo, he had been old enough to fight in the army of Arista during the war between the United States and Mexico. After the treaty of 1848, he had moved with his mother and brother to their ranch a few miles above Brownsville, Texas. Here he seems soon to have earned the reputation of a lawless, dangerous man. Though uneducated and not very attractive personally, he had great influence among the

---

[45] Notes from Mex. Leg., Vol. 8.

[46] Bancroft, *History of the North Mexican States and Texas,* II, pp. 416–419; Linn, *Reminiscences of Fifty Years in Texas,* pp. 352–354.

[47] His proclamations are signed "Cortina," or "Cortinas," indifferently. In regard to the question of his citizenship, see Mexican Border Commission of 1873, *Report,* pp. 134–136; *House Ex. Doc.* No. 52, 36 Cong., 1 Sess. (Ser. 1050), pp. 70–72, 74.

large Mexican population of the section. Because of his value as a political asset, and on account of the constant presence of a band of armed desperadoes ready to do his bidding, he had managed to escape the agents of the law.

At length, in July, 1859, while he and a company of his armed friends were in Brownsville, the city marshal arrested a former servant of his, whereupon Cortina shot and wounded that official, and then, taking the prisoner up behind him, rode away, bidding defiance to the authorities.[48] Soon afterwards he crossed the river and entered Matamoras, where he is said to have been lauded as the defender of Mexican rights.

On September 28, 1859, he re-entered Brownsville, having with him this time a body of mounted men variously estimated at from forty to eighty in number. He soon had the entire population at his mercy. Taking up his quarters at the deserted barracks of Fort Brown, he and his party went through the streets in search of their enemies. They killed the jailer, broke open the jail, liberated the prisoners, and murdered in all some four or five persons. Indeed, Cortina threatened to kill all the Americans in the place [49] and might have carried out his threat had it not been for the timely intervention of the Mexican Consul and another influential Mexican friend, who at length had persuaded the desperado and his band to withdraw.

After leaving Brownsville he took up his quarters at his mother's ranch where he received various mediators and finally agreed to cross over with his property and friends to Mexico. Previous to taking this step, however, he robbed the United States mail, threatened to burn Brownsville, and issued a proclamation setting forth his reasons for invading the town, representing himself as the champion of Mexican rights in Texas, expressing the hope that the authorities of the state would save him the trouble of punishing the base man who had wronged his fellows, and claiming to be a Texas citizen.[50]

For several days after the events of September Cortina remained

[48] Cortina claimed that the marshal was abusing the prisoners. *Ibid.*, pp. 64–68, 70–72.

[49] The American population probably did not amount to more than 150 or 200. *Ibid.*, pp. 34–43.

[50] *Ibid.*, pp. 70–71. Cortina declared that certain land-greedy individuals and lawyers had formed a clique to deprive the Mexicans of their lands and to force them to leave the country. The Mexican Commission of 1873 also made much of this point (*Report*, pp. 129 ff.), but the Texans bitterly denied the charge, citing as proof to the contrary numerous legal cases. *House Ex. Doc. No. 343, 44 Cong., 1 Sess. (Ser. 1709), p. 43.*

at Matamoras in comparative quiet, but the arrest of Cabrera, one of the officers of his band, by a posse of Brownsville citizens on October 12, again aroused him. When Cortina heard of the seizure of Cabrera he told some of the influential men of Matamoras that he would lay Brownsville in ashes, if the officer was not immediately released. A citizen was sent over to the American side to persuade the people of Brownsville to comply with Cortina's request. When compliance was flatly refused,[51] Cortina and his men recrossed the river, took up their quarters once more at his mother's ranch, and began preparations for vengeance.

Meanwhile an expedition was preparing to drive them out of their rendezvous. At the time of his first invasion a company of Mexican national guards had been called over by the people of Brownsville, and they were now invited to return. In conjunction with about twenty Americans and forty Texan Mexicans they stormed Cortina's stronghold, but were repulsed, leaving two pieces of artillery in the hands of the enemy. This triumph emboldened Cortina and brought new volunteers into his camp. He now began not only to levy contributions of arms and supplies, but also to conscript recruits from the neighboring ranches, while he kept himself informed as to the movements against him by intercepting the mails. On November 10, Texas Rangers under Captain Tobin arrived and soon began to harass him; but they either met with defeat, or being divided as to what policy they should pursue, withdrew without a battle.

All of this of course only served to increase Cortina's fame. A party of forty joined him from Nuevo León and another consisting of sixty convicts from Victoria, Tamaulipas, soon followed suit, so that he now had an army of several hundred. Hoisting the Mexican flag over his quarters, he published another proclamation, more verbose and drastic than that of September 30, in which he denounced in bitter terms the Americans of Texas, set forth a program for the redemption of the Mexicans in that State, and declared himself the divinely appointed agent to break the chains of his enslaved compatriots.[52]

But at last the slow-moving federal authorities began to take action. Immediately after the first invasion of Brownsville the collector of Brazos de Santiago had given notice of the occurrence to Twiggs, the commander of the United States forces in Texas.[53]

---

[51] On November 10, Cabrera was hanged by a mob.
[52] *House Ex. Doc.* No. 52, 36 Cong., 1 Sess. (Ser. 1051), pp. 79–82.
[53] *Sen. Ex. Doc.* No. 2, Part II, 36 Cong., 1 Sess. (Ser. 1024), pp. 378-379.

Upon receipt of this letter, the latter had issued orders for the dispatch of two companies of infantry, one to the junction of the Leona and the Frio Rivers, and the other to the Rio Grande below Fort Duncan. At the same time he had sent a company of artillery and one of cavalry to scout between Forts Duncan and Clark.[54] When news of the raid reached Washington the immediate reoccupation of Fort Brown was ordered.[55] It was not, however, until the latter part of November that these forces reached Brownsville; and Major Heintzelman, who was to have charge, did not arrive with his command until December 5.[56]

Finally, on December 14, Major Heintzelman with 165 regulars and 120 rangers advanced from Brownsville upon Cortina's position. The latter retreated northward avoiding a serious engagement until December 27, when his forces were overtaken and routed near Rio Grande City. Cortina fled into Mexico, leaving his "guns, ammunition and baggage carts, provisions, and everything he could throw away to lighten his flight." He had lost about sixty men who had been either killed or drowned in the river. The rest escaped into Mexico without their arms. Cortina afterwards moved down the Rio Grande, collecting the remnants of his scattered forces and eventually establishing his camp at La Bolza, on the Mexican side about thirty-five miles above Brownsville, with the intention of capturing the American steamboat *Ranchero* on its way down the river.

On February 4, 1860, he apparently attempted to seize this vessel, but a party of Texas Rangers who were on guard crossed over to the Mexican side and administered a sound defeat.[57] Cortina then set up at La Mesa ranch, but once more the Rangers, this time accompanied by a company of regulars, entered Mexico and forced him to flee.[58]

By this time Robert E. Lee, who had been chosen for his superior fitness, took charge of the Eighth Military Department (Texas). He was instructed to demand that the Mexican authorities break up the bands of Cortina, and, in case they failed to accomplish this plain duty, to cross into Mexico and disperse them with the forces under his command.[59] Lee immediately entered into tactful communi-

[54] *Ibid.*, p. 378.
[55] Adjutant-General to Twiggs, October 25, 1859, *House Ex. Doc. No. 52,* 36 Cong., 1 Sess. (Ser. 1050), p. 36.
[56] *Ibid.*, p. 64; *House Ex. Doc.* No. 81, 36 Cong., 1 Sess. (Ser. 1056), p. 7.
[57] *Ibid.*, pp. 2–14.
[58] *Ibid.*, pp. 80–99.
[59] *Ibid.*, pp. 84–85, 100–104, 133–134.

cation with these authorities, making known to them his instructions. Further measures on his part were not required. In 1860, Cortina was forced by the Mexicans to seek a hiding in the Burgos mountains some forty miles from the frontier.[60] He was the first conspicuous Mexican leader to raid the American border.[61] More was to be heard of him and his tribe in the future.

These difficulties in Texas were the most severe that grew out of the race hatred of the time; but the New Mexico frontier was not entirely free from such disturbances. The tragic death of the Crabb party inaugurated a sort of reign of terror. The Mexicans in the region were maltreated, retaliatory parties raided back and forth, desperate Mexicans committed robberies and murders and then fled across the boundary. Moreover, these disorders were given more than a local significance by the fact that they retarded the development of a section believed to be rich in mineral resources and threatened, along with the Indian raids, to interrupt communications with California.[62]

Before concluding this chapter it will be necessary once more to refer briefly to these Indian depredations. Raids both upon the Mexican settlements and upon those of the United States continued; and irritation north of the Rio Grande was increased by the belief

---

[60] Mexican Border Commission of 1873, *Report*, pp. 21, 143.

[61] In reporting the total results of the Cortina raid Heintzelman said:

"The whole country from Brownsville to Rio Grande City, one hundred and twenty miles and back to the Arroyo Colorado, has been laid waste. There is not an American (left), or any property belonging to an American that could be destroyed in this large tract of land. . . .

"Rio Grande City is almost depopulated, and there is but one Mexican family in Edinburgh. On the road this side I met (sic) but two ranches occupied, and those by Mexicans. The jaceles and fences are generally burned. The actual loss in property can give but a faint idea of the amount of the damage. The cattle that were not carried off are scattered in the chapparal, and will soon be wild and lost to their owners. Business as far up as Larido (Laredo), two hundred and forty miles, has been interrupted and suspended for five months. It is now too late to think of preparing for a crop and the whole season will be lost.

"The amount of claims for damages presented is three hundred and thirty-six thousand eight hundred and twenty-six dollars and twenty-one cents; many of them are exaggerations, but then there are few Mexicans who have put in any.

There have been fifteen Americans and eighty friendly Mexicans killed. Cortinas has lost one hundred and fifty-one men killed; of the wounded I have no record." (Heintzelman to Lee, March 1, 1860, *House Ex. Doc.* No. 81, 36 Cong., 1 Sess. [Ser. 1056], p. 13.)

[62] Mowry, *Memoir of the Proposed Territory of Arizona*, p. 19 ff.; Buchanan, *Works*, X, 256.

that the Indians, who in constantly increasing numbers were finding homes south of the boundary line, were encouraged by the Mexicans themselves. Since 1846 the Indian office and the military authorities had struggled almost in vain with the whole problem; and it was felt that their failure was due, at least in a measure, to the ease with which the Indians crossed the boundary and eluded pursuit and to the lack of a vigorous policy on the part of the Mexican government.[63] For the situation there were three remedies the adoption of which would result in mutual benefit to both countries—namely, a provision for the reciprocal crossing of the border in pursuit of fleeing bands, better co-operation between the American and the Mexican forces, temporary occupation of posts south of the boundary by the United States troops themselves—and unless one or more of these were adopted communication over the southern routes to California would continue to be interrupted, settlement of the southwestern frontier of the United States would be retarded, and the population of the North Mexican states would be imperiled, if not annihilated.

[63] Pinart Transcripts, Sonora, VI, 25½; *House Ex. Doc.* No. 81, 36 Cong., 1 Sess. (Ser. 1056), p. 90 ff.; *Sen. Ex. Doc.* No. 2, Part II, 36 Cong., 1 Sess. (Ser. 1024), p. 325 ff.; Commissioner of Indian Affairs, *Report* (1856), pp. 173–178 (1857), p. 296 ff.

CHAPTER X

GROWING IMPORTANCE OF THE QUESTION OF CLAIMS

As already has been noted, the irritating question of outrages committed upon the persons and property of American citizens living in Mexico or having intercourse with the country, had arisen again soon after 1848; and an attempt had been made to include a provision for the settlement of claims in the Gadsden Treaty. After 1853 these outrages continued with accelerated frequency; for while there was no interruption in the political disorders in Mexico and no abatement in the ill-feeling toward the Anglo-Americans, commerce between the two countries showed a considerable increase, and increase of business relations could mean, under the circumstances, only an augmentation of complaints.

Indeed, as early as November 2, 1853, James Gadsden had urged a modification of Mexican commercial regulations as one of the best methods of settling the difficulties between the two countries. On this occasion he had declared, as heretofore observed, that "most, if not all of the unpleasant collisions which occur on our respective frontiers, originate in a restringent system on one side antagonistical to a more free and liberal policy on the other"; and he had proposed to Bonilla a "Treaty of Free and Reciprocal Trade."

Gadsden had the Texas frontier in mind. As a matter of fact, however, the Mexican tariffs and irregularities in their application also occasioned a great deal of trouble on the maritime frontiers; and so important was this factor in the years immediately subsequent to 1853 that the numerous claims which arose at that time cannot be clearly understood unless prefaced by an examination of the Mexican revenue system, or—perhaps more properly—lack of system.

The duties and restraints placed upon commerce by the Mexican government were very vexatious to American merchants engaged in the Mexican trade. Not only were the rates high [1] and the prohibitions sweeping, but the laws were frequently modified or applied in an arbitrary manner, so that there was neither certainty

---

[1] See Dublán y Lozano, *op. cit., passim.*

nor uniformity, and special concessions and injurious discriminations seem to have been an ever-present evil. Between October, 1845, and January, 1856, for instance, six general modifications in the tariff were authorized by the federal government, to say nothing of the changes inaugurated by local leaders who took occasion to decree and exact duties to suit their own convenience. Furthermore, besides the general tariffs levied on virtually all imports, there were often municipal, sale, and transportation taxes.

The situation from the standpoint of the United States can perhaps best be set forth by means of brief extracts from the reports of the American consuls in Mexico. On June 17, 1854, Franklin Chase wrote from Tampico:

> The privileges and restrictions which have governed the commercial intercourse between the United States and this port, have been in accordance with the following tariffs, which have been in force in this district during the period hereinafter mentioned, that is to say, the tariff of 1845 was in force until the revolution of Colonel F. G. Casanova, which occurred on the 29th November, 1852, and on the 2d day of December next following he published his tariff, which remained in force until March 1, 1853, when the successor of General Casanova published another tariff known as that of Colonel Carlos Oronoz. The tariff of Oronoz continued in force until the 1st of June, 1853, at which period the tariff of Ceballos, under date Mexico, January 24, 1853, was recognized by the authorities of this district, and governed until the 3d of August last, when the existing tariff of June 1, 1853, was enforced in all its parts on vessels arriving from the United States . . .
>
> The disorganized state of political and military affairs in this country between the years 1851 and 1853, gave rise to many abuses in the revenue department, each military commander assuming the right to regulate a tariff to suit the emergencies of his own jurisdiction . . .[1a]

Writing from Vera Cruz, on June 25, 1854, and speaking of the treaty of 1831 still in force between the United States and Mexico, John T. Pickett said:

> It [the treaty of 1831] is violated by special permits which have recently been granted for the importation of the goods at the ports of San Blas, Matamoras, and Mazatlan, under the "Ceballos" tariff, whilst merchants at all other ports are compelled to pay the higher duties imposed by the tariff of June 1, 1853; thus subjecting many American merchants to a very heavy and ruinous discrimination, it being impossible for them to compete with the favored individuals. This privilege was sold to an English house at Matamoras for and in consideration of a loan to the supreme government of $100,000 . . .
>
> It has been and is being violated by the unlawful seizure and confiscation, under all manner of frivolous pretexts, of the goods imported by American merchants at this and other ports. In these cases some charge of an attempt

[1a] *House Ex. Doc.* No. 47, Part III, 34 Cong., 1 Sess. (Ser. 856), pp. 412–413.

to evade the revenue laws is, of course, trumped up; but as the property confiscated is divided between the collector of customs and his subordinates, . . . it will readily be supposed that a condemnation is easily had, especially as the power of arbitrary decision rests with the collector himself. When such cases are taken before the proper judicial tribunal at this place, the collector is invariably sustained; and, upon appeal to the superior court at Puebla, the decisions of the lower court are affirmed frequently . . . These matters have come to my particular notice, in consequence of the protests which have been made before me, and I now dwell upon them, inasmuch as they will be grounds for future claims of American citizens against this government.[2]

On October 10, 1855, the Consul at the same port, wrote:

Nothing can be more corrupt, false, unjust, unequal, and generally pernicious, than the entire Mexican commercial system. There are now no less than four distinct tariffs in operation and counter-operation here; not to mention concessions and special privileges granted to certain places and favored individuals—all to the great prejudice of the regular American merchant transacting business under the protection guarantied by solemn treaties.[3]

In a report dated March 31, 1856, the Consul of Tampico again said:

This return exhibits the meagre state to which the commerce between the United States and this port is now reduced, which can only be attributed to the irregular but adroit manner with which special favors are granted by the revolutionary chiefs to a few favorite foreign merchants, at the city of Mexico and in this place, who are rewarded for advances of funds, in payments at this custom-house, with enormous high rates of interest in the form of discounts . . .
The skilful [sic] manner with which these special favors are conducted precludes the possibility of preferring charges with sufficient evidence to sustain them; and although the American merchant sees and feels their consequences almost daily, yet the business is transacted in the customs under the coloring of law, and in such a manner as to shield the parties from any further responsibility . . .[4]

The consuls were unanimous in their conviction that a new commercial convention should be negotiated, and such an agreement was arranged in 1857, but Pierce declined to submit it to the Senate so near the expiration of his official term. The evils therefore continued, and almost a year after the close of the Pierce administration, E. P. Johnson reported from Tabasco:

Mexico makes treaties of commerce with foreign nations, offering to all equal advantage in her trade, and then, forced by her constantly increasing

[2] Ibid., p. 407 ff.
[3] Ibid., No. 2 (Ser. 844), p. 191.
[4] Sen. Ex. Doc. No. 35, 34 Cong., 3 Sess. (Ser. 887), pp. 202–203.

necessities, sells the monopoly of the most profitable part of it at half price to capitalists in Mexico and Vera Cruz; these, in their turn, perhaps, contract with the custom-house officers, introduce double the quantity in heavy cargoes, and divide the plunder between them . . .

In the frequent revolutions that desolate this unhappy country, the law, always a feeble and uncertain protection, becomes a dead letter or worse, and the foreigner is frequently insulted and treated with personal violence; heavy extortions are practiced upon him, often followed by imprisonment on any or no pretext whatever, until ruined in fortune and broken in spirit, he retires from the country with a light purse and a heavy claim on a government every day less able and less willing to pay.[5]

At least two of these officials advocated radical measures in dealing with the situation. Johnson complained in 1858 that the treaties made by the United States with Mexico were based upon the "erroneous conception" that it was a "civilized country." He urged the desirability in all cases of injury to American citizens of holding the offender personally responsible and exacting "complete satisfaction." A few examples, he thought, would "check future persecution." [6] On September 30, 1859, R. B. C. Twyman, Consul at Vera Cruz, wrote that it was ". . . an acknowledged fact that unless peace is [was] restored to Mexico, she must continue to be degenerated." He declared that pacification could be accomplished only by foreign intervention, and that "all honest hearts are [were] turned to the United States of America for that intervention—the only salvation for Mexico." [7]

Of course, it must be remembered that the foregoing is the American side of the story told by men who had probably been sufferers from the disorders which they described; but even when something is allowed for exaggeration, the situation must still have been bad, and one will not be surprised to learn that numerous claims arose from such irregularities. Moreover, it was primarily upon these consular accounts that American opinion and policy were of necessity based, and this is an important consideration.

The relatively complete list of the claims of citizens of the United States against all foreign countries which was submitted to the Senate in January, 1859, included approximately two hundred and fifty against Mexico for the period since the Treaty of Guadalupe Hidalgo. The complete list for the twelve years subsequent to 1848 is shown by the report of the Joint Claims Commission organized under the treaty of 1868, to be approximately four hundred and

[5] Report of February 24, 1858, *ibid.,* no. 37, 35 Cong., 2 Sess. (Ser. 991), p. 392.

[6] *Ibid.*

[7] *House Ex. Doc.* No. 4, Part I, 36 Cong., 1 Sess. (Ser. 1044), p. 400.

forty-eight. The majority of those in both lists arose from murder
and personal injury, imprisonment, and alleged irregularities connected with commercial relations. Aside from these, the most important causes of complaint were robbery, breach of contract, forced
loans, and expulsion from the country. The incomplete list of 1859
included sixty-one arising from trade relations, thirty-five from
imprisonment, ninety-six from murder, twenty-two from personal
injury. The report of the Joint Claims Commission contained
eighty-nine on account of commercial irregularities, one hundred and
seventy-eight on account of imprisonment, and something over one
hundred on account of murder and personal injuries. It also showed
a marked increase in the number of complaints against forced loans
and breaches of contract.[8]

The most important example under the last category continued
to be the Garay contract. The American citizens who were interested in the Isthmus of Tehuantepec, after a silence of almost three
years, began to renew their complaints. The Sloo, or "Mixed,"
Company had been compelled by the precarious state of its funds to
borrow $600,000 to make the necessary payments to the Mexican
government. They had obtained the loan from a British subject,
giving as security a lien on the grant; and Peter A. Hargous, still
game in spite of his former difficulties, managed to obtain this lien.
But the Sloo interests, who had incorporated themselves as the
Louisiana Tehuantepec Company, ignored the lien as well as a secret
clause in their contract which provided for the indemnification of
its former owners, and began work on a plank road across the
isthmus. Hargous was not thus to be outdone, however. On
March 31, 1856, his attorney addressed a letter to Gadsden, informing him that on November of the preceding year Hargous had entered
into an agreement with Falconnet (the British subject who had
advanced Sloo the loan) whereby he had acquired all the rights of
the former; that these rights, according to the agreement under which
the loan was made, embraced the entire control of the privilege;
that the Mexican government had recognized Falconnet as the sole
owner of said privilege; and, finally, that, contrary to the express
agreement which authorized Falconnet, in case the loan was not re-
paid, to dispose of it without the intervention of judiciary authority,
the Mexican government had refused to recognize the transfer of
Hargous. The attorney, therefore, respectfully requested that Gadsden take measures effectively to protect the rights of Hargous, and

[8] *Sen. Ex. Doc.* No. 18, 35 Cong., 2 Sess. (Ser. 981), p. 82 ff.; *ibid.*, No. 31,
44 Cong., 2 Sess. (Ser. 1720), p. 18 ff.

to "insure his acknowledgment by the Mexican government as owner of the privilege." [9]

But Gadsden, as Hargous thought, assumed an attitude of "lukewarmness, if indeed not of actual hostility." Hargous therefore appealed to Secretary of State Marcy, summing up the situation in the following paragraph:

It will, of course, be obvious to you that all the rights of the citizens of the United States in the Sloo grant were extinguished by its transfer to Falconnet, who is a British Subject, it must remain in the possession of the latter until his transfer to me shall be approved by the Mexican government. It is unquestionably, I should suppose, the policy and interest of our government that citizens of the United States and not British subjects should have exclusive control of the privilege referred to. If, therefore, the Mexican government should be countenanced in much longer delaying my request, the danger to the policy and interests to which I have adverted will be subjected is submitted to your wise consideration.[10]

The Pierce administration then instructed its Mexican Minister on the subject, directing him to call the attention of Mexico to the deep interest felt by the government and people of the United States in the completion of the communication across Tehuantepec, and to request that the Mexican government use all its power to remove the obstacles which lay "in the way of giving effect to" the disputed grant.[11] But an arrangement of any kind proved difficult to obtain; and disorders along the route itself interfered with traffic and threatened almost constantly to suspend the work.[12]

It is unnecessary to enter into further details with reference to the important and, in some respects, grievous list of claims which arose after 1848. It will suffice to note that they were more numerous and valuable than those over which Jackson, Van Buren, and Tyler were willing to go to war, and even more numerous and valuable than those which figured so prominently in Polk's Mexican policy.

There are some two or three factors which must not be overlooked, however, in seeking a correct appreciation of these claims and of Mexico's responsibility with respect to them. Ninety-three cases of so-called murder were connected with the Crabb expedition. One hundred and eight cases of imprisonment arose from the Zerman enterprise, and some six or eight in connection with the American passengers who, in 1854, entered the port of Guaymas on board the brig

[9] *Sen. Ex. Doc.* No. 72, 35 Cong., 1 Sess. (Ser. 930), p. 33 ff.
[10] *Ibid.*, pp. 35–36.
[11] Marcy to Forsyth, August 16, 1856, *ibid.*, p. 36.
[12] *Sen. Ex. Doc.* No. 31, 44 Cong., 2 Sess. (Ser. 1720).   Cases No. 792, 921 and 930.

Patrita (formerly the *Anita*, used in connection with Walker's raid on Lower California) without passports and under circumstances which aroused suspicion of filibustering intent.[13]   Resort to extreme measures by the Mexican officials under such circumstances may be somewhat palliated, even if it cannot be justified.   Moreover, there occurred during the time frequent instances of maltreatment of Mexicans in California and Texas; [14] and Indians of the United States continued to make destructive incursions upon Mexico, while the Mexican frontiersmen who had suffered from the raids of 1848–1853 had not yet obtained a penny of indemnity.[15]   In brief, the injuries and outrages were by no means unilateral: the United States was not so guiltless as to be justified in casting the first stone.

Nor could statesmen of the United States afford to overlook the fact that Mexican internal disorders which were largely responsible for the American claims, were likewise responsible for that interruption of industry and that depletion of the treasury which were making a settlement of these claims exceedingly difficult.   Unless Mexico could negotiate a loan on very inadequate security, unless she were willing to sell another strip of territory, there would be little chance for the immediate liquidation of claims.   On the other hand, unless the United States were determined to resort to war in case neither of these alternatives was acted upon by the Mexican government, moderation and patience were imperative.

Immediately after his return to Mexico in the summer of 1854, James Gadsden began to press the question of claims; and he persisted in this course during the remainder of his mission.   In fact, his aggressiveness in the matter did much to render him *persona non grata* to the Mexican Minister of Foreign Relations.   Gadsden had a singular way of doing as he pleased, however; and in respect to claims he often acted without instructions.[16]   The attitude of Presi-

[13] For the details of the *Patrita* affair, see Cripps to Marcy, No. 27, undated, No. 26, Apr. 18, No. 30, May 19, 1854, and Gatton to Cripps, May 24, 1854, all of which are found in Mex. Desp., Vol. 18; and Almonte to Marcy, July 24, 1854, Notes from the Mex. Leg., Vol. VII.

[14] See De la Rosa to Clayton, Oct. 19, 1849, Notes from the Mex. Leg., Vol. 5; Larrainzar to Marcy, Apr. 14, and May 3, 1853, *ibid.*, Vol. 6.

[15] The Mexican government maintained that the Gadsden Treaty had not absolved the United States from this indemnity obligation.   (Almonte to Marcy, May 27 and July 31, 1856, and Feb. 27, 1857, Notes from Mex. Leg., Vol. 8; Marcy to Almonte, July 10, and Dec. 11, 1856, Notes to the Mex. Leg., Vol. 7).
For a summary of Indian incursions into Mexico subsequent to the ratification of the Gadsden Treaty, see Mexican Border Commission of 1873, *Report*, p. 253 ff.

[16] For Gadsden's remonstrances, too numerous to cite in detail, see Mex. Desp., Vol. 19.   Bonilla requested Gadsden's recall in a letter dated Oct. 3,

dent Pierce, as revealed in his annual messages, was much more moderate than the course of his Mexican Minister would suggest. In December, 1854, Pierce stated that the Legation of the United States in Mexico had been "earnest in its endeavor to obtain from the Mexican government a favorable consideration of these claims, but hitherto without success." This failure he attributed in a measure to the "disturbed condition of that country." During the course of the next two years, outrages against American citizens increased in frequency; Gadsden declared that nothing but a resort to force could bring about a settlement; [17] and Great Britain, France, and Spain assumed a vigorous attitude regarding alleged injustices suffered by their citizens; [18] but Pierce displayed an extraordinary amount of forbearance, and remained firm in his policy of moderation. Referring to Mexican relations in his third annual message, he remarked:

The unhappy situation of that country for some time past has not allowed its Government to give due consideration to claims of private reparation, and has appeared to call for and justify some forbearance in such matters on the part of this Government. But if the revolutionary movements which have lately occurred in that Republic and in the organization of a stable Government, urgent appeals to its justice will then be made, and, it may be hoped, with success, for the redress of all complaints of our citizens.[18]

And in his last annual message, when he came to speak of the wrongs suffered by citizens of the United States in the Hispanic American countries, he said:

Unfortunately it is against the Republic of Mexico, with which it is our special desire to maintain a good understanding, that such complaints are most numerous; and although earnestly urged upon its attention, they have not as yet received the consideration which this Government had a right to expect. While reparation for past injuries has been withheld, others have been added. The political condition of that country, however, has been such as to demand forbearance on the part of the United States. I shall continue my efforts to procure for the wrongs of our citizens that redress which is indispensable to the continued friendly association of the two Republics.[19]

But obviously this situation could not continue indefinitely. The execution of the Crabb party, or its murder according to the Ameri-

1854, but Marcy refused to comply and Bonilla did not press the matter. (Bonilla to Almonte, Oct. 3, 1854, Notes from the Mex. Leg., Vol. 7; Marcy to Gadsden, No. 41, Dec. 19, 1854, Mex. Inst., Vol. 17.)

[17] Riva Palacio, *México á través de los siglos*, V, 155, 180, *passim;* Bancroft, *History of Mexico*, V, 716.

[18] Richardson, *Messages and Papers*, V, 336.

[19] *Ibid.*, V, 414.

can viewpoint, sent a wave of indignation over the country,[20] and Congress demanded an investigation of the matter.[21] Charles P. Stone and others interested in the public lands of Sonora protested loudly because they had been expelled by the Governor of that state; [22] Texas demanded that its frontiers be defended from Mexican outlaws and Indians who found their rendezvous on the south side of the Rio Grande; [22a] and citizens of the United States residing in Mexico earnestly invoked the interposition of their government.

Moreover, there was something of the expansionist spirit mingled with these complaints, and but little inducement was required to set in motion a wholesale filibustering enterprise. The people in that portion of New Mexico which later became the state of Arizona assumed the annexation of Sonora almost as a matter of course. They needed convenient communications with the Pacific, and the best routes lay through that state; they were largely dependent upon Sonora for their supplies, but its tariff system was provoking; they considered themselves more capable of developing the vast resources of the state than the Mexican inhabitants living there: why then should not the United States acquire the country immediately? [23] Nor was interest in Arizona and Sonora confined to the Anglo-Americans residing in the region. When the Thirty-fifth Congress met in December, 1857, numerous petitions poured in not only from the residents of the Gadsden Purchase, but from citizens of New York, Illinois, Ohio, Tennessee, and Missouri, praying for protection of the southern mail route to California, for the organization of the territory of Arizona, and for the grant of a quarter-section to actual settlers.[24] And these petitioners did not confine their interest to Arizona alone: they were much concerned about the mines and fertile valleys of Sonora. Some of them were influenced, also, by the additional motive of avenging the murder of the Crabb expedition. Accordingly, in 1857, 1858, and 1859 there was much talk of buying lands in Sonora, and plans were said to have been set on foot to form emigrant aid societies or filibustering parties designed to accomplish the ultimate absorption of the country.[25]

[20] House Ex. Doc. No. 54, 35 Cong., 2 Sess. (Ser. 955), p. 70; Bancroft, North Mexican States and Texas, II, 695.

[21] House Ex. Doc. No. 64.

[22] Memorial of Aug. 25, 1859, Sen. Ex. Doc. No. 2, 36 Cong., 1 Sess. (Ser. 1023), p. 49.

[22a] House Ex. Doc. No. 81, 36 Cong., 1 Sess, p. 90 ff.

[23] Mowry, Memoir of the Proposed Territory of Arizona.

[24] Sen. Journal, 35 Cong. 1 Sess., pp. 41, 52, 196, 202, 281, 341.

[25] Charles P. Stone published at Washington a twenty-eight page pamphlet on the resources of Sonora in which he hinted strongly that he expected the

Some such designs were likewise meditated in regard to Chihuahua, and other frontier states. Sam Houston wrote the Secretary of War in 1860 that for the past three years he had been urged by prominent persons from all sections of the country to invade Mexico. "Since 1857," said Houston, "I have been written to from various parts of the United States, urging me to invade Mexico, with a view to establishing a protectorate, and assuring me that men, money, and arms would be placed at my command if I would engage in the enterprise." [26]   At the same time Simeon Hart, a prominent American merchant in Chihuahua, revealed some of the schemes of his fellow-citizens residing in that portion of the country. After having importuned the President and the Secretary of War to intervene in their behalf, Hart wrote John H. Phelps, one of the Texas Representatives in Congress:

> You can assure Mr. Buchanan that his order to the army to protect our persons and property . . . will much gratify the people on the other side of the river, and still more will they be gratified by having the military stationed in their towns. If the order comes, . . . in six months there will be a prospect for annexation. You must hint this to judge Hemphill and Colonel Wigfall [other Texas Representatives in Congress], as also to the president. The present outside pressure against Chihuahua from Durange and the church party will tend to bring about what was so nearly accomplished by myself and friends a year since—that is, to have that State, by her congress, ask for annexation to us. [27]

Meantime, James Buchanan, who had succeeded Pierce in March, 1857, was being urged by his friends and political allies to lend renown to his administration by solving the Mexican problem. George L. Stevens requested an interview for the purpose of presenting a plan for the pacification of this turbulent neighbor.[28] The chief executive's old friend, Albert C. Ramsey, laid before him a scheme for the purchase of Mexican territory.[29]   Robert P. Letcher, formerly Minister to Mexico, implored the President to take up the Mexican question, pointing out with emphasis the grievances suffered by American citizens at Mexico's hands and suggesting the

region soon to become a part of the United States. See also letters written during 1857–1860 by residents of northern Mexico and published in a pamphlet put out by the Cincinnati and Sonora Mining Association in 1867, and *Sen. Journal*, 35 Cong., 1 Sess., as cited above.

[26] Houston to Floyd, March 12, 1860, *House Ex. Doc.* No. 52, 36 Cong., 1 Sess. (Ser. 1050), pp. 139–142.
[27] Hart to Phelps, Jan. 21, 1860, *ibid.*, pp. 99 ff.
[28] Stevens to Buchanan, May 14, 1859, Buchanan Papers.
[29] Ramsay to *idem*, Jan. 17, 1859, *loc. cit.*

purchase of Sonora.[30] Honorable Theodore Sedgwick, District Attorney in charge of the Southern District of New York, counseled radical measures. He declared that the "Principle of the Treaty of Guadalupe Hidalgo" had been "wrong"; that "instead of *paying* money we should have exacted it, or if an advance was necessary to buy peace . . . it should have been granted under a nominal *loan,* & accompanied by a military *occupation long* enough and *strong* enough to have given our people a chance to go in and acquire a foothold & Control over the Country"; that Buchanan should avoid Polk's error by sending American soldiers into Mexico to occupy the chief towns and maintain order until Anglo-Saxon immigration could gain the ascendency and dominate the country.[31]

[30] Letcher to *idem,* Aug. 12, 1859, *loc. cit.*
[31] Sedgwick to Buchanan, Jan. 10, 1859, *loc. cit.*

CHAPTER XI

THE SHADOW OF EUROPE

BEFORE turning to the Mexican policy of Buchanan's administration it will be necessary to treat more at length a topic which has already received brief consideration in a former chapter of this work. Attention was then called to the fact that it was during the quarter-century subsequent to 1840 that the Monroe Doctrine was given its severest test, but the discussion has now reached the point where it will be appropriate to take the matter up in greater detail. Again, however, it must be remarked that the chief concern here is not so much with what actually happened as with what the United States believed to be taking place.

Difficulties with European powers in the Hawaiian, or Sandwich, Islands began as early as 1842. At that time Sir George Paulet entered Honolulu harbor and demanded as redress for alleged maltreatment of British subjects, terms so humiliating that the King of the islands resigned his sovereignty and gave up his possessions rather than comply with them. Paulet immediately accepted the cession, set up a commission government, and organized a regiment of soldiers. Upon protest of the United States, Her Britannic Majesty disavowed the act, but both Great Britain and France, who had likewise appeared upon the scene and showed a disposition to seize territory in the region, continued to keep their agents at the Hawaiian court. Each of these European governments succeeded in negotiating commercial treaties, and violation of the treaty with France gave her an excuse for making extraordinary demands upon the sovereign of Hawaii, and for taking possession of public property in Honolulu when compliance was refused. Although another protest from the United States led eventually to the virtual withdrawal of the French demands, the French and British agents still sought to defeat American interests in the islands, and when plans for annexing the group to the United States were being considered, agents of the English and the French governments came together to the American Minister in London and entered a joint protest.[1]

---

[1] Johnson *America's Foreign Relations*, I, 520 ff.; *Cong. Globe*, 33 Cong., 2 Sess., p. 830 ff.; *Sen, Ex. Doc.* No. 77, 52 Cong., 2 Sess. (Ser. 3062), p. 119 ff.

It is well known that in 1851 the navies of France and England were instructed to prevent filibustering operations against Cuba, and that in April, 1852, the British government proposed a tripartite agreement to preserve Cuba to Spain. It is not commonly known, however, that certain American statesmen were constantly disturbed during the entire period under consideration by reports that the English and French navies were moving about and meddling in the West Indies, nor that the agents of these two powers interposed to prevent the negotiation of a commercial treaty with the Dominican republic.

On December 23, 1854, the commercial representative of the United States in Santo Domingo forwarded to the Secretary of State documents which he considered as constituting conclusive evidence that the French and the British had been responsible for the interruption of friendly relations between the United States and the Dominican republic. The documents showed that authorized agents of these European governments had attempted to persuade the authorities of the island republic to sign an agreement "never to sell, to lease, to mortgage or give away, either absolutely or temporarily, any portion of the Dominican territory . . . ; never to contract a financial engagement with any foreign State, nor accept a subsidy from such, or mortgage or hypothecate to it any branch of the revenues of the State of St. Domingo," and never to consent to any alienation of the "sovereign jurisdiction" over its territory to "any foreign State." [2]

While speaking in the Senate in 1855, Cass said that he had received news of the recent dispatch of British and French vessels to the vicinity of Cuba; and during the following year the report that England had sent men-of-war to the West Indies caused considerable excitement in the United States and led Buchanan, then Minister at London, to demand an explanation. During the next three years the efforts of the British government to stop the slave trade and prevent filibustering, and the fear of a renewal of its pretensions to the right of search, caused constant uneasiness.[2]

It is likewise a matter of common knowledge that England pursued an aggressive policy with regard to Central America, and that France also showed considerable interest in the region. British subjects had long been interested in Belize and the Mosquito Kingdom, and had displayed the usual Anglo-Saxon vigor. In 1848 a

[2] Dunning, *The British Empire and the United States*, p. 170 ff.; Johnson, *American's Foreign Relations*, I, 548–549; *Cong. Globe,* 33 Cong., 2 Sess., p. 832 ff.; *ibid.,* 34, and 35 Congresses, index under Great Britain and Central America.

British officer had put in his appearance with a warship and taken possession of the port of San Juan as a part of the Mosquito Coast over which Great Britain was exercising a protectorate. At the same time the English in Belize had evinced a disposition to seize some of the islands adjacent to the colony. These acts of aggression aroused uneasiness and bitterness in the United States. The Clayton-Bulwer Treaty represented an attempt at settlement, but it appeared to the people of the United States that England showed no inclination to comply with its provisions. They expected the withdrawal of the British government from the Mosquito Coast and from the islands near Belize. The British argued, however, that the treaty would not admit of such an interpretation, and not only refused to give up the protectorate, but organized the islands, now known as the Bay Islands, into a crown colony.[3]

British desire to maintain a hold upon the region was probably due mainly to its proximity to the proposed interoceanic communication across Nicaragua. The French government and individual Frenchmen had a similar interest in Central America, but their attention had at first been directed to Panama. It was reported that Louis Napoleon, while a prisoner at Ham, had appealed to Louis Philippe for release on condition that he engage in a canal enterprise on the isthmus of Panama. This permission had been refused. A decade later, after he had become the Emperor of the French, Napoleon again directed his attention to Nicaragua, however. Walker's raids were attracting general notice, and a French adventurer, Felix Belly, had conceived the idea of counteracting Yankee influence in the region and of constructing a canal across Nicaragua by the employment of French capital. Belly's denunciation of the Anglo-Americans and his attempt to persuade the president of Nicaragua to withhold his signature from a treaty which the United States had negotiated with the republic, led the United States to demand an explanation; whereupon the French Minister of Foreign Affairs declared that Belly had no connection with the French government. This official admitted, in December, 1858, however, that France was negotiating with Nicaragua and Costa Rica a treaty guaranteeing the neutrality of the transit route, and that the French squadron in the West Indies had orders to assist these states to suppress filibuster operations while the negotiations were pending. At about the same time, also, there were rumors that England, France, and Sardinia were preparing to comply with

[3] Dunning, op. cit., 154–163; Bigelow, Breaches of Anglo-American Treaties, p. 43 ff.; or a fuller account in Williams, Anglo-American Isthmian Diplomacy.

the alleged request of two of the Central American states for a protectorate.[4]

Nor were indications of European interference in South America
lacking. In May, 1848, Niles of Connecticut had called the attention of the Senate to the recent remarkable increase of British
territory in Guiana. He had likewise remarked upon the recent
disturbances in the La Plata region where England and France had
been acting as "mediators and invaders."

The synchronous and apparently joint interference of England
and France at numerous points in the western hemisphere led
to a belief in some quarters that this was the settled policy of the
two countries. On February 25, 1854, Cass read to the Senate a
portion of a recent speech of Lord Clarendon, British Secretary of
State for Foreign Affairs, in which the latter declared that the co-
operation of the English and French governments was "not confined
to the Eastern question," but that "on the question of policy, there
is [was] no part of the world in either hemisphere with regard to
which we are [they were] not entirely in accord." Cass thought
there was no doubt that these two countries meant to forestall any
designs of expansion entertained by the United States.[5] The affair
assumed such importance that Buchanan, United States Minister to
England, requested a conference with Clarendon. The latter denied
that the agreement was to have a general application to the western
hemisphere, but admitted that it was intended to apply to "the
navigation of the Plata, the Paraguay, the Amazon, & other rivers,
& to the countries of South America bordering upon them."[6]

On February 20, 1855, Cass again quoted from Clarendon's
speech. He also quoted a paragraph from an address of Louis Napoleon to the Legislative Chambers, in which the Emperor said in
regard to England and France, that the "same views and the same
intentions" animated the two governments "in every corner of the
globe." He then read an extract from a Spanish paper published in
Cuba, which showed that Spain was pleased with the formation of
such an alliance. In the mind of Cass, this evidence left no doubt
of the intentions of the allies; but if more proof were needed, he
believed it could be found in their actions for the past few years.
"They seem to have followed us," said Cass, "all over the world,

[4] McMaster, *History of the People of the United States,* VII, 556 ff.; Lewis
Cass to John Y. Mason, No. 146, June 9, 1858, and No. 169, Nov. 26, 1858,
France Inst. Vol. 15; Mason to Cass, No. 328, July 30, 1858, France Desp.,
Vol. 44, and No. 368, Dec. 16, 1858, *loc. cit.*
[5] *Cong. Globe,* 33 Cong., 1 Sess., pp. 483-484.
[6] Buchanan, *Works,* IX, 166-183.

watching, counteracting, and opposing, from the loading of a cargo of Guano to the acquisition of a kingdom." [7]

The kingdom to which Cass referred was probably Hawaii. The meaning of the allusion to the loading of guano was made clear by Senator Mason during the same day. He said that the United States had been attempting to make a treaty with Ecuador relating to guano and other commercial subjects, but that England and France had sought to interfere. The French *chargé* had been particularly obtrusive. He had remarked to the Ecuadorian Minister of Foreign Affairs that it seemed strange to him that Ecuador would seek the protection of a nation whose ambitious views and unscrupulous desires of extending its territory were notorious. As for the emperor of France, it was his purpose to turn his attention to the United States when the Russian war had been finished. [8]

Although European intervention in Mexico did not actually occur until near the close of 1861, uneasiness as to the likelihood of such a step was felt in the United States for at least sixteen years prior to this time. This was due in part to the interference of Europe elsewhere in America and in part to certain occurrences in Mexico itself. The apprehensions of the Polk administration have already been noted. Reference has likewise been made to the forebodings of Congress and the press subsequent to 1848. The misgivings of the agents of the United States in Mexico and across the Atlantic must now be examined.

In November, 1852, Alfred Conkling, at that time Minister of the United States in Mexico, reported what he considered reliable information that England and France had entered into a secret convention for the purpose of "extorting" from Mexico the "management of its custom houses" with the view of collecting the debts due to English and French subjects and of "excluding American influence and interference in Mexican affairs." [9] A month later he discussed unofficially with the French Minister the advisability of establishing a tripartite protectorate,—consisting of England, France, and the United States—over Mexico, "so far at least as relates to commerce." [10] In the following January a confidential agent of the Mexican President approached Conkling with reference to the possibility of obtaining the support of England and France, and especially of the United States, in safeguarding foreign commerce

[7] *Cong. Globe*, 33 Cong., 2 Sess., p. 826 ff.

[8] *Ibid.*, p. 832 ff. Mason quoted from a despatch written by Clay, the envoy of the United States in Peru, to Secretary W. L. Marcy.

[9] Conkling to the Secretary of State, Nov. 22, 1852, Mex. Desp., Vol. 16.

[10] *Id.*, No. 7, Dec. 24, *loc. cit.*

with Mexican ports against the lawless interference of Mexican insurgents.[11]

On May 30, 1853, Consul John Black of Mexico City wrote Marcy a long account of political conditions in Mexico, in which he reported the opinion of "some" Mexicans to the effect that Santa Anna had made "alliances with England, France, and Spain in order to check the growth of the United States, and draw its attention from the Island of Cuba." Black remarked that he had no doubt with reference to the determination of Santa Anna to "avenge himself on the United States," but that he believed and hoped the dictator's "expectations of assistance from other powers" were "visionary." [12]

Gadsden's suspicion of European interference in the negotiations resulting in the treaty of 1853 have already been noted. Soon after the ratification of this agreement, he began to complain of a growing hostility to the United States and a growing disposition on the part of the government of Santa Anna to seek European aid. Bonilla, the Secretary of Relations, carried on in the press a series of attacks upon North American policies and institutions; and Gadsden thought a determined effort was being made to transform the Mexican government into an hereditary absolutism, the succession to "pass from Santa Anna, to some member of the Royal family of Spain." In this manner, the Mexican conservatives hoped to engage the sympathy of European absolutism and enlist its support against the United States. "Every development and movement under the governing but deluded powers in Mexico," said Gadsden, "imposes on the United States the obligation which self preservation always sanctifies *openly* and *without disguise,* to sustain the liberal party in this misnamed Republic." [13]

In 1855, Gadsden shared the general apprehensions of his countrymen regarding the possibility that the European allies in the Crimean War would eventually turn their attention to the western hemisphere. He declared that the Gulf of Mexico was destined to be the Black Sea; the Sierra Madre Federation, the Danubian provinces; and Havana, another Sebastopol in the "American conflicts which threaten[ed]"; and that the European allies were dreaming of the "restoration of Legitimacy in one of the Royal families of Spain." In order to prevent this step, he urged the United States to support

[11] *Id.,* No. 9, Jan. 1, 1853, *loc. cit.*
[12] Mexico City Cons. Let., Vol. 10, No. 21.
[13] Gadsden to Marcy, No. 38 *bis,* Sept. 2, 1854, Mex. Desp., Vol. 18.

the liberal party and to let it be known that it was "prepared to meet the crisis at every hazard." [14]

In November of the same year, soon after Santa Anna had been overthrown and a Liberal government with "American predilections" established, Gadsden wrote that the European countries were redoubling their efforts and that the new Administration was in danger of succumbing." "I feel obligated," said Gadsden, "to reaffirm that Another Crisis at this capital is threatened which may give a triumph to European 'recolonization' and expel American influences from Mexico until recovered by another revolution and the sword." [15]

During the course of the year 1856, and in spite of the continuance of the Crimean War, the European powers appeared to assume a more aggressive attitude towards Mexico. England presented an ultimatum respecting alleged injuries inflicted upon a British consul, Spain prepared to send a fleet to Vera Cruz in order to exact satisfaction for outrages perpetrated upon Spaniards in southern Mexico and to compel the payment of sums due Spanish creditors, and France seemed inclined to coöperate with these European nations. These movements disturbed both Gadsden and George M. Dallas, Minister of the United States at London. The latter thought they "involved an ulterior purpose" on the part of Louis Napoleon either to "send a scion of his imperial house to the hall of the Montezumas, or to extirpate Walker, or so to involve Spain and Mexico in a war as to furnish the former a plausible excuse for transferring Cuba to England." [16] Gadsden feared even more elaborate schemes. He believed the European nations intended not only to dominate Mexico, but to form an offensive and defensive alliance with Guatemala and all the South American countries, restrict the maritime power of the United States, control Tehuantepec, preserve Cuba, return Santo Domingo to Spain, place Haiti under the protection of France, and check the progress of American expansion and ideas in general. [17]

Moreover, John Forsyth, who succeeded Gadsden in the late summer of 1856, soon evinced signs of alarm also. He was partic-

[14] Id., Feb. 5, April 3, May 18, Nos. 55, 60, and 63, loc. cit. Gadsden was accused of supporting the revolutionists fighting under the plan of Ayutla with more eagerness than propriety. (Id., Nos. 70–72, Sept. 3, 18, 19, loc. cit.)

[15] Id., No. 77, Mex. Desp., Vol. 19.

[16] Dallas, Letters from London, I, 60.

[17] No. 97, Oct. 4, 1856, loc. cit. For European movements against Mexico, see Riva Palacio, op. cit., V, 155, 180–186, passim.

ularly apprehensive in regard to Great Britain. In reporting the suspension of diplomatic relations on the part of England and the daily anticipation of the British fleet, he said that there was in Mexico a widespread opinion that British demands cloaked an ulterior design. Forsyth said that he found the Liberal party in Mexico desirous of forming with the United States an "alliance, offensive and defensive, the basis of which is [was] to be an honest purpose to do immediate justice to American Claimants, to protect American persons and property, a liberal Commercial Treaty, a Postal Convention, . . . an Extradition Treaty and, in short, an American protectorate," provided the United States were willing to loan the newly established Liberal government several million dollars. Forsyth believed that the Liberals also favored the infusion of American soldiers and officers into the Mexican army.[18]

The coming of the British fleet was delayed, but the rumor stimulated Forsyth to action. Early in 1857 he completed the negotiation of a series of conventions designed to strengthen the Mexican government and remove the European danger. The disapproval of these treaties by the Buchanan administration exasperated Forsyth, and the language of his protest is worth quoting as typical of the line of thought followed frequently by Americans since the days of James K. Polk. Forsyth said:

It is not safe for statesmen of the United States, to ignore the fact, that other nations besides our own have their eager gaze fixed upon this rich and superb country. Whether Mexico maintains her personality or falls to pieces, we have a deep interest in her future, and should secure an influence in her counsels. If she cannot stand without the aid of some friendly power, and the late appeal to our country is a confession of it, what Power . . . should occupy the commanding position of benefactor and friend? If the United States refuse, some other must. What if it comes in the form of a French Prince supported [by] ten thousand French bayonets? Or of British gold, effecting that floating mortgage on her territories which we decline? Believe me Sir, we cannot play the "dog in the manger" with our Monroe Doctrine. Mexico cannot afford to perish for the want of a Medical interventor, because we choose not to be the physician. She must lean upon some power. Shall it be Europe or the United States? I answer unhesitatingly the United States, by every consideration of humanity, good neighborhood, and sound policy. For if it be Europe, I can see a multitude of contingencies that will make Mexico the battleground for the maintenance of American [U. S.?] supremacy in America; the theatre for the practical illustration of the value and the virtue of the Monroe Doctrine.[19]

Was there ever a clearer instance of the close connection between a desire for expansion and for Anglo-American supremacy on the

[18] Forsyth to Marcy, No. 5, Nov. 8, 1856, *loc. cit.*
[19] No. 29, April 4, 1857, *loc. cit.*

one hand and the fear of European intrusion on the other? The words of Forsyth have a prophetic ring. The imperialists in the United States to-day would perhaps find little to add to this justification of an aggressive American policy.

During the next eighteen months Forsyth's letters were filled with alarms and pessimistic comments upon Mexico's future. In July, 1857, he reported the prospect of an immediate outbreak of hostilities between Spain and Mexico—a conflict which the people of the United States could not view as "indifferent spectators." [20] "The triumph of Spain here," said Forsyth, "would be a triumph of principles, opinions and purposes wholly at variance with the interests and settled policy of the United States." In the approaching crisis Mexico would be compelled to look to the United States for succor. A year later he expressed the conviction that the head of the ambitious, unscrupulous, anti-American French Minister, M. Gabriac, was "filled with the dreams of a European protectorate to be followed by a Mexican kingdom or Empire." [21] In September, 1858, he reported an interview with the British Minister regarding the question of outrages suffered by foreigners in Mexico in which this official declared that either Great Britain or the United States would have to take the Mexicans in hand and teach them to respect treaty rights and the law of nations.[22] And, according to Forsyth, the danger of European interference in Mexico was greatly increased by the hopeless incapacity of the Aztec nation. "What Mexico wants is a firm & good master to hold her destinies in his hands & save her from her worst enemy—herself."—But "regeneration must come from abroad in the shape of new ideas and a new blood."— "Mexican institutions are crumbling to pieces and interposition, to gather up the wreck, from some quarter, is as certain as it is indispensable." [23]

Although the diplomatic agents of the United States at Madrid, Paris, and London did not share the full measure of Forsyth's apprehensions, they were by no means free from uneasiness. Throughout 1857 and 1858 they kept a close watch over the Hispano-Mexican difficulty and the attitude of England and France toward it. During most of the time, while far from confident that European interference in the political affairs of Mexico would not take place, they were encouraged by what appeared to be the reasonable hope that France

[20] No. 43, July 2, 1857, Mex. Desp., Vol. 20.
[21] No. 80, June 25, 1858, *ibid.,* Vol. 22.
[22] No. 90, Sept. 18, 1858, *loc. cit.*
[23] No. 51, Sept. 26, and No. 58, Nov. 25, 1857, Mex. Desp., Vol. 21; No. 74, May 2, and No. 80, June 25, 1858, *ibid.,* Vol. 22.

and England would prevent Spain from attacking Mexico. They knew that France and England were attempting to mediate and they half expected the attempt to be successful. They made it clear, however, that they were not entertaining the illusion that the European powers were exercising this restraint out of love for the United States. These powers were busy with their own affairs: England with India and China and domestic problems; France with China, plans for playing an important rôle in Europe, and industrial depression at home. Moreover, these powers feared that the United States would support Mexico in a war with Spain in order to find a pretense for seizing Cuba, and they were not prepared for a general war in America. The Ministers to Spain and to France, Augustus C. Dodge, and John Y. Mason, even clung to the hope that England and France would hold Madrid in check in November, 1858, when war between Spain and Mexico seemed all but certain; and although the Minister at the court of St. James thought that Spain might, "under the auspices of England, be tempted to make a spasmodic effort for the restoration of her Mexican dominion," he contended that "a word, a single word, importing American unanimity and inflexibility on the topic, would crush the egg-shell project forever." [24]

As will appear in another connection, Forsyth broke relations with the reactionary government in Mexico in the summer of 1858 and returned home. For the next few months the United States had no plenipotentiary in Mexico, but in the spring of the following year Robert M. McLane took up his residence at Vera Cruz as Minister to the Juárez government. And McLane, like Gadsden and Forsyth before him, soon found much to disturb the equanimity of one opposed to European intrusion in the western hemisphere. On May 7, 1859, he forwarded a letter written by Consul Black of Mexico City in which the latter reported that the clergy, who had long been endeavoring to secure European aid, now had the special favor of Gabriac; that Gabriac was eager to curb the "dangerous expansive designs of the Colossus of the North"; and that exasperation because of inability to settle claims against Mexico was likely at any time to impel the British Minister to join his French colleague in recommending intervention. This apprehension led Black to advise the United States to seize the castle of San Juan de Ulua to prevent its capture by the French. Soon afterwards McLane reported that the

---

[24] This paragraph is based upon an examination of Spain Desp., Vols. 40 and 41, France Desp., Vols. 42–44, and Great Britain Desp. Vols. 71–73; also Dallas, *Letters from London.*

British Minister had urged him to join in an attempt to mediate between the Liberal and the Conservative leaders in Mexico. The
British Minister hoped that these Mexican chiefs might "submit to
a conference of the three allied powers [England, France and the
United States] in Washington—keeping truce meanwhile—sending
three delegates"; that "a new constitution might be decreed— . . . a
first president named for eight years—and some material aid to
ensure tranquillity afforded . . ." And so McLane continued to
sound the alarm until the end of his mission, going so far on one
occasion (March 30, 1860) as to predict that there would soon be
an attempt to establish European ascendency not only in Mexico,
but in the Central American states as well.[25]

But the envoys in Europe told a different story, particularly during the year 1859. They were unanimous in reporting that the
European nations were so busy with difficulties relating to Europe,
Asia, and Africa that they could not take a hand in American affairs. Two of these reports are worth quoting. In a despatch
dated October 21, 1859, and received by Cass on November 7, Dallas
enumerated the questions of foreign and domestic politics which were
agitating the British Cabinet.

Of the former description [said Dallas] are the retribution to be visited
upon China; the attitude proper to be taken to guard British interests should
Spain persevere in her threatened invasion of Morocco; the delicate position
of matters at the Island of San Juan; the contemplated European Congress;
the new treaties at Zurich; and the Italian complications: of the latter description are the indispensable Reform Bill for next Parliament: the forlorn
finances of India; the armaments of all sorts against possible invasion; the
attack of the Catholic Prelates of Ireland upon the national educational system
there; the proved bribery at elections and the penal laws required as remedies.[26]

An even more vivid description of the tensity of the situation is
given by William Preston, Minister at Madrid, in a letter dated
November 1, and received by Cass on November 26. Reporting the
commencement of war between Spain and Morocco, Preston wrote:

The cardinal question of the day, is whether the hostilities between Spain
and Morocco will lead to a general European war. Look where we will, the
signs of distrust are more clear than before the Italian campaign. Universal
anxiety prevails. The convention of Villafranca inspired no confidence, and
the peace of Zurich will give no repose . . . Wherever we turn . . . we see
the signs of an impending struggle. Whether in the Italian Duchies or Sardinia

[25] McLane to Cass, No. 12, May 7, 1858, and enclosure "C;" No. 18, June
25, and enclosure, Mex. Desp., Vol. 23; No. 72, March 30, 1860, *ibid.*, Vol. 25.
[26] Great Britain Desp., Vol. 74.

. . . ; or at Zurich; or Antwerp; or on the Isthmus of Suez; or at Tangiers, Madrid, or Gibraltar; we find the rivals present, on the point of dropping their masks, to commence one of those fierce conflicts which have signalized their history . . .[27]

If such reports are to be relied upon, Mexico was certainly not in danger of immediate European occupation during the last few months of 1859. But the question has its obverse side. The preoccupation of the powers of Europe would furnish the Buchanan administration a splendid opportunity for carrying out measures designed to remove the causes for Old World intervention in the future, or for the adoption of an aggressive policy towards certain American states and colonies. Nor did the agents of the Buchanan government residing in Europe overlook this phase of the matter. Writing from Rome in the spring of 1859, W. B. Lawrence said: "Any circumstance that diverts the attention of the great maritime powers from our continent cannot but have an advantageous bearing on our relations with the other states of America, as well as on the question of Cuba." [28] At about the same time Preston advised that England was on the point of opposing France in the Italian question and urged that Cuba "should be boldly seized at the first dawn of war" between these two powers. Otherwise, Preston maintained, it would be taken over by one of these belligerents.[29]

To check up these rumors with established fact has not been found practicable. How long the scheme of Mexican intervention had been entertained by the European powers cannot be certainly known until the archives of England, France, and Spain have been diligently searched, and perhaps not until the private correspondence of the statesmen of the time has been perused. It has been said that the French Empress told two prominent Mexicans in 1857 that she had often thought of how nice it would be to have a Mexican throne. It is known that as early as 1858 the French and Spanish Ministers in Mexico discussed the advisability of joint intervention in order to place a check upon the "expanding and unrestrainable people who occupy the north of the new hemisphere"; and that in May, 1860, the Spanish Minister of Foreign Affairs urged upon England the necessity of joint action for the purpose of preventing the absorption

[27] Spain Desp., Vol. 42.

[28] Lawrence to Buchanan, March 7, 1859, Buchanan Papers.

[29] Preston to Cass, No. 9, April 25, 1859, Spain Desp., Vol. 42; Preston to Buchanan, May 8, 1859, Buchanan Papers.

of Mexico by the United States.[30] And of course it is known that
the convention which definitely provided for joint intervention was
signed on October 31, 1861. What is more important to the present
discussion is the fact that the fear of such intervention was felt in
the United States as early as 1844 and that apprehension grew
more pronounced in the late fifties, for, after all, the State Department had to base its policy upon the facts as reported and not as
they may have been in reality.

In the face of what appeared to be almost constant threats of
European intervention had the United States taken any definite and
consistent stand? Would its previous attitude furnish any indication
of the action which might be expected of the Buchanan administration in the crisis of 1858–1860? The Monroe Doctrine which was
likely to be the precedent for whatever measures should be taken
was either silent or vague in certain particulars. It did not indicate
what action would be taken by the United States in the event that
the European powers undertook to impose their system upon any of
the American states or sought further to colonize the western hemisphere; it was silent regarding the attitude to be assumed by the
United States in case of the transfer of an American colony from
one European power to another or of the voluntary acceptance of
European dominion by an American state. Moreover, the doctrine
was promulgated without the previous positive assurance that it
had the backing of the legislative branch of the government. Before
long, however, situations arose which demanded a decision with reference to each of these points.

In 1825 a French fleet appeared in the West Indies and there were
rumors that Spain intended to transfer Cuba to one of the European
states. This occasioned the first distinct statement of policy regarding the transfer of a colony. France was plainly told by Henry
Clay, at that time Secretary of State, that the United States would
not allow Cuba and Porto Rico to pass into the hands of any other
European power. This statement was often reiterated during the
next thirty years, one of the best known instances being that of
Secretary Everett in 1852. Everett declared that the United States
would consider the acquisition of Cuba by any other European
power in "somewhat the same light as France and England would
view the acquisition of some important island in the Mediterranean
by the United States . . .", and called upon these countries to con-

[30] John Musser, *The Establishment of Maximilian's Empire in Mexico*, pp.
14–16; Arrangois, *México desde 1808 hasta 1867*, II, 353.

sider what their attitude would be in regard to an island that guarded the mouth of the Seine or the Thames.[31]

In regard to California and Oregon, the Hawaiian Islands, and Yucatán, a more directly belligerent policy had been declared. Polk had stated with reference to British advances on the Pacific coast that the United States could not "in silence permit any European interference on the North American continent, and should any such interference be attempted will [would] be ready to resist it at any and all hazards." [32] In speaking of the possibility of Yucatán's being transferred to England or Spain, Polk declared in 1848 that "in no event" could the United States permit Yucatán to become a "colony of any European power"; and, as has been noted, he and Walker were in favor of annexing the peninsula in case this should become necessary to prevent it from falling into European hands.[33] In 1851 Webster, then Secretary of State, expressed in no uncertain terms the attitude of the Fillmore administration towards the interference of the powers of Europe in the Hawaiian Islands. He said:

> The Government of the United States . . . can never consent to see these islands taken possession of by either of the great commercial powers of Europe . . .
> The Navy Department will receive instructions to place, and to keep, the naval armament of the United States in the Pacific Ocean in such a state of strength and preparation as shall be requisite for the preservation of the honor and the dignity of the United States and the safety of the government of the Hawaiian Islands.[34]

With reference to Central America and the various prospective routes for interoceanic communication, the policy of the United States, as is well known, was hampered by the Clayton-Bulwer Treaty and the prior establishments of Great Britain in the region. In regard to the Isthmus of Tehuantepec, however, it will be recalled that Webster had declared the policy of his government as early as 1851. With respect to rumored British interference he had instructed Letcher to "say to the minister of foreign affairs, that . . . the United States . . . could not see with indifference that isthmus, or any part of it, pass under the sway of any European State." [35]

[31] Hart, *The Monroe Doctrine*, p. 101 ff; *Sen. Ex. Doc.* No. 13, 32 Cong., 2 Sess. (Ser. 660), p. 15 ff.
[32] Richardson, *Messages*, IV, 398.
[33] Polk, *Diary*, III, 444–445; Richardson, *op. cit.*, IV, 581–583.
[34] Webster to Severance, July 14, 1851, *Sen. Ex. Doc.* No. 77, 52 Cong., 2 Sess. (Ser. 3962), pp. 95–97.
[35] Webster to Letcher, Dec. 22, 1851, *ibid.*, No. 97, 32 Cong., 1 Sess. (Ser. 974), p. 56.

Moreover, there is another statement of policy which had specific reference to Mexico. Instructing John Slidell on March 12, 1846, Buchanan, then in charge of the State Department, took occasion to remark that "should Great Britain and France attempt to place a Spanish or any other European Prince upon the throne of Mexico, this would be resisted by all the power of the United States." [36]

Thus it will be seen that the executive branch of the United States government had expressed itself prior to 1857 with reference to most of the situations to which the Monroe Doctrine could conceivably be applied and that these declarations of policy had come from both parties. If Buchanan's administration gave any weight to the reports of European designs in Mexico, it would be forced in deference to unequivocal and reiterated statements of American policy to take some action, regardless of the claims question or any other complaint.

Concerning the attitude of Congress, however, it was of necessity uncertain. The Monroe Doctrine and its subsequent interpretations still remained *dicta* of the executive department; Congress as a whole had never expressed itself on these subjects. Clay had sought an expression in 1825, the Senate was apparently on the point of taking a vote in 1848, and Cass had labored arduously from 1853 to 1856 to force an expression of policy; but no action had ever been taken.[37] Yet the consent of Congress would be necessary before any very effective measures could be put into operation in support of these declarations. Unless this could be obtained executive utterances would be almost as impotent as the vain boasting of a child.

[36] Buchanan, *Works,* VI, 405.
[37] Hart, *The Monroe Doctrine,* p. 101 ff.

CHAPTER XII

THE MEXICAN POLICY OF BUCHANAN'S ADMINISTRATION

THE events narrated in the last three chapters indicate that the Buchanan administration would probably be called upon to formulate a definite Mexican policy. Railway routes across northern Mexico, more satisfactory arrangements for the holders of the Tehuantepec concession, and less embarrassing commercial regulations were being persistently sought. Redress for the increasing number of outrages against the persons and property of American citizens was being emphatically demanded, and closely connected with the demand was the idea of securing Mexican territory as indemnity. Moreover, the ever-present shadow of European intervention was eliciting impetuous counsels and tending to lead to the adoption of decisive measures.

Would the administration pursue a bold and aggressive policy? If the Democratic platform of 1856 and the previous records of James Buchanan and Lewis Cass, Secretary of State, could be taken as criteria, such a policy might be anticipated with confidence; for that platform was boisterously belligerent, and both Cass and Buchanan had not only evinced dissatisfaction with the amount of territory acquired from Mexico in 1848,[1] but had frequently expressed alarm at the prospect of European intrusion in the western hemisphere.

Appointed as Minister to Mexico in 1856, John Forsyth of Alabama had been at his post only a short time when Buchanan entered the White House. Forsyth had been instructed by the preceding administration to allay Mexican suspicion regarding sinister designs which the United States was supposed to cherish in respect to Mexico, but to urge a new agreement with reference to the Tehuantepec grant, trade reciprocity, a settlement of claims, and a postal convention.[2]

By February 10, 1857, he had succeeded in negotiating five

[1] Polk, *Diary*, index under Mexico and Yucatán; Dodd, "The West and the War with Mexico," in Ill. State Historical Society, *Trans.* (1912), pp. 15-23.
[2] Marcy to Forsyth, No. 1, Aug. 4, 1856, Mex. Inst., Vol. 17.

treaties, two relating to commercial affairs, one embracing a postal convention, one providing for a claims commission, and still another granting a loan to Mexico. These agreements represented a line of policy remotely similar to that which, a half-century later, the United States was to pursue in the Caribbean. The loan of fifteen million dollars was to be extended by the government of the United States to the Mexican government, but three millions were to be retained to pay the claims of American citizens against Mexico, and four millions were to be applied to extinguish the British convention debt. The seven millions thus set apart were to be secured by 13% of the import duties collected in the Mexican ports. The remaining eight millions were to be extinguished by a reduction of 20% in both the import and the export duties on the trade between the United States and Mexico. In other words, the latter sum was to constitute a sort of subsidy for the American-Mexican trade—a trade to be further stimulated by reciprocity on certain stipulated articles.[3]

In Forsyth's mind these treaties would, if ratified, bring about a profound change in the Mexican situation. Not only would they stabilize the Mexican government and enable it to satisfy American claims, but they would also contribute to the elimination of European influence by removing all excuse for British interference in Mexico and capturing a lion's share of Mexican commerce for the United States. Moreover, Forsyth believed these agreements represented a kind of floating mortgage on Mexican domain. In this latter connection, he wrote:

I regarded a loan to Mexico as a species of floating mortgage upon the territory of a poor neighbor, useless to her, of great value to us, which in the end would be paid, could be paid with honor, and could only be paid by a peaceable foreclosure with her consent. In short, finding it impossible to acquire territory immediately, I did the next best thing,[4] which was to pave the way for the acquisition hereafter . . .

The Pierce administration was not ready, however, to adopt the policy suggested by Forsyth, and the treaties were not submitted to the Senate.

Although Buchanan was no more favorably disposed toward the agreements,[5] he soon made it plain that an attempt to acquire ter-

[3] Forsyth to Marcy, No. 24, Feb. 10, 1857, and enclosures, Mex. Desp., Vol. 20. The treaties were printed in La Nación, 14 de abril de 1857.
[4] Forsyth to Cass, No. 29, April 14, 1857, Mex. Desp., Vol. 20.
[5] The grounds for objection to these treaties were not fully set forth. It was merely stated that they "would make important changes in the inter-

ritory was to be a prominent feature in his Mexican policy. Soon after his inauguration, Buchanan was approached by Émile la Sère and Senator Judah P. Benjamin, president and attorney respectively of the Louisiana Tehuantepec Company, who persuaded him to send new instructions to Forsyth. These authorized the American Minister to pay Mexico twelve or fifteen million dollars for Lower California and a large portion of Sonora and Chihuahua,[6] together with the perpetual right-of-way and privilege of transit, under the guaranty of the United States that it would be kept neutral, over any line of interoceanic communication across Mexican territory. A mutual settlement of claims was also authorized, the United States to retain two million dollars for the satisfaction of American claims against Mexico. Forsyth was further instructed to make use of Benjamin and La Sère in obtaining the desired cession, and, at the same time, to coöperate with them in securing the modification of the terms of their grant.[7]

The American Minister reluctantly approached the Comonfort government with offers for a purchase of territory, but he resented the intrusions of the agents of the Tehuantepec Company and refused to assist them. They nevertheless succeeded in procuring a private contract with Mexico and returned to the United States to decry Forsyth in a private letter to Buchanan.[8] To this contract Forsyth objected because he thought it jeopardized American interests in Tehuantepec, secured the government of the United States no benefit, and violated the instructions of the Secretary of State. At the same time, he attempted to negotiate in regard to the transit

national relations of the contracting parties" and that they presented to the mind of the President "weighty objections." See Marcy to Forsyth, No. 11, March 3, and Cass to Forsyth, No. 12, March 12, 1857, Mex. Inst., Vol. 17. The treaties were attacked in Mexico on the ground that they represented a scheme on the part of the United States to acquire Mexican territory. (*La Nación*, 15 de februar, 1857, and following.)

[6] From the mouth of the Rio Grande to its intersection with the parallel of thirty degrees, the boundary was to remain as it then existed. From that point it was to extend out the thirtieth parallel to the easternmost tributary of the Rio Chico, thence down the middle of said tributary and river to the Gulf of California and thence down the middle of said Gulf and around Lower California to the termination of the boundary as defined in the treaty of 1853. See map facing p. 139.

[7] Cass to Forsyth, Nos. 27 and 28, July 17, 1857, Mex. Inst., Vol. 17; Butler, *Judah P. Benjamin*, pp. 185–188.

[8] Forsyth to Cass, No. 48, Sept. 15, No. 57, Nov. 24, 1857, and Private of Jan. 4, 1858, Mex. Desp., Vol. 21; Callahan, "The Mexican Policy of Southern Leaders under Buchanan's Administration," p. 139.

an agreement more favorable than that contained in the eighth article of the Gadsden Treaty, but he failed in his effort.[9]

In defending his course, Forsyth took occasion to assert that had
his overtures not been hampered by direct attempts to obtain territory from a government already pledged not to alienate any part of
the national domain, he could have secured indirectly everything
the administration desired by means of a treaty providing (1) for
a kind of protectorate over the Isthmus of Tehuantepec, and (2)
for the cession of a right of way for a railway along the line which
the United States desired as a new boundary.[10]

In keeping with this idea, he asked permission to offer twelve
million dollars to the Mexican government for a treaty of transit
and commerce; and when his government declined to expend this
sum unless it could "obtain a consideration equally valuable in
return," [11] he sought to "make it clear that the purchase of commercial privileges was contemplated, & in fact, desired, merely as a
means to a political end—that end being to sustain Mexico & to
keep her from falling to pieces, perhaps into the hands of Foreign
Powers, until such time as we were ready to 'Americanize' her." [12]
Moreover, on several occasions before the close of the year 1857,
seeing what he considered a chance of sustaining the Comonfort
government and at the same time of profiting by its difficulties, he
asked permission to offer a price for the desired territory so large as
to prove "an irresistible temptation" to President Comonfort and
the Mexican Congress. Although the United States refused to increase the maximum, Forsyth persisted in his attempts to acquire
territory, urging his government to place a million or a half-million
at his disposal "to be applied as part payment immediately upon
the signing of a Treaty of cession." [13] In other words, the distinguished Alabaman was desirous of resorting to the tactics of his
noted precursor from South Carolina. Pierce and Gadsden had
found it profitable to prolong the existence of the despotism of Santa
Anna, why should not Buchanan and Forsyth adopt the same procedure with reference to Comonfort?

When in January, 1858, Comonfort was overthrown and Zuloaga

[9] Callahan, op. cit., p. 138; Sen. Ex. Doc. No. 72, 35 Cong., 1 Sess. (Ser. 930),
pp. 50–51.

[10] Despatches No. 51 and 52, Sept. 26 and 28, 1857, Mex. Desp., Vol. 21.

[11] Cass to Forsyth No. 33, Nov. 17, 1857, Mex. Inst., Vol. 17.

[12] No. 68, Feb. 13, 1858, Mex. Desp., Vol. 21. Quoted in Callahan, op. cit.,
p. 139.

[13] Nos. 56, 58, and 62, of Nov. 18, 25, and Dec. 17, 1857, loc. cit.

was placed at the head of the Conservative government, Forsyth
immediately recognized the new administration and bid for a territorial cession; but once more he met with disappointment.[14] He
then urged his government to resort to more vigorous measures in
order to compel Mexico to meet her obligations, remarking in a
despatch to which reference has already been made:

You want Sonora? The American blood spilled near its line would justify
you in seizing it. . . . You want other territory? Send me the power to make
an ultimate demand for the several millions Mexico owes our people for spoliations and personal wrongs. . . . You want the Tehuantepec transit? Say to
Mexico, "Nature has placed that shortest highway between the two oceans,
so necessary to the commerce of the world, in your keeping. You will not
open it yourself nor allow others to open it to the wants of mankind. You
cannot be permitted to act the dog in the manger. . . . Give us what we ask
for in return for the manifest benefits we propose to confer upon you for it,
or we will take it."[15]

This excerpt reveals the extremely close connection between desire
to obtain Mexican territory and exasperation because of alleged
outrages committed against citizens of the United States in Mexico.
Since the beginning of his mission Forsyth had indeed had many
examples of alleged violence to his countrymen called to his attention. He had made persistent efforts to secure redress for the
execution of the Crabb party and of those suspected of complicity
with it. His exertions had been in vain, however, as they were to
be in numerous other cases which he pressed for settlement. As
early as June 1, 1857, he had urged upon his government the importance of an "occasional display of the American flag in the ports
of Mexico and on both coasts," in order to shield his countrymen
who were bitterly complaining of their "unprotected condition, especially in contrast to that of British and French subjects."[16]
Again, on September 26, he declared that the condition of citizens
of the United States residing along the Pacific coast of Mexico was
"such as to imperatively demand some example which shall [would]
strike home to the minds of the officials and inhabitants of that
region the conviction that there is [was] a power, though distant,
yet certain, willing and able to protect American citizens from plunder, imprisonment, and death." He then referred to the insults
which he declared had been heaped upon the American Consul at
Mazatlán, and to the alleged murder of four Americans on the

14 Callahan, *op. et loc. cit.*
15 Private of April 15, 1858, Mex. Desp., Vol. 21. Quoted, in part, by Callahan, *op. cit.*, p. 140.
16 *House Ex. Doc.* No. 64, 35 Cong., 1 Sess. (Ser. 955), pp. 38–39.

Sonora border, imploring his government "for the sake of outraged humanity" crying out "for justice in American accents from so many dungeons on the Pacific coast, not to let pass these two ripe occasions to dissipate the dishonoring and fatal belief . . . that the United States lacks either the will or the power to protect her children and their flag abroad." [17]

These grievances of American citizens and personal dislike for the Zuloaga administration finally led Forsyth to break off relations. The occasion for the step was the attempt of Zuloaga to levy what Forsyth considered a forced loan. On May 15, 1858, a decree was issued placing a tax on all property valued at more than a certain stipulated sum, whether owned by Mexicans or foreigners. Forsyth and the British Minister protested against the decree on the ground that it constituted a forced loan, and, as such, was contrary to the tenth article of the Anglo-Mexican treaty of 1826, to the benefits of which citizens of the United States were entitled under the most favored nation clause. They also advised their countrymen to pay the contribution under protest. In spite of these remonstrances, when Solomon Migel, a citizen of the United States, refused to pay, he was ordered to leave the country within three days. Forsyth thereupon notified the Mexican Minister of Relations that the decree of banishment would be executed "upon peril of . . . responsibility to the sovereignty of the United States." Nevertheless, Migel was expelled from the country; and Forsyth decided to suspend relations until the pleasure of his government could be learned.[18] Cass did not consider the contribution in question a "forced loan" in the strict sense of the word; but on account of the disturbed condition of the relations of the two countries, he instructed Forsyth to ask for his passports.[19]

President Buchanan now determined to recommend vigorous measures. His purpose had probably been foreshadowed by a resolution, introduced by Senator Houston of Texas on February 16, 1858, which provided for the appointment of a committee to investigate and report as to the advisability of establishing a protectorate over Central America and Mexico. Congressional action on this measure furnished little encouragement; [20] but Buchanan nevertheless proceeded to set forth a part of his policy in his annual message of 1858. It consisted of two closely related features centering around the subjects of claims and frontier difficulties, and prob-

[17] *Ibid.*, p. 55.
[18] *Sen. Ex. Doc.* No. 1, 35 Cong., 2 Sess. (Ser. 974), p. 41 ff.
[19] Cass to Forsyth, July 15, 1858, *ibid.*, p. 48.
[20] *Cong. Globe,* 35 Cong., 1 Sess., pp. 715, 738, 750, 1598, *passim.*

ably embraced the design of acquiring another strip of Mexican territory. In regard to indemnity for claims, the President declared: "It would be vain for this government to attempt to enforce payment in money . . . , because she [Mexico] is destitute of all pecuniary means to satisfy these demands." Any doubt as to the meaning of these words is dispelled by a more explicit statement in the same message, to the effect that had he not expected the ultimate triumph of the Constitutional party in Mexico, he would already have recommended that Congress "grant the necessary power to the President to take possession of a sufficient portion of the remote and unsettled territory of Mexico, to be held in pledge" until the injuries of the citizens of the United States should be redressed and their just demands satisfied. Such a method of reprisal he considered as "recognized by the law of nations." [21] Since the Mexican government was not likely soon to have sufficient funds to settle its outstanding obligations, this step probably would have meant occupation of a permanent nature.

Of the frontier Buchanan drew a dark picture. He spoke of bands of predatory Indians roaming promiscuously over the border states of both countries, of anarchy, violence, and helpless local governments on the Mexican frontier, of lawless Mexicans preying upon the inhabitants of Arizona, arresting its development, and threatening to break up stage and postal communications with the Pacific. He then announced his conviction that the only possible remedy for these evils was the assumption of a temporary protectorate over the northern portions of Sonora and Chihuahua, and the establishment of military posts there. He had "no doubt but that this measure will [would] be viewed in a friendly spirit" by the states concerned, for it would "prove equally effectual" for the citizens of both Mexico and the United States.[22]

The President's recommendation was referred to the Committee on Foreign Relations which brought in a bill, on January 11, 1859, authorizing him to employ the public forces of the nation in the protection of American citizens in Mexico.[23] This bill was given no immediate consideration; and on February 18, Buchanan sent a special message to Congress asking authority to use the land and naval forces to protect Americans and their property while in transit across the isthmian routes, as well as from outrages committed by the republics to the south.[24] This led to a motion to take

[21] Richardson, *Messages*, V, p. 521 ff.
[22] *Ibid., loc. cit.*
[23] *Cong. Globe*, 35 Cong., 2 Sess., pp. 1118–1143.
[24] Richardson, *Messages*, V, 538–540.

up the bill of January 11. Considerable debate followed, and the motion was eventually defeated by a vote of thirty-one to twenty-five.[25] No further consideration was given to the bill.

It is probable that Buchanan set forth in his message of December, 1858, only a portion of the policy which his administration had under consideration. Another important feature which may already have been contemplated was the recognition and support of the Liberal, or Constitutional, government of Juárez, then established at Vera Cruz. Buchanan's reference in this message to the possibility of the triumph of this leader may well be taken as foreshadowing this step. On December 27, William M. Churchwell was sent as special agent to investigate conditions in Mexico and to report the prospects of the contending parties. While writing Churchwell's instructions Cass took occasion to remark:

From the President's message to Congress at the opening of this session, you will have gathered the views of the administration upon the subject of Mexican affairs. The liberal party in Mexico has our hearty sympathy, and we are disposed to give it any moral support which may result from our recognition of its supremacy, whenever such recognition can take place in conformity with our usual policy on such occasions.[26]

Churchwell sent back reports favorable to the Liberal government and a memorandum signed by Juárez in which this chief expressed his willingness to cede, under certain conditions, not only Lower California, but perpetual rights-of-way over Tehuantepec, and from the Rio Grande to Guaymas and to Mazatlán, respectively.[27] Thereupon Robert M. McLane of Maryland was appointed Minister and instructed, on March 7, in the following somewhat unusual and enigmatic fashion:

The first question presented to you, on your arrival in Mexico, will be in reference to the recognition of a Government there, with which you can transact business. . . . If you find a Government in Mexico, which exercises general authority over the country, and is likely to maintain itself, you will, of course, recognize it, without reference to any opinions which you may have as to the rightfulness of its existence. The question whether there is a government in any country, is not a question of right, but of fact, and in the ascertainment of this fact in Mexico very much must be left to your discretion.

[25] *Sen. Journal,* 35 Cong., 2 Sess., p. 343. The vote on this measure was influenced by sectionalism and by a general aversion to placing too much power into the hands of the executive. The affirmative vote numbered thirteen southern and four northern men, and the negative, eleven southern and twenty northern men. Partisan considerations also exerted an influence.
[26] Cass to Churchwell, Dec. 27, 1858, Mex. Inst., Vol. 17.
[27] McLane to Cass, No. 1, April 7, 1859, Mex. Desp., Vol. 23; Callahan, *op. cit.,* p. 142.

Undoubtedly, however, the sympathies of the United States have been strongly enlisted in favor of the party of Juarez which is now established at Vera Cruz, and this government would be glad to see it successful. This arises not only from the fact that it is believed to be a constitutional party, but because, also, its general views are understood to be more liberal than those of the party opposed to it, and because, moreover, it is believed to entertain friendly sentiments towards the United States. Notwithstanding this preference, our government cannot properly intervene in its behalf without violating a cardinal feature of our foreign policy. Yet, it would be an agreeable duty to give it the full weight of our recognition, at the earliest period when its condition and prospects would justify us in doing so. The single fact that it is not in possession of the City of Mexico, ought not to be a conclusive consideration against it . . .

You are authorized, whenever under your instructions you shall have recognized a Government in Mexico, and shall find it willing to negotiate a satisfactory treaty of commerce and limits with the United States, to enter upon such negotiation without delay.

McLane was then authorized to offer ten million dollars for Lower California and transit privileges across northern Mexico and Tehuantepec, a portion of which sum was to be retained to satisfy the claims of American citizens against Mexico.[28]

From these instructions the Buchanan administration appears to have been in a state of perplexing indecision occasioned by several motives. On the one hand there was an indisposition to depart from the *de facto* principle; on the other, a professed preference for liberalism and an intense desire for territory and, possibly, for the settlement of claims. The knowledge that the Conservative government of Mexico was to a great extent under the domination of the agents of the European powers may also have had some weight. It is likely, however, that desire for territory was the most influential of these motives. If Cass had expressed frankly the sentiments of the administration, he would perhaps have instructed McLane somewhat as follows:

The Conservative government at Mexico City has steadfastly refused to alienate territory or grant indemnity for injuries perpetrated upon American citizens residing in Mexico. Moreover, it appears to be under the domination of the agents of the monarchical governments of Europe. The Liberal government now established at Vera Cruz has, on the contrary, evinced a friendly disposition towards the United States; and it has expressed a willingness to settle all outstanding difficulties by the sale of territory and transit privileges. As yet, however, its authority is limited to a small area. In fact, it does not even hold the capital city of the country. Recognition at this time might therefore be considered premature. You are accordingly instructed, if possible, to pursue a line of action calculated to safeguard this government from the

[28] See Mex. Inst., Vol. 17.

charge of having departed from the *de facto* principle, but while so doing, you should be extremely careful not to lose an opportunity of acquiring a portion of northern Mexico and concessions for interoceanic communications.[29]

Just one month after these instructions had been written McLane recognized Juárez and entered upon negotiations for the objects of his mission. But his task proved far more difficult than he had anticipated. He was hampered from the beginning by the action of the Conservative government which alleged that the United States, having previously broken relations with it because of its refusal to alienate territory, had now recognized Juárez solely for the purpose of despoiling Mexico of its national domain.[30] For the next few months McLane's efforts were, in fact, fruitless. The Liberal Ministers of Foreign Affairs, who followed each other in rapid succession, objected that a treaty embracing the proposals of the American Minister would not be ratified by the Liberal Congress, or urged that the immediate payment of the pecuniary consideration would be necessary in order to stem the tide of opposition until ratifications could be exchanged. Although he thus found it impossible, for the time being, to obtain the transit privileges and a cession of territory on suitable terms, he did find the Juárez government willing to enter into a sort of alliance by which the United States would have been obligated both to maintain order in Mexico and to guarantee the integrity of its national domain. Into such an agreement McLane declined to enter and Cass approved his conduct.[31]

McLane then urged (1) that the President of the United States "ask Congress for the power to enter Mexico with . . . military forces . . . , at the call of its authorities, in order to protect the citizens and treaty rights of the United States,"[32] and (2) that Juárez be sustained by a military alliance.[33]

Influenced by this advice and perhaps by the knowledge that the European states were too busy with their own affairs to interfere,

[29] Gadsden had rushed down to Cuernavaca and recognized the government of the Ayutla insurgents before it had been fully established; and Forsyth had extended recognition to Zuloaga within forty-eight hours after he had seized the reigns of power. In neither instance does the act of the Minister appear to have been disapproved. See Gadsden to Marcy, Nos. 73 and 74, Oct. 19, 1855, and enclosures, Mex. Desp., Vol. 19; and Forsyth to Cass, Nos. 66, 67, and 68, Jan. 29 and 30, and Feb. 13, 1858. Mex. Desp., Vol. 21.

[30] McLane to Cass, Nos. 1, 10, and 12, April 7 and 30, and May 7, 1859, Mex. Desp., Vol. 23.

[31] McLane to Cass, Nos. 8 to 30, *loc. cit.;* and Cass to McLane, No. 14, July 8, 1859, Mex. Inst., Vol. 17.

[32] Despatch of Aug. 28, 1859, Mex. Desp., Vol. 19.

[33] Unofficial note of Oct. 31, *ibid.,* Vol. 24.

Buchanan added a new feature to the Mexican policy which he had recommended in 1858. In his annual message of 1859, he dwelt at length upon the outrages perpetrated upon American citizens domiciled in Mexico, mentioning numerous instances of violence and declaring that there was "scarcely any form of injury which has [had] not been suffered" by them "during the last few years." [33a] It was evident that this feature held a large place in the President's mind; but he tried to put the Mexican question upon the still higher plane of duty toward one's neighbor and defense of the established policy of the United States.

Mexico ought to be a rich and prosperous and powerful republic. She possesses an extensive territory, a fertile soil, and an incalculable store of mineral wealth. She occupies an important position between the Gulf and the ocean for transit routes and for commerce. Is it possible that such a country as this can be given up to anarchy and ruin without an effort from any quarter for its rescue and its safety? Will the commercial nations of the world, which have so many interests connected with it, remain wholly indifferent to such a result? Can the United States, especially, which ought to share most largely in its commercial intercourse, allow its immediate neighbor thus to destroy itself and injure them? Yet, without support from some quarter, it is impossible to perceive how Mexico can resume her position among nations. . . . The aid which she requires, and which the interest of all commercial countries require that she should have, it belongs to this government to render, not only by virtue of our neighborhood to Mexico, along whose territory we have a continuous frontier of nearly a thousand miles, but by virtue, also, of our established policy, which is inconsistent with the intervention of any European power in the domestic concerns of that republic. . . . If we do not [lend such aid] it would not be surprising should some other nation undertake the task, and thus force us to interfere . . . , under circumstances of increased difficulty, for the maintenance of our established policy.[34]

He therefore recommended that a military force be sent into Mexico in order to aid in the establishment of the Constitutional government and in the extension of its authority, as well as to obtain redress for the outrages committed against United States citizens by the Conservatives. He believed that Juárez would agree to such a step and that he would work in concert with the United States forces; but even if Juárez refused, Buchanan professed himself to be unable to see how the obligation to protect American citizens could be evaded. Accordingly, he asked Congress to authorize the President to employ a "sufficient military force to enter Mexico for the purpose of obtaining indemnity for the past and security for the future." [35]

33a Buchanan, *Works*, X, 335–356.
34 *Ibid.*, X, 367.
35 *Ibid.*, X, 358.

In regard to Sonora and Chihuahua, Buchanan repeated the recommendations of the previous year. He likewise repeated the request for permission to employ the naval forces to protect the "lives and property of American citizens passing in transit across the Panama, Nicaragua, and Tehuantepec routes, against sudden and lawless outbreaks and depredations." [36]

But the appeal of Buchanan fell upon deaf ears. "These recommendations . . . were wholly disregarded by Congress during the session of 1859–1860. Indeed, they were not even noticed in any of its proceedings. The members of both parties were too exclusively occupied in discussion of the slavery question, and in giving their attention to the approaching Presidential election, to devote any portion of their time to the important Mexican question." [37]

Before the attitude of Congress could be known on the recommendations, and, in fact, even before his third annual message had been communicated to that body, Buchanan decided to go a step further than he had been willing to go a few months before, and to authorize McLane to negotiate a treaty providing for intervention in Mexican affairs, in connection with a treaty of transit and commerce. [38] "By this means he thought something might be accomplished, both to satisfy the long deferred claims of American citizens, and to prevent foreign interference with the internal government of Mexico." [39]

When he returned to Mexico in November, 1859, McLane found the Juárez government more disposed to negotiate. It had failed to secure a loan which Lerdo de Tejada had been sent to the United States to obtain, and it was now almost in desperation. [40] The resumption of negotiations promptly [41] resulted in a treaty and a convention to enforce treaty stipulations which embraced everything the United States had desired. For a consideration of $4,000,000, one-half of which was to be retained to pay the claims of United

---

[36] *Ibid.*, X, 360.

[37] "Mr. Buchanan's Administration," *ibid.*, XII, 251.

[38] The statement, in "Mr. Buchanan's Administration," that "the President, having failed in obtaining authority from Congress to employ a military force in Mexico, as a last resort adopted the policy of concluding a treaty with the Constitutional Government," is only a partial truth. He may have been relatively certain as to the action Congress would take, however.

[39] "Mr. Buchanan's Administration," *loc. cit.*, XII, 259.

[40] No. 54, Dec. 7, 1859, Desp. Mex. Vol. 24; Callahan, *op. cit.*, p. 146. Callahan gives wrong citation, however.

[41] No. 57, Dec. 14, 1859, *loc. cit.* The treaty bears the date of December 14, 1859.

States citizens against Mexico,[42] the United States was ceded perpetual rights-of-way across Tehuantepec, and also from Matamoras, or Camargo, or any other convenient point on the lower Rio Grande, *via* Monterey to the port of Mazatlán, as well as from Nogales to Guaymas.[43] Mexico furthermore agreed to establish ports of entry at both ends of these routes, and to allow the United States to transport troops and supplies of war over Tehuantepec and from Guaymas to Rancho de Nogales.[44] Along with these transportation privileges, the United States was to be permitted, with the consent, or at the request of the Mexican government, to employ military force for the protection and security of persons and goods passing by any of these routes; and, in cases of extreme and imminent danger, to have the right to intervene without having previously gained the consent of Mexico.[45]

Besides these stipulations relating primarily to transit privileges, the treaty provided for perfect reciprocity with reference to certain natural and manufactured products of both countries, and contained a guaranty to citizens of the United States residing in Mexico of freedom of religious worship and of exemption from the payment of forced loans.[46]

The treaty was accompanied by a convention of two articles, the first of which designated the manner of enforcing treaty stipulations in the following language:

If any of the stipulations of existing treaties between Mexico and the United States are violated, or the safety and security of the citizens of either Republic are endangered within the territory of the other, and the legitimate and acknowledged Government thereof may be unable from any cause to enforce such stipulations or to provide for such safety and security, it shall be obligatory on the Government to seek the aid of the other in maintaining their due execution, as well as order and security, in the territory of that Republic where such violation and discord occur; and in every such special case the expense shall be paid by the treasury of the nation within whose territory such intervention may become necessary; and if discord shall occur on the frontier of the two Republics, the authorities of the two Republics nearest the place where the disorder exists shall act in concert and co-operation for the arrest and punishment of criminals who have disturbed the public order and security of either Republic, and for this purpose the parties guilty of these offences may be arrested within either Republic and delivered over to the authorities of that Republic within which the crime may have been committed; the nature and character of such intervention, as well as the expense thereof, and the

---

[42] Article X.
[43] Articles I and VII.
[44] Articles III, IV, and VI.
[45] Article V.
[46] Article IX.

manner of arresting and subjecting to punishment the said criminals, shall be determined and regulated by an agreement between the executive branches of the two Governments.[47]

The extraordinary character of this agreement, which became known as the McLane-Ocampo Treaty was recognized from the beginning in both the United States and Mexico. The Constitutional government had been very reluctant to consent to the first article of the convention, and probably did so only because McLane gave it to understand that the United States would intervene sooner or later in defense of treaty rights and to protect American citizens, regardless of whether the convention was signed or not.[48] The Conservatives, of course, were violently opposed to the treaty. Both Miramón and his Minister of Relations sent protests to the United States and to other foreign countries, and the Conservative press attacked it in energetic terms. This was to be expected; but even in Vera Cruz, the seat of the Juárez government, the agreement was badly received. The artisans and soldiers in this city were displeased, officials of the national guard resigned in order to show their disgust, and the dwelling of Juárez was daily placarded with lampoons accusing him of being a traitor to his country.[49] Some of the papers of the Constitutional party supported the treaty, however, and saw in such arrangement the only method of securing the triumph of their cause and the salvation of Mexico.[50]

Officials of the United States in Mexico were impressed with the importance of the treaty. Consul Black of Mexico City, who had been for years a close and friendly observer of Mexican affairs and was familiar with the terms of the agreement, said: "Our country has a solemn duty to perform to *itself*, to the *world*, to the cause of *justice* and *humanity*, and to that of *Freedom* and *human rights*,— from which it will never shrink." [51] Mingled with this spirit of altruism, was the desire for the national security of the United States and the predominance of its influence in Mexico. In submitting the-

[47] The Spanish text of the treaty and the convention is given in Zamacois, *Historia de Méjico*, App., Doc. 6. The quotation given above is from Callahan, *op. cit.*, pp. 147–148. Article II of the convention set a time limit for the exchange of ratifications.

[48] McLane to Cass, No. 57, Dec. 14, 1859, Mex. Desp., Vol. 24; Callahan, *op. cit.*, pp. 146–147.

[49] Rivera, *Historia de Jalapa*, V, 273.

[50] These journals are quoted and paraphrased in Zamacois, *Historia de Méjico*, XV, *passim*.

[51] Letter to McLane, Dec. 5, 1859. Mex. Desp., Vol. 24, quoted with slight inaccuracy in Callahan, "The Mexican Policy of Southern Leaders under Buchanan's Administration," p. 148.

results of his negotiations, McLane declared that unless the treaty were ratified, there would be no way of preventing the continuation of anarchy which would lead to intervention from some quarter and possibly force upon the United States the "responsibilities of a general war and a conquest that few would desire to undertake or consummate." [52]

On January 4, 1860, the President submitted the treaty of transit and commerce and the convention to enforce its stipulations to the Senate, and on the same day they were referred to the Committee on Foreign Relations. They received occasional attention during the next four months, and on May 31, after being seriously considered, they were rejected by a vote of eighteen to twenty-seven. A subsequent motion to reconsider was agreed to on June 27, but it was at length decided to postpone further discussion until the assembling of the next congress. [53] All these proceedings, as in the case of the Gadsden Treaty, were carried on in executive session of the Senate and it appears that none of the expressions of opinion on the measures have been revealed; but the rejecting vote and occasional bits of comment indicate that the sectional issue was the deciding factor. Of the eighteen who voted for ratification, all were Democrats and fourteen were from the South. The negative vote numbered twenty-three northern and four southern, twenty-one Republicans and six Democratic Senators. [54] The New York *Tribune* declared the treaty a plot of the slave interests to extend their territory and to augment their population; it was opposed by the *National Intelligencer* and the *Boston Courier;* and F. P. Blair in a letter to Crittenden expressed the belief that its main purpose was to promote the expansion of southern institutions. [55]

The attempt to settle the Mexican difficulties had therefore failed, and as on former occasions, the President and his Cabinet were now left to face the European danger without a definite declaration of Congress regarding American policy. What attitude would be assumed? Near the close of the year of 1858 and before the sentiments of Congress regarding the treaty had become known, Dodge,

[52] No. 57, Dec. 14, 1859, Mex. Desp., Vol. 24, quoted in Callahan's "Evolution of Seward's Mexican Policy," p. 11, but with incorrect citation.

[53] *Sen. Ex. Journal*, XI, 115 ff.; Wilson, "Buchanan's Proposed Intervention in Mexico," pp. 696–697.

[54] The list is given by Wilson, *op. et loc. cit.*, but his count does not correspond to his list.

[55] *Ibid.*, pp. 698–699. Those who feared the political power of the Catholics in the United States may have hesitated because of the anti-Church politics of Juarez.

United States Minister to Spain, had been instructed to the effect that the United States would not "consent to the subjugation of any of the Independent states of this continent by European powers, nor to the exercise of a protectorate over them, nor to any other direct political influences [designed] to control their policy or institutions." [56] In March, 1860, McLane, who had become vexed at the dilatory policy of the Senate, urged that the Legation should be withdrawn from Mexico in case the treaty was finally rejected.[57] In reply to this communication, Cass said that he did not believe that England and France contemplated interference for the purpose of influencing the political destiny of Mexico, and that all nations had a right to intervene for the purpose of redressing outrages and injuries perpetrated against their citizens.[58]

In July, 1860, Lord Lyons attempted to induce the United States to join England and France in addressing identical notes to the Conservative and the Liberal governments, asking them to arrange some method of settling their difficulties; but the State Department replied that the United States was opposed to the interference of other powers in the domestic affairs of the independent nations of the New World, and especially of Mexico, and communicated the substance of this reply to Vera Cruz. These two European powers and Spain had, however, already entered into a tentative agreement whereby they, together with Prussia, were to intervene in Mexico even without the consent of the United States.[59]

After news of the Senate's rejection of the McLane-Ocampo Treaty reached Mexico, McLane, probably at the suggestion of Juárez, obtained permission to visit the United States for the purpose of a personal interview with Cass. He remained at Washington during a portion of August and September and had several conferences with the Secretary of State, during the course of which he asked for instructions to make a more definite and elaborate statement to the countries of Europe. He thought such a statement would limit their operations and give encouragement to Juárez. Cass saw no necessity for a formal declaration of policy, but he declared that any attempt to establish European ascendency in Mexico would be met by the armed opposition of the United States, provided Congress should adhere to the avowed policy of the country.[60] He therefore

[56] Callahan, "Evolution of Seward's Mexican Policy," p. 7.
[57] *Ibid.*, p. 12.
[58] *Ibid.*, pp. 12–13.
[59] Ibid., p. 14; Bancroft, *History of Mexico*, V, 788–789, and notes.
[60] *Ibid.*, p. 15; Callahan, "The Mexican Policy of Southern Leaders under Buchanan," p. 149.

directed McLane to return to Vera Cruz and resume friendly relations with Juárez, and while watching every movement of the European governments, to give them to understand that the United States meant to uphold its former policy regarding European intervention.[61]

Cass had refused to give the desired formal declaration of policy, he said, because England, France, and Spain already knew that policy and had disavowed any intention of acting contrary to it.[62] When McLane returned to Vera Cruz, he obtained from the Spanish Minister a confirmation of these disavowals. He then made an attempt to secure an extension of time for the exchange of ratifications of the McLane-Ocampo Treaty; and, failing in this, he decided there was nothing left for him to do, and not only offered his resignation, but advised the withdrawal of the Legation. Buchanan accepted his resignation, but decided to continue the Mexican mission in the person of John B. Weller.[63]

Before leaving his post McLane was disturbed by a report, alleged to have been given out by the European governments, to the effect that the United States had refused to coöperate in an attempt at mediation because it desired the continuance of the civil war in Mexico. He accordingly sent H. R. de la Reintrie to the interior to deny the assertion, and to declare the policy of the United States both to Juárez and to the European representatives.[64] From San Angel, near Mexico City, on December 20, 1860, La Reintrie sent a circular to the representatives of the leading European powers in which he declared:

The United States has determined to resist any forcible attempt to impose a particular adjustment of the existing conflict against the will and sanction of the people of Mexico, and, also, any forcible intervention by any power which looks to the control of the political destiny thereof. . . .

The government of the United States does not deny to the European powers the right to wage honorable warfare for a sufficient cause, anywhere, or against any nation; nor does it deny their right to demand redress for injuries inflicted on their respective subjects . . . but it does deny them the right to interfere, *directly*, or *indirectly*, with the political independence of the republic of Mexico, and it will to the extent of its power, defend the nationality and independence of said republic.[65]

[61] Cass to McLane, September 20, 1860, Mex. Inst., Vol. 18, summarized in Callahan, "Evolution of Seward's Mexican Policy," p. 15.

[62] *Ibid., loc. cit.*

[63] *Ibid.*, p. 16.

[64] *Ibid.*

[65] *House Ex. Doc.* No. 100, 37 Cong., 2 Sess. (Ser. 1136), pp. 17–18.

Such a policy was consistent with the numerous declarations which the apprehension of European intervention had called forth during the past fifteen years; and if Seward, who succeeded Cass in March 1861, was not willing to take so bold a stand, it was not from any change of opinion which had come over American statesmen, but because the nation had become involved in a civil war which made such declarations dangerous and the enforcement of such a policy impossible. The United States at that time had nothing to lose, and much to gain, in assuming the sincerity of European disavowals of any intention to influence the political system of Mexico until its own domestic problems had been settled and it was left free to turn its attention to the maintenance of established policy.

CHAPTER XIII

MEXICAN PROJECTS OF THE CONFEDERATES

In October, 1861, the long apprehended European intervention in Mexico actually began. The motive announced by the Powers— France, England and Spain—was the desire to avenge the outrages suffered by their nationals and to force the Mexican government to live up to its financial obligations, but it soon became evident that France entertained the ulterior design of conquest.

The attitude of the Lincoln-Johnson administration towards Mexico and this French scheme would obviously depend in large measure upon the prospects of subduing the Southern rebellion and the ambitions and the projects of the Confederates towards the neighbor across the Rio Grande. The force of the latter factor has not been fully appreciated, however; and until it has been given adequate attention, the history of the period will remain incomplete and Mexican policy during the Lincoln-Johnson administration imperfectly understood. Why, for instance, were some two or three proposals of compromise on the basis of a joint war upon one or more of the intervening European nations presented to the Confederate leaders? Why the great anxiety on the part of the North to land troops at Guaymas, to purchase Lower California, and to occupy and hold the southwestern frontier? Why the persistent effort of Northern agents to foment Mexican suspicion with reference to alleged sinister designs and ambitions of the South? A satisfactory answer to such questions as these is only to be found in a careful examination of the Mexican projects of the Confederate leaders.

That these leaders contemplated the ultimate absorption of a part or the whole of Mexico hardly admits of doubt. Why the great pains to establish the principle that the slaveholder had the right which the federal government must vouchsafe to him of carrying his property into new territory, when most of the new territory the United States then possessed was known not to be adapted to the institution of slavery? Evidently eager southern eyes were turned towards Mexico. This fact was so clearly set forth in the discussions evoked by the various compromise proposals that the Mexican

230

tiate with the United States a treaty guaranteeing the integrity of Minister at Washington, alarmed at the prospect, sought to nego-Mexico.[1]

It is further demonstrated by the correspondence of the Confederate government. J. T. Pickett, formerly consul of the United States at Vera Cruz, in presenting his views to a prominent Southern statesman on March 13, 1861, remarked:

I do not deem it necessary to do more than allude in this hasty note to the immense advantages to accrue to the Confederate States in the future from the boundless agricultural and mineral resources of Mexico—as well as the possession of the invaluable inter-oceanic transit of the Isthmus of Tehuantepec. *Southward* is our destiny and we may not look with indifference upon the very potent designs of our enemies in that quarter . . .[2]

And this was the man chosen by Jefferson Davis as special agent to Mexico!

In the following January a prominent military official of the Confederacy wrote John H. Reagan, a member of Davis's cabinet, that their cause had warm and influential friends in Chihuahua and that this "rich and glorious neighbor" would "improve by being under the Confederate flag." He then added,

We must have Sonora and Chihuahua . . . With Sonora and Chihuahua we gain Southern [Lower] California, and by a railroad to Guaymas render our State of Texas the great highway of nations. You are at liberty to lay this note, if you see fit, before President Davis.[3]

For the realization of these territorial ambitions, however, the Confederacy must bide its time. While it was engrossed in a struggle for its existence, it could not afford to dissipate its energies by assuming the burden of defending additional territory. Indeed, a few months after the Civil War began, a Mexican governor who had control of two of the frontier states proposed to annex them to the new nation, asking only one thousand Texan troops and a detachment of flying artillery for the consummation of the act, and Jefferson Davis declined the offer.[4] Annexation ultimately, but

[1] *House Ex. Doc.* No. 1, Part III., 39 Cong., 1 Sess. (Ser. 1246), pp. 535–537. Romero to Seward, May 4, 1861.

[2] Letter to John Forsyth, Pickett Papers (Library of Congress, Manuscripts Division).

[3] *Official Records,* Series I, Vol. L, Part 1, pp. 825–826. Hereafter referred to as follows: *Of. Rec.,* I, L, i, 825–826.

[4] Quintero to the Sec. of State, Confidential, Aug. 19, 1861; Wm. M. Browne (Asst. Sec. of State) to Quintero, Sept. 3, 1861, Pickett Papers. The latter despatch is printed in Richardson, *Messages and Papers of the Confederacy,* II, 77–78.

other matters first. The more immediate interest of the South in its neighbor resulted from the fact that Mexico not only served as a medium through which passed the Confederate European trade, but also furnished a good market for the sale of cotton and the purchase of arms, munitions, and other supplies. For this reason it was extremely important to cultivate the friendship of Mexico, and particularly of the authorities of the Mexican frontier.

Later, after French intervention in Mexico had gotten well under way, the Confederates sought Napoleon's recognition and support by opening communications with the monarchical party and Maximilian. Finally, as the Southern cause became more and more hopeless, a new aspect was introduced by discontented Confederates turning toward Mexico in search of vengeance, adventure, and new homes.

On May 17, 1861, Robert Toombs, the Confederate Secretary of State, instructed J. T. Pickett to proceed to Mexico in order to sound out the members of the Juárez administration on the subject of an alliance for the purpose of resisting the enemies of both governments. Although he was not at that time to demand recognition, he was to assure them, in case he found them favorably disposed, of the readiness of his government to conclude a "treaty of amity, commerce, and navigation with that Republic on terms equally advantageous to both countries." Pickett was instructed, further, to feel the pulse of merchants and ship-owners on the subject of privateering and to grant letters of marque and reprisal to those desiring to obtain such; to remind Mexico of the long-standing friendship of the Southern statesmen and diplomatists; and to express his confident anticipation that the Mexican authorities would grant to armed vessels sailing under the flag of the Confederate government the right to enter the ports of Mexico with such prizes as they might be able to capture on the high seas.[5]

Pickett's conduct in Mexico did not reflect credit upon the government which he represented. Somewhat lacking both in tact and dignity, he was vigorous and pugnacious. Upon landing at Vera Cruz, he took steps to open negotiations with the Governor of that state, suggesting that this South Carolina of Mexico might desire again to assert its independence! On July 28, he wrote from Mexico City that he had established friendly and confidential relations with the Minister of Foreign Affairs. The main purposes of his mission would already have been accomplished, he thought, had it not been

[5] Richardson, *op. cit.*, II, 20–26.

for the disturbances in the internal affairs of the country.⁶ Pickett had evidently not learned of the decree of the Mexican Congress granting the request of the North for the privilege of transporting troops and supplies from Guaymas across Sonora to attack the Confederates in Arizona. When he finally received this news, he said privately that if Mexico did not annul the decree, she would lose Tamaulipas in sixty days, while he officially informed the government that its action would probably lead the Confederate forces to invade the North Mexican states.⁷ On October 29, he informed Toombs that a treaty was pending between Juárez and the United States which probably hypothecated Mexican lands to the United States and at the same time granted the privilege of establishing Northern military posts in Mexican territory. He asked whether it would not be wise, under the circumstances, to occupy Monterey with the purpose of permanently holding this city and the adjacent region. "Our People," said Pickett, "must have an outlet to the Pacific. Ten thousand men in Monterey would control the entire Northern part of this Republic. Commerce—not the sword—would soon finish the work." ⁸ Pickett's entire mission was characterized by expressions of a similar nature, and his pugnacity got him into the guard house upon one occasion. In the intervals between threats he proposed the re-cession of California and New Mexico in return for a treaty of free trade between Mexico and the Confederacy.⁹ Near the close of the year he was instructed by his government to return to Richmond.¹⁰ While returning thither by way of Vera Cruz, the presence of the Spanish fleet in that port suggested to him a novel idea:

The part for the Confederate States to play at this crisis is clear to my mind. Our revolution has emasculated the "Monroe doctrine" in so far as we are concerned. The Spaniards are now become our natural allies, and jointly with them we may own the Gulf of Mexico and effect the partition of this magnificent country.¹¹

Pickett's experience revealed that the Confederacy could expect little encouragement from the Juárez government. Had that government been well disposed towards the Confederates, it could not

⁶ Pickett Papers.
⁷ See Callahan, *Diplomatic History of the Southern Confederacy*, p. 73.
⁸ Pickett to Toombs, No. 13, Nov. 29, 1861, Pickett Papers.
⁹ Callahan, *op. cit.*, pp. 73-75.
¹⁰ *Ibid.*
¹¹ Despatch No. 13, Nov. 29, Pickett Papers.

have rendered any very great service; for it was throughout the
period rather a flying squadron than a governing body.[12]   But the
members of the Juárez administration evinced little friendliness
toward the Confederacy, showing rather a disposition to play into
the hands of the United States, which was putting forth every effort
to secure their friendship and to counteract the influence of the
Southern agents. As early as April 22, 1862, John S. Cripps, one
of these agents, remarked upon the "cordiality . . . prevailing between the United States minister and the Mexican Cabinet.' He
said that the animosity previously directed at the American Union
was then being "concentrated in single intensity upon the Southern
Confederacy"; that both the Mexican government and the Mexican
press were untiring in their efforts "to identify, in the popular belief,
the salvation of Mexico with the subjugation of the South; on which
happy consummation, men, money and arms would be lavishly supplied by her sister Republic in vindication of the national integrity
of Mexico so intimately enlaced with assertions of the Monroe
Doctrine." [13]   Somewhat later Hamilton P. Bee, a citizen of Texas
and well informed on the Mexican situation, declared that owing
to the influence of Thomas Corwin, the Minister of the United
States, the tone of the Juárez government had been hostile to the
Southern cause, and various annoying and injurious measures had
been initiated. They had "decreed martial law on their frontiers,
forbid the export or import of any article whatsoever from Texas,
and closed their custom-houses." [14]

When it became obviously useless to expect encouragement from
Juárez, Confederate leaders looked elsewhere in Mexico for aid.
The three considerations which they were most desirous of obtaining
were arms and supplies, the extradition of criminals and deserters,
and the nullification of the privilege of the United States to transport troops over Mexican territory.   Since the bonds of the Mexican
Union were extremely weak, they pursued the course which immediately recommended itself and began negotiations with the frontier
leaders.

The most influential man in northern Mexico was Santiago
Vidaurri. He had united Coahuila and Nuevo León under his sway,
and the weakness of the Mexican central government, together with
his wide popularity, enabled him to wield great influence in his
own and neighboring states.[15]   In 1861, he was nominally a sup-

[12] Bancroft, *Mexico*, VI, 54 ff.
[13] Despatch to the Confederate Secretary of State, Pickett Papers.
[14] *Of. Rec.* I, XV, 881–882.
[15] Bancroft, *Mexico*, V, 698, 705, *passim*.

porter of Juárez, but he had for years been dominated by the ambition to establish a so-called Republic of Sierra Madre in northern Mexico. The value of the friendship of such a man soon became apparent.

Vidaurri had first been approached, however, in the interest of border security before the value of the region under his control as a source of supplies for the Confederacy had been fully realized. Soon after the establishment of the Montgomery government, the Governor of Texas and the Texan delegation in the Confederate Congress had urged upon Davis the importance of this matter, alleging that failure to protect this frontier would increase the adherents of Sam Houston who cherished the idea of establishing Texas as an independent republic. In deference to these representations, Juan A. Quintero, a native of Cuba who had spent several years in Mexico and knew Vidaurri personally, was dispatched to Monterey to request in forceful terms the coöperation of this chief in putting down the lawless bands along the frontier.[16]

When Quintero returned to Richmond, he reported that Vidaurri was not only ready to comply with the request regarding the protection of the international border, but that he was anxious to ally himself with the Confederacy, and even to annex to the new nation the states under his control. At the same time the importance of northern Mexico as a market began to be observed. It was accordingly decided to confer upon Quintero a more permanent commission to Vidaurri's government.

On September 3, Quintero was instructed to establish friendly relations with the Governor of Nuevo León and Coahuila; to express the gratification of the President upon learning of the amicable disposition of that and adjacent Mexican states; to inquire as to the possibility of securing arms and ammunition; and to seek to induce Vidaurri to interfere in the proposed transportation of munitions and troops of the United States across Mexican territory. Quintero was not, however, to take any steps for the time being with regard to the proposed union of the Confederate states with those under Vidaurri's control.[17]

Upon his arrival at Monterey, the agent of the South was once more cordially received. He had little trouble in obtaining from Vidaurri the promise that he would not only protest against and oppose the passage of troops of the United States through Nuevo León and Coahuila, but that he would address communications to

[16] Toombs to Quintero, May 22, 1861, Pickett Papers.
[17] Richardson, *op. cit.*, II, 77–81.

the Governors of other frontier Mexican states urging them to take similar action.[18] During the next three years Quintero resided at the Nuevo León capital where he was permitted to purchase lead, sulphur, copper, and saltpeter for the South and to lend his able assistance to the very important trade between the Confederate and North Mexican states in general.[19]

Meanwhile Vidaurri was growing more and more hostile toward the Juárez government. Having at last made a complete break in the spring of 1864, he was soon forced to flee to Texas. There General Magruder of the Confederate army received him with open arms and the two apparently entered into plans looking towards an alliance between the Confederacy and the monarchical forces of Mexico.[20] It was not long thereafter until Vidaurri's friendship for the Imperialists led him to their capital where he was made Counsellor of State. In April, 1865, however, he visited Monterey, whence he wrote the Confederate commander of Brownsville that he had much information which he could not safely "submit to writing." [21]

The relations of the Confederates with Vidaurri were the most noteworthy and profitable of any of their attempts in the frontier states of Mexico. The Southern military leaders, and not the Secretary of State, negotiated with the other North Mexican Governors. To Hamilton P. Bee was given the task of preserving friendly relations with the executives which followed each other in quick succession in Tamaulipas. Brigadier-General H. H. Sibley of New Mexico made appeals to Luis Terrazas of Chihuahua and to Ignacio Pesqueira of Sonora.

Sibley sent out as his agent Colonel James Reily, who with virtually the same instructions proceeded first to Chihuahua and then to Sonora. The great hospitality with which he was received upon his arrival at Chihuahua City led him to assume that his government had been recognized, and so he informed Sibley, congratulating him on "having been instrumental in obtaining the first official recognition by a foreign government of the Confederate States of America."

[18] *Ibid.*, II, 151.
[19] Among the Pickett Papers there are some seventy despatches of Quintero, extending over the period from June 1, 1861, to December 7, 1864. A perusal of these not only removes all doubt as to the great importance of the Confederate Mexican trade and the strong influence of the South in the region, but it explains, in large measure, the anxiety of the North to occupy the Mississippi and the southwestern frontier.
[20] *House Ex. Doc.* No. 1, Part III, 39 Cong., 1 Sess., pp. 497–498; Bancroft, *op. cit.*, VI, 129–131.
[21] *House Ex. Doc.* No. 1, 39 Cong., 1 Sess., p. 509.

Reily delivered a letter which Sibley had directed to Terrazas and, having received one in reply, set out upon his return journey to Fort Bliss, New Mexico.

Sibley's letter has not been found, but from the response of Terrazas it may be inferred that the Confederate commander asked for favorable trade concessions, for an agreement allowing mutual crossing of the border in pursuit of Indians, and for opposition on the part of the Chihuahuan Governor to the transportation of the troops of the United States across his state. The second proposal was politely declined; the first Terrazas promised gladly to grant; with reference to the third, Terrazas declared in his communication to Sibley that he would take orders from the Supreme Congress and not Juárez, but Reily said that the Governor told him personally that he would not allow the forces of the United States to cross over the territory of his state even if this body should demand it.[22]

Reily had set out on his mission to Chihuahua in the early part of January, 1862. Before the close of the month he had returned. Writing John H. Reagan with reference to the matter, he declared enthusiastically that he had accomplished the entire task in twenty-one days.[23]

March 14, 1862, found him in Hermosillo, whither he had come on his journey to Sonora. From this place he addressed a note to Governor Pesqueira, who happened to be there at the time, asking for a personal interview. He also transmitted to the Governor a letter from Sibley, in which the latter made inquiries concerning reports to the effect that the central government of Mexico had granted to the United States certain privileges regarding the transportation of troops and munitions of war across Mexican territory; proposed that the forces of Sonora and the Confederacy should coöperate in the pursuit of marauding Indians; and asked the privilege of establishing a depot at the port of Guaymas, and of transit from there through the territory of Sonora.

Three days later Reily received a reply to his own note as well as to the letter of Sibley, and before setting out for his command, he apparently boasted that he had obtained favorable concessions. In a letter addressed to the Federal commander, George Wright, on August 29, 1862, Pesqueira said, however, that he had managed Reily with considerable precaution, but had promised him nothing, and assured Wright that a "step" through Sonora "by any force

[22] Of. Rec., I, IV, 167–174.
[23] Ibid., I, L, i, 825–826.

from the South under any pretext whatsoever" would be considered "an invasion by force of arms." [24] It is probable that Pesqueira, finding himself between two dangers, sought to conciliate both.[25]

Had Pesqueira and Terrazas been never so friendly toward the Confederates they would perhaps have found it difficult to extend them any effective aid; for the Federal officers of California, who had kept a close watch on Sonora since the very outbreak of the war, soon occupied New Mexico and northwestern Texas, and hence were in a position to keep the Confederate schemers under close surveillance. The Federal commander, Carlton, addressed a letter to each of these dignitaries, expressing his unbounded confidence in their disinclination to help those who were defending a cause condemned by all Christian nations; and although J. R. West reported in December, 1862, that the Confederates "plotted with impunity in El Paso [Ciudad Juárez]" and other sections of Chihuahua, less than a year later the Federal agent in Chihuahua City declared that reports of powder leaving that state for the Rebels originated in malice and were emphatically false.[26] Trade in other articles than arms and ammunition did continue, however.[27]

Free and friendly intercourse with the state of Tamaulipas was very important to the Confederacy, because the port of Matamoras furnished the best, and almost the only, means of communication with the outside world. Matamoras was to the South what New York was to the North.[28] Arms, ammunition, and supplies of every description from Europe were landed here, and then conveyed across the Rio Grande into the heart of the Confederacy. Moreover, a quantity of supplies could be purchased from the population of Tamaulipas, and it was found convenient to transport goods bought from the district farther north, down the right bank of the Bravo to a point opposite Fort Brown, Texas. To handle this important and somewhat delicate situation a man of tact and knowledge of Mexican character was needed, and General Hamilton P. Bee, a citizen of western Texas who spoke the Spanish language fluently, was chosen for the task.

Before Bee took charge of the "Sub-Military District of the Rio Grande," in April, 1862, this section of the frontier had given considerable trouble. The outbreak of the Civil War in the United States found Tamaulipas, as usual, in the grip of a civil feud be-

[24] *Ibid.*, I, L, ii, 93.
[25] *Ibid.*, I, L, i, 988–992, 1030.
[26] *Ibid.*, I, XXVI, i, 919; I, L, ii, 245.
[27] *Ibid.*, I, L, ii, 225–226.
[28] *Ibid.*, I, XLVIII, i, 512–513.

tween contending aspirants for the executive authority. The difficulties arising from this confusion soon became apparent. Before
the close of the year 1861 the subordinate commanders of the
Confederacy on this frontier complained of the destructive operations of these Mexican militarists, of the vexing problem of maintaining a friendly neutrality, of the virtual impossibility of obtaining
supplies and preventing the desertion of Confederate troops.[29]

Under the leadership of such chieftains as Juan N. Cortina, Albino
López, Manuel Ruíz and José María Carvajal, and occasionally
complicated by the appearance of Santiago Vidaurri or an agent of
President Juárez, these disturbances were to continue; and General
Bee, familiar with Mexican frontier conditions, may well have taken
them as merely to be expected. When he took charge of the
sub-district of the Rio Grande, however, he found the situation
further involved by two other factors: the intrigues of the Federal
agents at Matamoras and the unfriendly decrees of the Juárez
government. Not only did these agents offer inducements to
deserters which rendered it extremely difficult for the Confederate
officers to maintain the morale of their troops, but they actually
organized companies of soldiers and bandits, Mexican and North
American, who under the command of such desperadoes as Zapata
preyed upon Southern commerce and frequently committed depredations in Texas. And while such bands were rendering life
and commerce unsafe on both sides of the Rio Grande, President
Juárez was issuing decrees of non-intercourse with Texas.

To remedy these evils and at the same time to maintain peace
was the extremely difficult task assigned to General Bee in the spring
of 1862. Its accomplishment depended largely upon the control
of the local situation. Bee began by an appeal to Vidaurri, and
ably assisted by Quintero and the allurements of the Confederate
trade, he soon prevailed upon this leader to defy the decrees of
Juárez. The latter, determined that his authority should be respected, then proclaimed martial law on the frontier and attempted
to displace Vidaurri. This effort likewise proved futile and Bee
complacently wrote that "with the glittering attraction of our cotton
the whole available resources of Mexico are being brought to us.
Shoes, blankets, cloth, powder, lead, saltpeter, sulphur, &c. are now
coming in in quantity which will soon supply our wants."—"The
decree prohibiting the export of goods from Mexico to Texas is not
enforced on this line." [30] Having thus succeeded in nullifying the

[29] *Ibid.*, I, IV, 97, 149–150, 152–153, 164–165.
[30] *Ibid.*, I, XV, 881–882; I, XXVI, ii, 399, 434.

decrees of the national government of Mexico, Bee entered more energetically upon the task of counteracting the influence of the Federal agents at Matamoras. With a happy combination of tact and vigor he began to remonstrate with the Governor of Tamaulipas. He soon had this official coöperating with him in matters of commerce as well as in his efforts to annihilate border raiders and recover deserters from the Confederate ranks. In fact, on February 25, 1863, he secured an agreement providing for the rendition of criminals and deserters and the return of stolen property and granting the privilege of crossing into Mexico in pursuit of marauding banditti.[31] What wonder that the Lincoln government evinced great anxiety to occupy the line of the Bravo!

After the Northern army took Brownsville (late in 1863) and stationed troops along the lower section of the Rio Grande communications along the right bank of the river became extremely risky for the Confederates. Bee, gloomily anticipating that the Yankees would completely dominate Matamoras and possibly the whole of Tamaulipas, wrote Quintero requesting him to make arrangements with Vidaurri for crossing the trade along the borders of Coahuila. Fortunately they found this chief still ready to grant them favors, and Monterey now became a more important center than ever for Confederate commerce and diplomacy.[32]

While seeking to cultivate cordial and profitable relations with the officials of the frontier Mexican states, the Confederates were also making appeals to the French party in Mexico. Since Louis Napoleon was their avowed friend, it was natural to expect that he might extend aid to them through Mexico, especially if he could promote his Mexican undertaking thereby. The policy of appealing to monarchy was perhaps not entirely agreeable, but the Southerners were willing, if it should become necessary, to sacrifice their sentiments and use their "powerful friends" in order to rescue themselves from what they considered a "worse fate." [33] Accordingly, on January 1, 1863, long before the fall of Puebla and the entrance of the French forces into Mexico City, Hamilton P. Bee sent A. Supervièle with instructions to communicate with the French naval officials who were supposed to be in the vicinity of Tampico and urge upon them the advantages to be gained by taking Matamoras. Learning upon his arrival at Matamoras that the French had evacuated Tampico, Supervièle set out for Havana and reached this port

[31] *Ibid.*, I, XV, 197, 996, 1051, 1127 *passim;* I, XXVI, i, 284, ii, 67–68.
[32] *Ibid.*, I, XXVI, ii, 395–401, 567.
[33] *Ibid.*, *loc. cit.*, 142; García, *Documentos . . . para la historia de Méjico*, XXXIII, 54.

early in February. While here he had a conference with the French Consul in which he stated in a general way the importance of his mission for the French expedition, explaining that the occupation of Matamoras would enable them to procure mules and the "means of keeping alive their cotton manufactories, suffering greatly for the want of raw material."

From Havana Supervièle proceeded to Vera Cruz where he had an interview with the French Admiral and found him a "great sympathizer in" the Confederate "cause, and a man well convinced of the importance of" his "proposals." The Admiral declared that if he were invested with the necessary power and men he would not "hesitate a moment to carry out immediately an expedition against Matamoras," but under present circumstances it was impossible. The yellow fever was fast reducing the number of his sailors, some of the men-of-war having lost two-thirds of their crews already. Moreover, the Admiral said that the best of understanding did not exist between him and General Forey, the commander of the French land forces, and he advised Supervièle to seek an interview not with Forey but with De Saligny whom the next mail from France would probably re-establish in his diplomatic powers.

Supervièle took the Admiral's advice and set out for the interior. When he reached Orizaba he was detained several days owing to the recent issuance of general orders of non-communication. During this time he had several conferences with General Woll, with whom he established "not only ordinary relations, but intimate friendship." In taking this step Supervièle said that he had an eye to the future, for he knew that Woll had been appointed Minister of War and commissioned by Maximilian to organize the army of Mexico.

Having at length obtained a permit, he left Orizaba on April 10, and five days later he reached the neighborhood of Puebla where he called upon De Saligny at his headquarters. This dignitary appeared very cordial. He assured Supervièle that his sympathies were with the Confederacy, "that he himself was a Secessionist, and that his best friends were all engaged in the Southern cause." Thus encouraged, the Confederate agent explained his mission at length. Said Supervièle:

I exposed to him for the first time, in detail, the importance acquired by the port of Matamoras since the blockade . . . ; that the conduct of the Emperor from the beginning of our struggle had gained all the sympathies of our government and people; that we looked upon France as our natural ally; . . . that our government and people would give the preference to the French for the acquisition of our cotton; . . . that by taking possession of Matamoras they could avoid great expense by sending agents into the States of Coahuila and Nuevo Leon to purchase at low prices any quantity of mules they wanted, and, by crossing them on the left bank of the river, they could be driven in safety down to the mouth with the protection of our authorities; . . . that for the supply of beeves they could have the same advantages; that as for the difficulties presented at the mouth of the river in crossing the bar, we could manage things in such a way that, without compromising either France or the Confederacy officially, we could . . . in secrecy furnish them with three lighters flying Mexican colors, but, in fact, belonging to us.

De Saligny asked whether recognition was the price expected for these favors, and Supervièle refused to put the matter on this basis, declaring that for the moment he considered recognition of little importance but admitting that such a step on the part of France would have a good moral effect.

The question of the occupation of Matamoras was referred to Generals Woll and Almonte, both of whom reported favorably. But the opposition of General Forey and other factors delayed action until after the fall of Puebla and the occupation of Mexico City, whereupon he gave his assent to the step. Moreover, the mail which arrived from France on June 2 brought a letter from Louis Napoleon directing the seizure of the important Mexican ports. Accordingly, when Supervièle set out for the Trans-Mississippi Department near the close of the same month he carried a message of friendship from Regent Almonte to the Confederate authorities and the assurance from Saligny that Matamoras would soon be occupied.[34]

But further procrastination occurred and every moment was precious to the Confederates, for a Federal attack upon Brazos Santiago and Brownsville was expected at any time. Accordingly, E. Kirby Smith, commander of the Trans-Mississippi Department, wrote out (September 2, 1863) an urgent appeal to John Slidell, the Confederate agent at Paris. He called attention to the great scarcity of arms in the department under his command and declared that the intervention of the French government alone could save Mexico from "having on its border a grasping, haughty, and imperious neighbor." If Louis Napoleon ever intended to intervene, now was the time for him to take the right bank of the Rio Grande in order to keep open to the Confederates the only channel for the introduction of supplies.[35]

To carry this letter to Slidell, Supervièle was chosen. He was instructed first to proceed to Mexico in order to secure the release of certain vessels laden with arms designed for the Confederacy

[34] Of. Rec., I, XXVI, ii, 140–151.
[35] Ibid., I, XXII, ii, 993–994.

and now held by the French authorities under the impression that they were being imported by Juárez. If he should become convinced while in Mexico that the Admiral of the French Navy was still friendly, he should hand Smith's letter to him "for perusal." In case he found that there was an official in Mexico with power independently to control the movements of the army, he was directed to show the letter to him also. He was then to proceed to France.[36]

When Supervièle finally reached Paris in December, 1863, the forces of the United States had already occupied Brownsville. Vicksburg had been taken, the battle of Gettysburg had been fought, and the Federal authorities had at last concluded that they could afford to take this long-contemplated step. Scarcity of troops and indisposition to come into close contact with the Northern forces were perhaps the decisive factors in occasioning French delay to send troops to the lower basin of the Rio Grande.[37] It would be interesting to speculate as to what influence the occupation of Matamoras by the French in the early spring of 1863 would have had upon the course of the civil war, but there is no space for speculation here. The plain fact of history is that the French did not occupy that city until the Northern forces had come and gone, and that when they did, they entered into most cordial relations with the Confederates.[38]

Meantime, the State Department of the Confederacy made overtures to the Mexican Imperialists. In December, 1863, a confidential agent of Almonte, now head of the Imperial government in Mexico, called upon Quintero in Monterey and informed him that the Regent had already suggested to Napoleon the advisability of recognizing the Confederacy and was now anxiously awaiting the arrival of a commissioner from the South. The communication of these facts led Judah P. Benjamin, who had now become Confederate Secretary of State, to send William Preston as Envoy Extraordinary and Minister Plenipotentiary to Mexico. He was instructed (January, 1864) to ascertain whether he would at once be received as the accredited ambassador of an independent government. Upon the arrival of Maximilian he was to propose a treaty of alliance of ten years' duration for mutual defense against the United States. A treaty of amity and commerce was to be effected, also, and likewise a free passage across Sonora and Chihuahua to the Pacific. When the new Emperor arrived, however, he gave no intimation of

[36] *Ibid.*, I, XXVI, ii, 308–309.
[37] *Ibid.*, I, LIII, *Supplement*, 960–961.
[38] *Post*, p. 246.

a desire for official relations with the Confederacy, and Preston was at length recalled.[39]

Maximilian was no doubt influenced in this course of action by Louis Napoleon. The Minister of the Juárez government at Washington and the Minister of the United States in France had kept Seward well informed, and his constant watch over, and protest against, Napoleon's actions had led the French ruler to assume an attitude of cautious duplicity very exasperating to the Confederate Secretary of State. In fact, Benjamin virtually despaired of Imperial aid after June, 1864.[40]

But the compatriots of Benjamin west of the Mississippi were not so easily discouraged. They probably did not expect either Louis Napoleon or his tool, Maximilian, openly to recognize their government so long as there was a possibility of the North acquiescing in France's Mexican enterprise, but at the same time they felt that when once the French and their Mexican allies were convinced of the irrevocable hostility of the United States to Maximilian's empire, they might then be led to accept the assistance offered by the Confederacy. At any rate they were determined to make a last desperate appeal in the hope of securing an alliance and, failing in that, of obtaining homes and employment south of the Rio Grande.

Accordingly, in February, 1865, General Kirby Smith instructed Robert Rose, to whom he was granting a permit to cross the border on private business, to make known to Maximilian his intention, in the event that a catastrophe should befall the Confederacy, to seek refuge at the Imperial court. Smith suggested further, and with the idea that Rose would use his suggestions for what they were worth, that his influence might be of considerable value to His Majesty's government in inducing intelligent and daring soldiers of the South to espouse Maximilian's cause in case of a collision with the United States, or at any rate to settle in and strengthen his empire.[41] In keeping with this same general purpose, Brigadier-General James E. Slaughter, of the Western Sub-District of Texas, turned over to one of the Imperialist commanders of the line of the Bravo all the correspondence relating to the Lew Wallace scheme for the reconciliation of the Confederate states by means of a joint expedition against the French forces in Mexico.[42]   And on May 2,

[39] Richardson, *Messages and Papers of the Confederacy*, II, 611–613, *passim*. Several of Preston's despatches may be found in the Pickett Papers.

[40] *Ibid.*, III, 675; Pierce Butler, *Judah P. Benjamin*, 341–342.

[41] *Of. Rec.*, I, XLVIII, i, 1358–1359.

[42] García, *Documentos*, XXVII, 30–38, 68–70, *passim*.   See *post* p. 266.

after the news of Robert E. Lee's surrender had probably already reached him, Smith developed his plans more fully. He instructed Rose while disclaiming diplomatic capacity, to give assurance to the Imperial authorities that the Confederates desired to enter into a liberal agreement "for mutual protection from their common enemy." Smith declared that evidence from many sources clearly revealed that the North was looking with "jealous eyes upon the neighboring empire of Mexico" and meditating a "blow aimed for its destruction." And, lastly, he ventured to suggest that the gallant troops under his command, some anxious to render military service in return for homes, others ready to "rally around any flag" promising to "lead them to battle against their former foe, . . . would be of inestimable value" to the Imperial cause.[43]

For some time after the surrender of Lee the Confederates west of the Mississippi expected President Davis to flee to Texas; and they accordingly attempted to organize an army of 15,000 at the town of Marshall, in that state. Davis was perhaps expected to place himself at the head of this force and put it at the disposition of Maximilian. When these plans miscarried, however, and Smith was forced to surrender the Trans-Mississippi Department, the soldiers managed to retain their guns and considerable ammunition. Thus supplied, they returned home boasting that there would still be a day of reckoning for the North.

In the course of the next few months some three or four thousand of these disbanded Confederate soldiers made their way into Mexico, where they continued their appeal to the Imperial authorities.[44] Recently there has come to light the somewhat daring proposal of one of these refugees who had found service in the French army. In a letter marked confidential but bearing no date, A. W. Tewell [Terrell] [45] submitted a plan to Count Noüe of Bazaine's staff. Before coming directly to the point, Terrell expressed his admiration for the "flag of the great French nation" and intimated that he still clung to the idea of delivering the South. He then asked, in view of the diplomatic complications which had kept him inactive for the "last month," to be granted the following favors:

1st.—Permit me publicly to dissolve my connection with the French army. The news of that connection has perhaps reached the United States, and the

[43] Of. Rec., I, XLVIII, ii, 1292–1293.

[44] Ibid., loc. cit., i, 297–303, ii, 775.

[45] The writer's account of his career in the army, his statement that he was a lawyer, the well-known fact that Judge Terrell went to Mexico immediately after the surrender of his department, all point to him as the author. The double "r" could easily be mistaken for a "w."

fact that my connection with the French Government has ceased to exist should be publicly known to prevent Yankee suspicion of my future purposes.

2nd.—Furnish me with six months' pay and permit me to go to the Capitol of Texas [where no oath will be required of me by my former law partner and friend, Governor A. J. Hamilton]. Through the Governor of that State I can obtain accurate information of the plans and purposes of the Yankee Government at all times, and can obtain the earliest information of every secret filibusterous enterprise intended for Mexico.

. . . Should war begin between France and the United States I would be on the ground, and would fall on the right flank of the Yankee force on the Rio Grande in 30 days with from 2 to 4000 cavalry and open communication with your forces at Piedras Negras or Monterrey.

. . . My brigade *was never surrendered* but *disbanded* by me, each soldier taking home an Enfield rifle and 100 rounds of ammunition, they were ordered by me to keep their arms concealed.

In the event of war I could reassemble them in 20 days.[46]

These Confederate overtures to the Imperialists met with considerable encouragement. Tomás Mejía, one of the commanders of the forces of the French party in northern Mexico, seems to have entered into a quasi-alliance with them; and there appears to have been a general understanding that the "Confederate Government and authorities would use all their efforts to continue and perpetuate the most friendly relations with the Imperial Government," treating with "every consideration" the vessels sailing under its flag in Confederate waters, while, in return for these favors, the officials of Maximilian were to permit "all the arms, ammunitions, and supplies of war the Confederates desired to be introduced and passed." Moreover, reports of plans for a more extensive and significant understanding were not lacking. Quintero was said to have had an interview, early in 1865, with Marshal Bazaine, and rumors were afloat to the effect that bearers of despatches from Maximilian through Kirby Smith to Jefferson Davis had passed simultaneously through Mobile, Alabama, and Jackson, Mississippi.[47]

Bazaine in fact seems to have given the idea of a secret Confederate alliance careful consideration, even going so far as to ask the advice of the Belgian Minister in Mexico. This official advised great caution with respect to the Confederate machinations. He said that while he did not think that open hostilities between the French and the United States were probable, he nevertheless deemed it wise in view of the state of excitement existing in the latter country not to furnish a "rallying cry for the popular passions." Far from giving aid to the rebels who were contemplating a last stand in Texas so

[46] García, *op. cit.*, XXXIII, 50–54.
[47] *House Ex. Doc.*, No. 1, Part III, 36 Cong., 1 Sess. 503–510; *Of. Rec.*, I, XVIII, i, 1379–1380, ii, 307–308, 771.

soon as Jeff Davis should arrive, it might even be wise to oppose their project; for a final resistance on the part of the South in Texas would be a source of grave danger to the Maximilian empire. The North was gradually disarming and disbanding its troops. In six months, if matters were quietly allowed to take their course, the crisis would pass. If, however, it should become necessary for the North to send a large army to the southwestern frontier, deplorable occurrences might follow. The Belgian Minister advised, therefore, that when the Confederates came across the Rio Grande a great show (*luxe*) of neutrality and respect for a neighboring nation should be made, and that they be compelled to lay down their arms; and advised that if Jefferson Davis sought refuge in Mexico he should be "shown all the consideration due a great character," but given every encouragement to proceed to Europe, "for, unfortunately, he could be in Mexico only a source of provocation, a centre of conspiracy. . . ."[48] There were very good reasons for ordering General Philip Sheridan to the Rio Grande in the spring of 1865!

The presence of Sheridan's "Army of Observation" on the frontier and the advice of the Belgian official may have been responsible for the great caution which characterized the movements of Bazaine and the Mexican Imperialists. They disarmed an organized force which General Shelby had conveyed across the Rio Grande and surrendered to the North arms which another band of retreating Confederates had left in their charge. They apparently refused to accept Terrell's proposal. Nevertheless, the Confederate officers did not meet with a complete rebuff; for the French foreign legion serving in Mexico was augmented by Southern soldiers, Shelby's detachment appears afterwards to have been enlisted in the Imperial Army, and it was reported that another Southern officer was recruiting his friends in Matamoras.[49]

Moreover, colonization projects which appear to have been designed mainly to attract Southern immigrants were devised. Perhaps the most persistent promoter of these was William M. Gwin of California, Ex-Senator, Jacksonian Democrat, and Unionist. September 3, 1863, found him in Paris, whither he had gone after a term of confinement in a Federal prison.[50] He soon had interviews with several statesmen, and eventually with the Emperor

[48] García, *op. cit.*, XXVII, 245–249.

[49] *Ibid.*, XXXIII, 45–49, *passim; Of. Rec.*, I, XLVIII, ii, 1015, 1077, 1148–1149, 1192.

[50] William M. Gwin, Memoirs (MS. in Bancroft Library, Univ. of California), 187–199; *Alta California*, November 17 and 23, 1861; *Overland Monthly*, Second Series, XVII, 499.

Napoleon himself. The latter questioned him closely concerning the development of California, the prospects of a Pacific Republic, and the possibility of settling a mining population in the North Mexican States. As a result of these conferences Gwin left France for Mexico, in the early summer of 1864, "fortified," as he thought, "by the whole power of the French Government and the Mexican Imperial Government about to be established, and by direct orders to the French general in Mexico, to give him what military aid he might require to lay the foundation" of a colony embracing Eastern Sonora and Western Chihuahua.[51]

There appears to have been, at the time, some uncertainty as to the type of colonists which Gwin hoped to interest in his undertaking. Gwin's comments which were set down more than ten years later indicate that he expected immigrants mainly from the mining regions of the United States and British Columbia, while he hoped they might be augmented ultimately by French, Germans, Spaniards, and South Americans. He said, also, that Napoleon advised him to "abstain from all connection with the Civil War in the United States" and not to show any sectional partiality. Nevertheless the plan was interpreted as purely Confederate not only by the government of the United States and by the Mexican Minister at Washington, but also by the agents of the Richmond government itself. On June 2, 1864, John Slidell, who had been associated with Gwin at Paris, wrote Benjamin that Gwin was on his way to Mexico where he intended to establish a colony with settlers of southern birth or sympathy and that he thought the project would be beneficial to the Confederacy if carried out. During the same month William Preston wrote Jefferson Davis from Havana to the effect that Gwin was anxious to cultivate friendly relations between Mexico and the Confederacy, since his scheme depended upon the emigration of Southern men from California. In fact, Preston thought that Gwin might be expected to succeed in persuading Maximilian to recognize the Confederacy. On July 8, Matias Romero, the Mexican Minister at Washington, transmitted to Seward documents which the former considered as plainly showing that the project of Gwin proposed to "take to the frontier of Mexico all the discontented citizens of the United States living in the South, with the design of organizing them under the protection and with the assistance of France." One of these documents, a clipping from the New Orleans *Times,* was an article written by a correspondent

---

[51] Gwin, Memoirs, 224; John Bigelow, *Retrospections of an Active Life,* II, 190.

who seems not to have been in sympathy with the Gwin scheme, but who nevertheless thought there was no doubt of its ultimate success. "He [Gwin] goes out," the writer declares, "as director-general of emigration for . . . Sonora, Chihuahua, Durango, and Tamaulipas, with extraordinary powers and *eight thousand* French troops to back him. Ten thousand confederates are to be armed and paid by the empire, but kept in the above-mentioned states as protection to the emigrants. Strategical points are to be fortified and garrisoned on the frontier. Dr. Gwin's son has applied for and will get an exclusive privilege for all the railroads in Sonora. The southerners are elate and golden visions float before them." Indeed, according to this correspondent, they "seriously" proclaimed that Maximilian's empire would be saved by the emigration of their comrades who would "rally by thousands at the call of Gwin, and raise an impassable bulwark against American aggression," and the commander-in-chief of the French forces believed them.[52]

Such were the contemporary views of Gwin's plan. It is unnecessary to relate the delays and anxieties through which he passed during 1864 and 1865. His undertaking was somewhat hampered, perhaps, by the evident disfavor of the United States, but it would not be far from the truth to assert that it was wrecked by Mexican prejudice against foreigners. Before the end of July Gwin had given up all hope of success and asked for an escort out of Mexico. He had requested to leave *via* the Rio Grande in order to warn the Confederates interested in his scheme not to enter Mexico! [53]

But many Southerners were still unbaffled. Gwin had scarcely gotten safely out of the country when they entered enthusiastically into another project. On October 10, 1865, the industrious Romero sent to Seward extracts from the *Mexico Times*, a journal published in English in Mexico City, showing, as Romero declared, that Maximilian had thrown aside "all dissimulation" and made public his plans for colonizing Mexico with discontented citizens of the United States. As agents, such prominent Confederates as ex-Governor Sterling Price of Missouri, Judge John Perkins of Louisiana, ex-Governor Isham G. Harris of Tennessee, and W. T. Hardeman and [M. O.] Roberts of Texas had been chosen. M. F. Maury, ex-Lieutenant in the United States Navy and sometime Confederate

[52] *Overland Monthly*, Second Series, XVII, 502 ff.; Gwin, Memoirs, 201–224; Bigelow, *op. cit.*, II, 190, 197–198; *House Ex. Doc.* No. 1, 39 Cong., 1 Sess., Part III, 517.

[53] Bigelow, *op. cit.*, III, 122; Gwin, Memoirs, 246–248.

commissioner to Europe, had been appointed Commissioner of Immigration.

The *Mexico Times* became the organ of the project. Speaking through its columns on September 23, 1865, the promoters stated that two of their agents had proceeded to Córdova and the *tierra caliente* region and two others had set out for Tepic and the country bordering on the Pacific. They urged patience on the part of their friends, promising them that in a short time the whole country would lie out before them, where they might be as free to choose their lands as Lot when Abraham sought to conciliate him. The following week the same paper gave a list of more than a hundred prominent Confederates who had recently arrived in Mexico City; and also reported rumors that Sterling Price had "taken service under Maximilian" with authority to "recruit a cavalry force of thirty thousand men from the late Confederate army," and that the Emperor intended to assemble one hundred thousand rebel soldiers in less than a year "in order to face General Sheridan on the Rio Grande." [54]

Early in November the Mexican Minister transmitted to Seward certain decrees of the Maximilian government which shed further light upon the project. Maury had been made both Commissioner of Colonization and Counsellor of State. J. B. Magruder had been named chief of the colonization land office. The nature of the immigration expected was revealed by the fact that while Maury was authorized to establish agencies in Virginia, North and South Carolina, Texas, Missouri, Louisiana, and California, nothing was said about the Northern states. [55]

During the next few months "golden visions" once more began to "float before" the Confederates. Generals Price, Shelby, and Harris were preparing to settle with their friends near Córdova where they expected to raise coffee, and perhaps cotton and tropical fruits; Generals Hardeman and Terry, with others from Texas, were negotiating for the purchase of *haciendas* in Jalisco; Reverend Mitchell of Missouri had "already commenced a fine settlement on the Rio Verde, in San Luis Potosi." [56]

Such was the auspicious beginning, but disillusionment soon came. The Federal commanders in Texas and California rigidly guarded emigration; Terry and the Texans failed to put the Jaliscan deal through; and the little settlement founded at Carlotta, near Córdova, was destroyed by the Liberal forces. Always unfriendly towards

[54] *House Ex. Doc.* No. 1, 39 Cong., 1 Sess., Part III, 522–525.
[55] Romero to Seward, Nov. 4, 1865, *ibid.*, 526–527.
[56] *Ibid.*, 528–535.

foreign settlers, the Mexicans of the Liberal party in particular were not likely to evince a kind disposition toward immigrants brought in by a foreign prince and established in a colony bearing the name of a foreign princess. The New York *Tribune* of June 22, 1866, reported that Price, Harris, and Perkins were preparing to return to the United States.[57] Magruder, Maury, and others were not permitted long to bask in the imperial light, for that light with all its power to produce golden visions and awaken the dying hopes of the Confederates was soon to be forever extinguished at Orizaba.[58] The day for American colonization in Mexico had not yet arrived. Perhaps these projects were doomed to failure from their inception. But the statesmen who had charge of affairs at Washington during the critical days of 1865 and 1866 did not possess the gift of prophecy. To them the danger may have appeared more real than they were willing to confess.

[57] A. E. Waggner, *Life of David Terry*, 230 ff.; *Of. Rec.* I, XLVIII, i, 297–303; García, *op. cit.*, XXVII, 96–97; *House Ex. Doc.* No. I, Part III, 39 Cong., 1 Sess., 214–215.

[58] Maximilian was executed on June 19, 1867. On November 4, 1870, Thomas Nelson, Minister of the United States in Mexico, wrote that there was not "a single notability remaining out of the many Confederate refugees." *U. S. Docs., For. Rel.* (1870), p. 295.

CHAPTER XIV

SEWARD AND FRENCH INTERVENTION

THE career of the man who took charge of the State Department in March, 1861, had been characterized by an ardent desire for the extension of the national boundaries of his country. In 1846 he had declared that the United States had reached a new stage in its development—the stage of "territorial aggrandizement." He said that he believed the popular passion for domain would prove "irresistible." "Our population is destined," he wrote, "to roll its resistless waves to the icy barriers of the North, and to encounter oriental civilization on the shores of the Pacific. The monarchs of Europe are to have no rest while they have a colony on this continent." This idea he repeated in 1850 and again in 1852. While making a tour of the western states in 1860 he said at Detroit that the annexation of "New Brunswick, Nova Scotia and Canada, what remains of Mexico, all of the West Indies and Central America" would be "very desirable." At St. Paul during the same tour he predicted that Russian America and Canada would one day form a part of the Union, and that "convulsions," "rapid decay," and "dissolution" within the Spanish American states were but the "preparatory stage for their reorganization in [to] free, equal and self-governing members of the United States of America." Indeed, his son and biographer says that one of Seward's favorite topics of conversation was his desire to extend his country "up to the pole and down to the tropics"; and a re-reading of his published letters and speeches will reveal that one of his stock arguments against slavery was that it tended to delay or prevent national expansion.

It does not appear strange, therefore, in the light of his previous record, that he should be seized by the impulse to adopt a defiantly aggressive policy when he assumed the rôle of Secretary of State and confronted the prospect of a disrupted Union and a general campaign of European interference in the American states. His advice to Lincoln in his now familiar "Thoughts" is worth quoting in connection with these expansionist tendencies. He said:

I would demand explanations from Spain and France, categorically, at once. I would seek explanations from Great Britain and Russia, and send agents

into Canada, Mexico, and Central America, to rouse a vigorous continental
spirit of independence on this continent against European intervention.

And, if satisfactory explanations are not received from Spain and France,
Would convene congress and declare war against them.

It was thus that he proposed to meet the crisis. He would heal a
local quarrel by a "continental crusade . . . , smother a domestic
insurrection" by a "war of conquest, . . . supplant the slavery
question by the Monroe Doctrine," and perhaps ultimately change
a "threatened dismemberment of the Union into the triumphant
annexation of Canada, Mexico, and the West Indies!" And one
familiar with Seward's career will find no reason to be startled at
this proposal. He did not hate slavery more than he loved expansion.[1]

Seward's official correspondence during the spring of 1861 has
something of the tone and the purpose of these "Thoughts." On
April 2, he sent Señor Tassara, the Spanish Minister at Washington,
a strong protest against Spain's action in Santo Domingo. "This
reported attempt," said Seward, "cannot fail to be taken as a first
step in a policy of armed intervention by the Spanish government in
the American countries which once constituted Spanish America,
but have since achieved their independence." Seward then reminded Tassara that the United States had adhered to the policy
of respect for the title of Spain to Cuba largely because it had expected the Catholic Kingdom not to become an aggressive neighbor;
and, referring to alleged plans of the Spanish government to reconquer Santo Domingo, he concluded in the following vigorous manner:

I am directed to inform you and also the government of His Catholic
Majesty in a direct manner, that, if they should be found to have received
at any time the sanction of that government, the President will be obliged
to regard them as manifesting an unfriendly spirit toward the United States,
and to meet the further prosecution of enterprises of that kind in regard to
either the Dominican republic or any other part of the American continent
or islands with a prompt, persistent and if possible, effective resistance.[2]

[1] Seward, *Works* (Baker ed. of 1887–1890), I, 109, III, 109, 409, IV, 311–312,
333, 399; Frederick W. Seward, *Seward at Washington,* III, 372; Nicolay and
Hay, *Abraham Lincoln,* III, 445–447.
Seward argued (1) that slavery tended to create dislike for the United
States abroad and therefore to prevent the voluntary entry into the union of
the other states and provinces of the New World; (2) that the slave states
deprived the federal government of the funds necessary for a strong army
and navy by their opposition to a high tariff; (3) that the fight for a balance
in the Senate caused the North to object to expansion to the south and the
South to object to expansion toward the north, thus bringing about a deadlock.
[2] As quoted in Callahan, "Evolution of Seward's Mexican Policy," pp. 19–20.

Seward immediately communicated with the Ministers of Mexico, Guatemala, Salvador, Nicaragua, Costa Rica, Honduras, and New Granada and confidentially enclosed a copy of this note to Tassara. In the letter to Romero, which may be taken as typical, he said: "The President suggests that you bring this subject to the government of Mexico to the end that it may adopt such measures in this exigency as the safety and the welfare of the respective states existing on the American continent, and its islands, including perhaps Mexico, shall seem to require." [3]

In line with the same general policy, also, were the instructions to Thomas Corwin, who was sent out as Minister to Mexico in April, 1861. Corwin was directed, among other things, not to press for a settlement of claims against Mexico, but to call attention to the dangerously aggressive designs of the Confederacy and of Europe; to give assurance of the desire of the United States that Mexico should "retain its complete integrity and independence"; to oppose any recognition of the Confederacy; and, lastly, to endeavor to impress upon Mexican statesmen the idea that the struggle which the United States was then waging for the integrity of a republican nation was of great concern to every American state, since they all were trying out the republican experiment. In this latter connection Seward took occasion to remark that the American states "in some respects hold a common attitude and relation towards all other nations. . . . It is the interest of them all to be friends as they are neighbors, and to mutually maintain and support each other so far as may be consistent with the individual sovereignty which each of them rightly enjoys, equally against all disintegrating agencies within and foreign influences or power without their borders." [4]

Moreover, there was something of his early audacity in his despatch to Corwin regarding alleged Confederate designs upon Lower California, Sonora, and Chihuahua. After notifying the American envoy that the commanders of the land and naval forces of the United States on the Pacific were to be authorized to prevent this threatened violation of Mexican territory and sovereignty, Seward directed him to stimulate the government of Mexico to an energetic effort in defense of its sovereignty, to ask consent for the intervention of the forces of the United States if they should be needed, to assure Mexico that his government was not desirous of acquiring Mexican soil, but to make known its willingness to pur-

[3] Note of April 2, quoted in *op. et loc. cit.*
[4] Seward to Corwin, No. 2, April 6, 1861, Mex. Inst., Vol. 17.

chase "Lower California or any part of it in preference to seeing it
inevitably fall into the hands of the insurrectionary party of this
country by purchase or conquest." [5]

But the extremely critical state of the Union after the first battle
of Bull Run, and perhaps the tempering influence of Lincoln's
moderation, soon transformed this perilous impetuosity into the
sagacious sobriety of a great statesman. One of the earliest indications of the change which was coming over Seward appears in his
instructions to Corwin with reference to the defiant manifesto which
La Reintrie had issued on December 29, 1860.[6] In this connection
Seward said:

> I am very sure that this Government cherishes the actual independence of
> Mexico as a cardinal object to the exclusion of all foreign political inter-
> vention, . . . yet the present moment does not seem to me an opportune one
> for formal reassurance of the policy of the Government to foreign nations.
> Prudence requires that in order to surmount the evils of faction at home we
> should not unnecessarily provoke debates with foreign countries, but rather
> repair as speedily as possible the prestige which those evils have impaired.[7]

Thus the Secretary of State was gradually assuming an attitude
of cautious moderation. His proposal of a loan to Mexico based
upon securities which would probably have led to the absorption
of another portion of her territory was to mark the end of the earlier
phase of his aggressive policy.

This proposed Mexican loan possesses an element of Seward's
early aggressiveness and, like the Forsyth convention of 1857, con-
stitutes another precedent for the more recent Caribbean policy
of the United States. It should therefore not be passed over in
silence. One of the important motives behind it was the desire to
remove what appeared to be a strong provocation for European
intervention in Mexico; namely, the decree of the Mexican government (dated July 17, 1861) suspending payments on the foreign debt.
This could be accomplished either directly or indirectly. Seward
preferred the former mode and instructed Corwin accordingly.
The American envoy was authorized to negotiate a treaty providing
for the assumption by the United States of the payment of the
interest at three per cent upon the funded debt of Mexico

. . . for the term of five years from the date of the decree recently issued
by the government of Mexico suspending such payment, provided that that

[5] No. 8, June 3, 1861, *ibid.*
[6] *Ante*, p. 228.
[7] No. 16, Aug. 24, 1861, Mex. Inst., Vol. 17. Printed in *House Ex. Doc.* No.
100, 37 Cong., 2 Sess., (Ser. 1136), p. 19.

government will pledge to the United States its faith for the reimbursement of the money so to be paid, with six per cent. interest thereon, to be secured by a specific lien upon all the public lands and mineral rights in the several Mexican States of Lower California, Chihuahua, Sonora, and Sinaloa, the property so pledged to become absolute in the United States at the expiration of the term of six years from the time when the treaty shall go into effect, if such reimbursement shall not have been made before that time . . .[8]

These instructions were conditioned upon the acceptance of such an arrangement by England and France. When these powers declined, Seward did not specifically authorize Corwin to negotiate a loan on any other basis. He permitted him to proceed with the negotiation, however, and submitted the resulting treaty to the Senate.

Whatever stipulation it might include as to the application of the funds granted, the projected loan appeared to Corwin to have far-reaching possibilities; and this envoy, evidently thinking of Seward as the audacious character which he had known in April, 1861, and not as the adroit, calculating statesman which he was rapidly becoming, did not fail to point them out. This he did, however, in very gradual fashion, perhaps for the good reason that the full significance of the transaction did not occur to him at once. With reference to the proposed pledge of the public lands and mineral rights in Lower California, Chihuahua, Sonora, and Sinaloa as security for the loan, Corwin first remarked:

This would probably end in the cession of sovereignty to us. It would be certain to end thus if the money were not promptly paid as agreed on. By such an arrangement two consequences would follow: First, all hope of extending the dominion of a *separate* southern republic in this quarter or in Central America would be extinguished, and [second,] any further attempt in all time to come to establish European power on this continent would cease to occupy the mind of either England or continental Europe. If the republics of Mexico or Central America could maintain themselves against southern filibusters or European cupidity, I should not desire either to intermeddle in their concerns or add any of their territory to ours, except, perhaps, Lower California, which may become indispensable to the protection of our Pacific possessions.

The reasons, however, for a departure from this rule, arising out of our present apparent weakness, stimulating aggression, as well by filibusters as Europeans, seem to demand serious consideration. The United States are the only safe guardians of the independence and true civilization of this continent. It is their mission, and they should fulfil it.[9]

Then in the fall of 1861 when a supposed projected Confederate seizure of Northern Mexico was giving him considerable uneasiness,

[8] Seward to Corwin, No. 17, Sept. 2, 1861, *House Ex. Doc.* No. 100, p. 22.
[9] No. 3, July 29, 1861, *ibid.*, pp. 15–16.

Corwin revealed another significant feature of the loan project. He maintained that the holding of a mortgage on the public lands of the Aztec republic would justify the United States in meeting the rebels on these lands and assisting Mexico to expel them.[10] And this he did at the very time that the Mexican government was giving its consent to the mortgaging of the public domain, mineral rights, and church property throughout the entire republic to the United States. By this logic the United States would have been at liberty to expel an enemy from any part of Mexico!

Again, writing early in the following year with respect to the anticipated procedure of the Board of Commissioners which according to the loan treaty was to take charge of the pledged lands, Corwin remarked enthusiastically:

Part of this commission being citizens of the United States, would certainly attract purchasers from our own country, who being dispersed among these peoples everywhere, would teach them lessons in morals, religion, and politics, which they have yet to learn, and which alone are wanting to make them citizens of a free Republic. Let it be remembered that Mexico is our neighbor, and enlightened self interest requires that we should not be indifferent to the welfare of such. We have by one means or another taken from her about half her original territory. We have done more to weaken her than has been done by the whole world besides. . . . Whilst we were fighting her and wrestling [wresting] her territory from her, England was lending her money. Hence England has three fourths of her trade, we one tenth. Is not this the time, by a friendly policy, to reverse this order of things? Especially now, when unless we extend a helping hand, Europe will take from Mexico what we have left her, and with it her right to govern herself.[11]

And, once more, in connection with Lincoln's plans for colonizing the free negroes, Corwin pointed out the possibility of disposing of some of the Mexican public lands for this purpose. He said that for "a trivial outlay" appropriate lands in the *tierras calientes* of the Atlantic and Pacific coasts and on the Isthmus of Tehuantepec could be procured, and that, in Mexico, the negro would not be subjected to racial or political discrimination.[12]

Is it not somewhat startling that all this should come from the stanch opponent of the Mexican War, the man who expressed the hope that Mexico might welcome American soldiers with bloody hands to hospitable graves? Wherein does his loan policy differ from that advocated by such avowed apostles of manifest destiny

[10] No. 7, October 29, 1861, *ibid.*, pp. 31–32. This is the date of the original. The despatch, as published, is erroneously dated October 21.
[11] Corwin to Seward, No. 21, April 16, 1862, Mex. Desp., Vol. 29.
[12] *Id.*, No. 24, May 20, 1862. *loc. cit.*

as John Forsyth, or from the benevolently pacific penetration of the European powers concerning which so much has been heard in the last few years? And does it not also suggest to citizens of the United States the recent Caribbean policy of their own country?

But the first seven months of the year 1862 were perhaps the most critical period of the Civil War, whether viewed from the standpoint of the domestic difficulties of the Federal government or from that of the danger of European interference in behalf of the Confederacy. Largely on this account the Senate of the United States refused to accept the Mexican loan treaty in any form.[13] It was therefore necessary for Seward to formulate a new policy.

Anticipating the final refusal of the Senate to ratify the Corwin treaty, Seward had already sketched the outlines of this policy in two documents whose importance warrant extensive excerpts. The first was a circular to the Legations of the United States abroad written (March 3, 1863) just after the receipt of the first definite evidence of ulterior designs on the part of the European powers. In this despatch Seward said:

. . . The President has relied upon the assurance given his government by the Allies that they were in pursuit of no political object, but simply the redress of their grievances. He entertains no doubt of the sincerity of the Allies; and if his confidence in their good faith has been disturbed, it would be restored by the frank explanations given by them that the governments of Spain, France and Great Britain had no intention of interfering to procure a change in the constitutional form of government now existing in Mexico, or any political change which should be in opposition to the will of the Mexican people . . .

Nevertheless the President regards it as his duty to express to the Allies, in all kindness and candour, that a monarchical government established, in the presence of foreign fleets and armies, occupying the waters and soil of Mexico, has no promise of security or permanence; in the second place, that the instability of such a monarchy would be enhanced if the throne were assigned to a person alien to Mexico; that in these circumstances the new government would instantly fall unless sustained by European alliances, which . . . would be practically the beginning of a permanent policy of armed intervention by monarchical Europe, at once injurious and inimical to the system of government generally adopted by the American continent.

These views are based upon some knowledge of the opinions and political habits of American society. There can be no doubt that in this matter the permanent interests and sympathies of our country would be on the side of the other American republics.

We must not be understood as predicting on this occasion the course of events which may ensue, both in America and Europe, from the steps which are contemplated. It is enough to say that in the opinion of the President the emancipation of the American continent from the control of Europe has been

[13] Callahan, *op. cit.*, p. 33; *Correspondencia de la Legación mexicana*, II, 286.

the principal characteristic of the past half century. It is not probable that a revolution in the opposite direction can succeed in the age which immediately follows this period, and while the population of America increases so rapidly, while its resources develop in the same proportion, and while society forms itself uniformly to the principles of the American democratic government . . .[14]

The second of the documents in which Seward had set forth his new policy was his instructions to Dayton after the procedure of the French south of the Rio Grande had given considerable evidence that Louis Napoleon was to be the champion of a proposed new monarchy in Mexico. Dayton was directed to adopt the following adroit course:

You will intimate to Mr. Thouvenel that rumors of this kind have reached the President and awakened some anxiety on his part. You will say that you are not authorized to ask explanations, but you are sure that if any can be made, which will be calculated to relieve that anxiety, they will be very welcome, inasmuch as the United States desire nothing so much as to maintain a good understanding and the most cordial relations with the government and people of France.

It will hardly be necessary to do more in assigning your reasons for this proceeding on your part than to say that we have more than once . . . informed all the parties to the alliance that we cannot look with indifference upon any armed European intervention for political ends in a country situated so near and connected with us so closely as Mexico.[15]

Such was Seward's Mexican policy as outlined early in 1862. It was founded upon expediency and dictated by sound common sense. Confronted by a victorious Southern army at home and a friendly disposition toward the Confederacy in Europe, and with the evidence of French plans for Mexican domination before him, he could afford neither to remain silent nor to utter a vigorous protest. The French government must be informed that its intervention in Mexican affairs was disapproved, but this must be done in such manner as to avoid its active disfavor; and, above all, the way must be kept clear for the adoption of a firmer policy in the future. Seward's course was admirably adapted to this end. Gently, politely, tactfully, he notified France that the sympathies of the American people ran counter to monarchy and the interference of Europe in American affairs. While conveying the general impression that he accepted as honest and trustworthy French disavowals of political designs in Mexico and assuming that such designs were impossible of realization even if they should exist, while repeatedly dwelling upon the

[14] As quoted in Callahan, *Evolution of Seward's Mexican Policy*, pp. 31–32. Seward had already refused to coöperate with the allies in their Mexican undertaking.

[15] *House Ex. Doc.*, No. 100, p. 218, instructions of March 31, 1862.

traditional friendship of France and the United States, he frequently subjected the French government to sharp interrogation and sometimes let fall the implication that its disavowals and its actions were inconsistent. And it is a noteworthy fact that at no time during these critical years did he mention the Monroe Doctrine. Between the danger of provoking Napoleon into supporting the Confederacy and declaring war on the United States under conditions that might have assured him of the backing of the French people, on the one hand, and that of maintaining a silence which might be interpreted as acquiescence, on the other, there lay only a very narrow path; and this path became more and more difficult to follow with the passing of time. A less astute statesman than Seward might have lost his way or deliberately turned aside; for in pursuing his course he was compelled not only to match wits with clever European diplomats but to expose himself to the criticism and opposition both of his constituents and of the Hispanic Americans whose best interests his policy eventually served.

Agents of the Spanish-American states, stimulated by what appeared to be a threat of general European intrusion in America, and perhaps also by Seward's occasional Pan-American expressions, sought to commit Seward to aggressive policy. As early as January, 1862, Don Manuel Nicolás Corpancho, the newly appointed Minister of Peru to Mexico, had a conference with Seward for the purpose of urging upon him the expediency of forming a Pan-American alliance to expel France from Mexican territory. Seward politely refused to discuss the matter with him on the ground that he was not accredited to the United States.[16] In the following March Señor Asta Buruaga, Chilean Minister at Washington, approached the Secretary of State with the proposal that the United States should take the lead in a continental demonstration against the establishment of a foreign monarchy in Mexico. According to Buruaga, Seward replied that the Washington government "would not consent to the establishment of a monarchy in Mexico"; but of course no such demonstration was made.[17] Early in April the Minister of Peru, who had just arrived in Washington, attempted to persuade Seward to sign the bases of a continental alliance for the purpose of mutually guaranteeing the American states against foreign intervention or the establishment of foreign protectorates. As an inducement, the Peruvian Minister had written into the bases a stipulation binding the Spanish-American states to the strictest non-recognition

[16] *Correspondencia de la Legación mexicana*, II, 7-8.
[17] *Ibid.*, II, 75.

of the Confederacy.[18]   Once more Seward refused, justifying himself
on the ground that the delicate state of relations with Europe rendered such a course dangerous.   The envoys of the American states
then began to discuss the calling of a Pan-American congress; but
even before the United States had been invited to send a delegation, Seward let it be known that his government would not be able
to participate.[19]

At length, having tried persuasion in vain, the Spanish Americans
resorted to compulsion.   They attempted to force Seward's hand by
carrying on a campaign of propaganda in the English language press
of the United States and also in *El Continental*, a Spanish newspaper which they had just set up.   Searching through the published
diplomatic correspondence of Seward they found a document which
appeared to be adapted to the purpose of representing him as having
pusilanimously abandoned principles long cherished by his constituents.   In the summer of 1862 the government of New Granada,
confronted by a revolution which was proving difficult to quell, had
asked the United States to land troops in Panama in order to maintain the neutrality of the transit route in accordance with the stipulations of the treaty of 1846.   Loath to take hasty or independent
action under the circumstances, Seward had asked the advice and
coöperation of England and France.   The despatch in which he
solicited this advice was now published with elaborate comment and
scathing criticism of Seward's whole American policy, and Seward
was approached by the Minister of New Granada and asked to explain his attitude.   The Secretary of State shrewdly replied that it
was not the custom of the State Department to notice anonymous
communications or careless newspaper comments.[20]   The Spanish
Americans had played their trump card and had lost.   They might
continue their propaganda, but there was little likelihood of effecting
any immediate change in Seward's policy.

While in the midst of difficulties which were being created for
him by the envoys of Hispanic America Seward was forced to restrain the agents of the State Department in Europe.   Early in 1863,
just after Napoleon's famous letter [21] to Forey had found its way

[18] *Ibid.*, II, 119–122, 153.
[19] *Ibid.*, II, 396, Romero to Mexican Minister of Foreign Relations, Sept. 18,
1862.
[20] *Ibid.*, III, 86, *id.* Jan. 6, 1863, and enclosures.
[21] It will be recalled that, in this letter, Napoleon expressed the intention
of limiting the growth and prestige of the United States by establishing a
strong government in Mexico.   A French copy of the letter, taken from the
archives of Bazaine, is published in García, *Documentos*, XIV, 8–20.

into the journals of Europe and America, Gustave Koerner, Minister of the United States at Madrid, had had an interview with the Spanish Minister of State in the course of which he had declared, unofficially, that the United States would take proper action to prevent France from establishing a permanent monarchy in Mexico. When Seward received an account of what had taken place, he mildly rebuked Koerner. Calling attention to his former policy of accepting French disavowals and assuming the impossibility of establishing a foreign monarchy in America, he reminded Koerner that the United States must assume an attitude of strict neutrality. A copy of this despatch was sent to the Minister of the United States in France with the direction that it should be read to the French Minister of Foreign Affairs.[22]

In the following September the American envoy to Austria was disturbed by indications of an early transportation of Austrian troops to Mexico, and reminding Seward of the Monroe Doctrine, asked leave to enter a protest and a statement of American policy. Seward warned this agent not to provoke an unnecessary debate with the Austrian government and restated his policy of neutrality in most explicit fashion. He said:

France has invaded Mexico, and war exists between the two countries. The United States hold in regard to the two states and their conflict the same principle that they hold in relation to all other nations and their mutual wars. They have neither a right nor any disposition to intervene by force in the internal affairs of Mexico, whether to establish or maintain a republican . . . Government there, or to overthrow an imperial or foreign one, if Mexico shall choose to establish or accept it.[23]

And, as in the previous instance, Seward saw to it that a copy of this instruction was placed into the hands of the American Minister at Paris.

Finally, even John Bigelow, the American Consul-General in France, became impatient with Seward's soft words and "charming compliments," and advised him to be more outspoken. To this counsel Seward responded in characteristic fashion that, "with our land and naval forces in Louisiana retreating before the rebels instead of marching toward Mexico" it was not "the most suitable time . . . for offering idle menaces to the Emperor of France."— "We have compromised nothing, surrendered nothing," said Seward, "and I do not propose to surrender anything. But why should we gasconade about Mexico when we are in a struggle for our own life?" [24]

The wisdom of Seward's course was revealed in the fall of 1863 when the circulation of reports to the effect that the United States only awaited the termination of its domestic troubles to expel the French from the land of the Montezumas caused the Emperor to think seriously of active measures against the power which seemed to menace his projected American kingdom. He inquired of the French Minister of Foreign Affairs whether the United States government had made a formal protest. Finding that no such protest had been made and that Seward's attitude revealed no indications of hostility, Napoleon decided that a change of policy was not necessary.[25] Nor did the Emperor depart from this decision when Seward politely declined to recognize the Maximilian régime.

It did not become necessary for Seward further to interpret his policy to the Anglo-American Ministers in Europe. A hint to the wise proved sufficient. But this danger had hardly been averted when another arose. From the beginning the Democratic and Radical Republican members of Congress, under the encouragement, assistance, and counsel of the Mexican Minister at Washington, had been subjecting his Mexican policy to an irritating scrutiny. At length, in January, 1863, the opposition members in the Senate decided upon a bold step. One of their number, Senator McDougall of California, introduced resolutions declaring that French intervention in Mexico constituted an act of hostility against the United States which it was the duty of the government to meet by a demand for the immediate withdrawal of the French troops. The able generalship of Charles Sumner forced these resolutions to the table, and during the following year McDougall renewed his attempt only to meet a second defeat. But Seward's friends in the House did not prove so strong. On April 4, 1864, Henry Winter Davis put through this body without a dissenting vote a resolution declaring that it would be contrary to accepted American policy to acknowledge a monarchy erected upon the ruins of a republican government in America.

In the face of the extremely delicate situation which this brought about, Seward once more evinced his diplomatic skill. Early in January, 1864, he had taken the precaution to notify Dayton that the extravagant views of the Capitol were not in harmony with the neutral forbearance of the White House. As soon as the Davis

[24] Bancroft, *Seward*, II, 430.
[25] *Ibid.*, II, 427.

resolutions passed, he instructed Dayton to say to the French government that the Executive and not Congress had charge of the foreign affairs of the United States; that no change of policy was contemplated; and that when a change should be decided upon France would be duly apprised. The House resolutions had caused considerable consternation in France; and, as Seward's biographer has well said, "but for such declarations as these—in opposition to the prevalent opinion of the people of the United States—it is practically certain that Napoleon would have felt compelled to strike at the Federal government while it was weak, and while he was still master of affairs at home and in Mexico." [26]

The next fifteen months witnessed the last desperate efforts of the Confederates to sustain their slowly declining cause. While they were defending Richmond, attempting to obstruct Sherman's advance to the sea, and manfully facing the enemy west of the Mississippi, they were pleading with France to allow the departure of the newly constructed Confederate vessels lying in French ports and bidding for an alliance with Maximilian or seeking employment in his army and homes in his empire. But the approaching termination of the Civil War brought no substantial modification in the policy which Seward had determined upon in 1862. As the end drew near he became more and more convinced that the wisest course would be to continue in the path of moderation and prevail upon France, if possible, to withdraw her forces without resort to hostilities. Accordingly, he wrote the American Minister in France in March, 1865, that

. . . the policy of this government toward Mexico as hitherto made known by the President remains unchanged. It rests with France to decide whether this is satisfactory. If we have war with her, it must be a war of her own making either against our ships or upon our territory. We shall defend ourselves if assailed on our own ground. We shall attack nobody elsewhere . . .

. . . All parties must abide the trial of the [French] experiment, of which trial it must be confessed that the people of Mexico must ultimately be the arbiters. This government has not interfered. It does not propose to interfere in that trial. It firmly repels foreign intervention here and looks with disfavor upon it anywhere; therefore, for us to interfere in Mexico would be only to reverse our own principles. . . . I remain, however, of the opinion I have often expressed, that even this vexatious Mexican question in the end will find its solution without producing any conflict between the United States and France. The future of Mexico is neither an immediate, nor even a vital question for either the United States or France. For both of them it is a

[26] Callahan, *op. cit.*, pp. 37–48; Bancroft, *Seward*, II, 428–430; *Correspondencia de la Legación mexicana*, III, 123–124.

foreign affair, and therefore time and reason may be allowed their due influence in its settlement . . .[27]

And, at the beginning of the following June, Dayton was authorized to inform the French government that the policy of the United States still remained unchanged.[28]

Having thus determined to persist in his moderate course, it became necessary for Seward, while exercising utmost vigilance with reference to the desperate schemes of the declining Confederacy, to hold in restraint the ever-enlarging group of his own countrymen who were growing more and more eager, as their domestic struggle came to a close, to drive the French out of Mexico. Violent threats from the platform and the press, or summary proceedings along the Rio Grande, or some indiscreet project of the radicals, might offend the French people, provoking them into supporting a scheme which they had formerly disapproved and furnishing Napoleon a much-needed opportunity of covering up his failures and regaining his popularity in a patriotic war. Such eventualities had to be strictly guarded against if Seward's pacific policy was to be given a full trial.

Two projects which must have sorely tempted Seward—because they had in them an element of that impulsive audacity which the New York statesman often revealed—were undertaken by his opponents early in 1865. Both were based upon the supposed desire of the Confederacy for territory to the south and the idea of "smothering domestic insurrection in a war of conquest." One was evolved by the fertile brain of Francis P. Blair; the other by General Grant and Lew Wallace.

On December 28, 1864, Blair was given a permit signed by President Lincoln and allowing him to pass through the lines of the Union army and return. The main purpose of his mission was to ascertain whether the Confederate leaders were inclined to listen to proposals of peace. He seems to have undertaken it on his own account and without authority to speak for the President. On January 12, he arrived at Richmond where he had a conference with Jefferson Davis. Blair proposed that the two hostile governments enter into negotiations looking toward as armistice as preliminary to the union of their military forces for the purpose of driving the French out of Mexico and maintaining the Monroe Doctrine. Blair insisted that slavery was "admitted on all sides to be doomed," that Louis Napoleon clearly intended to establish a permanent monarchy

[27] Instructions of March 6 and 17, as quoted in Callahan, *op. cit.*, pp. 57, 58.
[28] Bancroft, *Seward*, II, 433.

in Mexico and make the Latin race supreme in the southern portion
of the North American continent, and that, consequently, further
hostilities toward the Union became a war in support of monarchy
and French supremacy in America. The present suicidal struggle
was most pleasing to the Emperor and, if continued, would enable
him to realize his designs. Jefferson Davis was the only man whose
"fiat" could "deliver his country from the bloody agony now covering it in mourning." What if an armistice could be entered into—
an armistice the secret preliminaries of which might enable Davis
to "transfer such portions of his army as he may [might] deem
proper" to the banks of the Rio Grande? Here they could form
a junction with the Liberal forces under Juárez who no doubt would
devolve all the power he could upon Davis, even a dictatorship if
necessary. And if they were needed, Northern troops could easily
be induced to join the enterprise. Thus supported and strengthened,
Davis could drive the Bonaparte-Hapsburg dynasty out of Mexico,
"ally his name with those of Washington and Jackson as a defender
of the liberty of the country," and perhaps, in reorganizing Mexico,
he could mould the Mexican states so as to adapt them to subsequent
annexation to the North American Union.

Here was clearly a return to something of Seward's "Thoughts."
The peace proposals of Blair amounted to a joint filibustering enterprise designed to extend the boundaries of the United States to the
Isthmus of Darién. Davis appears to have given the matter serious
consideration, and it seems to have interested other high officials of
the Confederacy and figured rather prominently in the preliminaries
of the Hampton Roads Conference. "But," in the words of Nicolay
and Hay, "the Government councils at Washington were not ruled
by the spirit of political adventure. Abraham Lincoln had a loftier
conception of patriotic duty and a higher ideal of national ethics."
The mission, like the conference to which it give rise, ended in
failure.[29]

Before the fate of the Blair project had become known, General
Lew Wallace had conceived another of similar nature. On January
14, 1865, Wallace wrote Grant that he had reliable information indicating that the Confederates of the Trans-Mississippi Department
would come to terms with the North in order to make a joint attack
upon the French in Mexico. He asked permission to proceed to
Brazos Santiago while Blair was in Richmond, and upon his own
authority to invite the commander of the Confederate forces at
Brownsville to a conference on the old battle field of Palo Alto.

[29] Nicolay and Hay, *Abraham Lincoln*, X, 93 ff.

There he would suggest as the basis of a reconciliation the champion-
ship of Juárez, the invasion of Mexico, and the expulsion of the
French. Wallace was very optimistic with reference to the importance and success of his project. He urged that its accomplishment
would stagger the rebellion and ventured to wager a month's pay
that he would win and that "Blair and Company" would lose.

Soon afterwards Wallace was given permission by Grant to visit
the Rio Grande and Western Texas on a "tour of inspection." [30]
Early in March he had interviews with John S. Ford and James E.
Slaughter, both of whom he found, as he alleged, not only anxiously
in search of "some ground upon which they could honorably get
from under what they admitted to be a failing Confederacy," but
also favorably disposed toward his scheme. At their request formal
proposals for the cessation of hostilities were presented. These met
their approval, and Ford agreed to carry them in person to Major-
General J. G. Walker, who in turn was to forward them to E. Kirby
Smith, Commander-in-Chief of the department.

With high hopes regarding the outcome of his mission, Wallace
proceeded from western Texas to Galveston where he awaited the
responses of Walker and Smith. When on April 1, Walker's reply
came, it must have occasioned no little surprise. The peace overtures were flatly rejected. After declaring the loyalty of the states
of his department to the Confederacy, Walker added:

It would be folly in me to pretend that we are not tired of a war that has
sown sorrow and desolation over our land; but we will accept no other than
an honorable peace. With 300,000 men yet in the field we would be the most
abject of mankind if we should now basely yield all that we have been contending for during the last four years, namely nationality and the rights of
self-government. With the blessings of God we will yet achieve these, and
extort from your government all that we ask . . . .

Wallace seems never to have succeeded in getting into direct or
even indirect communication with Smith. From Galveston he proceeded to New Orleans and thence to Baltimore and to Washington.
From the latter address he wrote on May 16, that he had despaired
of the success of his project and that he was convinced of the existence of a secret alliance between the Texas Confederates and the
Mexican Imperialists. [31]

With these two aggressive schemes Seward appears to have had
no connection. Though they may have appealed to his adventurous
audacity, they were contrary to his best judgment and they cut

---

[30] Grant to Wallace, Jan. 22, 1865, *Of. Rec.*, I, XLVIII, i, 612.
[31] *Ibid.*, I,. XLVIII, i, 201, 512, 1166, *passim*, ii, 457–458.

across the course which he had resolved to follow. On February 7, 1865, he wrote Bigelow:

> You will read of projects on the part of our insurgents to suspend the present contest, or end it, by a combined war against France alone or France and England. If they come in question, you may confidently say that this government prefers to fight this civil war out on the present line, if no foreign state intervenes in behalf of the insurgents.[32]

With the close of the Civil War the forces which threatened to drive Seward from his determination to avoid a rupture with France over the Mexican question became more formidable. The platforms upon which the politicians of 1864 had come into office uniformly contained clauses denouncing European intervention and demanding the withdrawal of the French troops. The press, with scarcely a discordant note, was demanding a more aggressive policy. And, more dangerous still, was the too evident assumption on the part of the high officials of the Northern army that the splendid machine which had crushed the Confederates was to be transferred to Mexico for the purpose of expelling the French.

In the summer of 1865 this latter factor brought Seward's remarkable genius for the management of men into bold relief. After the Civil War ended streams of letters poured into the mail of Romero, the Mexican Minister at Washington, and throngs of men called at the Mexican Legation inquiring what inducements would be given for service in the army of Juárez and offering to enlist. This suggested to Romero, who had been in touch with the Blair project and approved so much of it as looked toward the expulsion of the French, the idea of securing some prominent Northern general to "direct" these emigrants and to organize them into an army, once they had arrived in Mexico. The Minister conferred with General Grant and found him not only favorably disposed toward the plan but apparently not unwilling to accept the position of director and future commander of the troops. Both Grant and Romero decided later, however, that the general could serve the undertaking better by remaining in the United States and exerting his influence upon governmental policy. Sherman was then approached, but he evinced an indisposition for adventures outside of the United States. Finally Grant and the Mexican Minister decided upon General J. M. Schofield as the man best fitted for this daring enterprise. This commander accepted the offer, provided the War Department would give him a leave of absence after it had been informed of the matter.

[32] *Foreign Affairs* (1865), III, 363.

Grant and the Mexican envoy then undertook to convince the administration of the wisdom and expediency of the plan. Numerous interviews with the President, the Secretary of State, and the Cabinet followed. Seward opposed the scheme on the ground that it would lead to an unnecessary war with France; and the Secretary of War and the President were not inclined to overrule him. At length, however, the dogged persistence of Grant wrung from President Johnson permission to give Schofield a leave of absence. The hero of Appomattox then wrote out instructions for Sheridan, who, it will be remembered, had charge of the army of observation on the Rio Grande. He directed Sheridan to place the ordnance and ordnance stores along the river at the disposal of Schofield and to muster out such of his troops as cared to participate in the expedition against the French. In the meantime, Romero and Schofield drew up a contract defining the powers and stipulating the pay of the General. · At last Seward appeared to be on the point of being over-reached and driven from his determined line of action.

But Schofield hesitated at the last moment and sought a final interview with the Secretary of State before launching out upon this risky undertaking. The meeting took place at Cape May early in August, 1865. Seward obtained from the General a complete revelation of the whole plan, convinced him that he agreed with him in purpose and differed with him only in regard to method, and flattered him into believing his talents were more needed in diplomacy than on the battlefields of Mexico. Seward said to the general in his own impressive fashion: "I want you to get your legs under Napoleon's mahogany and tell him he must get out of Mexico." He also suggested to Schofield the advisability of making a tour of inspection along the southwestern frontier in order to be enabled to represent the actual situation to the Emperor in more forceful fashion. Without seriously suspecting that such experienced diplomats as Seward and Bigelow had little need of the assistance of a novice, Schofield eagerly accepted the offer of a special agency to France. After nearly three months' delay the General left for Paris, "where he was allowed to remain and do some feasting in the outer circle of court and military society" until the crisis had passed. "The soldier had done no harm in diplomacy, where he had had no important authority; Seward and Bigelow had been laughing in their sleeves." [33]

The funds for the execution of the project were to have been obtained by the sale of Mexican bonds to American purchasers who

[33] Bancroft, *op cit.*, 433–435. Romero's interesting account of this scheme may be found in *Correspondencia de la Legación mexicana*, V, 77, 223, 265, 281, 296, *passim*.

were in sympathy with the Juarist cause. Its temporary interruption by the detachment of Schofield did not seriously interfere with this financial feature. Considerable progress had been made before Schofield left for Paris; and soon after his departure the brokers and other interested parties descended upon Congress. They found members of that body ready to champion a bill providing for governmental guaranty of these bonds. But their movements displeased Seward, who still evinced great anxiety to avoid giving the slightest cause for offense to France at a time when the Emperor was facing a critical decision between his pride and his judgment, and argued that the official guaranty of a loan to Mexico would enable the Constitutional forces to offer a more vigorous opposition to the French and therefore constitute a breach of neutrality. On account of Seward's well-known opposition and the large national debt accumulated during the war, the majority of Congress was not prepared to support the measure; and the numerous attempts to put it through utterly failed.[34]

Meantime Seward resolved to assume a more peremptory tone in his management of the Franco-Mexican situation. While formulating his policy in the summer of 1862, he had been careful to keep the way clear for a change. At this time, likewise, he appears to have perceived that the attitude of the American people might come to constitute a weapon which could be brandished at the opportune moment. The increasing difficulties of the Emperor at home and in Europe, and the impatient hostility now being evinced by all classes in the United States toward the Franco-Mexican project seemed to indicate that this moment was now approaching. Replying to Bigelow's report of French apprehensions with reference to the apparent opposition of the American people to the Mexican empire, Seward took occasion to remark (March, 1865) that "even if it were necessary on our part to labor for its removal, the traditions and sympathies of a whole continent could not be uprooted by the exercise of any national authority and especially could it not be done by a government that is purely democratic like ours." "The Emperor's persistence implies," Seward added, "that he yet believes to be certain what we have constantly told him that the people of the United States, reasoning upon preconceived sentiment and national principles, can not even apprehend to be possible, namely: that a new European monarchical system can and ought to

[34] For the various schemes concocted for the purpose of raising money in the United States and the connection of various members of Congress with them, see Plumb Papers and *Correspondencia de la Legación mexicana,* the index to volumes V, VII, and VIII.

be permanently established on the American continent and in territory bordering on this Republic." [35]

Here was the sword which Seward could flash before Napoleon's eagle gaze. The American people could be represented as straining at the leash—Congress irritated and preparing to demand action, the officials and soldiers of the heroic Northern army spoiling for a fight with the French in Mexico. Perhaps this would induce the Emperor, in view of growing domestic opposition to his Mexican enterprise and the approaching crisis in European affairs, to hasten his withdrawal from the Aztec republic. If it failed, then Seward could undertake to restrain all these impatient elements, or else accept war.

For the next few months Seward used his weapon with great dexterity. In September, 1865, after the French government had made a shrewd attempt to commit the United States to an admission that the republican system of government had not been successful in the Spanish-American states and that the form of government which the Mexican people might choose to adopt would be a matter of indifference to the United States, Seward authorized Bigelow to present to France what amounted almost to an ultimatum, but it was an ultimatum in the form of a suggestion as to what the American people might insist upon doing if the French failed to withdraw from Mexico. The Secretary of State said:

It can hardly be deemed necessary to repeat on this occasion what has been so often and so constantly avowed by this government, namely, that the people of the United States cherish a traditional friendship towards France. We also habitually indulge a conviction that the existence of friendly relations between the United States and France is by no means unfavorable to the interests of that great nation. These sentiments have survived the many interesting national changes which, during the present century, have occurred in the two countries concerned, and they may therefore be deemed to be independent of all merely partisan or dynastic influences in the one country or in the other.

It is perceived with much regret that an apparent if not a real, a future if not an immediate, antagonism between the policies of the two nations seems to reveal itself in the situation of Mexico. . . . The United States have at no time left it doubtful that they prefer to see a domestic and republican system of government prevail in Mexico rather than any other system. This preference results from the fact that the Constitution of the United States itself is domestic and republican, and from a belief that not only its constituent parts ought to preserve the same form and character, but that, so far as is practically and justly attainable by the exercise of moral influences, the many American states by which the United States are surrounded shall [should] be distinguished by the same peculiarities of government. I think it not improper to add, that although the Constitution of this government and the habits

[35] Instructions of March 17, as quoted in Callahan, *op. cit.*, pp. 58–59.

of the American people formed under it disincline us from political propagandism, and although they still more strongly disincline us from seeking aggrandizement by means of military conquest, yet the nation has, at various times since its organization, found it necessary for expansion, and that the like necessity may reasonably be expected to occur hereafter. That expansion has thus far been effected by the annexation of adjacent peoples, who have come into the Union through their own consent as constituent republican States under the Constitution of the United States. To these two facts may be added the general one that peace and friendship between the United States and other nations on this continent, and, consequently, the advance of civilization in this hemisphere, seem to us more likely to be secured when the other American states assimilate to our own.

Seward then remarked that administrations in the United States frequently found themselves under the necessity of adapting their policies to the demands of the national will, and stated his conviction that the deliberate expression of that will could usually be relied upon as pointing out a line of action contributing to the "safety and welfare of the Union." In conclusion he said:

. . . It may reasonably be anticipated that henceforth the Congress of the United States and the people in their primary assemblies will give a very large share of attention to questions of extraneous character, and chief among these is likely to be that of our relations towards France with regard to Mexico. Nor does it seem unwise to take into consideration the fact that the presence of military forces of the two nations, sometimes confronting each other across the border, has a tendency which both of them may well regret, to produce irritation and annoyance. . . . A time seems to have come when both nations may well consider whether the permanent interests of international peace and friendship do not require the exercise of a thoughtful and serious attention to the political questions to which I have thus adverted.[36]

Before these instructions reached Bigelow the French Minister of Foreign Affairs had expressed to him a strong desire to withdraw the French troops "as soon as circumstances would allow it," and ventured the suggestion that the adoption by the United States of a friendly attitude towards Maximilian would hasten the process of withdrawal. The French Minister now attempted to obtain the recognition of Maximilian as compensation for such a step. In reply to this proposal, Seward instructed Bigelow to notify the French government that the United States "are not prepared to recognize, or to pledge themselves hereafter to recognize, any political institutions in Mexico which are in opposition to the republican government with which we have so long and so constantly maintained relations of amity and friendship."[37] In announcing his refusal to the French

[36] *Foreign Affairs* (1865), III, 412–415, instructions of Sept. 6, 1865.
[37] *Ibid.*, III, 421–422, instructions of Nov. 6, 1865.

Minister at Washington, he once more wielded the weapon which had been forged for him. He informed him that this step had been in accord with the imperative demands of the American people who were not likely to become reconciled to a monarchy which had been established by a foreign army in a neighboring republic. Said Seward:

> . . . The principal cause of the discontent prevailing in the United States in regard to Mexico is not fully apprehended by the Emperor's government. The chief cause is not that there is a foreign army in Mexico; much less does that discontent arise from the circumstances that the foreign army is a French one. . . . The real cause of our national discontent is, that the French army which is now in Mexico is invading a domestic republican government there which was established by her people, and with whom the United States sympathize most profoundly, for the avowed purpose of suppressing it and establishing upon its ruins a foreign monarchical government, whose presence there so long as it should endure, could not but be regarded by the people of the United States as injurious and menacing to their own chosen and endeared republican institutions. . . .[38]

The President's annual message of December, 1865, contained a thinly veiled threat and the congressional session which it inaugurated soon revealed exasperation and eagerness for more aggressive action. Once more Seward seized upon the occasion to brandish what had now become his favorite weapon. He directed Bigelow to inform the French government that the legislative department had become keenly interested in the Mexican question; that Congress was authorized and entitled under the constitution to "direct by law the action of the United States in regard to that important subject"; and, furthermore, that while there was an "earnest desire to continue and to cultivate sincere friendship with France," this traditional policy "would be brought into eminent jeopardy, unless France could deem it consistent with her interest and honor to desist from the prosecution of armed intervention in Mexico." [39]

Soon after this despatch reached France the Emperor began to show a disposition to recall the French army from Mexico. After considerable parleying, with the view of effecting the evacuation with as much grace and as little loss as possible, Napoleon promised to withdraw the troops in three detachments, the last to be embarked by November, 1867. Seward had completed his greatest achievement in diplomacy.[40] But not to Seward alone belongs the credit for

[38] Seward to Marquis de Montholon, Dec. 6, 1865, in Seward, *Works* (Baker ed.), V, 426; Callahan, *op. cit.*, p. 70.

[39] Instructions of Dec. 16, 1865, in *For. Affs.* (1865), III, 429.

[40] Bancroft, *Seward*, II, 419.

the failure of Napoleon's Mexican undertaking. The withdrawal of the French troops was due as much to powerful opposition in France, the menacing attitude of Prussia,[41] and the dogged persistence of the troops of Juárez, supported and encouraged by the clandestine introduction of American arms and munitions.

[41] Duniway, "Reasons for the Withdrawal of the French from Mexico," in Amer. Hist. Assoc., *Ann. Rept.* (1902), I, 315–328.

CHAPTER XV

THE DAWN OF A NEW ERA

The French troops appeared to be preparing to withdraw from Mexico, and a protest from Seward amounting virtually to an ultimatum perhaps was the decisive factor in preventing the dispatch of Austrian reënforcements. But the Mexican problem remained. The evident precariousness of Maximilian's hold upon the country indicated that he must soon abdicate. The Mexican leaders would then be left to fight among themselves as formerly or else to compose their difficulties and establish order.

Unfortunately the prospects for stability did not appear to brighten as the end of the Maximilian régime approached. The constitutional term of Juárez had expired in December, 1865, but his friends had prevailed upon him to assume the patriotic duty of continuing in power; and, as usual, rival claimants to the chief executiveship were springing up. Two of these—González Ortega, a former chief justice of the supreme court, and the ex-dictator, Antonio López de Santa Anna—had for some time been in the United States, urging their claims upon the government and soliciting the support of intrepid speculators and adventurers. They were planning to seize the first favorable opportunity to inaugurate a revolution south of the Rio Grande and establish themselves in power in Mexico City.

If revolution and chaos should follow the departure of French troops from Mexico a heavy responsibility would rest upon the United States. Not only would Mexico be exposed to the aggressions of the surviving remnants of the manifest destiny school, of disbanded soldiers who had not yet found their place in the normal pursuits of life, and of adventurers and speculators of all kinds, but Europe would be likely to charge the United States with a "dog-in-the-manger" policy. It was therefore necessary for Seward to prepare for this new emergency.

This he had done in statesman-like fashion more than a month before the departure of the first detachment of the French troops. He had decided to send to the seat of the Juárez government a

Minister Plenipotentiary accompanied by the Commander-in-Chief, or some distinguished officer, of the United States army. In his instructions to Lewis D. Campbell, whom he had appointed to the former position in the summer of 1866, Seward showed that he had grasped the situation in all its ramifications and formulated a very definite policy. He directed Campbell not to embarrass or obstruct the departure of the French troops, if they appeared to be attempting in good faith to evacuate the country. He cautioned him not to recognize any government in Mexico other than that of Juárez. Moreover, Seward virtually authorized Campbell to place the army and navy of the United States at the disposition of the constitutional government. He said:

> The president of the republic of Mexico may desire the good offices of the United States, or even some effective proceedings on our part, to favor and advance the pacification of a country so long distracted by foreign invasion, combined with civil war, and thus gain time for the reestablishment of national authority upon principles consistent with a republican and domestic system of government; it is possible, moreover, that some disposition might be made of the land and naval forces of the United States, without interfering within the jurisdiction of Mexico, or violating the laws of neutrality, which would be useful in the restoration of law, order, and republican government in that country . . .

Thus far there is nothing very unusual or startling about Seward's policy. Gadsden had urged the United States time and again to champion the cause of the Liberal government in Mexico and President Buchanan had proposed to send the army into the country in order to back Juárez. The striking feature of these instructions is Seward's denial of aggressive designs upon Mexican territory. In this connection he remarked:

> What the United States desires in regard to the future of Mexico is not the conquest of Mexico, or any part of it, or the aggrandizement of the United States by purchases of land or dominion, but, on the other hand, they desire to see the people of Mexico relieved from all foreign military intervention, to the end that they may resume the conduct of their own affairs under the existing republican government, or such other frame of government as, being left in the enjoyment of perfect liberty, they shall determine to adopt in the exercise of their own free will, by their own free act, without dictation from any foreign country, and, of course, without dictation from the United States.[1]

It may be doubted whether any administration since that of James Monroe could have made an honest disavowal of all desire to acquire Mexican territory whether by purchase or conquest; and no sub-

[1] Seward to Campbell, Oct. 25, 1866, in Seward, *Works*, V, 470–474.

sequent official document emanating from the executive department
was to be couched in language so friendly to Mexico until the days
of Wilson.

Is it not a little strange that such a document should have come
from the pen of a statesman who, at that very moment, was planning
to bargain for Alaska and the Danish West Indies and to annex
Santo Domingo and the Hawaiian Islands? Was it because he
was not yet sure he would not have to support Mexico in a war to
expel the French, and was therefore desirous of removing all suspicion from the mind of his prospective ally? Possibly; but there
does not appear to have been any modification of his policy subsequently, for he frequently took occasion to warn Romero against
the schemes of Anglo-American speculators and adventurers; he
refused to be offended at the rejection of his proposals of clemency
towards Maximilian or the alleged seizure of Santa Anna from the
deck of a vessel of the United States by a Mexican man-of-war; and
he sought, by the negotiation of a claims convention, to remove all
ground for difficulty, aggression, and offense in the near future.[2]

The truth is, Seward's later Mexican policy was largely determined
by two motives; namely, the expectation that Mexico would eventually be acquired by the gradual process of Americanization which
would result from the emigration of capital and colonists from the
United States; and the conviction that "the desire for the acquisition
of territory had sensibly abated in the United States," that his compatriots had come to "value dollars more, and dominion less." In
May, 1864, he had written Bigelow confidentially that

those who are most impatient for the defeat of European and monarchical designs in Mexico might well be content to abide the effects which must result
from the ever-increasing expansion of the American people westward and
southward. Five years, ten years, twenty years hence, Mexico will be opening
herself as cheerfully to American immigration as Montana and Idaho are
now. What European power can then maintain an army in Mexico capable
of resisting the martial and moral influences of emigration?[3]

In like manner, soon after the close of the Civil War he began
once more to dwell upon his favorite prediction that Mexico City

[2] Campbell's unexampled inefficiency defeated Seward's plans for immediate
assistance to Juárez. Seward's later Mexican policy is most clearly set forth in
his interviews with Romero, an account of which may be found in *Correspondencia de la Legación mexicana*, VIII, 530, 625, 674, 786, *passim*, X, 89,
199, *passim*. Seward made a friendly visit to Mexico in 1869. (See Bancroft,
Seward, II, 519–521, and authorities there cited.)

[3] As quoted in Callahan, "Evolution of Seward's Mexican Policy," p. 52.

would one day become the seat of power of the Anglo-Saxons in America. He now told his friends that he expected this to come about in thirty years.[4] In view of the rapidly cooling ardor of the people of the United States for territory, why attempt to accelerate the operations of natural law and anticipate the work of time?

In fact, Seward was standing at the threshold of a new era in the relations of the United States and Mexico. Formerly the attitude of the Anglo-Saxon Americans toward their Indo-Hispanic neighbor to the south had been characterized mainly by an aggressive eagerness for territory, for dominion. Thereafter its most salient feature was to be a strong desire for investment opportunities and commercial intercourse, with only an occasional resurgence of the former motive. Manifest destiny was giving place to economic penetration, or economic infiltration, if one prefers the term. And economic penetration was to proceed with more moderation and tranquillity. It was not to be hurried forward precipitously under the impetuous demand for empire. It was destined to proceed slowly with the gradual accumulation of capital demanding investment opportunities in Mexican trade and resources. Nor was it to be given immediate momentum by the vivid apprehension of European aggression, for the danger of European intervention had vanished and the hostility of the Mexican people toward the leading nations of the Old World furnished reasonable assurance that it would not soon reappear. The new movement was eager for amity and peace; and it is an interesting and striking occurrence that Seward, one of the leading exponents of manifest destiny, should become one of the precursors of economic penetration.

The Mexican government, on its part, reciprocated this friendly disposition. The open sympathy of Northern Senators and Congressmen, of Northern military leaders and periodicals, the secret aid which Northern men had extended to Mexico in the critical days of 1865 and 1866, the stand taken by Seward after the Confederacy had been subdued, had left a favorable impression upon high official circles in Mexico City. From the beginning of French intervention Mexican Liberals had felt that the fate of their cause was somehow closely linked with the preservation of the North American Union.[5] Acting in accordance with this view, the Juárez government, as has been seen, had evinced an unwillingness to aid the Confederacy but had granted the North about the only favor within

---

[4] *Works*, IV, 331–332; Pierce, *Sumner*, IV, 328, note.
[5] Corwin to Seward, June 29, 1861, *Sen. Ex. Doc.* No. 1, 37 Cong., 2 Sess. (Ser. 1117), p. 70.

its power to bestow—permission to land its troops at Guaymas and march them across Mexican territory to attack the Southern armies in Arizona and New Mexico. At the close of the Civil War Minister Romero reminded Seward of the anxiety with which "the government of Mexico had been waiting the termination" of this struggle. The success of the Union, said he, "insures our own, whilst its overthrow would have made our situation more difficult." [6] President Juárez declared in a message to the first congress which convened after the overthrow of Maximilian that "the constant sympathy of the people of the United States and the moral support given by their government to" the Mexican "cause justly deserve the sympathy and the regard of the people and government of Mexico," to which sentiment the President of that congress responded with the remark that "the republic of Mexico will always reckon among its best friends the statesmen that directed American policy during the period of our crisis," and that "the principle of non-intervention faithfully observed by the oldest of the republics of this continent, the only ally of Mexico, has proved the salvation of our country." [7] Edward Lee Plumb, who took up his duties as *chargé ad interim* near the Mexican government in October, 1867, was highly pleased with his reception and the "strong" and "repeated" expressions of appreciation and satisfaction with the "course of the Government and people of the United States towards Mexico during the late long and severe struggle." [8]

Nor were these demonstrations of friendship confined to mere words. The Mexican government granted the United States army the privilege of transporting supplies overland from Guaymas to Arizona, and the navy the privilege of coaling at La Paz, Lower California. At the same time it entered into an agreement for the settlement of the claims difficulty which had for more than twenty years been a source of irritation between the two countries, no important adjustments having been made since the treaty of Guadalupe Hidalgo. [9]

[6] Romero to Seward, July 23, 1865, *House Ex. Doc.* No. 73, 39 Cong., 1 Sess. (Ser. 1261), p. 176.
[7] For the speech and the response, see *ibid.*, No. 1, Part II, 40 Cong., 3 Sess. (Ser. 1365), pp. 379–380.
[8] Plumb to Seward, No. 11, Oct. 9, 1867, Mex. Desp., Vol. 31.
[9] Malloy, *Treaties, Conventions,* etc. I, 1129 ff.
The commission created under this convention did not complete its work until November, 1876. The total number of claims presented by American citizens against Mexico was 1017 amounting to the enormous sum of $470,126,-613.70. Mexican citizens presented against the United States 998 claims totaling $86,661,891.15. One hundred and eighty-six awards amounting to

But if the relations of the United States and Mexico appeared to be approaching a state of harmony quite unusual for the two neighbors when Seward prepared to lay down his portfolio, factors which augured unpleasantly for the future were not totally lacking. The costly struggle against French intervention had, as was natural, given rise to widespread hostility to foreigners and this hostility almost inevitably tended to extend itself to citizens of the United States. Edward Lee Plumb, *chargé* of the United States in Mexico, said on May 20, 1868:

> The conviction is being forced upon my mind, by my observations here, that, whatever may be the official action of this Government or however enlightened and friendly may be the sentiments personally of President Juarez and his cabinet, there is a feeling existing in this country towards foreigners in general, to which the citizens of the United States do not form an exception.[10]

Two years later United States Minister Nelson wrote that the "feeling of jealousy and dislike" toward foreigners, including his own

---

$4,125,622.20 were made in favor of the former. One hundred and sixty-seven awards amounting to only $150,498.41 were allowed the latter. Of the claims presented against the United States almost the entire number falls into two classes—Indian depredations, and excesses committed by North American soldiers; and of these two the former was far more important. Three hundred and sixty-six claims aggregating more than $31,000,000 arose from this source between the Guadalupe Hidalgo and the Gadsden treaties. These were dismissed, however, on the ground that the Gadsden Treaty released the United States from "all liability." (Moore, *History and Digest of International Arbitrations*, 1305). The most important of the claims of the second class arose from the spoliations of the returning soldiers of 1847–'48, from the burning of Piedras Negras by the troops of Callahan in October, 1855 (see *ante*, p. 174 ff.), and from the pillaging of Bagdad by a company of Negro soldiers in 1866. Nearly $24,000 was awarded Mexican claimants because of the raid of Captain Lewis and his Texas volunteers upon the village of Sabinas Hidalgo, and 150 of the total claims allowed Mexican citizens were given to inhabitants of Piedras Negras who had suffered from the raid of 1855.

Of the claims presented against Mexico, the most common were those for the seizure and destruction of property, for forced loans, for illegal arrests and imprisonment, and for murder. Most of these claims arose prior to 1861, and have been analyzed elsewhere (*ante*, Chs. III and X). It is sufficient to notice here that the majority of them were for the illegal seizure and destruction of property; that the most important under this category were those of the Louisiana Tehuantepec Company, of the La Abra Silver Mining Company, and of Benjamin Weil, the last two of which were shown to be stupendous frauds long after the umpire had awarded them the aggregate sum of $1,152,046.94; and that something of the nature of the frontier difficulties of the seventies was forecast by the appearance of fifteen claims for the theft of cattle. (*Sen. Ex. Doc.* No. 31, 44 Cong., 2 Sess., Ser. 1720, pp. 18–67.)

[10] Plumb to Seward, No. 131, Mex. Desp., Vol. 33.

countrymen, was probably "more intense . . . than ever before." [11] Moreover, the disaffection of Porfirio Díaz and his brother led to armed contests for the chief executiveship, kept the treasury in a state of exhaustion, gave opportunity for brigandage and interior disorders of all kinds, and rendered the protection of the frontier exceedingly difficult. Occasional remonstrances from the Washington government and frequent protests and threats from the Anglo-American Southwest were sufficient to fan into flame the smoldering embers of fear and hatred which no amount of official amity, nor the kindly words of President Grant, nor the sensational Mexican tour of Seward [12] could remove from the bosom of the Mexican people. Signs of amity there were; and for a brief period these signs were general, but the amity was more apparent than real, or at best only very ephemeral.

[11] Nelson to Fish, No. 165, Jan. 20, 1870, *ibid.*, Vol. 38.
[12] For an account of Seward's tour see Bancroft, *Seward*, II, 519–521.

CHAPTER XVI

BORDER IRRITATIONS, 1868–1877

PERHAPS the greatest impediment to friendly relations between the United States and Mexico for more than a decade subsequent to 1867 was the state of affairs on the international frontier. During this period conditions on the border, and especially along the Rio Grande, were probably more unsettled and irritating than ever before or since. Texas was suffering grievously from the disorders of reconstruction and establishing an appalling record for crime.[1] Law and order had not yet been effectively introduced into New Mexico and Arizona. The Mexican states south of the international line were being disturbed by the revolutions and counter-revolutions characteristic of the section. Smugglers, robbers, cattle-thieves, and all kinds of dangerous and desperate characters had collected along the lower Rio Grande. Indians and bandits infested the region above Laredo and westward to the California line.

Formerly Mexico had borne the brunt of frontier lawlessness. For many years, as has already been frequently noted, Indians, smugglers, filibusters, and border ruffians had defied her laws, laid waste her fields, and murdered her population. But now the movement was reversed and the frontier of the United States soon felt the force of the change. Cattle-thieves from the Mexican side of the Bravo stole Texas cattle in large numbers. Smugglers attracted by the Mexican Free Zone—a strip of country some six or eight miles wide and extending northward for more than five hundred miles along the meanderings of the river—, which presented an opportunity of introducing without duties large quantities of goods designed for the markets of the southern states of the North American union, defrauded the United States treasury to the extent of several millions annually.[1a] Above Laredo, Texas, savage Indians who had their lodges in the mountain fastnesses of Coahuila and Chihuahua laid waste northwestern Texas and southeastern New Mexico. North of the Sonora border frontier settlers were frequently terrified, robbed, and killed by Indians who found hiding-places in that state.

[1] Ramsdell, *Reconstruction in Texas.*
[1a] See *Senate Report* No. 166, May 16, 1870, 41 Cong., 2 Sess. (Ser. 1409).

The first of these irregularities to occasion trouble was the tariff frauds along the Rio Grande. Scarcely had the French left Mexico when protests were heard against this "objectionable arrangement on the Mexican frontier." [2] Soon afterwards the treasury department of the United States, much concerned over the loss of revenue in the region, called Seward's attention to the immense amount of smuggling which was taking place.[3] Thereupon Seward instructed Plumb, American *chargé* in Mexico, to confer with the Mexican government regarding the matter.[4]

Plumb took advantage of an early occasion to carry out his instructions, but the result of his interview was not entirely satisfactory. Although a Mexican tariff commission had reported against the continuance of the Free Zone, which was undoubtedly causing much of the difficulty, and several prominent Mexicans, the Secretary of the Treasury included, were in agreement with the commission, the Secretary of Foreign Affairs was quite reserved and evinced uneasiness lest any action adverse to the zone might turn the frontier against the government. Nevertheless Plumb was of the opinion that the objectionable region stood a good chance of being abolished by the congress then in session.[5]

In this he proved himself a poor prophet. Congress not only refused to revoke the decree, but even debated the advisability of extending the Free Zone. News of this action found its way into the newspapers of the United States and the American Congress soon felt called upon to investigate these irregularities.

On May 16, 1870, the Joint Select Committee on Retrenchment made a "Report on the Protection of the Revenue of the United States." The report was based upon the testimony of a few witnesses from the border country who had at one time or another been connected with the United States treasury department. These witnesses were not conspicuous for a kindly disposition toward Mexico. They declared, for instance, that Mexico was a nation of grafters and smugglers, that the Mexican people were incapable of self-government, and that the only solution of the frontier problems was to be found in the annexation to the United States of the "whole country" north of the Sierra Madre range and extending from the Gulf to the Pacific. With such evidence before them the Senate Committee presented a somewhat drastic report. It advised that merchants be permitted no longer to transport commodities in bond

2 Plumb to Seward, Dec. 3, 1868, *Dip. Cor.* (1868–1869), II, 626.
3 McCulloch to Seward, Sept. 26, 1868, *ibid.*, II, 595.
4 Seward to Plumb, Sept. 30, 1868, *ibid.*, II, 594.
5 Plumb to Seward, Dec. 3, 1868, *ibid.*, II, 627–628.

to the southwestern frontier. It maintained that the United States in this way would do all within its power to eliminate smuggling. It took occasion to remark, however, that the coöperation of Mexico would be indispensable to a complete solution. Nor was it optimistic with respect to the possibility of securing Mexican assistance. In concluding its report the Committee declared:

> The hope of successful negotiation seems to have been exhausted. In violation of her own constitution, which prevents the enactment of revenue laws unequal in their effect, Mexico still persists in maintaining along our frontier a belt of territory to which goods are admitted free, while imports to all other portions of the country are required to pay heavy duty. Unfriendly is the mildest term by which such conduct can be characterized. A due consideration for the protection of our own interests may render other measures requisite to induce Mexico to regard the comity of nations, and observe toward us such a course of conduct as is essential to the maintenance of friendly relations . . .[6]

This committee report created a sensation in Mexico and brought on a lively debate over the Free Zone in the Mexican Congress. Matías Romero, Mexican Secretary of the Treasury, appeared and made the most able speech against the continuance of the zone. Romero rebuked certain members of Congress who, because a foreign nation was concerned in the matter, were deciding the question "rather with the heart than with the head." Romero declared that the decree establishing the zone was unconstitutional because it granted a special privilege to Tamaulipas, that it was no longer necessary to the prevention of the migration of the Mexican frontier population to the American towns along the Rio Grande, and that it encouraged smuggling into the Mexican interior and involved large loss of revenue to the Mexican treasury. He took occasion also to lament the report of the United States Senate Committee on Retrenchment, declaring that it had been based on very inadequate testimony.[7]

The ablest advocates of the maintenance of the Free Zone were Don Ramón Gúzman and Don Emilio Velasco. Of the latter Romero said that during a recent illness which his friends feared might prove to be his last, he had been more concerned with the zone and ports of deposit than in his own existence. In his address before Congress Gúzman revealed considerable hostility toward the United States. He declared that Tamaulipas had been saved from depopulation and ruin by the establishment of the zone. When it

---

[6] *Senate Report* No. 166 (Ser. 1409), pp. 7–8.
[7] See "Debates in the Mexican Congress," in *Foreign Relations* (1870), p. 437 ff. The Debate occurred in Oct. and Nov., 1870.

was erected in 1858 the population of that state was only 18,000; by 1863 it had increased to 50,000; now it numbered 70,000 souls. Prosperity in this region would mean an ultimate increase in the federal revenue. In order to remove the contraband evil insofar as it related to Mexico, increased vigilance over the morality of the employees of the Mexican treasury was all that was necessary. The Mexican inhabitants of the frontier would not suffer the abolition of this zone. They would surely take up arms; and if the Mexican government should attempt to conquer them they would "cross in a body to the American shore, leaving the ashes of their homesteads as trophies to their oppressors." Of course the Yankees considered the zone detrimental to the prosperity of the Anglo-American frontier, but that was no reason for its abolition. On the contrary, "that fact speaks [spoke] louder in its favor than anything my [his] feeble voice can [could] utter." Officials of the Washington government might be expected to protest against the measure and even to bring pressure to bear upon Mexico. In fact they had already approached him with "*suggestions . . . tending to the suppression of the Free Zone,*" but he had "*energetically repelled them,*" as all patriotic Mexicans should.[8]

After protracted debate in which the Mexican executive, through Romero, attempted to effect the abolition of the zone, Congress not only formally sanctioned the measure on November 5, 1870, but voted to extend it over the frontier of Coahuila and Chihuahua and the northern district of Nuevo León.[9] Gúzman and Velasco had won.

During the course of the next year the revenue question continued to attract considerable attention in the press of both countries, and in 1871, as in 1870, President Grant devoted to the dispute a few sentences in his annual message.[10] Soon afterwards, however, tariff frauds were overshadowed by other enormities which had begun to occur on the frontier.

The raids of Mexican Indians and the theft of cattle in Texas had been attracting attention for some time. Witnesses appearing before the Senate retrenchment committee had had something to say about the latter evil. At length, on May 7, 1872, Congress passed a joint resolution authorizing the President to appoint a commission of three to proceed to Texas and inquire into the extent and character of the crimes committed along the Rio Grande frontier.[11] On

[8] *Ibid.,* p. 495 ff.
[9] Nelson to Fish, Nov. 10, 1850, *ibid.,* pp. 497-498.
[10] Richardson, *Messages and Papers,* VII, 146.
[11] "Report of the United States Commissioners to Texas," *Senate Report* No. 39, 42 Cong., 1 Sess. (Ser. 1565), p. 1.

hearing of this action the Mexican government appointed a similar committee with the view of being prepared to present its side of the matter and to counteract the alleged plots of "malicious claimants and ambitious private parties" in the United States.[12]

The border had now definitely taken the center of the stage in American-Mexican relations, but more was to be heard of cattle stealing and Indian raids than of revenue frauds. The commissioners of the United States proceeded to the Rio Grande in the Summer of 1872 and examined witnesses for more than two months. They then submitted an extensive report confined mainly to the lower Rio Grande. They presented a depressing picture of conditions in this region. At the close of the Civil War vast herds of cattle had roamed over these grassy plains, but now they were a perilous and dreary waste, the herds decreased to about one-fourth their former number, the lonely ranchmen mourning the loss of their friends and the members of their families who had been murdered because they chanced to cross the path of the robbers. That the thieves were Indians and Mexicans residing south of the river was established by the unimpeachable (?) testimony of Texas witnesses and the well attested fact that 25% of the hides transported northward through the Brownsville customs-house bore Texas brands and another 25% gave evidence of having been altered and defaced. Aside from the loss of their friends and loved ones which could not be estimated in dollars and cents, the committee reckoned that the cattlemen had suffered theft of stock and other outrages to the extent of $27,859,363.97. And, in the opinion of this committee, insult was added to injury by the connivance of the Mexican frontier officials, state and national, in these outrages; for according to the testimony of witnesses considered reliable by the committee these officials either shared the plunder or, actuated by hostility toward the United States, winked at the crimes perpetrated upon the Texas border. In view of this appalling situation the committee recommended an increase of the United States cavalry force along the southwestern frontier.[13]

The members of the Mexican commission went much more fully into the frontier problem, setting forth their findings in two elaborate reports presented after they had already perused the report of commissioners of the United States. They made an exhaustive study of

---

[12] *Reports of the Committee of Investigation sent in 1873 by the Mexican Government to the Frontier of Texas* (American ed.), Preface, p. iii, hereafter and heretofore cited as Mexican Border Commission of 1873, *Report.*

[13] See "Report of the United States Commissioners to Texas," *loc. cit.*

the border troubles since the year 1848 and set forth their nature and origin in great detail. They complained bitterly of the Indian depredations suffered by the North Mexican frontier. They declared that these outrages were largely the result of the American policy of thrusting these natives back upon the frontier and virtually forcing them to prey upon Mexico for a livelihood. Compared with the atrocities thus committed against Mexico, the occasional injuries inflicted upon the United States by the small bands of *American* Indians now residing south of the international line paled into insignificance. They declared, moreover, that the Mexican frontier had been the victim of horse-thieves organized north of the Rio Grande and directed by Texans; that the losses of the Texas cattlemen had been greatly exaggerated; that most of the thieves stealing cattle from the Texans were Texans themselves; that some few Mexicans had been guilty of cattle stealing but these had been trained in this disgraceful practice by Americans; and, lastly, that American complaints against alleged outrages committed by Mexicans on the Texas border, like their complaints regarding the Free Zone, were raised with the view of finding a plausible excuse for annexing a portion of northern Mexico.[14]

In concluding their report the Mexican commissioners advised that inasmuch as the local officials of both countries had proved inefficient, control of the frontier should be turned over so far as possible to federal officials of the governments concerned. To this end they recommended that Mexico increase the national army and organize a national police. They also advised the amendment of the extradition treaty then in force between the United States and Mexico and urged that the Mexican frontier states pass more simple and effective legislation. In this way, according to the commissioners, Mexico and the Mexicans would do their part toward alleviating the unfortunate situation, but they took occasion to declare that neither laws, nor treaties, nor any other arrangements on the part of their nation would prove effectual until the spirit on the left bank of the Rio Grande changed from one of aggressive hostility to one of friendly and sympathetic tolerance.[15]

Thus it will be seen that the commissions were by no means in agreement. The Americans reported only the outrages and injuries suffered by citizens of the United States and charged the Mexican officials, local and even national, with neglect or collusion. The

[14] Mexican Border Commission of 1873, *Report, passim.*
[15] *Ibid.*, pp. 213–223, 438–443. The Mexican government sent a commission to the Sonora frontier also.

Mexicans, on their part, saw only their own woes while minimizing those of their neighbors and questioning the integrity of American frontier officials. Both groups were unfair and inaccurate, but the truth perhaps corresponds more nearly with the findings of the Mexican commissioners. A large part of the sufferings of the Texas frontier was no doubt due to the disorders of the reconstruction period; and a lingering of manifest destiny added to a desire to shift attention from internal politics or to find an excuse for maintaining the army at as large a figure as possible may have been responsible for magnification of the evils.

Nevertheless, when all due allowances have been made, conditions must have been far from satisfactory. Nor did such reports as these cultivate a spirit likely to take the matter seriously in hand. As might almost have been expected under the circumstances, neither government made any serious attempt to apply a remedy. Meantime the robbers, the cattle- and horse-thieves, and the Indians plied their trade and followed their course.

It was not long, however, until impetuous army officials of the United States stationed on this frontier began to act of their own accord. In fact their expeditions into Mexico were so numerous during the next few years that when the late President Carranza sought proof that the recent violations of Mexican soil by the United States had not been confined to his administration, he did not have to go outside of the decade subsequent to 1873. Within that period alone he was able to find some twenty-three instances.[16]

The first in Carranza's list and perhaps the first of the expeditions of this character was the Mackenzie raid of 1873. It was occasioned by Indian depredations. For several years the Kickapoo Indians who had recently taken up their abode in Mexico had been making bold incursions far into the interior of western and northwestern Texas. Their operations had been so well planned and executed as to arouse suspicion that they were being directed by Mexicans. As early as 1869 the United States had been urging upon the Mexican government the necessity of coöperation in an attempt to bring the culprits back to their reservation in the United States and the advisability of permitting troops of the United States to cross the line in pursuit of the hostiles. The Mexican foreign office had replied at the time that permission thus to pursue the Indians could only be granted with the consent of the Mexican congress and showed great reluctance to ask this consent. The Mexican government had

[16] Message of September 1, 1919.

then been warned that action might be necessary without its permission, but it had been later decided, out of consideration for the embarrassments occasioned by disturbed political conditions in Mexico, not to press the matter further for a time.[17] Meantime, Mexico offered assistance in the "just and humane object" of removing the Kickapoos to the northern side of the boundary, but the agents of the United States who had been sent down in the summer of 1871 to accomplish the removal met with opposition on the part of the local inhabitants and officials and returned home in disgust. Nor did another attempt, made the following year, prove more successful.[18]

Thus matters stood when in May, 1873, news reached Colonel R. S. MacKenzie, who was stationed at Fort Clark, Texas, that the Kickapoos had made a raid and escaped with a drove of horses. He and Lieutenant Bullis took up the trail at once, and leading their troops into Coahuila, fell upon the Indian village of Remolino, killing nineteen of the savages, capturing some forty, and recovering sixty or seventy head of horses.[19]

Although it is possible that MacKenzie undertook this expedition on his own responsibility, there is some evidence that he may not have been acting contrary to the wishes of the Washington government. On January 16, 1873, Secretary of State Hamilton Fish suggested to the Minister of the United States in Mexico that the Mexican government appeared "so apathetic or so powerless to prevent such [Indian] raids that sooner or later this government [i. e., the United States] will [would] have no other alternative than to endeavor to secure quiet on the frontier by seeking the marauders and punishing them in their haunts wherever they may [might] be. Of course we should prefer that this should be done with the consent, if not with the co-operation of Mexico. It is [was] certain, however, that if the grievances shall [should] be persisted in, the remedy adverted to will [would] not remain untried."[20] On January 22, 1874, Fish wrote the Secretary of War that he believed that

---

[17] *House Ex. Doc.* No. 1, 41 Cong., 1 Sess. (Ser. 1412), Part II, p. 143; *Foreign Relations* (1871), pp. 635, 662–663; Moore, *Digest of International Law*, II, 435.

[18] *Foreign Relations* (1870), pp. 649–650; *ibid.*, (1872), Part 1, p. 416 ff.

[19] *House Misc. Doc.* No. 64, 45 Cong., 2 Sess. (Ser. 1820), pp. 187–188; Mexican Border Commission of 1873, *Report*, p. 424. In the fall of 1873 some four hundred Kickapoos were removed from Mexico to the United States and two years later about one hundred and thirty more were persuaded to return. See *House Ex. Doc.* No. 1, 43 Cong., 2 Sess. (Ser. 1634), Part I, p. 716; *ibid.*, 44 Cong. 1 Sess. (Ser. 1673), No. 1, Part I, p. 1896.

[20] *Foreign Relations* (1873), p. 643.

an incursion into Mexico when necessary for the dispersal of a band of Indian marauders was not a violation of international law.[21] Colonel MacKenzie does not appear to have been censured for his act; or if censured, he was certainly not removed from his post. Moreover, when the governor of Texas later referred to the raid as a precedent, the government of the United States seems to have acquiesced.[22]

The year 1874 witnessed unusual excitement along the Rio Grande. According to Governor Coke of Texas the murders and robberies were more numerous and destructive than they had been for some time. This official was compelled to organize three companies of minute-men for frontier defense. But bad as they were, the crimes of 1874 were only a small harbinger of evils to come. The year 1875 was destined to be the most perilous and harassing the Texas frontiersmen had suffered. Hardly a week passed without its raid, and hardly a raid without the loss of stock and other property, without murders and outrages perpetrated upon the inhabitants of the state. In fact a reign of terror held sway in a vast section extending from the banks of the lower Rio Grande to Corpus Christi.[23] And, as one would expect, enraged frontiersmen occasionally crossed the Rio Grande in their attempts to avenge the outrages of the marauders.

Indeed, the next important invasion of Mexican soil, but the fifth in the enumeration of Carranza, occurred in November, 1875. Captain Randlett of the United States army was encamped at Edinburg, Texas, when he received news that thieves with a herd of cattle were on their way to the Rio Grande. He immediately sent a courier to Ringgold Barracks for help and a telegram to Fort Brown for more specific orders, while he sent out scouts to ascertain the ford the robbers would be most likely to attempt to cross with

[21] Moore, *op. cit.*, II, 421.

[22] A large number of murders and robberies committed on the Texas border in the summer of 1874 and the lack of what appeared to be sufficient protection on the part of the federal army, led the Governor of Texas to raise minutemen to protect the frontier. To at least one of the captains of these companies the Governor gave orders to pursue the marauders into Mexican territory. When questioned in regard to his action by the Washington government, the Governor argued that if troops of the United States had a right to "cross the national boundary and continue pursuit of marauders on Mexican soil, . . . Texas forces which are doing the duty which ought to be performed by the United States troops . . . have the same right." See *House Report* No. 343, 44 Cong., 1 Sess. (Ser. 1709), pp. XVI, 161–167. In this conclusion the Attorney-General seems to have acquiesced. See *House Ex. Doc.* No. 13, 45 Cong., 1 Sess. (Ser. 1773), p. 62.

[23] *House Report*, No. 343, pp. I–XVI, 61, *passim*.

their booty. From Fort Brown on November 16 he received the command: "If you catch the thieves, hit them hard. If you come up to them while they cross the river, follow them into Mexico." From the scouts which he had sent out he learned, on November 17, that a herd of cattle were being driven toward the river with the probable intention of effecting a crossing near Las Cuevas during the day. Preparations for pursuit were hastily made, and shortly after four o'clock the troops reached the river, where they found the thieves forcing the cattle off of a steep bank into the stream. An encounter took place, but hostilities were interrupted by darkness. During the night Randlett sent a message to the *alcalde* of the little Mexican village of Las Cuevas demanding the return of the cattle and the delivery of the thieves, whose names he supplied. At the same time he prepared to move to the Mexican shore early the next morning.

But just before daybreak Major Clendenin of Ringgold Barracks arrived and, taking command, forbade Randlett to cross the river on the ground that it would be bad faith to do so while negotiations were in progress. A few hours later Randlett received a communication from the *alcalde* which informed him that a few of the cattle had been recovered, but that the thieves had escaped with most of the herd in the direction of Camargo. In the meantime Clendenin had reported on the situation to the commander of Fort Brown and asked for further instructions. In reply he had received the following order: "If you have not crossed when this reaches you, await arrival of Major Alexander, who will be at *Las Cuevas* to-morrow with two companies. General is afraid you have not men enough."

About noon, and before Alexander had brought up reënforcements, Captain McNally of the Texas Rangers came upon the scene and declared his intention of crossing the river as soon as his troop should arrive. Clendenin urged McNally to await Alexander's arrival, but the Ranger captain remained obdurate. Thereupon Clendenin remarked: "If you are determined to cross, we will cover your return, but cannot cross at present to help you." Clendenin then placed a Gatling gun in position on the left bank of the Rio Grande and ordered Randlett to protect McNally's return. Soon afterwards Clendenin departed for Ringgold Barracks, leaving Randlett in charge until Alexander should arrive.

By the early morning of the 19th McNally succeeded in transferring his men and five horses to the Mexican side. A considerable skirmish ensued, and about two hundred and fifty Mexican regulars soon put in their appearance. A part of the fighting took place within sight of the American troops; and Randlett, supposing that the Texas Rangers were on the point of being wiped out, began to dispatch federal troops to McNally's assistance. After the exchange of several volleys between United States and Mexican soldiers, a truce to last until nine o'clock November 20, was agreed upon. Just at this moment Alexander of Fort Brown arrived and ordered the immediate withdrawal of the United States forces. As for McNally, this impetuous Ranger captain declared he would not return until the Mexican authorities delivered up the cattle and the thieves in accordance with the terms of the truce. Nevertheless, he and the remnant of his men did return on the following day.[24]

Nor did the civil government of Texas bear these outrages inflicted upon its constituents with meekness and passivity. A joint committee of the state Legislature appointed to investigate conditions reported 105 murders and a 90% decrease in stock in the region below Eagle Pass. It also recommended the increase of state forces on the southwestern frontier and expressed the fervent hope that ere long the federal government would do its full duty, not only furnishing the border with adequate protection but indemnifying the Texans for their losses and reimbursing them for the sums expended in performing a duty rightly devolving upon the central authorities. The Governor not only forwarded this report to Washington but sent protest after protest and plea after plea for federal assistance.[25]

The vehement appeals of the Texans and the remonstrances of Mexico against the invasions of her soil forced the United States to take further notice of the conditions on the southwestern border. But little was done to remedy conditions. A small number of additional troops was sent to the region and a few war vessels dispatched to the Rio Grande,[26]—and a committee of the House undertook another investigation of the Rio Grande frontier.

This committee made its report on February 29, 1876. Although its findings were the result of a more thorough investigation than that of its precursor of 1872, still its researches were far from exhaustive and its conclusions by no means unprejudiced. On the ground that the report of the committee of 1872 was entirely satisfactory for the period it covered, the committee of 1876 reviewed

[24] On this whole affair, see *House Report* No. 343 and *House Ex. Doc.* No. 13, referred to in the previous note.

[25] *House Report* No. 343, 44 Cong., 1 Sess. (Ser. 1709), pp. 70–73, 169–170, *passim.*

[26] *Ibid.,* p. 81.

very briefly the events of these earlier years. It declared that disorders along the lower Rio Grande were becoming gradually worse. While robberies of cattle were increasing in frequency, these robberies, serious as they were, were not the most important grievance. The problem of the frontiersman was rapidly being transformed from merely one of pecuniary losses to one of personal security against outrage and the loss of life itself. The members of the committee vehemently denied that the sufferings of the frontier were mutual and reciprocal. They alleged in fact that it would be impossible for bands organized in Texas to make successful raids into Mexico, due to the efficiency of the newly established Mexican rural police, the organization of the population on the river ranches, and the facilities for the rapid transmission of news from one settlement to another. They declared also that the Mexican officials of the frontier, both local and national, continued to aid and abet these crimes and to grow rich off of the plunder. In short they found only desolation, robbery, murder, and terrorism on the left bank of the Rio Grande—ranches abandoned, villages in peril, highways unsafe, business at a standstill. In view of this intolerable situation, the committee, while declaring that it was "strongly in favor of avoiding all cause of dispute with the Mexican national government" and disclaiming any desire for a collision with Mexico or the acquisition of territory south of the international boundary, resolved that the President should increase the army on the frontier and that he should be permitted, at his discretion, "to order the troops when in close pursuit of the robbers with their booty, to cross the Rio Grande, and use such means as they may find necessary for recovering the stolen property, and checking the raids, guarding, however, in all cases against any unnecessary injury to peaceable inhabitants of Mexico." [27] The committee recommended this course of action in spite of the admitted conviction that the Mexican people in their pride would never allow their government to grant the United States permission to send its troops into Mexican territory. They contended that such defiance of Mexican sentiment was called for by the enormity of the outrages suffered and the danger that the Texans would "rise up in arms in their last despair, and themselves cross the border and wage a war of retaliation." [28]

This report called forth inflammatory articles in the leading newspapers of Mexico, and a petition of the students of one of Mexico's best schools implored the government to train them in order that

[27] Ibid., p. XVII.
[28] Ibid., p. XVI.

they might defend their beloved nation. In the midst of the general clamor and excitement, Romero once more took up his pen and counseled moderation. He pointed out the improbability that Congress would pass the resolution offered by the committee—and in this Romero was right, for the resolution did not pass—, that several of the leading men in the United States, such as Sherman, Sheridan, and Grant, were friends of Mexico, and that the people of the United States themselves had demonstrated more than once since the close of the Civil War in their country that they were not eager for further territorial acquisitions.[29]

While the Mexican press was thus engaged in violent denunciations of the United States Porfirio Díaz crossed from Texas into Mexico and launched a revolution which was destined some seven months later to seat him in the presidential chair. His success was insured in part by a clever manipulation of this Mexican hostility towards the United States and, indeed, towards foreigners in general.[30]

The operations of Díaz and the enlistment of some of the turbulent element of Tamaulipas under his banner, caused a lull in the raids along the Rio Grande, but the scene then shifted to that rough, mountainous country above Eagle Pass. In April and May, 1876, chief Washo Lobo and his Lipan braves murdered twelve Texans. Lieutenant Colonel W. R. Shafter, under orders of General E. O. C. Ord of the Texas military department,[31] determined to pursue the perpetrators into Coahuila. Accordingly, he sent Lieutenant Bullis across the Rio Grande at a ford about sixty miles above the Pecos with instructions to spy out the camp of the Indians and to fall upon it. The savages were warned of Bullis's approach and little was accomplished by this expedition; but in the following July a more successful raid was made. Shafter and Bullis passed over the river some twenty-five miles above its junction with the Pecos and marched southward into Mexico for five or six days. The main army of invasion then halted, and Bullis was sent ahead with twenty scouts and as many soldiers to search for an Indian village reported to be on the San Antonio River. At dawn on July 30, they discovered that they were near a Lipan camp. They made

[29] Foster to Fish, May 4, 1876, and enclosures, *Foreign Relations* (1876), pp. 398–400.

[30] *Id.*, Nov. 28 and Dec. 30, 1876, *ibid.*, (1877), pp. 385, 392.

[31] On Dec. 6, 1877, Ord testified before the congressional committee on military affairs as follows: "I gave orders nearly two years ago to cross over on a fresh trail, I stated my reason for giving the order and communicated the orders to the administration, and I received no instructions in regard to the matter. The order was not disapproved and consequently it was tacitly approved." *House Misc. Doc.* No. 64, 45 Cong., 2 Sess. (Ser. 1820), p. 103.

a hasty attack which resulted in the death of fourteen Indians, the capture of four squaws and ninety-six horses and mules, and the destruction of the entire Indian encampment. Bullis then turned northward, joining Shafter on the following day. Before reaching the United States they had another encounter with a band of Indians just returning from Texas, but with less success than on the recent occasion. Again, in January, 1877, Lieutenant Bullis and his company, assisted by Captain Keys with two hundred negro cavalry, pursued a band of Lipans and Mescalero Apaches about one hundred and twenty-five miles into Mexico, but were unable to overtake them or recover any considerable amount of stolen property.[32]

These punitive expeditions met with only partial success and failed to put a stop to the Indian incursions. Moreover, the Mexicans evinced less and less disposition to coöperate in the efforts to suppress the raids. On March 9, 1877, Shafter wrote that "not the slightest attempt" was being made by the Mexicans to prevent the Indians from raiding into the United States, but on the contrary they were "finding refuge in the towns when pursued, and a market for their stolen plunder at all times." [33] General Sheridan forwarded this letter to headquarters on March 19, with the recommendation that "the Mexican government be compelled to prevent these hostile incursions." [34] A few days later the hostility of one of the Mexican frontier officials was evinced by a threat to punish as traitors certain of the Mexican guides who had aided American troops in their pursuit of Indians upon Mexican soil. When news reached General Ord that two of these guides were being held in jail at Piedras Negras, he sent Colonel Shafter and Adjutant-General Taylor to rescue them; but the prisoners were hurried away before the jail could be seized. The American forces were then withdrawn, but Ord sent word to the Governor of Coahuila that any injury to the guides would be considered as tantamount to a declaration of intention to coöperate with the savages in their depredations.[35] Before the close of April reports of another Indian raid were sent to headquarters. On May 5, Sheridan repeated his recommendation of the previous March and this recommendation was reiterated by General Sherman on the 29th.[36] A crisis was now approaching.

[32] *Ibid.*, pp. 188–191.
[33] Shafter to the Assistant Adjutant-General. *House Ex. Doc.* No. 13, 45 Cong., 1 Sess. (Ser. 1773), pp. 4–5.
[34] *Ibid., loc. cit.*
[35] *Ibid.*, pp. 9–12.
[36] *Ibid.*, pp. 13–14.

CHAPTER XVII

THE CRISIS OF 1877–1879

NOT only had the border raids reached a very irritating and grave stage by the spring of 1877, but, what is more important perhaps, the exigencies of domestic politics now rendered it imprudent for the Washington government to continue longer in an attitude of semi-indifference towards the southwestern frontier or any other phase of Mexican relations. A bitter contest over the recent presidential election had brought the United States to the verge of another civil war. The successful candidate, Rutherford B. Hayes, just inaugurated after a questionable victory, was in need of an issue to draw the public mind away from the contest. "Certain gentlemen . . . conceived the idea that, in view of the tension . . . created by the partisans of Mr. Tilden [the rival candidate] and of the disturbed condition of affairs in the Southern States, it would divert attention from pending issues and tend greatly to consolidate the new Administration, if a war could be brought on with Mexico and another slice of its territory added to the union." [1] Others perceived that the recent advent of Díaz to power and his natural desire for the recognition of the United States furnished an excellent opportunity for the exertion of pressure in behalf of the ever-increasing number of Americans interested in Mexican trade and investments. During the course of his revolution Díaz had declared null certain concessions granted by his predecessors to foreigners. Some of these were held by citizens of the United States who now began to whisper to the Hayes administration in very depreciatory tones regarding the talents of Díaz and his ability to maintain his position. [2] Would it not be wise to give Lerdo more time to regain his lost power? Could not the new Mexican executive be forced to grant more favorable considerations to American economic interests in return for recognition, for moral and even material backing?

[1] Foster, *Diplomatic Memoirs*, I, 92.

[2] See in particular the letters of E. L. Plumb to the Secretary of State, copies of which are in the Plumb Papers (Library of Cong., Manuscripts Division). Plumb was agent of a railway company which held a concession from Lerdo de Tejada.

Such were some of the suggestions which began to be made. Furthermore, Texas had a special claim on the Hayes administration. Hayes's lifelong friend and trusted adviser, Guy M. Bryan, was a Texan; and the votes of the Texans in Congress were necessary to defeat the machinations of the President's enemies.[3] The Hayes government might therefore be expected to adopt an energetic Mexican policy.

The expiring Grant administration was inclined to follow the *de facto* principle and anxious to secure the first installment under the claims convention of 1868 as soon as it should become due. It had accordingly given United States Minister John W. Foster instructions which the latter deemed tantamount to an authorization of discretionary recognition. But Foster was already in touch with the commercial and capitalistic interests of his country,[4] and he was anxious not to embarrass the new administration at Washington. He accordingly contrived to secure the payment of the claims installment without committing his government on the question of recognition. Hamilton Fish, Secretary of State under the Grant administration, then approved his course and instructed him as follows:

In your intercourse with prominent men in public life, you will endeavor to leave an impression that the United States, prior to deciding in favor of that step [i. e., recognition], would expect the repeal of the law creating the "Zona Libre" . . . and efficient measures towards checking inroads into their States and Territories adjacent to Mexico. Though these measures might not in the

[3] See the "Bryan-Hayes Correspondence" (ed. E. W. Winkler), in *The Southwestern Historical Quarterly*, XXV (October, 1921), 98, *passim*, XXVI, *passim*, XXVII, *passim*.
Colonel Bryan writes thus in his Autobiography: "Shortly after President Hayes's inauguration he wrote me to come to Washington that I could 'help him,' which I did and was his guest at the White House for over three weeks—during the settlement of the Louisiana and South Carolina Legislative difficulties. When I left he told me I had been of great service to him and that much of his kindly feeling toward the South was due to me." (Quoted in *ibid.*, XXV, 101–102.) After Bryan's return he gave an interview to the Galveston *News* in which he said: "I believe that the interests of Texas will be more carefully looked after, better protected, and more summarily dealt with than heretofore." (Quoted in *ibid.*, XXVII, 70.)
On November 29, 1877, Sherman complained to Sheridan that it had been necessary to permit Ord to run his vigorous course on the Rio Grande in order not to give offense to the Texans whose votes alone would save the army from being reorganized and placed into the hands of those "who deserted it in 1861." (Sherman Records, Vol. VI.)
[4] Foster had returned to the United States and made several speeches before various commercial organizations in 1875.

end be deemed indispensable to a formal recognition of that government,
they are deemed so important to the preservation of friendly relations between
the two countries, that our earnestness upon the subject must not be left in
doubt.[4a]

Thus matters stood when Hayes entered the White House. On
the day of his inauguration Foster forwarded an autograph letter
from Díaz and stated by telegram that he would take no step toward recognition until further instructions had been received.[5]
Hays was now free to define his attitude and he was not slow
in doing so. On March 27, 1877, Secretary of State William M.
Evarts wrote Foster the following instructions: "It is deemed advisable . . . in view of the present condition of affairs in Mexico
to await the progress of events and the action of the Congress of that
country at its coming session, before taking any further steps in the
direction of a formal and official recognition of General Díaz." [6] On
the 15th of the following May the State Department received a
letter from Foster advising that the Mexican Congress was sure to
confirm the choice of Díaz as President and tactfully suggesting his
recognition as the best available man.[7] The Hayes administration
then assumed a still firmer attitude. Foster was informed that a
guaranty of concerted action for "the preservation of peace and
order and the protection of life and property" on the frontier "should
be made the condition precedent to any recognition." In the same
letter complaint was made also of the "forced loans" and "unequal exactions" to which American citizens residing in Mexico had
been subjected.[8]

Foster proceeded to give these instructions the broadest possible
significance. He forthwith drew up and submitted to the Mexican
government a memorandum of subjects for negotiation which included almost every conceivable phase of United States-Mexican
relations. Commerce was to be encouraged by a reciprocity treaty,
by a postal convention providing for the increase and maintenance
of mail facilities, by the establishment of steamship lines between
the leading ports of the two countries, and by the abolition or the
modification of the Free Zone. American investments in Mexico

[4a] No. 370, Feb. 12, 1877, Mex. Inst., Vol. 19. See with reference to the
claims installment, Foster to Fish, No. 487, Jan. 16, 1877, Mex. Desp. Vol. 58.

[5] Copy in Mex. Desp., Vol. 58.

[6] Mex. Inst., Vol. 19.

[7] Foster to Evarts (Unofficial and Confidential), April 28, 1877, Mex. Desp.,
Vol. 59.

[8] F. W. Seward (Acting Secretary of State) to Foster, May 16, 1877, *Foreign Relations* (1877), pp. 403–405.

were to be safeguarded by a joint guaranty of protection to the persons and property of those engaged in the construction of a railroad to unite the American system with the City of Mexico, by a stipulation as to protection of other American capital and companies employed in the development of the resources of Mexico, and by the exemption of American citizens from forced loans and other so-called illegal exactions. All claims, present and future, were to be settled by the establishment of a commission or a court of claims. Frontier affairs were to be adjusted by an agreement providing for reciprocal crossing of the border, by the modification of the extradition treaty of 1861, and by more specific agreements with reference to the property rights of citizens of one country residing in the frontier region of the other.[9]

But before negotiations could be fully entered upon with reference to these important matters news of the policy adopted by Hayes with reference to the disorders on the frontier had aroused a storm of protest which rendered such negotiations temporarily out of the question. On June 1, 1877, the Secretary of War had issued the following instructions to General Sherman with regard to the border raids:

The President desires that the utmost vigilance on the part of the military forces in Texas be exercised for the suppression of these raids. It is very desirable that efforts to this end . . . be made with the co-operation of the Mexican authorities; and you will instruct General Ord, commanding in Texas, to invite such co-operation on the part of the local Mexican authorities, and to inform them that while the President is anxious to avoid giving offense to Mexico, he is nevertheless convinced that the invasion of our territory by armed and organized bodies of thieves and robbers to prey upon our citizens should no longer be endured.

General Ord will at once notify the Mexican authorities along the Texan border, of the great desire of the President to unite with them in efforts to suppress the long continued lawlessness. At the same time he will inform those authorities that if the Government of Mexico shall continue to neglect the duty of suppressing these outrages, that duty will devolve upon this Government, and will be performed, even if its performance should render necessary the occasional crossing of the border by our troops. You will, therefore, direct General Ord that in case the lawless incursions continue he will be at liberty, in the use of his discretion, when in pursuit of a band of marauders, and when his troops are either in sight of them or upon a fresh trail, to follow them across the Rio Grande, and to overtake and punish them, as well as retake stolen property taken from our citizens and found in their hands on the Mexican side of the line.[10]

[9] Memorandum enclosed in Foster to Evarts, No. 968, June 6, 1877, Mex. Desp., Vol. 59.
[10] *House Ex. Doc.* No. 13, 45 Cong., 1 Sess. (Ser. 1773), pp. 14-15.

Porfirio Díaz could not afford to assume the attitude of a passive spectator with respect to these activities on the frontier or allow himself to appear coerced and intimidated into active coöperation with the United States. He too must keep an eye on the domestic situation, or else bring down upon his head the condemnation of the Mexican people at a time when he was in great need of their support in order to consolidate his power. If the tension could be maintained without an actual outbreak of hostilities it might enable him to silence opposition and augment his popularity. It would be a dangerous game, but the stakes were high. And if war came—well, Díaz was no coward. He accordingly instructed General Gerónimo Treviño to advance immediately to the border with a division of the Mexican army. This was to be done for the purpose of coöperating with the American forces in the suppression of the turbulent elements along the frontier, but Treviño was ordered, in case of an invasion of Mexican soil by troops of the United States, to "repel force with force." [11] The publication of this order rallied all parties to the support of Díaz. The newspapers, whether Conservative or Liberal, Lerdista or Porfirista, Spanish or Mexican, called upon every loyal son of Mexico to support the new President against the Yankee Colossus which was merely using the frontier as a pretext for despoiling a friendly nation.[12]

Negotiations in such an atmosphere would obviously prove very difficult. The despatches of Foster during the next few months present a vivid picture of the critical state of the relations between the two countries, and one can not read them without realizing something of the dramatic tensity of the situation.

On June 19, Foster made known to the Minister of Foreign Affairs the stand which the Hayes government proposed to take with reference to recognition, and a heated discussion ensued. Foster's report of the conference is worth quoting at length:

Mr. Vallarta insisted that the government of General Diaz possessed all the conditions of recognition required by international law and the practice of nations, and as a proof of this cited the fact that the European powers represented in Mexico, as well as the Central American republics, had already recognized the present government, leaving the United States in a singular and independent position, which he sought to explain by the unfriendly attitude of the administration of President Hayes. He claimed that the present Government of Mexico had manifested every possible disposition to comply with the obligations of treaty and comity toward the United States; that it had promptly paid the first installment on the Mexico claims awards under the

[11] Ogazón to Treviño, June 18, 1877, *ibid.*, pp. 19–20.
[12] Clippings enclosed in Foster to Evarts, June 21, 1877, *ibid.*, pp. 19–27.

most difficult circumstances; and that it had held itself ready to grant all reasonable guarantees for the preservation of peace on the frontier and for the protection of American interests in Mexico; but . . . the adjustment of these questions would probably follow recognition, especially where they required treaty stipulations.

Mr. Vallarta expressed regret that there had been an apparent change in the policy of the Government of the United States with the advent of the new administration; that Mr. Fish had interposed no objection to the receipt of the claims installment from the *de facto* government, and there appeared to have been good reason to believe that with the inauguration of General Diaz as constitutional president, he would be recognized as such by the United States as he had been by the European nations. He claimed to have had private advices from New York and Washington that the present administration had been operated upon by the machinations of ex-President Lerdo and certain American gentlemen who had personal and sinister purposes to accomplish, and that it had yielded too readily to the representations of General Ord, who was an annexationist and seeking to precipitate a war between the two countries.

Mr. Vallarta then referred with much feeling to the Order of June 1 of the Secretary of War to General Sherman, containing the instructions to General Ord. He said that when the substance of the order was telegraphed to the government here it refused to believe that it was true, because it could not comprehend that the United States would manifest such a hostile and aggressive attitude toward Mexico, especially without any previous notice of its intention. The government therefore awaited the arrival of the mail with much interest, hoping to be advised that the telegraphic account was untrue or exaggerated. But by this medium the hostile attitude of the government at Washington was fully confirmed. He said that in discharge of a solemn duty, the Mexican secretary of war had issued orders to General Trevino and the northern division of the army to repair at once to the frontier of the Rio Grande, and then gave me the instructions embraced in said order. He hoped for the preservation of peace, and General Trevino was instructed to exert himself to maintain it, but if the orders to General Ord were carried out and the Mexican territory were violated, the consequences might be of the gravest character. Mr. Vallarta said that Secretary McCrary in his order to General Sherman had disregarded all the rules of international law and the practices of civilized nations, and treated the Mexicans as savages, as Kaffirs of Africa; that an absolute declaration of war would have been more considerate, as the national honor and the sovereign rights of the republic would not in that way have been so completely disregarded.

If through diplomatic channels notice had been given to Mexico of an ultimatum regarding the frontier, and it had then neglected to render satisfaction to the United States, there might be occasion to consider the propriety of issuing orders such as those given to General Ord; but, in the manner in which the orders had been issued, the cabinet at Washington had sought to place Mexico beyond the pale of civilized nations. The government, he said, had just received intelligence from General Trevino that, upon the invitation of General Ord, he had gone to the frontier to hold a conference with him, and that General Trevino had been advised of the desire of the government that he should co-operate with the American troops in suppressing the raids, but that it would never permit its territory to be violated by American troops, in the manner indicated in the order of Secretary McCrary, without repelling various commercial organizations in 1875.

them by force of arms. No government could stand in Mexico for a moment against the popular indignation, if it did not assume this attitude.[13]

Less than two weeks later Foster again referred to the excited state of the Mexican public mind. He said that

the universal impression created with the Mexican public has [had] been, that the order to General Ord . . . was utterly without cause or provocation; that it was inspired by the President of the United States and his Cabinet, partly for political considerations, in order to maintain party ascendency at home, and partly . . . by filibusters and speculators, combined with the machinations of ex-President Lerdo; and that the object of the order to General Ord was to drive Mexico into a war, whereby the United States, taking advantage of the weakness and internal dissensions of this nation, could annex to its territory the northern Mexican states, and possibly establish a protectorate over the whole country.[14]

At the same time Foster called attention to a violent attack upon the motives of the Hayes administration which had appeared in the official journal of the Díaz government.[15] Foster later protested against the attack and demanded that the official organ publish in reply to it a memorandum which he submitted. President Díaz tactfully declined on the ground that such a course "might seriously embarrass his government." [16] The fact is, that the officials of the Mexican federal government appeared to be as much excited as the Mexican press. General Díaz told the Spanish Minister that he expected war and that he was rather pleased with the prospect. It would consolidate his government and completely destroy Lerdo's prestige; and, moreover, the United States would meet an entirely different reception than that accorded her in 1846–'47. Romero alone remained calm.[17] So great was the excitement that Foster deemed it unwise to attempt a Fourth of July celebration in the Mexican capital.

But while the relations of the two countries were strained almost to the breaking point, Treviño and Ord exercised prudent moderation on the frontier. Friendly interviews were exchanged and both commanders took pains to avoid occasions for a rupture. Although General Ord sent troops across the Rio Grande now and then in pursuit of raiders, he was careful not to do so when a detachment of Mexican troops was near. Only once, at the close of September

[13] Foster to Evarts, June 20, 1877, *Foreign Relations* (1877), pp. 410–413.
[14] Id., June 28, 1877, *House Ex. Doc.* No. 13 (Ser. 1773), pp. 28–34.
[15] It was alleged that the Hayes administration had been influenced by Lerdo de Tejada and by E. L. Plumb and other concession-seekers who were backing Lerdo in the hope of thus obtaining valuable grants.
[16] *Ibid.*
[17] Foster to Evarts (Private), June 30, 1877, Mex. Desp., Vcl. 59.

or the beginning of October, 1877, was a hostile outbreak between the frontier forces imminent. At that time Bullis with a company of ninety soldiers raided an Indian village near Zaragossa, Mexico. Shafter, apparently suspecting that the expedition might cause an unfriendly movement on the part of the Mexican regulars stationed in the region, crossed over the international line with some three hundred men to support Bullis in case of trouble. After attacking and burning the Indian village and capturing a number of Indian women, Bullis set out on his return to the Rio Grande. Soon afterwards the Mexican forces who had followed his trail put in their appearance; but Shafter's troops came up at the opportune moment and the Mexicans retired. Had Bullis been unsupported or the total number of United States troops been smaller, hostilities might have occurred.[18]

Nevertheless the greater part of the Mexican journals continued to keep a critical and even hostile watch over the situation. Such coöperation as Díaz was able to give was extended under rapid and galling fire of newspaper criticism. Treviño was denounced as a traitor because of his cautious procedure on the frontier.[19] Díaz was accused of a disposition to truckle to the Yankees.[20] Vallarta's friends hinted to Foster that Vallarta would be 'ground to powder by public sentiment' if he attempted to put through an agreement for the settlement of pending issues. Vallarta himself told the German Minister in Mexico that his enemies would use any treaty he signed with the United States for his utter destruction. Well might Foster complain that "it is [was] not so much a question of duty and justice, as of popular prejudice against the Yankees, which influences [influenced] the action of the government." [21]

In the face of this overwhelming sentiment against submitting to the demands of the United States it would require considerable spirit for the Díaz administration to make any concessions and one need not be surprised that it dared not do so. On September 11, Foster reported that the attitude of the Mexican government amounted virtually to the "rejection of all our terms." [22] On the 12th of the following November he said:

[18] *House Ex. Doc.* No. 13 (Ser. 1773), pp. 28, 53, 156, 163, *passim; Foreign Relations* (1877), pp. 418–418; *House Misc. Doc.* No. 64, 45 Cong., 2 Sess. (Ser. 1820), pp. 191, 269.

[19] Foster to Evarts, July 13, 1877, and enclosures, *Foreign Relations* (1877), p. 419 ff.

[20] *Id.,* No. 603, Sept. 14, 1877, Mex. Desp., Vol. 60.

[21] *Id.,* Sept. 11, (Confidential), *loc. cit.*

[22] *Loc. cit.*

All the indications of public sentiment here point to a growing bitterness of feeling towards the United States and a general belief that a war between the two countries is almost inevitable. The conviction appears to be unanimous that it is the settled policy of the government of the United States to provoke a conflict, and that its attitude in reference to the Rio Grande frontier and other questions is only a pretext to humiliate Mexico and to drive it into some act which will be construed . . . into a declaration or a cause of war.

At the same time Foster reported that the Mexican Senate had advised the executive to make no concessions.[23] Before the close of the month the Cabinet reached the decision to demand recognition as a right, to consider no question before recognition and make no concessions precedent thereto.[24] Evidently the Senate and the executive department of Mexico had made up their minds that they could not afford to yield to the demands of the United States in defiance of popular sentiment. To all appearances war and peace now depended upon the United States.

The wily Díaz played to his constituents and prepared for the worst by sending reënforcements to the frontier and taking steps to promote an alliance with the Hispanic-American states.[25] At the same time he probably indulged hopes that the Hayes administration might be forced to recede from its position. In the fall of 1877 he had set in motion plans designed to foment the divided councils which he thought he perceived in the United States. To Yankee financiers who were now coming to Mexico in considerable numbers he evinced a disposition to grant favorable concessions. These went back home to sing the praises of Díaz.[26] He even sent agents to the United States for the purpose of carrying on propaganda in favor of his recognition.[27]

In fact there was developing in the United States, as Díaz more than suspected, a growing conviction that the bellicose attitude of Hayes was not serving the interests of American merchants and investors. Already, in the summer of 1877, the President's Mexican policy had become the "news sensation of the day." "He was criticised for over-stepping the bounds of his authority, violating

23 Id., Mex. Desp., Vol. 61.

24 Id., November 28, 1877, No. 635, loc. cit.

25 Ibid.; Id. No. 639, Dec. 1, and No. 642, Dec. 12, 1877, loc. cit.

26 Id., May 16, 1877 (Personal), Mex. Desp., Vol. 59; Id., Oct. 6, 1877 (Confidential), ibid., Vol. 60; Id., No. 775, Sept. 5, 1878, ibid., Vol. 63, and enclosures; Foster to F. W. Seward, May 16, 1877 (Unofficial and Confidential), ibid., Vol. 59; id., Sept. 9, 1878, ibid., Vol. 63. Prominent among these financiers were John B. Frisbie, Simon Stevens, and N. S. Reneau.

27 Foster to Evarts, No. 775, Sept. 5, 1878, and enclosures, Mex. Desp., Vol. 63.

treaty rights, and making virtual war upon an impotent friendly power. It was even widely charged that the administration was actuated by a deep and malevolent purpose to provoke war with Mexico in order to divert attention from domestic problems and to bring about the annexation . . . of several of the northern states of Mexico." [28] Only these gestures of Díaz were needed to set in motion an organized attempt to force Hayes to abandon his policy.

The Congressional session which met in compliance with a special call of the President in October, 1877, scarcely opened before there was manifested a disposition to go thoroughly into the whole Mexican question. A military committee solicited information from the Secretary of War, from numerous army officials, and from civilians with knowledge of frontier conditions. And this committee did not hesitate to ask embarrassing questions. Who were the raiders on the southwestern frontier? Were not some of them Texans? Why did not the United States army apprehend them before they crossed into Mexico? What was Texas doing to repress the disorders? Were the Texans not anxious for federal military posts simply to give markets for their produce? How long had troops of the United States been permitted to pursue raiders across the Rio Grande? If American troops should meet a detachment of the Mexican army on Mexican soil, would a battle ensue? What kind of officers had charge of American troops on this frontier? Was not there a disposition among these officers to invade Mexico and bring on a collision? Was the sending of troops into a neighboring country not an act of war? What was the strength and purpose of Díaz with reference to the policy of the United States? What had been the effect of the Ord Order upon Mexican public opinion? [29] Such questions as these scarcely concealed the hostility of the committee towards the Mexican policy of the Hayes administration. The House Sub-Committee on Foreign Affairs was more kindly disposed, but the insurgents had amended its instructions so as to include a study of the means of "enlarging the commercial relations" between the United States and Mexico, and some of Hayes's opponents were found among its members also. Secretary Evarts was forced to come before this committee and defend the administration's Mexican policy and Foster was recalled from Mexico, perhaps in the hope that his testimony might strengthen Hayes's hand.

[28] Williams, *Hayes*, II, 209–210.
[29] For this lengthy testimony, see *House Misc. Doc.* No. 64, 45 Cong., 2 Sess. (Ser. 1820).

Evarts took occasion while before the committee to make an earnest plea for congressional support of the President's Mexican policy and for harmony between the two branches of the government. "I do not see . . . any reason," said Evarts, "for an antagonism between Congress and the Executive Department of the Government, if the subject is as well understood by Congress as it is by us; and all our correspondence is open to Congress."

The trouble in Mexico [he added] is that reproach is brought upon free government by the ease and frequency of their revolutionary changes; and if I were to express an opinion as to the effect of non-recognition thus far upon the Mexican administration at home it would be this [,] that it has really given more . . . stability . . . and more hope of stability to Diaz than if recognition had been made, and produced more actual and serious efforts on the part of Mexico to . . . discharge its duties to this country on the frontier.

Evarts urged the committee to put into any resolution which it might draw up on the question of recognition, a statement approving the policy of the executive and leaving the matter of negotiations before or after recognition to his discretion. He said he did not think the people of the United States were "ready or ought to be ready to have continual troubles on our [their] border excused by this or that reason." He did not believe a war with Mexico would be possible "unless our government or people desire[d] it." Mexico might bluster, but she would hardly think a war worth while. He went so far as to admit that he might have to abandon his attempt to secure an "understanding in advance of recognition," but he confessed that he did not see "how we can [could] avoid breaking diplomatic relations" if the Mexican government persisted both in its neglect of the border and its opposition to the pursuit of malefactors by American troops into Mexican territory.[30]

In the course of his testimony Foster put forth a similar plea. The committee's attempt to elicit from him a statement as to whether he would advise recognition gave him his opportunity. In this connection he remarked:

When the report came to Mexico that Congress was going to examine into the condition of our relations with that country the Mexican papers immediately said that there was now a prospect of justice being done them. They have interpreted the position of the executive as a hostile one. There is a widespread feeling there that our government is impressed with what we call manifest destiny; that sooner or later we will occupy the whole of Mexico; and they interpret everything as a deliberate plan on our part to provoke a conflict and acquire territory . . .

[30] This testimony is bound in Mex. Desp., Vol. 61.

Foster stated that the Mexican government was anxious for antagonism to arise between Congress and the President and that he hoped that no such antagonism would occur. He was decidedly of the opinion that if Congress should direct the President to recognize the Díaz government before the executive took voluntary action, the Mexicans would consider such a step as a condemnation of the past conduct of the executive and assume an attitude more hostile than ever.

But while Foster came gallantly to the aid of Evarts in appealing for harmony between the White House and the Capitol, a portion of his evidence must have pleased the mercantile malcontents who were impatient for early recognition of Mexico. He admitted that Díaz had "shown more energy in the direction of preserving order on the frontier than any previous Mexican government." He declared, moreover, that General Díaz was "ruling the country in peace and according to the constitution and has [had] made a very respectable administration." And, what was more important to these merchants and masters of finance, Foster stated that he believed delay in recognition was injuring the development of commerce between the United States and Mexico; that the Mexican government was anxious to foster this commerce; and that Mexico's neglect of the frontier had been due more to inability than to indisposition.[31]

Such testimony—and other witnesses expressed similar opinions—[32] was admirably adapted to their purpose. Perhaps it could be used to put through Congress a resolution condemning the President's Mexican policy and demanding immediate recognition.

This disconcerting prospect may have forced the hand of the executive. At any rate Foster was sent back to Mexico with instructions to extend recognition to the Díaz government; and this he did on April 9, 1878. As for the Sub-Committee on Foreign Affairs, on April 25 it came resolutely to Hayes's support by recommending a joint resolution (1) that the President be authorized to keep on the border, "from the mouth of the Rio Grande to El Paso, a military force of not less than five thousand men, of which at least three thousand shall be cavalry"; (2) that the Ord Order should not be withdrawn or modified until Mexico should agree to treaty stipulations insuring adequate protection to the border and to the lives and

---

[31] Testimony bound in *loc. cit.*

[32] For the published testimony, see *House Report* No. 701, 45 Cong., 2 Sess. (Ser. 1824), document entitled, "Texas Frontier Troubles."

property of American citizens in general as well as a satisfactory settlement of all outstanding issues.[33]

Having yielded the one point of recognition, Hayes now determined to pursue the remainder of his policy with vigor. Foster was directed to follow the act of recognizing the Díaz government by a request that it enter upon "a consideration of some permanent measures for the preservation of peace and the punishment of outlawry upon the frontier, the better protection of American citizens and their interests in Mexico, and the settlement of the various matters of complaint made by the Government of the United States." [34] In personal conferences it is probable that Foster was given more forceful instructions, and it is certain that he and Evarts discussed the possibility of war between the two countries.[35]

If Hayes expected the Díaz administration to yield with meekness to his demands, he was destined soon to be disillusioned. In the course of a few weeks after his return to Mexico City Foster became convinced that the repeal of the Ord Order would probably be the *sine qua non* to any successful negotiations on pending issues. New expeditions into Mexican territory in the summer of 1877 and the bitter and sustained discussions of the matter in the press soon removed all doubt on this score. Hostility to the United States probably reached the climax on the evening of September 15, when in the midst of the celebration of the national holiday at the leading theatre of the capital, cries of "War!" and "Death to the Americans!" suggested to Foster the advisability of withdrawing from his box-seat and seeking shelter under the American flag at legation headquarters; [36] but Mexican public opinion continued to be subject to paroxysms of unfriendliness which recurred so frequently that they rendered negotiations exceedingly difficult. On October 29, 1878, Foster threw up his hands in despair and declared that he had not been able to reach a satisfactory settlement on a single controverted point.[37] The Mexican Congress and press were determined that no agreements should be made until the Ord Order had been revoked and Díaz was no more inclined to defy public opinion on this question than he had been on that of recognition.

And why should he? His propagandists were at work, and reports continually came in of increasing impatience and growing opposition

[33] *Ibid.*, p. XLII.
[34] Evarts to Foster, March 23, 1878, *Foreign Relations* (1878), p. 544.
[35] Foster to Evarts, July 15, 1878 (Unofficial), Mex. Desp., Vol. 63; *id.*, Oct. 30, 1878 (Confidential and Unofficial), *ibid.*, Vol. 65.
[36] Foster, *Diplomatic Memoirs*, I, 101-102.
[37] Foster to Evarts, No. 822, Oct. 29, 1878, Mex. Desp., Vol. 65.

among American business men to Hayes's Mexican policy. The easiest way out of the difficulty evidently lay through the successful manipulation of American opinion.

Foster, influenced no doubt by what he assumed to be the attitude of his chief, urged firmness to the point of coercion, but he revealed at the same time grave doubt as to whether the American people were prepared to approve such a course. He saw as clearly as did Díaz that the matter was rapidly being resolved into a contest for the control of public sentiment in the United States. Nor was he slow to contribute his share to the support of Hayes's administration. The agents of the Mexican government, perceiving that the financiers of New York and the merchants and manufacturers of the Middle West were those most likely to become actively concerned in the President's Mexican policy, were making their most vigorous drives upon these centers. In the late summer of 1878, Señor Zamacona, Mexican Minister at Washington, visited Chicago and gave several addresses which set forth in glowing terms the prospects for rapid increase of trade with Mexico and the opportunities for American investors south of the Rio Grande. He made at least one appearance before the Manufacturers' Association of the Northwest. Foster, keenly aware of the damaging influence of such propaganda, responded to a letter of inquiry from Carlisle Mason, the president of this association, with a lengthy refutation of Zamacona's address and a full discussion of the impediments to the development of commercial relations between the two countries, of the lack of protection to American citizens and capital, of the opposition manifested to railway connections with the United States, and of the prejudices displayed against American enterprises in Mexico in general. Foster's polemic "was published in full in the Chicago papers, was reproduced in the annual volume of diplomatic correspondence, and by resolution of Congress it was printed as a public document." [38] It was also published by the association of manufacturers to whose president it had been written. It thus had a wide circulation in the United States where it may have made a few converts to Hayes's policy. Its influence may have been more than counteracted, however, by the able refutation immediately put forth by Matias Romero under the direction of the Mexican government; for in this elaborate monograph Romero contended that the Díaz administration was exceedingly eager to

[38] Foster, *Diplomatic Memoirs*, I, 115. For the letter to Mason, see *Foreign Relations* (1878), pp. 636-654 and *House Ex. Doc.* No. 15, 45 Cong., 3 Sess. (Ser. 1852),

attract American capital and enterprise and to develop American trade.[39]

At any rate financiers from New York and manufacturers and merchants from the West demonstrated their unflagging interest by organizing excursions to Mexico, while Congress entertained motions designed to stimulate Mexican trade or resolutions advising the appointment of commissions to negotiate a commercial treaty. Nor did the Hayes administration dare do more than cling tenaciously to the Ord Order and direct Foster to persist in what continued to prove useless negotiation.

At length a gradual improvement of conditions along the lower Rio Grande made it unnecessary to cross into Mexican territory and at the same time rendered it possible to revoke the Ord instructions without giving offense to Texas. This step was accordingly taken in February, 1880.[40] Díaz then evinced a disposition to yield an agreement for reciprocal crossing of the boundary in pursuit of marauders and the Hayes administration congratulated itself on the salutary influence of its firmness.[41]

The crisis had now passed, but in reality Hayes had been defeated in his contest with Díaz. He had been forced to grant unconditional recognition and had gained no concessions on the issues of forced loans, the Free Zone, the right to purchase real estate on the frontier, indemnity for alleged insults and injuries to American citizens, or protection of American life and property. Nor does it appear that Hayes's immediate successors accomplished more satisfactory results. At no time did Díaz prove himself more entitled to the sobriquet of "iron man" than when withstanding attempts of the United States to induce, persuade, or coerce him into signing formal, official agreements granting protection, guaranties, or exemptions to its citizens.[42]

[39] Secretaría de Hacienda, *Memoria* (1878–1879), p. 415 ff.; English version, New York, 1880, p. 325.

[40] *House Ex. Doc.* No. 1, 46 Cong., 3 Sess. (Ser. 1951), p. 735.

[41] In this connection see Rippy, "Some Precedents of the Pershing Expedition into Mexico," in *The Southwestern Historical Quarterly*, XXIV, 298 ff.

[42] But difficulties regarding the boundary and the shifting currents of the Rio Grande as well as several other important matters were settled by arbitration during the Díaz régime.

CHAPTER XVIII

PACIFIC PENETRATION

WHILE the two governments were wrangling over border disorders, formal guaranties to vested interests, and commercial concessions, hardy American pioneers were crossing the Rio Grande in ever increasing numbers. And when they reached Mexico they usually found the officials of the central government cordial and obliging. If they sought railway concessions they soon procured them. If they desired exemption from duties during the initial stages of a new enterprise this favor was not long denied.[1] The mining laws of 1884, 1892, and 1909 appeared to be satisfactory to those engaged in the mining of metals as well as to the coal miners and the oil men.[2] Citizens of the United States soon found it possible to evade the Mexican law which forbade them to purchase real estate on the frontier.[3] They were no longer troubled with forced loans; and if they complained of unjust treatment by the Mexican courts, Díaz is said eventually to have interfered in their behalf even here.[4] It may be that they were granted other favors either by Díaz or by the *Científicos*, counsellors of the dictator who, according to rumors, were not averse to lining their pockets with Yankee gold. In a word, what Díaz refused to grant by open and formal proclamation from the housetop he gradually yielded in the secret places of the palace.

Not that Díaz and his group showed marked favoritism to Americans. Certain special privileges may have been ceded, but it is probable that the Mexican government offered virtually the same advantages to all capitalists, whatever their nationality. Nor were the concessions generally such as would yield returns without ex-

[1] Powell, *The Railroads of Mexico*, pp. 167–169; for various railway concessions, see *Legislación sobre Ferrocarriles;* for concessions of other types, see Ministerio de Fomento, various *Memorias*.

[2] See, for instance, the lengthy testimony of Frederic R. Kellogg, in Fall Committee, *Report*, II, 2380 ff.

[3] Americans own land just across the boundary in Lower California, Sonora, and Chihuahua.

[4] Bulnes, *The Whole Truth About Mexico*, p. 193 ff.

pense, effort, or ingenuity. Americans frequently purchased them from Mexicans who had failed in an attempt to develop them or else had had no desire to do so. Some of the grants were certainly no better than had been secured from the United States or could then have been secured from various state governments of the American Union. But Mexico was more undeveloped and the central government of Mexico with its ever enlarging powers and functions had at its disposal more extensive, numerous, varied, and valuable concessions than Americans could easily have found elsewhere.

The railway builders of the United States were the first to enter Mexico on a large scale. Their agents began to visit Mexico City in quest of concessions soon after the Civil War, but they failed to acquire any until near the close of Díaz's first term. The list of promoters and speculators included such men as J. Sanford Barnes, Thomas W. Pearsall, R. S. Hays, Jay Gould, U. S. Grant, Russell Sage, Collis P. Huntington, and E. H. Harriman. Almost all of them eventually obtained railway grants, but most of the construction enterprises were carried forward by three groups: the Santa Fé, the Southern Pacific, and the Denver and Rio Grande, the latter apparently backed in part by Thomas A. Scott and J. Edgar Thomson of the Pennsylvania system.

Mexico does not appear to have suffered greatly from the evils of stock manipulation and wild speculation which had been so prevalent in the United States. Nor is it probable that the subsidies granted by the Mexican government, liberal though they were, were as valuable as those given to various railway enterprises in the United States. American capitalists made real investments in the country, and it is not likely that Mexican railroading has been as yet very profitable. Rates were usually high, however; and soon after the opening of the present century the tendency to pool and to consolidate became alarmingly apparent.[5]

By 1902 American holdings in Mexican railways were valued at well over $300,000,000. By the close of the year 1911 this amount had increased to almost $650,000,000. Americans had constructed about two-thirds of Mexico's sixteen thousand miles of railroad.[6]

Close upon the heels of the railway promoters and builders came the American miners. They did not often find *bonanzas*. In fact Americans usually bought abandoned or inadequately developed

---

[5] Powell, *op. cit.*, pp. 123–194. See also the Plumb Papers.
[6] U. S., *Commercial Relations* (1902), I, 433–435; Fall Committee, *Report*, II. 2553, *passim*; "Consular Reports," July 18, 1912. p. 316.

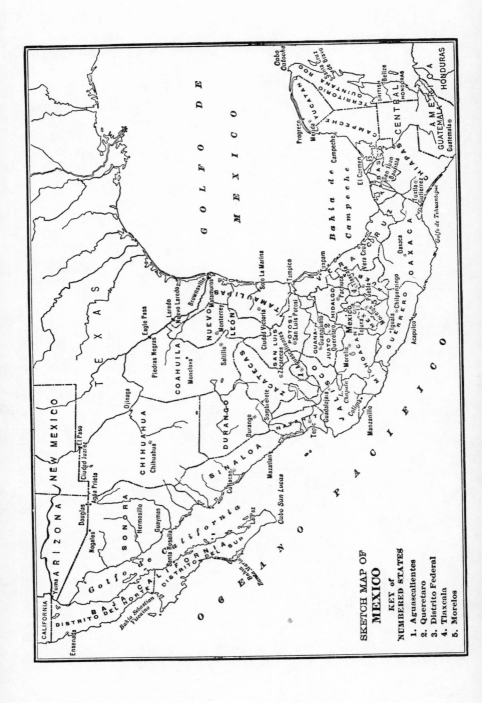

SKETCH MAP OF
MEXICO

KEY of
NUMBERED STATES

1. Aguascalientes
2. Querétaro
3. Distrito Federal
4. Tlaxcala
5. Morelos

mines. To these they brought large quantities of capital, improved machinery, and superior skill. By 1902 American mining properties in Mexico were valued at more than ninety-five million dollars and nine years later they had reached two hundred and fifty million, including the smelting industry. It was alleged that because of the large amount of initial capital necessary to put the abandoned mines in order many of these enterprises could be operated only by big companies. This is perhaps true. Certain it is that much of the mining was carried on by such huge interests as the Hearst Estate, the American Smelting and Refining Company (the Guggenheims), the Batopilas Company (of New York), the Anaconda group, the Greene-Cananea interests, the United States Steel Corporation, and other million dollar concerns.[7]

Along with the railroad men and the miners came the ranchmen, the planters, the land-speculators, and the small farmers. Sometimes ranching, farming, and timber lands were bought up by the large railway and mining companies themselves. Sometimes the lands were purchased by specialists in real estate, ranching, or farming. The large holding was the rule.

Into Lower California went Flores, Hale and Company of San Francisco, for the purpose of buying and leasing thousands of square miles of land for the production of orchilla. Into this territory went likewise the agents of the McCormick harvester interests of Chicago, to exploit the maguey fibre, and the representatives of great land and cattle companies or speculators in real estate, to purchase properties varying in area from fifty thousand to three million acres.

In 1902 the Sonora Land and Cattle Company, with headquarters at Chicago, was reported to own one million, three hundred thousand acres in Sonora. At the same time other important American holdings in this state were listed. M. M. Sherman of Kansas City was said to own five hundred thousand acres; the Sinaloa and Sonora Irrigation Company, four hundred thousand; William Bennett and Sons of Nogales, Arizona, seventy-five thousand; and the Greene Cattle Company, six or eight large tracts. A few years later the Richardson Construction Company, owned principally by Americans, bought out and enlarged to some six or eight hundred thousand acres the holdings of the Sonora and Sinaloa Company; the West Coast Cattle Company purchased two hundred and twenty-eight thousand acres; and the Alamo Cattle Company, ninety thousand acres.

[7] *Ibid., passim.*

In Chihuahua the Hearst estate acquired a tract of one-fourth of a million acres and the Corralitos Cattle Company, an equal amount. Just across the boundary of New Mexico and in Chihuahua, also, the Palomas Land and Cattle Company secured possession of two million acres. The famous T. O. Ranch embraced one million acres bordering on the Rio Grande in the same state. In Chihuahua, likewise, was situated the one hundred and forty thousand acre tract of the Mexican Irrigated Land Company, the some three hundred and sixty thousand acres of James D. Sheahan (near Jiménez), and the more than eight thousand acre holding of the Torreón Construction Company (near Santa Rosalie).

Into Coahuila went the Nelson and Weller Company, acquiring one hundred and sixty-five thousand acres; the Rosito Live Stock Company which bought up three hundred thousand acres; and several other investors. In this state also was situated the famous San José de las Piedras and the Piedra Blanca ranches, consisting of four hundred and sixty thousand and of one million two hundred and forty thousand acres, respectively.

Soon after the opening of the present century American land speculators and oil prospectors began to purchase large estates in Tamaulipas. In 1902 an Oklahoma Company purchased the Chemal Ranch which embraced a tract of more than three hundred thousand acres. This company was followed by an association of northwestern capitalists who purchased the Atascador estate comprising one hundred and thirty-five thousand acres; by the Comanche Land Company which acquired some eleven thousand acres; by the Valley of Paradise Development Association which bought up two hundred thousand acres; by the San Antonio (Texas) Land Company which secured possession of two hundred and fifty thousand acres; and by a dozen other companies purchasing tracts varying in size from six thousand to seventy thousand acres.

Nor were these holdings confined to the northern frontier. Large American holdings could be found in almost every Mexican state, and particularly in the tropical regions, where Americans engaged in the cultivation of sugar, coffee, rubber, cotton, and tropical fruits. It was reported in 1902, for instance, that San Francisco companies owned in the state of Chiapas five rubber plantations varying in area from six to twenty-five thousand acres; that an Omaha company claimed more than forty-six thousand acres and a Chicago firm, twenty-one thousand in this state. At the same time two Chicago companies were said to own five thousand acres each and another, seven thousand acres, in°Oaxaca, while other companies were accredited with estates varying from five to twenty thousand acres in Vera Cruz. The next few years saw a large increase in the number of these tropical properties. In 1906 La Esmeralda Plantation Company, composed of residents of Ohio, acquired almost four thousand acres in Vera Cruz. Two land companies, one from Peoria, Illinois, and the other from Norman, Oklahoma, purchased fifty-eight thousand acres near Medina, Oaxaca, during the same year. The Laguna Company of Delaware which had already acquired valuable holdings in 1902 soon increased them to six hundred and fifty thousand acres. The Vista Hermosa Company soon enlarged its Oaxaca holdings until they comprised twenty-five thousand acres. And before the fall of Díaz it is likely than ten or fifteen other associations went into these tropical states and purchased tracts varying in size from twelve thousand to a million acres. Mexico was rapidly becoming a land of large American estates.

Along with the big landlords were coming small farmers in ever increasing numbers. Soon after 1880 Mormons began to enter Mexico from Utah, Idaho, and other western states. By 1912 four thousand of them had settled in ten prosperous colonies, three in Sonora and seven in Chihuahua. Large profits for many of the land companies depended upon their success in inducing their countrymen to try their fortunes south of the Rio Grande. And, thanks in part to their efforts, many Americans from the West and Southwest were crossing the border and setting up agricultural establishments in almost every Mexican state. The Fall Committee of the United States Senate reported that there were in 1912 not less than fifteen thousand Americans residing permanently in Mexico and cultivating lands in small holdings.[8]

It is impossible to ascertain with accuracy the amount of money invested by Americans in Mexican lands during the Díaz régime. Consul-General Andrew D. Barlowe, who estimated these investments at somewhere between twenty-eight and thirty millions in 1902, has the following to say in this connection:

Estimates under this heading have been most difficult to make. It is certain that many of the so-called tropical agricultural companies have greatly exaggerated the amount of capital actually invested by them . . . The first cost of virgin lands in the tropics of Mexico is very small, say 50 cents to $1 per acre as a liberal average. Development work is expensive, and some of the older companies have no doubt spent considerable sums in improving their properties, but in a general way the "monthly payment" companies have not invested much in Mexico, however much the small investors may have paid

[8] "Consular Reports" (1880 ff.), index under *Mormons; House Doc.* No. 305, 57 Cong., 2 Sess. (Ser. 4520), p. 507; Fall Committee, *Report,* II, 3312.

the promoters for the privilege of holding stock in these companies . . . Promises of dividends by persons who propose to engage in the rubber-growing business are purely speculative and theoretical. Other American agricultural companies which propose to raise various tropical products may or may not be successful . . . It is safe to advise any person not to invest in any enterprise in Mexico without first visiting the country personally and thoroughly investigating the proposition and the local conditions . . .

While not much can be said in favor of the tropical agricultural companies, there are a great many legitimate agricultural enterprises in Mexico operated by American capital, some very successfully; and there is doubtless a large field here for conservative investments of American capital in this line.[9]

It is probable that American holdings in farms, ranches, and timberlands reached some fifty to eighty millions by 1912.[10]

Although the three classifications already analyzed constituted by far the most important American interests in Mexico until near the close of the Díaz régime, they by no means exhaust the list of American lines of endeavor. The money of citizens of the United States was invested in numerous enterprises in almost every Mexican state. As early as 1902 the following enterprises were listed in an official report: Manufacturers and foundrymen had interests in nineteen different states valued at nearly ten million dollars. Banks, trust companies, and investment companies had more than seven million dollars' worth of property in the three states of Puebla, Coahuila, and Nuevo León, and in the Federal District. Chemists, ore-testers, refiners, and so forth, owned almost seven millions worth of properties in Aguas Calientes, Chihuahua, Durango, the Federal District, Hidalgo, Jalisco, Lower California, Nuevo León, and Sonora. Public utility companies possessed properties valued at almost six millions in eleven different states, and wholesale and retail druggists, merchants, grocers, and hardware men, about two millions distributed through virtually all the states. During the next few years investments in most of these lines showed a rapid increase and new enterprises were added to the list. For instance, to mention only a few of the more conspicuous, the automobile business and the soap industry were introduced after 1902; the insurance business was insignificant until after that date; the oil industry was developed after 1901; and just at the opening of the Madero Revolution American capitalists were sending in experts from the American uni-

---

[9] *House Doc.* No. 305, 57 Cong., 2 Sess. (Ser. 4520), p. 436.
[10] A financier of long residence in Mexico and familiar with Mexican conditions estimated (1921) actual investments of Americans in "plantation, hacienda, and timber properties" at $105,000,000. Bureau of Foreign and Domestic Commerce, *Confidential Bulletin*, No. 40.

versities for the purpose of introducing the citrus fruit and the beet sugar industries.[11]

The most marvelous of all transformations occurred in connection with the development of petroleum and its products. Fuel oil had been known to exist in Mexico for centuries. It had been mentioned as an industry of Mexico in pamphlets published as early as 1857; and several attempts to develop and market it had occurred in the 'seventies and 'eighties of the last century. But all of these efforts, whether made by Spaniards, Mexicans, Americans, or even by such a renowned master of industry as Cecil Rhodes, ended in failure. It remained for Edward L. Doheny, C. A. Canfield, A. P. Maginnis, Herbert G. Wylie and their associates, all enterprising business men from California, to develop and market this "liquid gold" on a huge and immensely profitable scale. They brought in their first well in 1901. During the next few years they convinced themselves of the enormous potential productivity of the Tampico and Tuxpam oil regions, macadamized the streets of Mexican cities, demonstrated the practicability of using oil as fuel for the steam railways, and calmly prepared for the day when there should arise a tremendous demand for crude and refined petroleum. In May, 1905, their company signed a contract to supply the Mexican Central Railway six thousand barrels daily for fuel. A few years later similar contracts were entered into with other Mexican roads, large sales were made to the Standard Oil Company, and huge quantities were shipped to the Atlantic coast of the United States, so that the annual production of the Doheny group increased from one million barrels in 1907 to some sixty or seventy millions in 1922.[12]

Of course other American capitalists were attracted to the Mexican oil fields. The Standard Oil Companies, the Waters-Pierce Company, the Southern Oil and Transport Company, the Texas-Mexican Company, the Gulf Refining Company, the Penn-Mex Fuel Company, the Sinclair group, and the Panuco-Boston Company soon put in their appearance. They were accompanied and followed by scores of others until some two hundred and ninety companies owned by citizens of the United States had organized for the purpose of developing Mexican oil. Nor were these organizations confined to Americans. In 1906 the powerful Pearson in-

[11] *House Doc.* No. 305, 57 Cong., 2 Sess., I, 503-505; "Consular Reports," July 18, 1912, p. 316 ff.; Fall Committee, *Report*, II, 2739, *passim*.
[12] *Mexican Petroleum*, pp. 3-108; Fall Committee, *Report*, I, 207 ff., testimony of E. L. Doheny.

terests of Great Britain entered the field, followed by the Royal Dutch Company, the Spanish-Mexican Company, and other large interests. By 1912 it became evident, however, that the Mexican oil industry was likely to be developed and controlled largely by four great groups—the Doheny, the Standard Oil and Waters-Pierce allies, the Royal Dutch, and the Pearson interests—whose future relations many feared but none could predict. In that year the holdings of United States citizens in oil were estimated at the moderate sum of fifteen millions.[13]

The value of the total investments of United States citizens in Mexico was estimated in 1902 to be over five hundred millions American gold. In 1912 it was placed at one billion and fifty-seven millions. The Fall Committee of 1919, rejecting the estimate of 1912 as too low, valued them at one and one-half billions gold at the beginning of the Madero régime. According to Fall the Americans owned at the date last mentioned 78% of the mines, 72% of the smelters, 58% of the oil, and 68% of the rubber business of Mexico; and Letcher's report for 1912 stated that they owned more than all the other foreigners combined and even more then the Mexicans themselves. Somewhere between forty and seventy-five thousand Americans had established their homes in Mexico before General Díaz was sent into exile in 1911.[14]

It must be noted also that along with the master of finance, the captain of industry, and the colonist, came the Protestant minister, the missionary, and the distributer of Bibles and other religious literature. In fact the missionary led the vanguard more often than otherwise, for nine Protestant organizations had sent missionaries into the country before 1880 and Protestant colporteurs had sold Bibles and tracts in the wake of the American armies of 1846–'47. By 1902 agents of sixteen denominations had established churches, Sunday Schools, publishing houses, and institutions of learning both in the great centres of population and in the remoter district. In 1916, in spite of five years of revolution, there were in Mexico six hundred Protestant churches and places of regular wor-

---

[13] Middleton, *Industrial Mexico, passim;* "Consular Reports" July 18, 1912, p. 316 ff.

A *Confidential Bulletin* (No. 40) of the Bureau of Foreign and Domestic Commerce placed actual American investments in "oil lands and refineries" at $90,000,000 in 1921.

[14] *House Doc.* No. 305, 57 Cong., 2 Sess., I, 503; Fall Committee, *Report,* II, 3322, 3313.

A confidential estimate of the Bureau of Foreign and Domestic Commerce in 1921 placed the actual amount of American money invested at a little less than $652,000,000.

ship, with more than twenty-two thousand communicants, and more than four hundred Sunday Schools having a combined enrollment of almost eighteen thousand teachers and pupils, to say nothing of the numerous educational institutions some of which were among the best in the country. This perhaps represents a small showing compared to progress in other lines, but this Protestant missionary effort is nevertheless a factor that must not be ignored by the historian attempting to set forth the relations of the two countries in their proper light.[15]

Nor will the story of pacific penetration be complete without a page setting forth the marvelous growth of the commerce between the two countries subsequent to 1880. In 1860 this commerce amounted to a little more than seven million dollars. In 1870 it had not reached nine millions, but it had grown to more than fifteen millions by 1880, almost thirty-six millions in 1890, and more than sixty-three in 1900, while it mounted to the remarkable total of ninety-two millions in 1905 and one hundred and seventeen millions in 1910. By 1900 the United States had acquired a larger portion of Mexican trade than all of the European nations combined, and in 1912–13 about 51% of Mexico's imports came from the United States and more than 77% of her exports went to the same country.[16] Truly the Americans had become a tremendous force in Mexican life and progress. The process of pacific penetration had gone a long way in the short period of little more than three decades since the advent of Díaz to power.

[15] Beach and St. Johns, *World Statistics of Christian Missions,* p. 74. See, also, files of the *Missionary Herald* and the *Missionary Review.*

[16] Carefully compiled tables of United States-Mexican trade may be found in Robertson, *Hispanic American Relations of the United States,* App., p. 419 ff. See also Jones, *Mexico and Its Reconstruction,* for an extended treatment of this commerce.

CHAPTER XIX

THE CHALLENGE OF AMERICAN PREPONDERANCE

THE American movement into Mexico resulted in many advantages to the Mexican people. It brought unparalleled prosperity, raised the standards of living, sometimes stimulated the ambitions of the Mexicans, and, in a word, contributed a very large share toward placing Mexico temporarily among the great nations of the modern world. Without this movement Mexico could not have played so conspicuous a rôle at the Hague or in Central American arbitration, nor could she have challenged universal admiration by the splendor and magnificence of her centennial celebration in 1910. Mexico owed the dazzling brilliance of this latter occasion largely to the vision, the faith, the tenacity, the masterful ambition, and the constructive genius of American empire-builders who had received their early training in the great American West. But few Mexicans at this time appreciated the contribution which Yankee finance, enterprise, and ingenuity had made to Mexican progress. Most of them were thinking not so much of what the Yankees had done for Mexico as of the price which Mexico had paid for that service—of the unequal distribution of wealth, and of the prospect and possibility of Saxon domination.

In fact there never had been a time when Mexico had received foreigners with more than half a heart or looked upon them without suspicion, and the Americans were least likely to be an exception to the rule. Nationals from the United States had come to Mexico either of their own accord or at the urgent invitation of the Mexican chief executives. They had entered the country rather against the wishes of the Mexican people than at their solicitation. Successive Mexican presidents had been willing to make grants to American railway-builders and American masters of finance and industry for years before the popular branch of the Mexican Congress showed a disposition to ratify them.

A proposed concession to an American company for the construction of a railway from Guaymas to the Arizona border met with vigorous objection during the 'seventies on the ground that it would deflect Mexican trade from the centers of population, deprive the Mexican government of revenue, stimulate Yankee immigration, and eventually lead to the detachment of the frontier states from the Mexican Union.[1] Even more decided opposition had been evinced to granting an American company the privilege of connecting the northern frontier with the capital city. In 1878 this proposal had met with overwhelming defeat in the Mexican Congress where the leading speaker presented the following interesting line of argument:

> . . . I think, sir, that it is very poor policy, very injudicious, to establish within our country a powerful American company. Perhaps I should not venture to meet this question; but when I believe that I comply with my duty, although I fear for the good of the country, I have no fear of anything else. Let me suppose that this company is exceedingly rich; let me suppose that this company is going to build the railroad for us in five years, in five days; then I tremble at this, because we are going to establish within our territory an American influence . . .
>
> There are two severe laws in history and these laws are not to be forgotten. The first is this: Border nations are natural enemies . . . Who despoiled France of a section of territory? The bordering nation, Germany. Who is invading Turkey at the present time? The bordering nation, Russia . . . What war is there between Spain and Switzerland, between Italy and Russia? None. It is a natural law of history that border nations are enemies . . .
>
> There is also another law in history: Nations of the north necessarily invade the nations of the south. Let the history of the emigrations of the different races be read from prehistoric times, and the nations of the north will always be seen tending to conquer the nations of the south. Unfortunately, we do not need to recur to foreign histories; a rich part of our territory has become the prey of the United States; and we do not wish to learn, nor to open our eyes! . . .
>
> You, the deputies of the States, would you exchange your beautiful and poor liberty of the present for the rich subjection which the railroad could give you? Go and propose to the lion of the desert to exchange his cave of rocks for a golden cage, and the lion of the desert will reply to you with a roar of liberty. . . .[2]

The fact that in the early 'eighties Díaz and González were able to force through Congress numerous concessions to American railway companies by no means indicated that this opposition had completely subsided. Such semi-foreign papers as *Trait d'Union* continued to declare that "after having lost Texas, California, New Mexico, and Western Indian Territory, as well as the provinces east of the Rio del Norte, Mexico" ought certainly to "show great

---

[1] Foster to Evarts, No. 1013, August 15, and No. 1014, August 16, 1879, including enclosures, Mex. Desp., Vol. 68.

[2] Quoted in U. S., *Foreign Relations* (1878), pp. 551–552.

circumspection" toward her sister Republic, her powerful neighbor whose spirit of absorption, natural to the northern races, it could not afford to "ignore." [3] Such opposition journals as *La Patria* continued to maintain that the American companies would most assuredly involve the Mexican government in disputes which would furnish the United States a pretext for aggression and absorption.[4]

Several months after important grants had been made to the three companies who were to build Mexico's great trunk lines—the Central, the National, and the International—the American Minister in Mexico summed up the situation as follows:

> That there is a prejudice here against all foreigners everyone knows; that this prejudice is more decided against Americans than against any others it is useless to deny. . . .
>
> There are some men who speak as though they believed that a more extended intercourse with the United States would be conducive to the interests of Mexico. It is, however, reproached against these that they . . . are pecuniarily interested. . . .
>
> There are, on the other hand, many others, and these among the most prominent persons in the country, who look upon the Rail Roads which are in process of construction, as well as those which are in contemplation, as the agents of the country's destruction as a nation. They believe that the states bordering on the Rio Grande will, in a short time . . . be populated by Americans; that the mines as well as the [other] valuable property therein will be owned by them; that American school houses will dot the country; that the spires of Protestant churches will overtop the towers of their cathedrals, that the new population will not submit to the methods of Mexican rule, and that they will not delay to incite a revolution against the National Government with a view to annexation to the United States, to be followed by the absorption of the entire country . . .[5]

Opposition such as this could not be completely ignored at this time by the Mexican chief executives themselves. The early railway concessions usually contained provisions requiring construction to be commenced on the interoceanic portion or on the southern end of their lines, and virtually all of these concessions included a stipulation designed to denationalize the grantees.[6]

That these apprehensions would be confined exclusively to the railway builders no sane man could hope for a moment. A hint of Mexican attitude toward other American enterprises may be seen in the quotations already given. In 1879 there was published in Mexico a pamphlet which "attracted very general attention and

---

[3] June 16, 1881.

[4] July 6, 1881.

[5] Morgan to Blaine, No. 254, August 13, 1881, Mex. Desp., Vol. 73.

[6] Powell, *The Railroads of Mexico*, p. 167 ff.; see also various contracts in *Legislación sobre Ferrocarriles*.

occasioned much solicitude." It urged immediate preparations for the redemption of Mexican bonds held by citizens of the United States. These bonds were secured by lands and mineral rights in Tamaulipas and San Luis Potosí, and it was urged that if they were not redeemed at maturity they would furnish the United States a pretext for annexing those valuable states.[7] In 1884 the Mexican government granted several millions of acres of land in Lower California to Adolfo Bülle and Luis Hüller. Soon afterwards it was learned that they had sold their concession, or a part of it, to an American company of Hartford, Connecticut. Some of the leading newspapers of Mexico immediately called upon Díaz to explain the entire transaction and show reason why Lower California was not likely to become another Texas.[8] On June 15, 1887, *El Nacional*, a Mexican journal somewhat reactionary in tendency, contained a long article surveying the whole situation. It declared that every concession granted to Americans, no matter what its nature, was simply one link more in the chain of American subjugation. Financiers from the United States who were so rapidly making themselves "masters of the great industrial, mineral, railway, and agricultural enterprises" would eventually exercise a decisive influence on the politics of the country. The day would soon come when they would decide the local elections, serve as members of Congress, and choose the President. Indeed, if the present policy of the Mexican government was persisted in, the time would soon arrive when the "Catholic religion would give place to Protestantism, Judaism, Mormonism, and the thousand religious sects which exist in the United States"; when the English language would "supersede the Spanish"; when the Mexicans would find themselves "slaves" in their own fatherland!

Sentiments of this nature received more than occasional expression during the decades which followed. In what virtually amounted to an anti-Yankee campaign *El Nacional* had the energetic and often fanatical support of the Catholic *El Tiempo*, the *Correo de Español*, *La Patria*, and later *El Debate*, *El Pais*, and *El Diario del Hogar*.

El Tiempo, in particular, seized upon "every possible occasion to inflame the popular passion against the Government and people

---

[7] Tomás Mendoza, *El Porvenir de Mexico*. Reference is made to the Carvajal bonds of the Maximilian period. (See Callahan, "The Evolution of Seward's Mexican Policy.")

[8] *El Nacional*, November 19, 22, 26, 1887; *Las Novedades*, November 28, 1887; *El Tiempo*, November 29, 1887; *El Monitor Republicano*, December 1, 1887; *Diario Oficial*, July 21 and 22, 1884, December 1, 1887, *passim*.

of the United States." It took almost a fiendish delight in denouncing the "accursed Yankees" as "lynchers by profession," "assassins" of Chinese and Italians, "robbers of Mexican soil," "propagators of Protestantism," "meddlers in Hawaii and Cuba." Its persistent denunciations called forth from the *Mexican Herald,* a paper published in Mexico City by citizens of the United States, the following interesting and perhaps penetrating remark:

> One would like to have the *Tiempo* avow its real opinions, which would probably be found to favor the reestablishment of the Empire, an alliance with Spain for a war against the ever detested Yankees, the expulsion of all heretics with fire and sword, and the tearing up of the railways to the north.[9]

In 1895 *La Patria* came out in favor of the acquisition of Cuba by Mexico. The plan proposed was that of mediation and purchase; and it was urged that Mexico should prevent the United States from converting the Gulf into a Yankee *mare nostrum* and erect a barrier to Yankee expansion into Latin America. The proposal found a responsive chord in the heart of several Mexican journalists.[10]

Soon afterwards Cleveland's Venezuelan message became the subject of general comment, and the reaction of the Mexican press even on this occasion was not without its unfriendly phase. Its publication in Mexico led one of the journals to make the facetious and sarcastic announcement that a group of American statesmen, smitten with a stroke of conscience, had met and solemnly resolved to request their government to return to Mexico all the lands which had been usurped from her from "the infamous perfidy of Austin to the present time." Another journal remarked that if Cleveland's message should bring on a war in which England should defeat the United States, the Hispanic Americans would be benefited, for they would then be convinced of the "emptiness and impotence" of Monroe's manifesto and forced to give up the "delusion of North American aid against Europe and to assume an attitude of distrust with reference to the Yankees and their hypocritical protective rôle." At the same time a Mexican author published in Cuba a pamphlet roundly denouncing the Monroe Doctrine as the symbol of Anglo-Saxon preponderance, the expression of the design of the colossal Carthagenian invader of the North to absorb all of America.[11]

[9] *Literary Digest,* XII (April 4, 1896), 684.
[10] See a compilation of the articles published under the title, *Cuba Mexicana.*
[11] Romero, El *"Monroismo" y El General D. Porfirio Díaz.*

Even the more friendly and moderate papers accorded the message only a carefully qualified approval.[12]

Opposition to the Yankees was sometimes expressed in subsequent years in spite of the ever enlarging censorship of the Mexican press; and when the despotism of Díaz at last began to reveal unmistakable evidences of weakness, the pent-up forces of hostility assumed a violence which could not be controlled. With respect to the denunciation of the newspapers it will suffice to point out the fact that the American Ambassador, Henry Lane Wilson, frequently felt called upon to urge Díaz to curb the most vehement journals.[13] Other literature of this period demands more than a passing notice.

In 1908 Professor Carlos Pereyra published a small volume on *The Monroe Doctrine, Manifest Destiny, and Imperialism*, in which he maintained that there was nothing benevolent in the attitude of the United States towards the other American states. This fact had been amply demonstrated, he declared, by the refusal of the Washington government to participate unreservedly in the Panama Congress (1826), by its assertion in 1825 of a preference that Cuba and Porto Rico should remain under Spain, and by the various applications of the Monroe Doctrine. In fact, Pereyra expressed the conviction that the manifesto of Monroe had served merely as the handmaid of Manifest Destiny, as a convenient and effective rallying cry of imperialism; and as for Roosevelt's recent interpretation of that notorious doctrine, this *Big Stick* policy of his amounted, in effect, to the classification of the Hispanic-American states into three categories: those which are capable of maintaining order and which, accordingly, are not likely to be interfered with in the near future; those which are alleged to be incapable of leading an autonomous and progressive life and which must, therefore, accept Yankee tutelage; and those "which unfortunately possess . . . territory coveted by the United States." [14]

During the following year Andrés Molina Enríquez issued a work on the *Great National Problems* of Mexico, the main contention of which was that the *mestizos* should be looked to as the only hope of national salvation. He believed that it would be possible for this element to absorb and dominate foreigners and Creoles alike. This process would be likely to encounter the opposition both

[12] See Rippy, "Some Contemporary Mexican Reactions to Cleveland's Venezuelan Message," in *The Political Science Quarterly*, July, 1924, p. 280 ff.

[13] Lane to the Secretary of State, Nov. 10, 15, and 18, 1910, *For Rel.* (1911), p. 354 ff.

[14] See in particular pp. 1–60, 118 ff.

of the Creoles and the foreigners and these groups would perhaps appeal for the intervention of the United States, but this eventuality might be avoided by the exercise of great caution and moderation. The *mestizos* must conform to the Monroe Doctrine while consistently insisting upon its Pan-Americanization. They must stand with the United States upon the Japanese Problem. They must adopt the delicate policy of long-suffering acquiescence in the influence of the United States while at the same time working against the predominance of that influence. They must, in brief, seek to unite the interests of Yankee and *mestizo*. Patient and tactful pursuit of this line of action could alone be counted upon to ward off the menace of American intervention and save the Mexican soul.[15]

At about the same time Esteban Maqueo Castellanos published a volume entitled *Some National Problems*. In an interesting description of the types of Americans in Mexico the author evinces a friendly moderation somewhat unusual at the time—an attitude which may possibly be explained by his Porfirista affinity. Castellanos says in substance:

The American population which comes to make itself permanent is one-third composed of sane and judicious elements, well-educated men of enterprise, who have a proper conception of equity and justice, and are adaptable to environment. They know Mexico well, appreciate its institutions, follow its development, and analyze its history as a forerunner of the future . . . [This one-third] grows affectionate toward the country, likes to be here, and furnishes a most estimable contingent.

This type of American proceeds ordinarily from the centre or north of the United States, and is not a possible enemy but a good friend. It forms an important and intellectual part of the American colony. It finds here the same liberties as at home. It considers our laws good enough. It never speaks of war, annexation, or imperialism with reference to Mexico . . .

The second one-third is formed of that group of Americans who come to Mexico looking for work, to struggle for a future, for a better economic situation than they enjoyed in the States. They are modest in means and education, good Yankees, strong enough for rude tasks, or, sometimes, persons who are anxious to dress in style. These people have no proper judgment of the environment into which they come; they know our institutions very little, study us not at all, and have no propensity to become amalgamated with us. They neither hate us nor like us. For them a Mexican is always an intellectual, social, and political inferior. They come especially from the northwest and the southwest of the United States. They may be an enemy to us; they will not be our defender. Imperialism is a good thing for them, and if intervention comes they will be glad to see the frontier line carried down to the Suchiate . . .

The other one-third is our irreconcilable enemy. It is composed for the

[15] Priestly, "Mexican Literature on the Recent Revolution," in *Hispanic American Historical Review*, II (May, 1919), 293–294.

greater part of people driven from the United States by labor competition which they have not been able to meet. They have fled their country in order not to be restrained . . . In their own country they are hostile to order; here, any authority exercised over them they consider an affront . . . A standing percentage of these immigrants have accounts with justice to settle in their own country. Many are fortune hunters. They will never dominate a situation . . . though they are . . . undesirable.

Thus it will be observed that two-thirds of the Americans in Mexico—which, by the way, Castellanos estimated at about forty thousand—were considered dangerous or undesirable even by this friend of the Díaz régime. Moreover, he admits that the American government and nation might become a menace to Hispanic-American independence. He points, however, to the domestic and foreign problems of the Anglo-Saxon republic as a source of comfort and possible protection. Divergent class and economic interests, unassimilated foreigners, the threat of a caste war between blacks and whites, the impending struggle for the domination of the Pacific—all these factors he expected in the near future to tax the strength and ingenuity of the United States. Castellanos even suggested that some of the states of the southwestern portion of the United States might eventually come to feel a stronger affinity for Mexico than for the American Union!

The author then concludes with the declaration that the real danger to the Mexicans would come not from the United States so much as from Mexico itself. If the Mexicans "know how to preserve internal peace, foment progress, increase riches, and work quietly for their own evolution, they will have nothing to fear from the Americans . . . If on the contrary we renew our revolutionary past, . . . if we forget in our political vertigo the road along which peoples move to enjoy the respect and consideration of others, . . . if we prefer violence to prudence, . . . then it will not be the Yankee peril that shall wipe our country off the catalogue of the life of nations, but it will be ourselves—the Mexicans—unworthy of the right of possessing nationality." [16]

Further analysis of anti-Yankee literature is unnecessary. Already the causes of Mexican antipathy to the government and people of the United States must have become evident. They are to be found in diversities of religion, race, and temperament, in the lively memory of former injuries suffered at the hands of their neighbors, and in the exigencies of domestic politics which called for the exaggeration of the Yankee Peril. They may be detected, too,

[16] *Ibid.*, pp. 295–297.

in the European sympathies of reactionary Mexicans and in the insidious propaganda carried on by Europeans from motives of political jealousy or economic rivalry. In the 'eighties the Mexican Yankeephobes urged their government to checkmate American influence by calling in European influence,[17] and it was but natural that the Europeans should aid and abet this policy.[18] Lastly, it must be admitted that, as the years passed, the increasing aggressiveness and power of American Big Business constituted a factor whose contemplation could hardly fail to arouse alarm even in less prejudiced minds.

President Díaz clamped the shackles of press censorship upon these Yankeephobes because their diatribes often tended to assume an anti-Díaz tone, and because their discoveries, alleged or genuine, endangered his power. But there are indications that Díaz as well as his ministers and tools likewise shared these apprehensions of American preponderance and domination. The dictator complied with the earnest solicitations of American financiers, and in the early days even urged them to make investments, because he believed that Mexico was in great need of their enterprise and ingenuity, but the future historian may discover that he came more and more to resent not only their power and influence, but that of their government as well. It may be that this furnished one motive for his anxiety during the last twenty-five years of his rule to stimulate the influx of English, French, and German capital and to negotiate European loans. It appears almost certain that it was responsible in large measure for the railway, oil, and other valuable concessions which Lord Cowdray secured at the opening of the century.[19] The policy of nationalizing the Mexican railways was said to have been adopted in order to forestall the consolidating schemes of E. H. Harriman and H. Clay Pierce,[20] and the aged dictator took great pains to pledge Edward L. Doheny never to sell out to the Standard Oil interests.[21] That Díaz was somewhat restive in the face of the ever enlarging rôle of the United States in

---

[17] See, for instance, Mendoza, *op. cit.*, and *El Nacional*, June 15, 1887.

[18] See comments of the European press in *Cuba Mexicana,* and Rippy, "Pan-Hispanic Propaganda in Hispanic America," in *The Political Science Quarterly,* XXXVII (September, 1922), 389 ff.
American ministers in Mexico frequently complained that European propaganda against the United States was being carried on in the country.

[19] Powell, *The Railways of Mexico,* p. 152, 175–177; Fall Committee, *Report,* II, 2411 ff., testimony of Sherburne G. Hopkins.

[20] Powell, *op. et loc. cit.;* Marcosson, "Our Financial Stake in Mexico," in *Collier's Weekly,* July 1, 1916, pp. 22–23.

[21] Fall Committee, *Report,* I, 218–219.

the western hemisphere likewise seems probable. He was embittered more than once by what appeared to be the too persistent attempts of the United States government to serve as mediator in the various disputes between Mexico and Guatemala.[22] His suggestions in 1896 with reference to the advisability of the Pan-Americanization of the Monroe Doctrine furnish further evidence of this attitude.[23] His joint mediation with the United States in Central America in 1907 may have had a similar significance. But none of these measures could stem the rising tide of Mexican nationalism which was destined ere long to drive out both the foreigners and the ruler who had called them in.

Nearly all of the charges preferred against the Díaz régime are connected directly or indirectly with his policy toward the United States or toward immigrant capital, and particularly that from the United States. They were in substance as follows:

(1) The sale of "half of Lower California for a mere pittance to Louis Huller, of German extraction and a naturalized American citizen, who passed it on to an American colonizing enterprise." It was "held that Lower California would follow the fate of Texas."

(2) The modification of the "Mining Code, including the clause which assigns to the owner of the land the coal deposits that may be found upon it, for no other reason than that of enriching the grantees of unclaimed lands in the state of Coahuila, who had acquired the Sabinas lands for an insignificant sum with a view to selling them to the American multi-millionaire, Huntington."

(3) The granting of "concessions to foreign companies to exploit the oil lands, among which companies the American predominated." The exemption of these companies "from export duties on the crude and refined product, thereby depriving the Mexican people of the only means at their command to derive anything from the exploitation of their great national wealth."

(4) Failure to prevent the Guggenheims from monopolizing "almost completely the important metallurgic industry upon which the progress of mining in the country depended." It was alleged that the Guggenheims "controlled the smelting plants of Monterey, San Luis Potosi, Aguas Calientes and Velardena in Durango, and were trying to get a foothold in Pachuca & Real Del Monte . . ."

(5) The sale "for next to nothing" of "3,000,000 hectares of excellent lands in the state of Chihuahua to two favorites of the Mexican Government, that they might resell to Mr. Hearst, the celebrated millionaire . . ."

(6) "The granting to Colonel Greene, an American citizen, of enormous concessions in the copper lands of the state of Sonora, upon which he had established the famous Cananea plant, where the four thousand employees were treated like slaves, and with such inhumanity that there was an up-

[22] These attempts at mediation extended over a period of more than twenty years. Cf. *House Ex. Doc.* No. 154, 48 Cong., 1 Sess.; *Foreign Relations* (1895–1898), index under Mexico and Guatemala.

[23] Cf. Rippy, article cited in note 12.

rising among them, with the result that armed men from the United States passed into Mexican territory to protect the American oppressors."

(7) Allowing United States Ambassador Powell Clayton "to appear every afternoon at the National Palace with a list of recommendations for private American affairs, in order that they might be approved immediately by the administrative and judicial authorities in favor of the interested parties, even when the requests constituted an infamous injustice to the rights of the Mexican people."

(8) The granting of "personal concessions" to United States Ambassador Thompson "by means of which he organized the United States Banking Company and the Pan-American Railroad."

(9) The granting of "scandalous concessions in rubber lands . . . to the American multi-millionaires, John Rockefeller and Nelson Aldrich, which caused the ruin of a great number of poor towns in the state of Durango."

(10) The sale to "twenty-eight favorites" of some fifty millions of hectares of "marvelously fertile lands" merely that these favorites might alienate them for a song to foreign companies, mostly American.

(11) The expulsion of the Yaquis from their "magnificent lands" in order "to hand them over to thieving bureaucrats, who wanted them merely to sell to American investors.

(12) Failure to prevent Mexican and American financiers from "consummating a piratical financial stroke against Mexico and the holders of Mexican railroad stocks." It was alleged that these speculators, having procured inside information as to the intentions of the Mexican government, bought secretly and at a low figure the stocks of various railroads and later sold them at a great advance to the Díaz administration.

(13) The appointment of E. N. Brown, an American citizen, "to the important post of General Manager" of the nationalized railway system, and the assignment of all other important positions of the system, especially those paying large salaries, to Americans.

(14) The grant of a "monopoly to the house of Mosler, Bowen & Cook to supply all office furniture to Government offices, as well as to Government schools . . ."

(15) The placing of foreign loans with the New York banks, particularly "the New York house of J. Pierpont Morgan."

(16) "The complete prostitution of Mexican courts" to American litigants.

(17) "The servile and traitorous act of lending Magdalena Bay to the United States."

(18) The rejection, because of a desire "not to displease the United States," of "the honorable propositions of eminently respectable Japanese houses to establish Japanese colonies in various parts of the country, particularly on the Pacific Coast and in Lower California."

(19) Neglect "to pursue the Chamizal question to the end, which would have put the Mexican people in the possession of the territory upon which the city of El Paso is built . . ."

(20) The passage at the dictation of the United States of "an immigration law . . . against the Japanese and the Chinese . . ."

(21) The pursuit of "so degrading a policy toward the United States that any American, however insignificant or knavish he might be, felt privileged to repeat with haughtiness, . . . 'Civis romanus sum' " [24]

[24] Francisco Bulnes, *The Whole Truth About Mexico*, pp. 120-127.

And so the list might be continued. A popular adage declared that Mexico was the foreigner's mother and the Mexican's stepmother, which meant that Mexico was the mother mostly of Yankees, or as General Felix Díaz said, the mistress of the United States. Few unprejudiced men would dare assert that anything like all these charges were well founded. The documents necessary to put these matters in their true light are not now available, nor is it likely that they will be soon. Francisco Bulnes, who has summarized the charges against the Díaz administration, remarked that "some are false; others simply absurd; others grossly exaggerated; others demonstrate a wrong interpretation from lack of proper understanding; some are true." Perhaps one can not do better than leave the question there for the present. It is probable that with most Mexicans the counts in the Díaz indictment could not have had more weight if they had been true, for Mexicans believed that they were true and falsehood when accepted as truth is a potent factor in history.

When all the evidence is in, the future historian may find in the aged Díaz a tragic figure. Convinced of Mexico's great need of foreign capital, he had begun his long rule by encouraging foreign enterprises and investments in partial defiance of the will of the Mexican people themselves. He had done so, perhaps, in the hope that the enriching and civilizing influence of the outlander would eventually demonstrate the wisdom of his policy. But the Mexican people were hard to convince. Díaz might argue that the influence of the growing foreign element in Mexico was edifying, civilizing, progressive, but the Mexicans persistently maintained that it was proselyting, oppressive, and denationalizing. Meanwhile the foreigners, especially the Americans, were accumulating wealth and power with amazing rapidity and beyond the wildest dreams either of themselves or of Díaz, so that in his declining years the aged chief found himself between two formidable and virtually irreconcilable forces and in the difficult position of one trying to serve two mutually unfriendly masters. Then occurred what always occurs under such a condition: Díaz was forced to hold to the one and despise the other. He surrendered, or at any rate permitted his ministers to surrender, to foreign capital, and attempted to suppress the Mexican people. But the Mexican people proved more powerful than Díaz and the foreigners. The grey-headed dictator died in exile; the outlanders found graves in Mexico or fled before the destructive rage of the Mexican populace, crying out for the protection of the government of their native land.

CHAPTER XX *

PRESIDENT TAFT'S MEXICAN POLICY

THE Mexican revolution which began in November, 1910, was essentially an armed protest of Indians and mixed breeds against the exploitation of foreigners, native landlords and industrialists, and the Church heirarchy.[1] It was heralded by violent denunciations of the United States and its nationals in the newspapers of Mexico City and by anti-American riots in various parts of the republic. President Taft's first step with reference to the uprising was to telegraph Díaz, expressing confidence in Don Porfirio's ability to maintain order and protect American property and citizens. At the same time, Henry Lane Wilson, Ambassador of the United States in Mexico City, had numerous interviews with Díaz and the Mexican Minister of Foreign Affairs, in which he urged that the press be brought under control and the rioters suppressed. The Díaz government assembled its waning strength and began to act. The anti-American sentiment soon subsided or became latent.

Meantime, the diplomatic agents of Don Porfirio's government were complaining of the failure of the United States to maintain neutrality. They alleged that the revolution against Díaz was being planned and equipped on American soil, and there was much truth in the allegation. Owing to the large amount of personal liberty permitted under the American system of government, antiquated neutrality laws, and the rugged and desert nature of the frontier region, it was comparatively easy for the insurgents to carry on propaganda, collect munitions and supplies, and even to organize their forces on United States soil. Their operations were further facilitated by widespread sympathy among the border inhabitants and possibly by the indifference of some of the frontier officials of the United States. In this situation there was nothing exceptional, however. Many a Mexican revolution had been organized in part within the territory of the United States and the

* This and the following two chapters are adapted from the author's statement in pages 9 to 89 of *Mexico: American Policies Abroad,* with the permission of the Chicago Council on Foreign Relations and the University of Chicago Press.

[1] *Cf.* Tannenbaum, *The Mexican Agrarian Revolution,* and McBride, *The Land Systems of Mexico.*

revolution which brought Díaz himself to power had been one of them.

The unique feature of the affair now under consideration was the slowness with which the United States came to the realization that it was failing to meet its international obligations. As early as November 19, 1910, the Díaz government began to urge the United States to guard its frontier by "mobilizing the necessary forces." But it was not until the early days of the following March that extra troops were sent to the international border, and even then they were dispatched for "maneuvers" or for the purpose of invading Mexico and protecting American life and property in case such a step should be deemed neccessary.

This dilatory policy led the critics of the Taft administration to declare that perhaps the President—or, at any rate, Secretary of State Knox and Ambassador Wilson—was not unwilling to see Díaz overthrown. These critics charged that the Mexican dictator had in his old days given offense to certain powerful captains of industry who had the ear of the Taft government through Henry W. Taft (the brother of the President), through Attorney-General George W. Wickersham, and through Secretary Knox himself. These powerful interests had determined to unseat Díaz and were glad to take advantage of the general discontent in Mexico to effect their purpose. Of course the critics did not make the preposterous allegation that such interests preferred the radical dreamer Francisco Madero to Díaz or a man of his stripe. These captains of industry merely accepted Madero temporarily as the most available leader. Their choice and the choice of Taft and Knox was De la Barra, whom they expected to seize the reins of power and turn Madero aside at the opportune moment.

This explanation of the delay of the Taft administration in adopting measures which would fulfill to the limit its neutrality obligations can neither be proved nor disproved at this time. There is good evidence that De la Barra was the choice of Taft and Knox [2] and it seems significant that United States troops were not sent to the border until it appeared certain that Díaz would be driven from power. Did it accord with the purpose of the Taft administration to use the army in order to hamper the movement of the insurgents only after De la Barra had started on the path which led him directly to the portfolio of foreign affairs and the presidency? This version of the affair should not be pressed too far. The Department of Justice under Taft had coöperated with the Díaz government for some time prior

[2] See Edith O'Shaughnessy, *Intimate Pages of Mexican History*, pp. 93–97.

to the revolutionary outbreak, giving it assistance in the suppression of propaganda and of treasonable acts and utterance of Mexicans on American soil, and the Department had been severely criticized for its pains. In fact, a congressional investigation of its conduct had been demanded. Moreover, too great zeal on the southwestern frontier and the dispatch of an unwonted number of troops at this time might have intensified the Yankeephobia sentiment in Mexico and resulted in great injury to American life and property south of the Rio Grande. And, lastly, it should be noted that the international obligations of the United States were not totally neglected during the early stages of the Mexican revolution, and that Mexico expected too much of the United States. The Díaz government would probably have been overthrown even if the United States had guarded every foot of the frontier. Whatever the true explanation of Taft's conduct, the fact remains that the neutrality of the United States was enforced during the spring and summer of 1911 to a degree far beyond that of the previous four months.

It might also appear very significant that most of the troops of the United States were withdrawn from the frontier in August, 1911, after a personal conference with Henry Lane Wilson and after the *Chargé* of the United States in Mexico had reported the general belief among Mexicans of the capital that Madero was bound to succeed in the November elections. Yet it must be remembered that conditions in Mexico were comparatively quiet at this time. It should also be noted that Ambassador Wilson "earnestly" recommended on November 15, after Madero was already in power, that "energetic measures be taken on the border and . . . every possible assistance compatible with our laws be given to the Mexican Government." [3] And lastly, it should not be forgotten that the revolutionary projects of Bernardo Reyes at San Antonio, Texas, were greatly hampered by the vigilance of the federal officers of the United States; Reyes having been compelled to surrender to the Madero authorities near the close of the year.

In fact, by the beginning of the year 1912 Madero found himself more embarrassed by the zeal of the United States in guarding its frontier than by its indifference to matters of neutrality. Early in January "several newspapers of the capital" published articles which charged that Madero had received assistance from the government of the United States in overthrowing General Díaz and establishing himself in power and that for this reason he now found himself unduly obligated to the United States. Two weeks later Ambassador Wilson

[3] Wilson to Knox, *Foreign Relations* (1911), p. 521.

called attention to "venomous attacks" of Madero and his Cabinet, "to exaggerated stories of political and financial intrigue," and to bitter denunciations of "the United States in its relations wth Mexico. . . ." At the same time he reported revolutionary movements against the established order in some five or six states and maltreatment of Americans in as many more. Apparently Yankeephobia was becoming a potent factor. Well might Madero have prayed to be saved from his friends!

Indeed, this Apostle of the Mexican masses soon had reason to question the sincerity of the friendship of the Washington government. On February 4, 1912, President Taft ordered the concentration of 100,000 troops, regulars and volunteers, on the Mexican border. Twenty days later Acting Secretary of State Huntington Wilson and Ambassador Wilson exchanged telegrams discussing the advisability of intervention. The news reached the papers of both countries. On March 2 Ambassador Wilson was instructed at his discretion to advise Americans to withdraw from certain zones of danger which he might designate. The Ambassador published the substance of his instructions in the dailies of Mexico City and warned Americans to remove from so many sections that the advice was construed to apply to almost the entire country! These steps were interpreted as indicative of lack of faith in, and even of hostility toward, Madero. Opponents of the Madero régime in Mexico are said to have been greatly stimulated. The editor of one of the American newspapers in Mexico City declared that "no honest man, no friend of peace and order, received encouragement or help, but the children of the Devil ran riot." [4] Worse still, any move on the part of the Madero government to capitalize the situation was partially estopped by two proclamations of President Taft. The first of these (March 2) warned Americans not to participate in the revolutionary disorders of Mexico. The other (March 14) assumed more rigid executive control of the exportation of arms and munitions and contained a hint of the possibility that the authority of the American President might be exercised to the advantage of Madero. In view of these demonstrations of favoritism it would seem futile for the Madero administration to seek new strength by sounding the anti-Yankee note and posing as the victim of American persecution.

A month later, however, Madero found himself in a more favorable position. Taft not only had prevented the *insurrectos* of northern Mexico from importing arms while granting this privilege to the followers of Madero, but he had permitted Madero to transport

[4] Bell, *The Political Shame of Mexico,* p. 151 ff.

troops across the United States for the purpose of attacking the insurgents. This had aroused the ire of Pascual Orozco and other chiefs, and they had immediately assumed a more truculent attitude, seizing American mails, committing depredations upon American property, killing and wounding American nationals, and refusing to take cognizance of the protests of American consuls. This led to vigorous remonstrance on the part of the United States. On April 15 Henry Lane Wilson handed the Mexican government a drastic note couched in the following language:

"The enormous and constantly increasing destruction of valuable American properties, . . . the taking of American life contrary to the principles governing among civilized nations, the increasing dangers to which all American citizens in Mexico are subjected, and the seemingly possible indefinite continuance of this unfortunate situation, compel the Government of the United States to give notice that it expects and must demand that American life and property . . . be justly and adequately protected and that it must hold Mexico and the Mexican people responsible for all wanton and illegal acts sacrificing or endangering American life or property. . . ."

Wilson also issued a warning to Mexicans who were circulating false rumors and instigating attacks upon Americans and expressed alarm at the reports that General Villa intended to execute all Americans captured from the armies of the insurgents. The remonstrance concluded with a quotation from a recent warning to Orozco, in which a protest was made against the "practical murder" of an American and notice served that "any maltreatment of any American citizen" would be "deeply resented" by the United States and "must be fully answered for by the Mexican people. . . ." [5]

The transmission of this note and its publication in the newspapers of the United States gave the Mexican government an opportunity to represent itself as a defiant victim of Yankee ruthlessness. Pedro Lascurain, Mexican Minister of Foreign Affairs, proceeded immediately to capitalize the situation. On April 17 he replied to Wilson's note and handed the note and the text of the reply to the Mexican press.

"The Mexican government is fully cognizant of its duties," said Lascurain. ". . . It finds itself under the painful necessity of not recognizing the right of your Government to give the warning which the aforesaid note contains, since it is not based upon any action imputable to the Mexican government signifying that it has departed from the observance of the principles and practices of international law.

"Since one part of the country is in a state of revolution the Mexican government holds as its principal duty the suppression of the rebel movement, and if in the regions which have removed themselves from obedience to the legitimate authorities attempts are made against the lives and property of foreigners the legitimate Government of the Republic will not be liable in this regard except under the same conditions as the Government of the United States or that of any other country would be if a rebellion arose in its own territory."

Lascurain then proceeded to pledge Mexico to abide by international law and the laws of the Mexican nation in the treatment of Americans and other foreigners who might be among the prisoners captured from the rebel forces. He also deplored the continuance of disorders in Mexico, as well as the injuries to foreigners which attended the disturbances and the baseless rumors spread by Mexicans and certain sections of the press of all countries. He declared, finally, that it was the settled policy of the Mexican government to punish the Mexican perpetrators of outrages against foreigners, but he denied that the Mexican government and people could be held responsible for the "rebel leader" Orozco in the sense implied by the American Secretary of State.[6]

This diplomatic encounter appears to have brought new support to Madero. At any rate he revealed unusual strength during the next few months. By midsummer his troops not only had arrested Villa and sent him to Mexico City for trial but also had virtually annihilated the insurgents under Orozco. So great was his progress that he was able to negotiate a loan of $10,000,000 with Speyer and Company late in May.[7]—The menaces of the State Department apparently had come at an opportune time. Yet the main purpose of that Department in the spring and summer of 1912 appears to have been to furnish protection to American citizens and to mend its political fences in view of the coming election. And its exertions at the time did not end with the note of April 15. War vessels were sent to the various ports of the Atlantic and Pacific coasts of Mexico to furnish transportation to American citizens who desired to leave the country and to serve as a warning to the Mexican people.

The effectiveness of this procedure in shielding American life and property seems to have been very doubtful. Not only were rebels

[6] *Foreign Relations* (1912), pp. 792–793.
[7] *Commercial and Financial Chronicle*, June 1, 1912, p. 1472.

of the North irritated at the favoritism of the Washington government toward Madero in the matter of importing arms and munitions; in other sections likewise the menacing attitude of the United States appeared to be only so much oil on the flames of Yankeephobia. Something had to be done, however, and this was the policy which the Taft administration had decided to adopt.

Nor did the temporary defeat and dispersal of the insurgents of the North in July and August bring peace to Mexico or add greatly to the security of American life and interests in the country. The defeated rebels of the North split up into numerous small bands ranging in size from one hundred to one thousand men and resorted to robbery, murder, and pillage. In the South, in the states of Puebla, Oaxaca, Morelos, Guerrero, and Mexico, the country was being terrorized and laid waste by Zapata and his followers. Elsewhere there were no large revolutionary organizations, but the government had broken down in numerous regions and chaos appeared to impend. Indeed, if one may believe Henry Lane Wilson, American life and property in Mexico were in greater peril in August, 1912, than ever before. The Ambassador complained at the time of the numerous outrages committed against American citizens—the increasing frequency of murders, arrests, and imprisonments on frivolous charges, and the illegal and unjust seizures of American property. Declaring that conditions were rapidly becoming intolerable, he said: "This phase of the situation here is arousing profound indignation among the Americans resident in Mexico and, if I may judge by the number of letters received by the Embassy and by the utterances of the American press, criticism and dangerous public opinion in the United States. . . . I feel that usual diplomatic methods have failed . . . and I fear that, unless some well-defined and positive course is adopted the injustice, abuses, and murders of American citizens will increase in number." In fact, the Ambassador went so far as to accuse the Madero government, nominally pro-American and suffering from its supposed pro-Americanism as it was, of "really conducting a campaign against American interests in Mexico" apparently designed "to make the members of the Madero family and the personal and political adherents thereof the beneficiaries of American loss." [8] Such a charge was exceedingly grave and, taken in connection with certain previous and subsequent reports of Wilson, arouses a strong suspicion of personal grudge or ulterior motives.

Wilson's report found President Taft in no squeamish mood, however. His mild patience in dealing with Mexico had long been

[8] *Foreign Relations* (1912), pp. 828–832.

criticized by the press and certain elements in Congress. As early as the middle of April, 1911, Senator William J. Stone, Democrat from Missouri, had demanded a more energetic Mexican policy. His protest had been called forth mainly by the injury of American citizens during battles between the Mexican government and insurgents in the vicinity of El Paso, Texas, and Douglas, Arizona. He took occasion, however, to refer to the strong anti-American sentiment in Mexico, the injuries suffered by Americans residing in the country, the growing impatience of European powers, and the interruption by Mexican rebels of the Colorado River irrigation project. He demanded that a committee be appointed to make inquiries and recommendations. This attack proved to be a mere tempest in a teapot, however. No one came to Stone's support and such prominent Senators as Bacon, Lodge, and Root upheld the President's policy, urging a kindly sympathy for Mexico. But by the summer of the following year conditions had considerably changed. As hundreds and even thousands of American refugees, pursuant to the advice of the Taft administration, made their way to the United States, a wave of sympathy and irritation passed over the country, and this sentiment was but deepened by reports of injuries and outrages which appeared in American newspapers. A portion of the press soon began to demand intervention and Congress not only made appropriations for transporting, sheltering, and feeding the refugees but also directed the Secretary of War "to investigate the claims of American citizens for damages suffered within American territory and growing out of the . . . insurrection in Mexico." Moreover, Senator Albert Fall began in July to demand protection for the persons and property of citizens of the United States south of the Rio Grande, and Senator Smith of Arizona revealed a growing impatience. As important as any other feature of the situation, furthermore, was the fact that the national campaign of 1912 had already begun and the Democratic platform had pledged the party to protect its nationals abroad. The time for more vigorous action had arrived.

The Taft administration accordingly began to take steps which indicated a resolution to bring Mexico to terms. On September 2, the American Ambassador was instructed to demand that the Mexican government establish adequate garrisons along the northern frontier, from Matamoras to Mexicali, and to designate the number of troops which the United States deemed necessary for preventing uprisings in the region and protecting American inhabitants across the border in the United States. A garrison was also requested for the protection of the Mormon colonies in Chihuahua.

Two days later Taft had a grave interview with the Mexican Ambassador at Washington, who was on the point of departing for Mexico City. Referring to the proclamation of March 14 and the benefits which it conferred upon the Madero administration, the President pointed out how friendly and patient he had been toward Mexico. He declared that in return for all this "we had a right to expect a more hearty consideration for all American interests in Mexico." He "spoke solemnly of his duty to the American people . . . and also of the duty of the Madero administration to vindicate his [patient] policy by a satisfactory attitude. The President even went so far as to say that if things went on from bad to worse there would be no course open to him in the discharge of his duties but to summon Congress and ask them to consider how the situation should be dealt with. Señor Calero, the Mexican Ambassador, appeared to be a "good deal worried." "He spoke energetically about the bad feeling caused by Senator Fall's speech and by the Magdalena Bay legislation. The President disavowed any sympathy for either and remarked that . . . it was not the Senate but the Executive which conducted our foreign relations." Moreover, at this point Huntington Wilson (Acting Secretary of State), who had been present during the interview, came to Taft's support, remarking that the Lodge Resolution against the alienation of Magdalena Bay and Fall's oratory had little to do with the specific matter at issue and pointing out that murderers were going unpunished in Mexico, that too much anti-American sentiment was being revealed even in government quarters, and that the Madero régime was really lacking in zeal and energy. Taft then remarked that Mexico must not assume that his patience was perennial and urged Calero to use his influence to bring about an improvement in the situation. The Ambassador, somewhat cowed and, as the sequel was to reveal, out of sympathy with the Madero movement, could only apologize for conditions in Mexico and speak "rather disparagingly of their Indian population, their inheritance of Spanish and Indian traits, their unfitness for democratic institutions, and the consequent enormously difficult problems they had to face." [9]

On September 5 Huntington Wilson instructed Henry Lane Wilson to present to the Mexican government a note which amounted virtually to an ultimatum. The Ambassador, in accordance with his instructions, made some revisions in the original draft and then transmitted it to the Mexican Minister of Foreign Affairs on September 17, the process of revision being hastened because of the rumor that the Madero government was on the point of being overthrown by a *coup d'état*. That this procedure of the Taft administration was

[9] *Foreign Relations* (1912), pp. 833–834.

taken with the national campaign in mind appears to be indicated by
the fact that news of a contemplated change in policy was permitted to
find its way into the papers.

The final draft presented to the Mexican government by Ambassador Wilson listed by name seventeen citizens of the United States
whose Mexican murderers had been allowed to go unpunished. Reference was made also to "other cases (which need not here be set
down)." Against such indifference and inefficiency vigorous protest
was uttered. At the same time it was announced that the United
States was no longer disposed to permit its nationals "constantly to
be made the objects of the tyranny of petty local authorities, or of
intrigue of anti-American sentiment." The *Mexican Herald,* a newspaper owned by Americans, and the Associated Press had been the
victims of unfair treatment; Americans interested in a colonization
company (the Tlahualillo of Durango) had suffered injustice on account of an adverse court decision rendered under pressure "from
official quarters"; American oil interests in the vicinity of Tampico
were being "taxed almost beyond endurance"; an attempt was being
made to annul the concession of the Mexican National Packing Company in which "twelve hundred odd American stockholders" were
indirectly interested—these instances were mentioned as illustrative
and most recent. They did not "by any means constitute all which
might be made the subject of remonstrance." This "predatory persecution, amounting practically to confiscation," must "cease forthwith.
. . . The administration in Mexico must bestir itself to fulfill its
international duties toward American citizens and their interests" or
the United States would no longer forbid the exportation of arms to
those in rebellion against the constituted authority in Mexico. Moreover, a still further threat was brandished. Wilson declared that "the
time has [had] come when the administration at Mexico City . . .
must either demonstrate its determination and ability to handle the
situation by the early establishment of order and the effective administration of law, or frankly confess that conditions are [were] such
that it is [was] powerless to do so. In the latter case it would evidently become necessary for the Government of the United States to
consider what measures it should adopt to meet the requirements of
the situation."

The conclusion of the note differed from an ultimatum only in that
no time limit was set for a reply. It contained the following demand:

"The Government of the United States desires from your excellency as promptly
as possible a comprehensive and categorical statement as to the measures the
Mexican Government proposes to adopt: (I) To effect the capture and adequate
punishment of the murderers of American citizens; (II) to put an end to the

discriminations against American interests . . . ; and (III) to bring about such an improvement in general conditions throughout Mexico that American settlers in that country will no longer be subjected to the hardships and outrages attendant upon a more or less constant state of revolution, lawlessness, and chaos." [10]

The Mexican Minister of Foreign Affairs did not formally reply to this note until November 22. Meantime, Ambassador Wilson made another of his flying trips to Washington in order to give further adverse information regarding the capacity and disposition of the Madero government; and *Chargé* Montgomery Schuyler reported, despite the fact that the attempt of Felix Díaz to hold Vera Cruz had utterly failed, that Madero was "absolutely impotent to bring even a semblance of peace and order." Schuyler also advised that the United States should have "warships in every Mexican port, prepared to remain indefinitely." At the same time it was said that "consular officers throughout Mexico" had sent the State Department very alarming accounts of the dangers to which American nationals were exposed.[11] Accordingly, Huntington Wilson requested the Secretary of the Navy (October 25) to hold in readiness eight vessels, four for the Pacific and four for the Atlantic coast of Mexico, this number to include the two vessels which were already at Vera Cruz and Tampico respectively.

It was in the tensity of this situation that Pedro Lascurain, Mexican Minister of Foreign Affairs, framed his reply to the vigorous note of September 15. It was a masterpiece. With reference to the arrest and punishment of the Mexican murderers of American citizens, Lascurain maintained that the Mexican government had fulfilled its international obligations. Surveying briefly the seventeen cases of murder listed in Ambassador Wilson's note, he pointed out that four had occurred prior to the Madero Revolution, that the Foreign Office had on file no data regarding four others, and that still three others had been prosecuted as "pernicious foreigners" who had been engaged in a filibustering enterprise in Lower California. He then stated that judicial investigation had been instituted in ten cases, three convictions having already occurred and two of the accused having been "released for want of evidence." Before closing this part of his note he called attention to several instances of the murder and lynching of Mexicans in California and Texas and in order to place the treatment of American nationals in Mexico in its proper light, he reminded Wilson that while three Americans had been killed in Mexico during the month of September, 1910, when Díaz was in

---

[10] *Foreign Relations* (1912), pp. 842–846.
[11] Disorders appear to have been worse during the first week of November than during the last ten days of October.

power, only three had been the victims of violence in 1911 and "three more during the present year." [12]

Taking up the charge that Mexico had evinced hostility toward American business interests south of the Rio Grande, Lascurain "most earnestly" rejected the "imputation." The difficulties of the Associated Press had been of its own making. It had declined to enter into a satisfactory contract for the use of the telegraph wire between Laredo and Mexico City. The Mexican government had refused to grant it privileges amounting to a virtual monopoly. It would be permitted to use the wire in question when it evinced a willingness to pay the regular rates exacted from other news-collecting agencies. The manager of the *Mexican Herald* had been offended because the Madero government, in accordance with its general policy not to subsidize the press, had withdrawn its support from his journal. No order had been issued preventing the publication of the *Herald*, but another journal started by the same management had been suppressed because it had carried on "a terrific campaign against the Government" and its editor had "infringed the penal laws." The Mexican national authorities had not levied a tax on oil on account of any anti-American sentiment. They needed money to run the government and establish peace. The tax in question amounted to only three cents per barrel and there had been no discrimination against American producers, all of them—Mexican, English, Americans, and the rest—being accorded the same treatment. So likewise in the cases of the colonization company and the packing company. The Madero administration was determined to give justice to all and it invited the United States Embassy to "disclose those other cases which might be the subject of protest."

Lascurain then turned to the demand made by the United States to be informed of the measures Mexico intended to adopt in order to pacify the country. He made some general statements as to the success achieved by Madero in the suppression of the insurgents, declaring that it might have attained more immediate—but probably less permanent—success had it not decided to employ moral suasion and adopt the law as the rule of action. He also pointed out the obvious fact that "all the countries of the world have passed through similar crises." "The United States," said the Mexican Foreign Minister, "has not been an exception to this rule. After its war of Independence and the Confederate war, it had to suffer long periods

[12] According to a subsequent report only 37 Americans were killed in Mexico in 1911 and 1912 and the death of the majority of these could in no way be attributed to revolutionary disturbances (*Foreign Relations* (1916), p. 477).

of internal difficulties of all kinds. . . ." The burden of the Mexican government might have been somewhat lightened if the United States had prevented the organization of armed expeditions in its territory and the importation of arms and munitions to supply the insurgents. In referring to this matter he did not mean to suggest that the United States had been wanting in good will toward Mexico; he merely desired to point out that the United States had not been uniformly successful in this respect for the same reason that the Mexican government had not been more speedy in the restoration of complete order. Both were basing their policies upon democracy and the rule of law.[13]

A few days after transmitting this note to the American Embassy, Lascurain set out for the United States. He apparently had come to the conclusion that the Mexican situation and the attitude of the Madero administration were not being correctly reported by Henry Lane Wilson and the Mexican Embassy at Washington. At any rate, he had determined to seek personal interviews with President Taft and Secretary Knox. He desired also to ascertain the "American interests in Mexico by personal conversations with individuals and corporations having interests in his country."

On January 2, 3, and 4 Lascurain had interviews with President Taft, Secretary Knox, and the Assistant Secretary of State. Knox gives an excellent summary of what occurred. "Mr. Lascurain made a decidedly favorable impression. At the interviews with the President and at the Department it was sought to impress upon him that Mexico must protect American life and property; do justice to American citizens; restore order; respond to the great moral obligation to be especially considerate of American interests and promptly meet this Government's requests in specific cases; and, in general, exemplify that friendliness, earnestness and efficiency in protecting American interests necessary to justify before public opinion the continuance of the signally friendly and patient policy of the United States." This last point appears to have been much emphasized. Knox told Lascurain "that great pressure had been brought upon the President and upon members of Congress for the repeal of the resolution authorizing the President, by proclamation, to forbid the exportation of arms and ammunition to Mexico that would likely fall into the hands of parties engaged in revolution in that country." The Assistant Secretary of State alluded to the great danger that public opinion would "reach a point where it could no longer be resisted." As for Lascurain, he

13 *Foreign Relations* (1912), pp. 871–877.

"seemed sincerely anxious to make every effort along the lines suggested." [14]

Henry Lane Wilson embarked for Mexico before these interviews took place. Resuming his duties as ambassador and chief of the Diplomatic Corps in Mexico City (January 5), he began forthwith to urge and in some instances to pursue a drastic policy. Even as almost insuperable difficulties gathered around Madero and ruin and grim death stared the Reformer in the face, Wilson pressed his demands for claims upon a bankrupt government, urged Madero to resign, and apparently sought to terrorize him by the menace of armed intervention. The Ambassador had no kind word, no sympathy for the Apostle of Mexican democracy. He pronounced Madero's program Utopian and censured him for not carrying it out. He complained of the impotence of his government and in the same despatch criticized his interference in elections and his suppression of the opposition press. Even while he denounced the Madero régime as a "wicked despotism" he argued that the Mexican people could be ruled only by a dictator. When the Taft administration expressed mild disapproval of some of his policies the Ambassador evinced a disposition to exceed his authority.

His conduct was most unprecedented during the second and third weeks of February. When the fighting between the government troops and the insurgent forces, under Felix Díaz and others, began in Mexico City, Wilson advised that "formidable warships supplied with marines should be dispatched to points on the Atlantic and the Pacific and that visible activity and alertness should be displayed on the boundary." Taft prepared to follow this advice.

On February 11 the Ambassador asked for "firm, drastic instructions, perhaps of a menacing character, to be transmitted personally to the government of President Madero and to the leaders of the revolution movement." He declared that this step must be taken for the protection of 25,000 foreigners in Mexico City, 5,000 of whom were nationals of the United States. Reinforcing this request, came a telegram from Governor O. B. Colquitt of Texas demanding intervention for the purpose of restoring order, protecting American life and property, and upholding the Monroe Doctrine. Colquitt was informed that the President's policy would continue for the time being unchanged and Wilson's appeal for drastic instructions was refused on the ground that the course which the Ambassador suggested might imperil Americans and their interests in Mexico, radically affect the

[14] *Foreign Relations* (1913), p. 924 ff.

issue of the contest for supremacy in the Mexican capital, and even lead to armed intervention.

The Ambassador then asked that the battleships soon to arrive in the Mexican ports be placed at his orders, to be employed at his discretion in case of a crisis. Moreover, while awaiting a reply he called together the Diplomatic Corps of Mexico City and put through a motion that one of their number carry to Madero that body's advice that his resignation would be desirable.

This unprecedented advice was actually transmitted, but Madero declined to listen. At about the same time the Mexican President somehow got—or pretended to get—the impression that Wilson was bent upon the debarkation of American marines. He at once sent out the report to all the military and political leaders of Mexico that the United States intended to undertake immediate intervention. This called down upon the Reformer the wrath of President Taft, who had refused to grant Wilson permission to employ the battleships and marines and supposed that Madero had information of this refusal. Taft scolded Madero and informed him that events in Mexico during the last two years had occasioned "extreme pessimism" among Americans and given rise to the "conviction that the present paramount duty is the prompt relief of the situation." Madero may have been sincerely alarmed and Wilson may have given him sufficient ground for alarm. On the other hand Madero may have sounded the note of Yankeephobia as a last desperate measure. However this may be, the days of his government and even of his own life were numbered and Taft gave him no comfort in the crisis. On February 18 he was arrested through the treachery of Generals Blanquette and Huerta, officers of his own army. Two days later a provisional government with Huerta as President was installed. In the early morning of February 23 Madero and Vice President Pino Suárez were shot while being taken under escort from the National Palace to the Penitentiary. If Ambassador Wilson had not aided and abetted Madero's enemies during the Tragic Ten Days— February 9 to 19—he had certainly been guilty of conduct which exposed him to profound suspicion and he had made little effort to save the life of the Reformer-President.

Wilson's intemperate haste in recommending the recognition of Huerta and accepting the Huerta story of how Madero and Suárez met their death constitute a further reflection upon his conduct. On the very day that the provincial government headed by Huerta was installed, the American Ambassador telegraphed the State Department a broad hint that the new régime should be granted recognition. On the same day he called his diplomatic colleagues together and they "agreed that the recognition of the new Government was imperative." On the day following he sent a "circular telegram to all consuls, advising them of the situation and instructing them to do all possible to bring about a general acceptance of the provisional government." On February 24 he telegraphed Knox that he was disposed to accept the Huerta government's version of the Madero and Suárez murders and "consider it a closed incident." He asked the "coöperation of the Department in this direction." At the same time he declared that he found the new government ready and willing to settle all outstanding issues with the United States.

The Taft administration might have followed the course indicated by its Mexican Ambassador had it not been for the shock which the procedure of Huerta caused the American public. Wilson was given specific instructions on the matter of claims and there was no remonstrance against the ruthless conduct of the military dictator, but the State Department did not officially announce its acceptance of the Huerta version of the murders, nor did it decide upon immediate recognition. On February 28 Wilson was informed that "with practical unanimity the American press treated as inadequate the explanations made by the Huerta régime in regard to the death of Madero and Piño Suárez, and is consequently expressing its horror thereat." "Having by inadequate precautions made possible that horrible occurrence," said Knox, "those responsible can not expect to escape public suspicion, and this Department is naturally obliged to decline to express itself on that painful subject pending the results of the promised thorough judicial investigation." [15] Two days before, Wilson had been cautioned by the Secretary of State not to grant formal recognition except upon specific instruction from that department. During the few days which remained of the Taft administration it had no occasion to change its policy. Neither did it recall the Ambassador who had been all too eager for the overthrow of Madero and the establishment of Huerta. Perhaps it could find no better means of retaliation for the defeat administered by Woodrow Wilson in the national election of the previous November!

Thus it will be observed that Taft's Mexican policy was avowedly one of non-intervention but in reality not without its interventionist phase. Neither the army nor the navy was used to coerce Mexico or to shield American life and property. Mexico was merely urged through diplomatic channels to protect these interests and American nationals

---

[15] For Wilson's attitude and conduct during this crisis, see *Foreign Relations* (1913), p. 699 ff. For his defense, see his *Diplomatic Episodes in Mexico, Belgium and Chile*, p. 252 ff. See, also, M. Márquez Sterling, *Los Últimos Días del Presidente Madero*.

were recalled from the zones of danger, transportation and temporary sustenance being supplied at government expense. And yet—so closely is the destiny of the two nations linked—certain steps which the Taft administration took or failed to take, whether by accident or by design, were not without influence upon the Mexican situation. The revolution which overthrew Díaz was in large measure prepared and organized within the United States, and the subsequent failure of Madero was partially due to the favoritism of the United States in the matter of arms and munitions shipments, the lack of confidence implied and engendered by Taft's warning to Americans to withdraw, and the menacing hostility of Henry Lane Wilson. It is of course impossible to determine the influence of President Taft and Ambassador Wilson upon the trend of events in Mexico. It may well be, as already suggested, that the Díaz régime would have been demolished even if American neutrality had been more strictly observed. In the same way it seems likely that the impractical Madero would have met his fate sooner or later had the attitude of Taft been less friendly at the beginning and the conduct of Henry Lane Wilson less embarrassing near the end.

At any rate, it is certain that Taft had made little contribution toward the solution of the Mexican problem when he left the White House in March, 1912. American interests were still suffering and no indemnities had been obtained. Thanks in part to the machinations of the Ambassador who served him in Mexico City, a dictator was then in charge of the Mexican government and ready to make terms with Washington; but the dictator was a toper with bloody hands and there was little assurance either of his continued tractability or of his power to bring permanent order to Mexico, unless it may be assumed that a stubborn minority may definitely and finally subdue fourteen million people and forever curb their aspirations.

CHAPTER XXI

WILSON'S MEXICAN POLICY AND ITS CRITICS

IN ONE respect the Mexican policy of Woodrow Wilson was to be similar to that of his immediate predecessor: Taft intervened in Mexican affairs while disavowing intervention and Wilson was likewise to do so. In most other respects the policies of the two Presidents were different and carried out under very different circumstances.

With reference to Mexico Taft proceeded as a complacent jurist and moderate imperialist, observing only the political, the legal, and the national aspects of the problem. The diplomatic correspondence of the last two years of Taft's administration reveals little indication that the Mexican situation was viewed in the light of Pan America. Nor is there any considerable evidence that Taft was conscious of powerful domestic or European pressure. Some domestic pressure there was, to be sure, but it would have had little weight had it not come in the midst of an arduous campaign for reëlection.

Wilson took up the Mexican problem with the vision of a Pan American and even of a world reformer. He also revealed the zeal of a Democratic crusader, but hardly the patience of a Job. And his course was rendered more arduous by the novelty of his policy, increasing disorders in Mexico, and the growing impatience both of his constitutents and of the world about him.

Immediately upon turning his attention to foreign affairs, Wilson saw clearly several facts. First, the little states of Latin America were indignant at the United States. They were "whetting their wits on the Monroe Doctrine," denouncing the United States for officious meddling in America, lamenting our cold, calculating materialism, and viewing with trembling apprehensiveness the course of our empire.[1] Second, the powers of Europe were growing impatient with the continued disorders in Mexico. Third, Mexico's problems, whether external or internal, were similar to those of many other states of Latin America.

On March 11, 1913, Wilson announced that he would throw the moral weight of his administration into the balance in favor of re-

---

[1] Rippy, "Literary Yankeephobia in Hispanic America," in *Journal of International Relations,* XII (January and April, 1921), 350 ff., 524 ff.

sponsible governments in Latin America. "We hold," he declared, "that just government rests always upon the consent of the governed, and that there can be no freedom without order based upon law and upon the public conscience and approval. . . . We shall lend our influence of every kind to the realization of these principles . . . , knowing that disorder, personal intrigue and defiance of constitutional rights weaken and discredit government and injure none so much as the people who are unfortunate enough to have their common life and their common affairs so tainted and disturbed. We can have no sympathy with those who seek to seize the power of government to advance their own personal interests or ambitions." [2] This was a plain announcement of determination not to recognize the heavy-handed despotism of Huerta.

Such a policy was clearly one of intervention, moral but far-reaching in its consequences. Wilson had set out to unseat a dictator and help the Mexicans toward an era of democracy. In doing so he would run the risk of prolonging an era of disorder. The effectiveness of his course would depend upon the attitude of the Mexican people and of the governments both of Hispanic America and of the leading nations of Europe, who were showing more and more concern with reference to the Mexican situation. If all agreed to coöperate Huerta would no doubt be doomed. If the Mexican people resented Wilson's interference and the states of Europe and Hispanic America insisted upon the old principle of *de facto* recognition the bibulous despot might conceivably defy the United States. The Latin-American states soon relieved his anxiety and accepted his leadership, but not so the diplomats of Europe. By the middle of the summer (1913) all of them had recognized Huerta, and Japan had followed suit.[3] Evidently the Great Powers were unfavorably disposed toward Wilson's new departure. Nor was Huerta's hold on the Mexicans weakened by the evident determination of Wilson to eliminate him. It is probable that a current of Yankeephobia set in in the dictator's direction.

But Wilson's optimism was equal to almost any obstacle. Even as the European and Japanese diplomats one by one extended recognition to the *de facto* ruler of Mexico, the crusading President sent John Lind to the Aztec capital with instructions designed to eliminate Huerta and pacify the country by means of a free election and the loyal acceptance of its results by all parties. Lind's mission utterly failed,[4] European statesmen continued recalcitrant, but Wilson's pur-

[2] Robinson and West, *The Foreign Policy of Woodrow Wilson*, pp. 179–180.
[3] Hendrick, *The Life and Letters of Walter Hines Page*, I, 175, *passim;* U. S. *Foreign Relations* (1913), p. 799, *passim.*
[4] *Foreign Relations* (1913), *loc. cit.;* Hendrick, *op. et loc. cit.*

pose was in no way shaken. In the latter part of October he took the train for Mobile, Alabama. Here he addressed a Pan-American assembly and announced himself as the champion of American democracy against official economic imperialism. "We have seen material interests threaten constitutional freedom in the United States," said the President. "Therefore we will know how to sympathize with those in the rest of America who have to contend with such powers, not only within their borders but from outside their borders also." [5] This address amounted to a defiance of those European powers who, more interested in money than in morals, placed the security of the investments of their nationals above democratic progress in Mexico.

Wilson probably designed his remarks mainly for the British government. At any rate, American diplomacy had been busy for some time in the effort to bring Sir Edward Grey around to the Wilson view on the Mexican problem. And before the close of the year 1913 Wilson had his way. Sometime in November or December Sir Lionel Carden, British Ambassador at Mexico City, "led a procession of European diplomats to General Huerta, [and] formally advised that warrior to yield to the American demands and withdraw from the Presidency of Mexico. The delegation informed the grim dictator that their governments were supporting the American policy and Sir Lionel brought him the unwelcome news that he could not depend upon British support." [6] The Great Powers had at last acquiesced in Wilson's policy with reference to Huerta. Soon afterwards their energies were absorbed by the World War. The Mexican imbroglio then became strictly an American affair.

Thus freed from European pressure, Wilson could announce, on December 2, 1913, that he saw no reason to depart from his policy of "watchful waiting" for the overthrow of Huerta and the achievement of order south of the Rio Grande. Yet his attitude was not strictly that of watchful waiting. In reality he gave hands and feet to his prayer against the Mexican despot. His pressure upon the European diplomats shattered Huerta's prospects of a loan. And Wilson took an even more important step. Since the last of August he had been exercising the authority conferred upon him by the law of March 14, 1912, so as to prevent each of the contesting groups from "receiving aid from this side of the border." [7] This was indeed

---

[5] Robinson and West, *op. cit.*, pp. 199–203.

[6] Hendrick, *op. cit.*, I, 209. Wilson had been disturbed by machinations of Sir Lionel and Cowdray.

[7] Near the last of August (1913), also, American nationals were "earnestly" urged to "leave Mexico at once"—an exhortation destined to be repeated often during the next two years.

strict neutrality. But the removal of the embargo from arms and munitions on February 4, 1914, in order, as he remarked, that the conclusion of the fight might be hastened,[8] hardly accorded with the attitude implied in the term watchful waiting. It really amounted to favoritism toward Carranza, Villa, and Obregón, who were leading the anti-Huerta hosts in the North. Of similar import was the occupation of Vera Cruz in the following April. Avowedly provoked by Huerta's studied abuse of the American flag and his systematic persecution of American nationals [9]—a quite human reaction on the part of the dictator—, it was designed to administer a humiliating rebuke and to intercept the grim warrior's supply of arms and munitions. It was an effective blow delivered by a passive statesman. Victoriana Huerta soon embarked for Europe never again to set foot on Mexican soil.

All this was for the good of the Mexican people, Wilson said. If the "usurper" had been allowed to succeed, "in despite of the constitution of the Republic and the rights of its people, he would have set up nothing but a precarious and hateful power, which could have lasted but a little while, and whose eventual downfall would have left the country in a more deplorable condition than ever." But the articulate Mexicans—we know nothing of the thoughts of that pathetic eighty per cent of exploited Indians and *mestizos* to whom Wilson's sympathy was generously extended—showed little appreciation for the President's benevolence. They resented his occupation of Vera Cruz. In some quarters of Latin America Wilson was better understood, however. As some of the leaders of the Mexican insurgents scolded and fulminated and the friendly occupation of Vera Cruz, which was intended neither as formal intervention nor an act of war against the Mexican people, was on the point of degenerating into an ugly affair, the A B C powers extended a timely offer of mediation. Delighted to find a way of escape from the embarrassing situation, the President eagerly accepted the offer. Mediation accomplished little in the pacification of Mexico, but it promoted Pan-American friendship.[10] It also enabled Wilson to maintain the *status quo* at Vera Cruz until he could withdraw the armed forces without humiliation or serious alienation of popular support in the United States. And had not the Mexican nation been given riddance of a bloody tyrant and left free to move along the pathway of democracy and order?

8 This he did on February 4, 1914 (Robinson and West, *op. cit.*, p. 207).
9 Wilson's message of April 20, 1914, in Robinson and West, *op. cit.*, pp. 209–213.
10 U. S. *Foreign Relations* (1914), p. 488, *passim*. The Niagara Falls Conference.

During the latter half of the year 1914 and the early part of 1915 the victorious leader of the Democratic hosts of the United States watched and waited hopefully. The Mexican leaders who held the field, now that Huerta had been removed, were slow, very slow, in the arrangement of their difficulties. To one familiar with Mexican history this was to be expected. People who had been used to deciding presidential elections by terrorism and bullets could hardly be expected speedily to reach a decision to confine themselves to ballots even in response to the pressing exhortations of an ardent democrat such as Wilson. But Wilson had forgotten his Mexican history. Early in 1915 he contended that Mexico ought to be allowed to consume all the time she pleased in settling her internal troubles,[11] but this was probably done in the enthusiasm of the high hope that she would not require long. By the middle of the year he began to lose patience. "In the very hour of their success the leaders of the revolution . . . disagreed and turned their arms against one another." The President admonished them to get together and threatened drastic action.[12] When they failed to follow the admonition, he invited the diplomatic representatives of the leading states of Latin America to discuss the Mexican situation with him once more. The insurgent leaders were requested to lay their cases before the assembled diplomats.

Some of the military leaders of Mexico sent representatives, others refused. The chief result of the conferences of the assembled diplomats was the decision, reached on October 19, to recognize Venustiano Carranza as *de facto* head of the national government of Mexico. And this was done in spite of the fact that this insurgent had for two years shown himself to be least amenable to American advice. Wilson had not allowed himself to be provoked by such stubbornness. The movement championed by Carranza appeared to promise most for the submerged eighty per cent. Those associated with him seemed to be loyal both to their chief and his ideals.[13] For more than a year Wilson had been convinced that the triumph of the *Carranzistas* and their reforms was essential to the permanent pacification of Mexico. He had hoped that Huerta's scepter would pass directly into the hands of this bearded, spectacled gladiator of the North in the summer of 1914, but he had been disappointed. Now at last his point of view had been made to prevail. The governments of Europe soon followed in the path which the American states under the leadership of Wilson

[11] *Addresses and Messages* (Hart ed.), pp. 40–41.
[12] Robinson and West, *The Foreign Policy of Woodrow Wilson*, pp. 268–270.
[13] U. S. *For. Rels.* (1915), p. 723 ff.

had marked out.[14] Carranza's cause was immensely strengthened. For the second time Wilson had intervened.

Nor was the extension of a somewhat hasty recognition the extent of this intervention. Wilson proceeded forthwith to manipulate the export of arms and munitions in favor of Carranza. These supplies were permitted freely to enter into the areas dominated by this leader, but an embargo was placed upon their shipment into Chihuahua, Sonora, and Lower California, where the *Villistas* were threatening to gain the ascendency. And arms and munitions were allowed to proceed even into this northern area provided there was assurance that they would be received by the *Carranzistas*.[15]

Except for such interposition as was represented by these acts Wilson persisted in his policy of non-intervention. Having thus exalted Carranza's international status by securing for him the recognition of the leading powers of Europe and America and having instructed his subordinates to enforce the arms embargo so as to favor the *Carranzistas,* Wilson settled down once more to watch and wait. Mexico's "fortunes are in her own hands," he declared in his annual message of 1915. "We . . . now hopefully await the rebirth of the troubled Republic. . . . We will aid and befriend Mexico, but we will not coerce her." One is inclined to inquire what portion of the Mexican nation was included under the term "Mexico." Certainly somebody had been coerced and was being coerced by the Wilson policy! At any rate, the United States had not sent an army into Mexico for the purpose of protecting American life and property and restoring order. To have remained completely passive in the face of the tragedy which was now dragging into its sixth year south of the Rio Grande would have been a dangerous provocation of American vested interests and of the American public as well.

Even as early as April, 1914, there were not lacking those who appeared to hope that the seizure of Vera Cruz might eventuate in general intervention in behalf of our stake in Mexico. They seemed to favor one of the lines of action suggested by Henry Lane Wilson. The Ambassador's proposals were industriously read into the record. Wilson had pointed out three courses: the recognition of Huerta on condition that he satisfy our demands with reference to claims and other differences, dismiss his Foreign Secretary, and permit our troops to assist him in establishing order north of the 26th parallel; a more general invasion, preceded by a denial of any desire of permanent occupation and the recall of our nationals, and accompanied by the organization of a commission, composed of the American Ambas-

[14] U. S. *For. Rels.* (1915), p. 772 ff.
[15] Robinson and West, *op. cit.,* pp. 73–74.

sador, the commander in chief of the Army, the ranking officer of the Navy, and a member of the Senate Committee on Foreign Relations, which should follow in the wake of the invading force, reconciling Mexican factions, "establishing the rule of law, and dispensing justice in the name of the United States"; and, lastly, the establishment of a permanent buffer state north of the 26th parallel—and incidently including the most important mining area of Mexico.[16] Such were the suggestions which the aggressive members of the national congress appeared to favor in the spring of 1914, but thanks to the strength of Wilson's party and to the hold of the President on public opinion, they were easily held in check.

As the year 1916 opened, however, signs of more formidable opposition could be seen. Mexico appeared to be approaching the "verge."

The crisis was occasioned mainly by Francisco Villa's raids upon the American frontier and by the political stage-play on the eve of the national election in the United States. The *Villistas,* their natural marauding proclivities stimulated by hostility aroused by Wilson's partiality for Carranza, perpetrated outrages upon American life and property in northern Mexico and began a series of incursions into the United States.[17] The Republican party seized upon the Mexican problem as one of the issues of the national campaign.

Senator Albert Fall, for three years a chronic critic of Wilson's Mexican policy, was in the midst of one of his diatribes when news of the massacre of eighteen Americans by *Villistas* at Santa Ysabel furnished critics and interventionists a better theme. William E. Borah of Idaho declared: "I would protect the American passport when issued at whatever cost. I would make even the fiends of Mexico know its worth. I do not believe that anything is to be gained in the long run by this policy of waiting for a nation like Mexico to settle its difficulties when those difficulties involve the rights of our own people." Senator Lippitt of Rhode Island served notice that if he "had been President of the United States . . . when the reports of these Mexican murders arrived in Washington, . . . another sun would not have set over the Sierra Madre Mountains before American soldiers would be [have been] hot on the trail of those murderers." "The first scrap of paper that I would have used," he added, "would have been a telegram instructing those soldiers to use every possible effort to secure those murderers, dead or alive; and I would have had in it a strong intimation that they need not object to including in those

---

[16] *Congressional Record,* 63 Cong., 2 Sess., Vol. 51, p. 6979 ff.; *Investigation of Mexican Affairs* (Report of the Fall Committee), II, 2293.

[17] Robinson and West, *op. cit.,* p. 105, *passim.*

provisions some of their accomplices and sympathizers. . . . I would have kept up that policy until the life of every American ranchman was as safe as though he had been in Washington." Representative Humphrey of Washington remarked that he and the "American people" did not "believe in" Wilson's patient forbearance, which meant in reality a policy "of slaughter and savagery." "Certainly," he declared, "this has not always been the policy of this Nation. When the shrieks and groans of murdered and tortured men, the sobs and cries of starving women and children in Cuba reached us, the American people demanded that these atrocities should end; and when that demand was disregarded our answer was not 'watchful waiting,' . . . but the American people rose as one man, drove the yellow flag of Spain from the Western Hemisphere, and placed Cuba among the nations of the earth. And the day is not far off when the people of this country, regardless of the attitude of the administration, will see that peace is brought to unhappy Mexico."

The Democrats at once detected a political motive in this outcry. The Republicans did not mean all they said. They supposed Wilson could not be forced to intervene in Mexico. They meant to show him up as having in a most cowardly fashion abandoned American rights in Mexico. The Democrats warned their opponents, however, that they might be playing a losing game. They might create a war sentiment which Wilson could not assuage and dared not resist, and if a war with Mexico should be in progress in November, 1916, Democracy's success in the national elections would be assured.

This warning fell for the most part upon heedless men. Senator Lodge, Representative Mondell of Wyoming, Republican floor leader of the House, and Representative Madden of Illinois appear to have observed this danger, but the rest either continued confident that Wilson could not be forced to intervene or, eager for the "Cubanization" of Mexico, were probably willing to risk defeat in order to achieve this end. At any rate, the political stage-play continued along with Villa's depredations. Senator Ashurst of Arizona called for more "grapeshot" and less "grape juice"; Fall demanded the occupation of Mexico with an army of 500,000; Slayden of Texas presented evidence of a Mexican conspiracy to reconquer the Southwest and turn it over to Negroes, Japanese, and Mexicans; Senator Gallinger of New Hampshire agreed with ex-Senator Blair's view that "our southern boundary is Panama" and that we must pacify Mexico in order to make our borders secure.

Senator Fall was the most boisterous of the opposition orators. On June 2 he spread his final pre-convention speech over seventeen pages of the *Congressional Record*. He said that Carranza was more

despotic than Peter the Great had ever been and characterized the
First Chief and his followers as bandits and thieves; he appealed to
Catholic prejudices in the United States by recounting *Carranzista*
outrages against the Church, its properties, priests and nuns; he denounced Wilson for his cowardly abandonment of American interests
and his support of an unprincipled tyrant; he dwelt upon the great
benefits conferred upon Mexico by American enterprise and capital.
His peroration was a hymn of praise in honor of the Austins, Bowies,
Crocketts, and Frémonts, with their Lone-Star and Bear flags and
their defiance of the British Navy on the Pacific Coast. "At that
date, thank God," he shouted, "there was not an American who would
call these Americans criminals although they brought on a war with
one country and defied the 'Mistress of the Seas.'" "Those people
living at Columbus," he continued, referring to Villa's murderous raid
upon this little village of New Mexico, "those people who have been
carrying civilization into Mexico, are of the same blood, the same bone,
the same sinew as those who raised aloft the Lone-Star flag on the one
coast and the bear flag on the other, and added an empire to this
country." [18]   Oil was the important motive back of Fall's oratory.

During the spring and summer the war spirit began to develop. In
the latter part of January a careful survey of the press in the United
States showed a majority opinion opposed to intervention, but by the
last of May sentiment had changed and "some of the most sober
and responsible papers" had lost patience.[19]   If Wilson did not feel
the martial spirit he at least sensed the situation after Villa's attack
upon Columbus. He dispatched a punitive expedition under Pershing
in pursuit of the bandit, but continued to declare against intervention
and succeeded in writing a non-intervention plank into the Democratic
platform. This action was of little avail in holding the aggressive elements in check. The pursuit of Villa rendered him more popular
among certain classes of Mexicans, and Carranza, though at first apparently not opposed to the expedition, gradually assumed a more
hostile attitude toward it. The climax was reached during the third
week of June—just as the Democrats were publishing their platform
—when the *Carranzistas* at Carrizal killed, wounded, and captured
a number of Pershing's soldiers.

The whole country burst into a flame and even Wilson himself
either lost patience or feared to remain inactive. Release of the captured troops was demanded in none too diplomatic terms. For a moment Carranza refused to comply.[20]   The peace of the two countries

---

[18] For this debate, See *Cong. Record*, Vol. 53, p. 945, *passim.*
[19] *Lit. Digest*, LII (January 29 and May 27, 1916), 213–214, 1515–1516.
[20] The correspondence will be found in *Current History*, IV (1916), 835 ff.

was suspended by a thread. The entire militia of the United States was ordered to the border and available men for the Governor-Generalship of Mexico were discussed.[21] But just before the breaking point was reached the labor leaders of the two countries came together and, on June 28, Samuel Gompers sent a personal telegram to Carranza, imploring him in the name of humanity to release the American prisoners. A few hours later extras announced to the American public that the soldiers in question had been set free.[22]

The break was thus avoided but the situation continued to be tense. A *Villista* outrage or a hostile move by the pig-headed Carranza might at any moment lead to the outbreak of hostilities. Fortunately for the peace of the two countries, however, numerous moderate and pacific groups, with the industrious assistance of Mexican agents,[23] undertook to hold the war-spirit in check. Protestant churches, some of the Jewish organizations under the leadership of Rabbi Wise, several journalists and educators, all of the labor organizations, and many of the plain people urged moderation and peace.[24] President Wilson, perhaps in the hope that this step might keep "the Mexican situation from blowing up" during a "critical part of the campaign," [25] appointed a commission of three to meet with an equal number of appointees of the Carranza government. He then assumed an attitude of defiant confidence during the national campaign, but he kept General Pershing in Mexico.

With the victory of Wilson at the polls in November, 1916, and the entrance of the United States into the World War early the following year this particular crisis definitely passed. The Mexican issue receded to the background and remained there for almost two years.

Meantime, the Carranza government lent a willing ear to German intrigue, sought to undermine Wilson's influence in Latin America, demonstrated its inability to cope with conditions in Mexico, and issued decrees which brought down upon it the implacable enmity of American vested interests. These interests demanded the protection of the State Department—and they were given whatever protection protests, remonstrances, and threats could yield—, carefully collected evidence, organized, and grimly bided their time. A suc-

[21] Information based upon a reliable confidential source.

[22] The A. F. L., Thirty-Sixth Annual Convention, *Proceedings,* pp. 57–64.

[23] *Cf.* numerous pamphlets distributed by the American-Mexican Commission and the Latin-American News Association.

[24] See files of the New York *Times, Literary Digest, Survey, Independent,* and the *Nation* for June–November, 1916.

[25] *The Letters of Franklin K. Lane,* pp. 227–228; *Foreign Relations* (1917), p. 916 ff.

cessful war could be depended upon to strengthen the material and psychological foundations of imperialism; the pride of victory would diminish forbearance in the presence of real or alleged outrages suffered at the hands of Mexico. At the close of the World War the Mexican government would either have to make amends for these injuries and repeal legislation and decrees which citizens of the United States considered unfavorable to their interests or drastic measures would be pursued.

As soon as the titanic European struggle ended the apostles of an energetic Mexican policy began once more to appeal to the American public. During the last weeks of 1918 the *Christian Science Monitor* came out with an editorial entitled "Mexico Next," and a syndicated cartoon represented Uncle Sam in uniform with rifle by his side sitting on a box of ammunition and soliloquizing, "What was the name of that fellow down there in Mexico who congratulated the Kaiser on his birthday?" During the course of the spring and summer of 1919 the majority of the powerful journals, some of the southern papers included, gave expression to a demand for a radical change in the administration's Mexican policy. A "new régime more complacent to American capital," the punishment of Carranza for his hostile attitude during the World War, and the performance of the "same service for Mexico" which had been "performed for Cuba" appeared to be the prevailing sentiment. Henry Lane Wilson returned to his old idea of a buffer state, only now he desired that it should extend to the 22d instead of to the 26th parallel.[26] And while the press was urging these views, numerous members of the national congress were making a large contribution to the task of arousing popular resentment and passion against Mexico. Senator Cummins of Iowa expressed the conviction that "we ought to try hard to buy Lower California," and "if we could not buy it we ought to take it." Senator Watson of Indiana declared that a war with Mexico "would be entirely agreeable to him." Representative Norman J. Gould of New York presented a list of outrages perpetrated against American oil men and their agents in the Tampico zone. He declared that the government of Mexico was "half-bandit" and "half-Bolshevik." He quoted the late Roosevelt as favoring intervention in Mexico in his last message to the American people and read into the record a recent report of one of Wilson's Cabinet officers which maintained that Mexican petroleum was absolutely necessary for our prosperity and our national security. Gould was followed from time to time by other advocates of drastic action with similar appeals. Finally, in

[26] G. H. Blakeslee, ed., *Mexico and the Caribbean* (New York, 1920), pp. 150–153.

September, 1919, a sub-committee of the United States Senate began to issue its findings in free installments to the American people. Its "Preliminary Report and Hearings" filled two huge volumes of more than thirty-five hundred pages! [27]

The chairman of this committee was none other than Senator Albert Fall and its bulky report was the last word in imperialist propaganda. An appeal for a more drastic Mexican policy was made on the following grounds: The Carranza régime was represented as inefficient, corrupt, barbarously lascivious, anti-American, pro-German and pro-Japanese, violently anti-religious, dangerously radical. Carranza was alleged to be responsible for hundreds of grievous injuries and outrages to American citizens and represented as a threat to our prosperity and national security because of his confiscatory policy with reference to the oil properties of American nationals in Mexico. Conditions in Mexico were declared to constitute a standing menace to the Canal Zone and the Monroe Doctrine. This report furnished a splendid supplement to journalistic propaganda and congressional eloquence. It left little to be said or done in arousing the American public.

Moreover, the last weeks of 1919 witnessed a decided change in the attitude of Wilson's official family toward Mexico. Franklin K. Lane, formerly one of the most able defenders of the President's Mexican policy, lost faith and began to succumb to the wiles of the irresistible Doheny.[28] Attorney-General Palmer seems to have permitted his department to break down along the Rio Grande. Ambassador Fletcher returned from Mexico pleading for vigorous measures. Lansing, growing more and more out of harmony with the President, appeared now to be half-inclined to listen to Fall and his group. Woodrow Wilson was lying in the White House a very ill man.

And then, just at this critical time, somebody in northern Mexico seized the consular agent of the United States at Puebla (William O. Jenkins). To Lansing's demand for immediate release the Mexican Government responded with a request for delay pending a judicial investigation. At last the stage seemed to be set for intervention. Fall's friends called him to Washington for an interview with Lansing. The Secretary of State and the leader of the interventionists appeared to be in agreement. Another demand was made for the immediate release of Jenkins, and Fletcher was delegated to represent Lansing in "close and continuous contact" with the Fall committee.

[27] Published as *Senate Doc.* No. 285 (Ser. 7665 and 7666), 66 Cong., 2 Sess.

[28] *The Letters of Franklin K. Lane,* p. 309, *passim;* and see also his testimony before the Fall Committee (*loc. cit.,* II, 2369 ff.).

A resolution was drafted approving the "action of the Department of State in reference to the pending controversy" and demanding the severing of all relations with the Carranza government. It was immediately submitted to the Senate and referred to the Committee on Foreign Relations, but before further action could be taken first Fletcher and then Lansing hurried to the Senate chamber and urged delay upon the second portion of the document. Apparently Wilson, who had not been consulted in regard to Mexican affairs since he returned a broken man from his western tour, had received a hint of what was going on and called a halt.[29] Soon afterwards Jenkins was released—under suspicion of having connived at his own capture—and once more the war-cloud floated past.

The aggressives, though beaten a second time, were by no means discouraged. The national elections were approaching. They would pledge the Republican party vigorously to defend American investments and energetically to prosecute American claims and they would defeat the Democrats in November. Perhaps they might even frighten the Democrats into writing a vigorous Mexican plank into their platform!

But just as Mexico approached the "verge" for the third time, and while labor leaders, churchmen, liberal journalists and educators, plain people, and Mexican agents in the United States were pleading for respect for Mexican sovereignty, Alvaro Obregón overthrew the corrupt Carranza régime. The new head of the Mexican nation hastened to avow a friendly policy toward the United States and soon revealed leadership of a high quality. The American press responded with widespread favorable comment [30] and agitation for immediate armed intervention soon ceased. Not even Senator Fall, in the last installment of his report, saw fit to urge armed coercion until diplomatic and economic pressure had been tried and proved ineffective. The military and naval forces of the United States were to be employed only as a last resort and for the "restoration of peace and order; protection of our own citizens; protection of Mexican citizens; restoration of American citizens to their properties; the affording of opportunity for the opening of mines, fields, and factories; and last, to afford the opportunity for the Mexican people themselves . . . to constitute a Mexican government of serious, competent, honest, and honorable men who will meet the civilized world upon a friendly ground and bind themselves to deal with other people as they themselves would be dealt with." Thus the sword of

[29] Fall Committee, *Report,* I, 843A ff. Henry P. Fletcher had been the Ambassador to Mexico since March, 1917.

[30] *Lit. Dig.,* June 5, 1920, pp. 30–31; New York *Times,* May and June, 1920.

intervention, according to the plan of this most aggressive of aggressives, was to be displayed in the dim distance as an auxiliary of a milder form of coercion, but the milder form was all that was to be employed immediately.

The party platforms drawn up in the summer of 1920 indicated that both of the great political organizations were committed to diplomatic coercion. Both expressed unwillingness to recognize Obregón (or rather his tool Adolfo de la Huerta, who was acting as President *ad interim*) previous to an understanding with reference to American claims and vested interests.[31] What action was contemplated if this procedure proved unavailing does not appear, nor is it clear whether a formal treaty or an informal pledge was to be required. It may be inferred from Fall's recommendations and the subsequent course of each party, however, that both national groups were committed to the treaty idea.

Although Wilson's Secretary of State, Bainbridge Colby, had publicly stated on the eve of the national elections that he did not deem it necessary to "prescribe rigid and definite terms upon which a recognition of the Mexican government would be expressly conditioned," he nevertheless suggested a few days later that "commissioners be promptly designated . . . to formulate a treaty" which would embody informal pledges previously made by the agent of De la Huerta.[32] How much Wilson had to do with this policy of pressure in behalf of vested interests it is difficult to say. Certainly he had not demanded in 1915 that Carranza "sign on the dotted line" as a condition of recognition. Nor were such demands in line with the Wilson idea of leaving American masters of finance and captains of industry to shift for themselves in foreign fields. Possibly the President was no longer directing the State Department. It must be noted, however, that not even in the days of his high idealism did he entirely abandon American nationals who had acquired interests in Mexico. He had questioned Carranza sharply on this matter and had received favorable commitments and the files of the State Department are filled with remonstrances against the decrees, exactions, and other damaging proceedings of the Mexican chiefs against American life and property in Mexico. Perhaps Acting Secretary Polk aptly stated Wilson's policy when he wrote in 1918:

[31] *Republican Campaign Text Book*, pp. 68–69; *Democratic Campaign Text Book*, the platform.

[32] American Association for International Conciliation, *The United States and Mexico*, pp. 409–417.

"The President has drawn a sharp contrast between the policy of armed intervention and that of diplomatic interposition. He has, on numerous occasions, stated in effect that he would not countenance armed intervention in the affairs of another State for the purpose of gratifying selfish interests. . . . But the President has never stated that he would forego the right of diplomatic interposition in behalf of American citizens, a distinctly friendly method of supporting legitimate national interests in order to avoid injustice." [33]

Final judgment can no more be passed upon the Mexican policy of Wilson than upon that of Taft. The latter might have prolonged the system of Díaz by a more rigid enforcement of neutrality but he probably could not have perpetuated that system. The evil day could only have been put off at the risk of intensifying the final catastrophe. Neither can the effect of Taft's moral support of Madero at the beginning of his career nor of Henry Lane Wilson's opposition at the end accurately be determined. Perhaps their attitude had very little weight. At any rate it does not appear that Madero possessed those qualities of leadership which would have enabled him to ride the tide of opposition and direct the mass movement toward a liberal and stable régime. Immediate recognition of Huerta might have hastened the achievement of order and the establishment of a government more friendly to American vested interests, but such a course would have meant, once more, merely the postponement of the democratic and nationalist upheaval with its accompanying proletarian extravagances. Nor is it at all certain that Woodrow Wilson the Crusader would not have undone Taft's work. So likewise in the case of Wilson. His opposition probably hastened the overthrow of Huerta, but the overthrow was probably destined to be accomplished sooner or later anyway. The submerged masses could not long have been held in check. In opposing Huerta Wilson was attempting to hasten the process of democratization and nationalization and in backing Carranza he was working toward the same end. Whether he succeeded in his effort it is difficult to say. Possibly he chose the wrong man. At the time he picked Carranza both Obregón and Calles were in sight, but there is no absolute assurance that they would permanently have succeeded where Carranza failed. If they had been backed then their bones might now be lying where the remains of Carranza were placed to rest and Carranza might now be the champion of "Mexico for the Mexicans" and land for the masses. The only difference between the intervention of Wilson and the armed intervention of the aggressives is largely one of purpose and cost. Wilson looked toward

[33] Fall Committee, *Report*, II, 3166, quoting Polk.

a régime which respected two important sentiments of the age—nationalism and democracy—and his policy was comparatively inexpensive. The apostles of armed intervention would have acted in the interest of an imperialism which had little respect for either, and the bill of blood and money would have been presented to the American public at large. There would probably have been little difference in the length of time required for the final consummation. Those who are more tolerant and passive may criticize both Wilson and the aggressives upon essentially the same ground. Both were too impatient to permit Mexico to work out her own destiny by dint of her own efforts and without interference of any kind. But to point out this fact is but to emphasize another characteristic of the white civilizations of the Western World. In the case of nations as of individuals the slow must have their speed accelerated and the eccentric must be made to conform to the prevailing type—and above all it must be remembered that the white nations of the West are God's anointed and the world was made for them!

At any rate, Wilson left Mexico's future largely in her own hands. Nationalistic and democratic aspirations had not been seriously interfered with, even if the process of realization had not been speeded up. So far as improvement in Mexican attitude toward the United States was concerned, little had been accomplished. Neither the Mexican people nor their leaders saw in Wilson a bulwark standing against powerful aggressive forces which threatened to submerge Mexican leaders and Mexican nationality alike. But crosses are made for reformers who would help nations and peoples to save themselves. And the last days of Wilson's administration had been marked by an attempt at diplomatic coercion.

CHAPTER XXII

HUGHES AND KELLOGG AT THE HELM

WHEN the Republican administration took up the Mexican problem in March, 1921, it was concerned not so much with indemnity for the past as with security for the future. It was true that between two hundred and five hundred American lives had been lost as a direct result of the revolutionary disturbances which broke out in 1910. It was also true that hundreds more had been thrown into prison or wounded and that from forty to fifty thousand had left Mexico, permanently or temporarily, having abandoned their pursuits and their property either of their own accord or pursuant to the advice of the American State Department. But the Mexican government had already indicated a willingness to negotiate conventions relating to these matters, and soon after Hughes entered upon his official duties Obregón's agent submitted drafts of treaties designed to settle all claims since 1868.[1]

To the new Secretary of State there was something more important than immediate indemnity for all these losses and injuries. The program of reform in Mexico constituted a threat to American vested interests and the Mexican government must sign a pact furnishing adequate safeguards. The draft of a Treaty of Amity and Commerce was accordingly submitted to the Obregón administration on May 27. Sixteen articles of this draft were taken up with the usual formalities of such agreements. The other two—Articles 1 and 2— contained the crux of the difficulties. They embraced five important provisions: (1) assurances that nationals of either country residing in the other would enjoy all the rights and privileges of native citizens; (2) reciprocal guaranties against confiscation and expropriation, except for public purposes, and after "prompt payment of just compensation"; (3) assurances against the retroactive application to

[1] Only experts with power to summon witnesses can determine the losses of United States citizens occasioned by the ten-year revolution in Mexico. Their true total may never be known. The future alone can reveal the effects of Mexico's agrarian and nationalization policies upon American vested interests. Turlington (*Mexico and Her Foreign Creditors*, p. 320) estimates the value of the claims of United States citizens against Mexico at P. 142,000,000.

American citizens of Carranza's agrarian decree of January 6, 1915—providing for the grant or restitution of communal lands to the Indian villages—, of the provisions of the constitution of 1917, or of any other decrees or orders of any sort; (4) restoration to American citizens, whenever possible, of the property rights of which they may have been deprived since 1910 and adequate compensation for all losses suffered on account of such deprivation; (5) the reciprocal guaranty to the nationals of either country residing in the other of freedom of worship and the right to own church property. The last of these provisions was not pressed upon the Mexican government, but the first four became the subject of an extended argument.[2]

Although the Mexican government did not immediately make a formal reply to the proposals, Obregón at once let it be known to the press that he was very much opposed to signing such an agreement as a condition of recognition. Secretary Hughes then issued a public statement defining his policy with reference to the matter. "If General Obregón is ready to negotiate a proper treaty it is drawn so as to be negotiated with him and the making of the treaty in proper form will accomplish the recognition of the government that makes it. In short, when it appears that there is a government in Mexico willing to bind itself to the discharge of primary international obligations, concurrently with that act its recognition will take place." Diplomatic promises were not sufficient. "The question . . . is not one of a particular administration but of the agreement of the nation in proper form which has become necessary as an international matter because of the provisions of its domestic legislation. If Mexico does not contemplate a confiscatory policy, the government of the United States can conceive of no possible objection to the treaty." [3] The viewpoint of Hughes was strictly that of the legalist and the jurist.

To this statement of Hughes, Obregón rejoined in his annual message of September 20. "This draft of a treaty," said the executive, "contained stipulations contrary to some of the precepts of our constitution; hence its adoption would inevitably lead to a situation of privilege in favor of the American residents in Mexico, which would automatically become applicable to the citizens of other countries, owing to the well known most-favored-nation clause." Thus foreigners would obtain a favored position and Mexicans would become aliens in their own native land. Moreover, even if this were not so, the signing of a treaty as a prerequisite of recognition "would have

[2] For the text of this proposed treaty, see *United States Daily*, May 15, 1926.
[3] New York *Times*, June 8, 1921.

imparted to recognition a conditional character, and would have seriously impaired the sovereignty of Mexico." Accordingly, while expressing a determination to protect American interests in Mexico, he expressed a desire to avoid humiliating promises.

The formal reply (November 19, 1921) of Minister Albert J. Pani to the proposed draft of a treaty of amity and commerce indicated the extent to which Mexico would go in order to obtain recognition. The Obregón government would sign a special claims convention for the adjudication of claims of American citizens arising between November 10, 1910, and May 31, 1920. It then would expect recognition, and after this had been extended it would sign a general convention for the settlement of claims arising since the adjudications which took place in accordance with the agreement signed on July 4, 1868. But it would not make further concession. It was determined not to enter into obligations which would interrupt its politico-religious and agrarian reforms and defeat its program of nationalization. It would not agree to limit its control over its national resources and its domestic policies.

During the next eighteen months neither government formally receded from its position, and the diplomatic controversy continued. Meantime, Obregón set to work in such manner as to redeem the informal diplomatic pledges which he had made from time to time, and the Supreme Court of Mexico handed down decisions which brought some comfort to the oil interests of the United States. On June 16, 1922, an agreement was signed with the International Committee of Bankers which recognized the validity of important financial obligations, stipulated the terms under which they were to be fulfilled, and promised the return of the Mexican railways to private ownership. The decisions of the Supreme Court established the precedent that "petroleum properties in process of development before May 1, 1917, when the present constitution took effect, are protected from a retroactive application of the fourth paragraph of Article 27." Moreover, Obregón's government delayed action with reference to the program of nationalizing the lands and subsoil resources of Mexico.

In his note of March 31, 1923, Pani did not fail to point out some of these facts. He referred to the Bankers' Agreement and to negotiations in progress between the Mexican government and the oil men of the United States. He cited the court decisions and gave statistics indicating that the oil industry in Mexico was in a flourishing state despite the alleged apprehensions of the petroleum producers. The oil production for the year 1920 was 157,000,000 barrels and for 1922 more than 182,000,000. Citizens of the United

States still owned 57.7% of the oil business in Mexico, the British 33.8%, and the Mexicans only 1.1%! In the process of granting communal lands to the Indian villages, Pani admitted that citizens of the United States may have suffered losses, but he justified the Mexican government on the ground of expediency. The impulsive demands of the long-abused people necessitated speedy action and the state of the Mexican treasury did not permit of cash indemnity. Moreover, the explosive enthusiasm of certain agrarians and the machinations of political agitators often made it impossible to confine official action within the limits of strict legality, but it should be "remembered . . . that faulty administrative organization is an evil from which some of the most civilized countries of the world still suffer." The Obregón government had chosen the lesser of two evils. It had extinguished the fires of a destructive agrarian revolt at the cost of only slight injury to the land-owners, and only twenty-six Americans had suffered! "Considering all this, . . . it may be affirmed that the damages to the American agricultural properties . . . will never justify the systematic resistance, worthy of a better cause, which the United States has been opposing to the currents of sympathy . . . created and developed under the protection of the good will of the Government of Mexico. . . ." [4]

This exposition of the improving situation and of the difficulties under which the Obregón administration was working may have had some weight with Secretary Hughes. It was made at the very time that he was being hammered by merchants, bankers, boards of trade and commerce, citizens and officials of the Southwest, and humanitarians and plain people everywhere until the bruises were becoming painful. What did the bankers care about vested interests? They had their Lamont–De la Huerta agreement. What reason for regret had the mid-continent oil men if the Mexican government squeezed a few more dollars from their competitors or interfered with the development of their petroleum reserves? The chambers of commerce in the Southwest and elsewhere were primarily interested in Mexican trade, and they felt that recognition would promote their interests. Humanitarians and plain people thought more of equity and the future of the oppressed masses of Mexico than of the international rules of capitalistic nations and vested interests of United States captains of industry. It was the old story repeating itself. Mexico was finding protection in the rivalries and diverse views of the several groups which constituted the American nation. Obregón and Pani saw the situation and rejoiced. In his note of

---

[4] These diplomatic notes will be found in *United States Daily*, May 17-19, 1926.

March 31 Pani had referred to the resolutions demanding immediate renewal of diplomatic relations, which had been presented to the State Department "by the majority of the legislatures of the States of the American Union and many official and private institutions." In fact, the Mexican leaders deliberately cultivated American public opinion—a procedure not at all unusual on their part.

Evidently the time had come when diplomatic briefs no longer sufficed, and Hughes prepared to adjust his sails to the prevailing wind. In May, 1923, Charles Beecher Warren and John Barton Payne were sent as commissioners to Mexico for the purpose of negotiating concerning recognition. Apparently the resolution to force Mexico to sign a treaty prior to and as a condition of recognition was about to be abandoned. The main purpose now appeared to be to obtain a definite and formal statement of the position and intentions of the administration of Obregón.

Mexico seems to have made very few concessions during the conferences which followed. Special and general claims conventions were signed, but these could have been had two years before. The Mexican commissioners, Ramón Ross and Fernando González Roa, declared with reference to petroleum that the Constitution of 1917 "is not retroactive in respect to all persons who have performed, prior to the promulgation of said Constitution, some positive act which would manifest the intention of the owner of the surface or of the persons entitled to exercise his rights to the oil under the surface to make use of or obtain the oil under the surface: such as drilling, leasing, entering into any contract with reference to the subsoil, making investments of capital in lands for the purpose of obtaining the oil in the subsoil, and carrying out works of exploitation and exploration of the subsoil and in cases where, in the contract relative to the subsoil, it appears that the grantors fixed and received a price higher than would have been paid for the surface of the land because it was purchased for the purpose of looking for oil and exploiting same if found; and, in general, performing or doing any other positive act, or manifesting an intention of a character similar to those heretofore described." But this was merely an elaboration of the position of the Mexican Supreme Court, a repetition of the doctrine that a positive act was necessary in order to transform the privilege of extracting petroleum into an acquired right. In this connection, however, the Mexican commissioners did hold out an encouraging promise. They stated that persons who had not performed such positive acts prior to the date when the Constitution of 1917 became effective would be conceded preferential rights to the fuel products beneath the surface which they owned and, upon application to the

Mexican national government, would be granted permission to avail themselves of these rights. Warren and Payne dissented from this positive act doctrine and reserved to their government the privilege of future protest. The American commissioners, on their part, agreed that Mexico might compensate citizens of the United States in 20-year, five per cent bonds for such lands as had or should be taken from them, not in excess of a square league (4,335 acres) for each village, in restoring communal lands to the Mexican Indians. But the commissioners refused to admit that ten per cent in excess of the value of these lands for purposes of taxation would constitute just compensation and they made it clear that the acceptance of bonds for the *ejidos* was not to be considered a precedent in respect to lands of citizens of the United States expropriated under other circumstances.[5]

Warren and Payne returned to Washington near the end of August and reported the results of their conferences. On September 3 diplomatic relations were formally resumed. Matters then quieted down somewhat. Obregón attempted to negotiate another agreement with the International Committee of Bankers; and the Agrarian Commission of Mexico continued to restore community lands to the villages, but the execution of most of the other provisions of the Constitution was postponed. In the meantime, the United States government showed its approval of Obregón by discriminating against De la Huerta in his attempt to seize the reigns of power. Obregón's candidate, Plutarco Elias Calles, was successful in the national election of the summer of 1924, and in the following December he quietly took charge of the Mexican government.

On the surface, the relations between the two nations continued to be harmonious until June, 1925. And then, just as the American public were beginning to think that the Mexican "ship of state had reached an even keel," Secretary of State Kellogg, who had entered the Coolidge Cabinet after the resignation of Hughes, published a startling statement in the press. Kellogg said in part:

"I have discussed Mexican affairs with Ambassador Sheffield at great length. He has gone over the entire situation. It will be remembered that we entered into two claims conventions with Mexico under which joint claims commissions were appointed to adjust claims of American citizens for properties illegally taken by Mexico and for injuries to American citizens of their rights. These commissions are now sitting and will, in due time, adjudicate these claims. Conditions have improved and our Ambassador has succeeded in protecting American, as well as

[5] *Proceedings of the United States-Mexican Commission . . . 1923.* For a fuller analysis of the controversy of 1921–1923, *cf.,* Hackett, *The Mexican Revolution and the United States.*

foreign, interests. Our relations with the Government are friendly, but nevertheless conditions are not entirely satisfactory and we are looking to and expect the Mexican Government to restore properties illegally taken and to indemnify American citizens.

"A great deal of property of Americans has been taken under or in violation of the agrarian laws for which no compensation has been made and other properties practically ruined and, in one instance, taken by the Mexican Government on account of unreasonable demands of labor. Mr. Sheffield will have the full support of this Government and will insist that adequate protection under the recognized rules of international law be afforded American citizens. . . .

"I have seen the statement published in the press that another revolutionary movement may be impending in Mexico. I very much hope this is not true. This Government's attitude toward Mexico and toward threatened revolutionary movements was clearly set forth in 1923, when there was such a movement threatening the constituted Government of that country.

"The attitude taken by this Government at that time has since been maintained and it is now the policy of this Government to use its influence and its support in behalf of stability and orderly constitutional procedure, but it should be made clear that this Government will continue to support the Government in Mexico only so long as it protects American lives and American rights and complies with its international engagements and obligations.

"The Government of Mexico is now on trial before the world. We have the greatest interest in the stability, prosperity, and independence of Mexico. We have been patient and realize, of course, that it takes time to bring about a stable Government, but we cannot countenance violation of her obligations and failure to protect American citizens." [6]

This public warning called forth from President Calles a spirited reply. He cited the claims conventions as proof of Mexico's willingness to "comply with her international obligations and to protect the life and interests of foreigners." He declared that the agrarian laws could not be a subject of complaint because, in the first place, "Mexico has [had] issued them in the exercise of her sovereignty" and, in the second place, the State Department of the United States had accepted the form of indemnity prescribed by these laws. He declared also that Secretary Kellogg, in referring to reports of prospective revolts against the Mexican government, was destroying confidence in that government and inciting the very disorders which he pretended to deplore. He said that Kellogg's statement that the United States would continue to support the Calles administration only so long as it continued to protect American life and interests embodied a "threat to the sovereignty of Mexico" which could not be overlooked or allowed to remain unresented.

In taking this action President Calles appears to have voiced the sentiments of the majority of the Mexican people. Mexican Senators and Deputies sent congratulations and pledges of support.

[6] New York *Times*, June 16, 1926.

Leaders in the Mexican Army endorsed his statements and offered their swords in his defense. The press came valiantly to his aid. *El Democrata* dismissed Kellogg's charges as fanciful and false. *El Universal* quoted the statement of Calles with approval and remarked that the Mexicans had a clear sense of their rights and their honor as a sovereign people. It resented in particular Kellogg's suggestion of a revolution and the withdrawal of American support from Calles, denominating such procedure as an attempt to settle a diplomatic question by a threat to "unleash a catastrophe." *Excelcior* announced in its headlines that Kellogg's statements constituted a threat against the sovereignty of Mexico, while on its editorial page it carried such headlines as, "The False Friend" and "Will History Forever Repeat Itself?" The contention of the editor of this journal was that the announcement of the American Secretary of State would be taken by the Caribbean countries as an admission of the pursuit of policy of fomenting revolution, thus confirming the suspicions that they had long entertained. So far as Mexico was concerned he was half-inclined to believe that this was really the established procedure of Washington. Evidently the public warning of Kellogg had not placed Calles in a position to make concessions!

After this outburst the diplomatic atmosphere became calm [7] once more until the closing days of 1925, when it appeared certain that the Mexican Congress would pass laws relating to the nationalizing of petroleum and lands owned by aliens. This occasioned another duel of pens which lasted intermittently for five months. The issue of the contest was doubtful, both parties gaining certain advantages.

The petroleum law (December 31, 1925) declared, among other things, that petroleum was the property of the nation and that aliens could obtain permission to exploit this commodity only on condition of agreeing to become Mexicans in all that related to such a concession. It also confirmed without charge, but only for a period of fifty years: (1) all rights arising from lands on which works for the extraction of petroleum were begun prior to May 1, 1917, and (2) all rights arising from contracts made before May 1, 1917, by the owner of the surface or his successor in title for the express purpose of exploiting petroleum. With reference to all such lands, however, the law demanded that the companies concerned should apply to the government within a year for a fifty-year concession.[8]

[7] On October 23, 1925, another agreement with the International Committee of Bankers was signed.

[8] Text in *Diario Oficial*, Dec. 31, 1925.

The following are the main provisions of the alien land law (January 21, 1926): (1) Aliens are forbidden to acquire direct ownership of land or water in a strip of one hundred kilometers along the frontiers and of fifty kilometers along the seacoasts. (2) Aliens are not allowed to constitute a part of a Mexican company which may have or acquire ownership of lands and waters, or of concessions for the exploitation of mines, waters, or combustible minerals elsewhere in the republic, except on condition of obtaining a permit which will be granted to them only after they have agreed, on penalty of forfeiture, not to invoke the protection of their home government in regard to the property in question. (3) In the case of Mexican companies owning rural property for agricultural purposes, participation of aliens is not to be allowed after their acquisitions reach fifty per cent of the total interests of the company. So much for the provisions which relate to the future. The law then goes on to lay down certain stipulations in respect to alien property acquired before the law becomes effective: (1) Foreign individuals, partnerships, and corporations may retain their holdings in the maritime and frontier strips until death or dissolution, and their heirs and assignees are given five years to dispose of the property even after this. (2) The same conditions hold elsewhere in the republic in respect to the ownership of lands, waters, and mining and other concessions, with the exception of aliens who possess fifty per cent or more of the total interests of Mexican companies holding rural lands for agricultural purposes. In such cases individuals are to have the same privilege, but corporations are to be granted a period of only ten years in which to dispose of their interests in excess of the stipulated maximum.[9]

The proposed partial denationalization of aliens, the previously acquired subsoil interests, and the provisions of the land law which relate to alien property acquired before the law became operative furnished the occasion for Kellogg's protests and the replies of Aarón Sáenz, Mexican Minister of Foreign Affairs. With reference to the issue of requiring foreigners to waive their nationality and agree, on penalty of forfeiture, not to invoke diplomatic protection in respect to their land and oil properties in Mexico, Kellogg refused to admit that said waiver could annul the relations of a citizen to his government or cancel his government's obligation to accord diplomatic protection in case of a denial of justice. Sáenz admitted that an individual could not "compel the state of which he is a citizen to re-

[9] Text in *ibid.*, January 21, 1926.

frain from asserting a right that belongs to it," but he contended that the waiver agreement was an obligation "assumed individually between the contracting party and the Mexican Government," and, as such, in no way infringed "upon any of the rights of a foreign state." The other two issues involved a definition of the terms "retroactive" and "confiscatory." Kellogg appears soon to have decided that further protest against the positive act view with reference to petroleum rights would be futile, but he continued to maintain that "the exchange of a present title for a concession having a limited duration"—namely, fifty years—did not "confirm the title." He also pointed out that the owners of oil lands and oil concessions who had not taken positive steps to develop the commodity prior to May 1, 1917, had not, under the provisions of the recent petroleum law, been granted the preferential right of exploiting the oil underneath these lands. And lastly, with reference to the alien land law, Kellogg argued that the time limit which it set for the disposition of lands held by aliens would occasion serious losses to American citizens, for they would inevitably be forced to sell them in a very unfavorable market. To which the Mexican Foreign Minister replied that the difficulty could be obviated by the acceptance of Mexican citizenship and that the result of the operation of these provisions could not be determined until the time came for the sale of the lands in question. Moreover, he assured the United States government that the regulations putting both of the laws into effect would be moderate and reasonable.[10]

And this assurance proved genuine. The regulations were somewhat more lenient than the laws. In certain cases an extension of time was granted for the disposal of alien holdings affected by the land law and it was expressly declared that none of the stipulations of the law or the regulations would be "applied retroactively to the injury of any person." The petroleum regulations confirmed for fifty years, with a *promise of indefinite extension* of this period instead of merely for fifty years, all oil rights acquired prior to May 1, 1917 (Art. 155). They also provided that the beneficiaries of any contract for the exploitation of petroleum entered into between May 1, 1917, and December 31, 1925, should have the preferential right for a year to obtain concessions from the Mexican government in accord with the stipulations of the law and the regulations (Art. 157). This stipulation presumably will furnish a partial remedy for those who had failed to take positive steps looking toward the development of petroleum from their lands prior to May 1, 1917.

[10] The correspondence was published in *United States Daily*, April 12–15, 1926, and in *Sen. Doc.*, No. 96, 69 Cong., 1 Sess.

Preferential treatment for such persons is, however, not expressly stipulated.[11]

It was not a notable victory for those who had for six years indulged in criticism of Wilson's "watchful waiting," but diplomatic coercion had accomplished something. The future had not been made absolutely secure, the vested interests were not yet satisfied; but a few radical tendencies had been checked and a few safeguards set up.

And just as economic controversies approached a calmer stage, religious matters threatened to disturb the composure of the two nations. Calles was bent upon the complete achievement of the revolutionary program. To restore the communal holdings of the native races and put into operation laws designed to nationalize lands and subsoil resources was not sufficient. The power of the Church must be curbed, the performance of religious functions confined to native ministers, education completely secularized, and the dominance of the State over the Church effectively asserted. It was in February, 1926, that serious steps looking toward these ends were first taken. Even if several American ministers and priests had not been affected by these "reforms," the drive against the Catholic Church in Mexico would have aroused hostility in certain circles of the United States. Kellogg and Coolidge were called upon to protest and even to withdraw recognition from Calles.[12]

But neither the dissatisfaction of captains of industry nor the prodding of churchmen could ruffle the calm which had begun to settle upon the Coolidge administration since the beginning of April. After all of their boisterous protests and fulminations the Republican aggressives found their leader committed to viligant patience. At any rate, they would not call it "watchful waiting"—what it really was—and the reticence of their chief was not as offensive as the oratory of Wilson. Besides, there might be some advantage in keeping the bad men of Mexico in uncertainty as to whether the American cohorts would come marching across the border and when.

At the opening of the year 1927, however, the clouds which had long overcast the horizon of United States–Mexican relations once more began to thicken. During the closing days of 1926 American Marines were landed in the state of Nicaragua. One of the reasons given out by the Coolidge administration for the debarkation was that the move had been made necessary by the action of the Mexican government, which was supporting a revolutionary group hos-

[11] *Diario Oficial*, April 8, 1926 ff.
[12] New York *Times*, March 7, 1926, *passim*; Hackett, *The Mexican Revolution and the United States*, pp. 398–400, 440–446.

tile to the interests of the United States in Nicaragua. In this connection, it was said that Calles was supporting Russian Bolshevism in its attempt to drive a red wedge between the United States and the Canal Zone.

But critics of the administration arrived at other motives by inference. They suspected that Coolidge and Kellogg were attempting to bluff Mexico into compliance with their demands or seeking a pretext for a break with Calles and the occupation of the oil zones. Again the anti-interventionists collected their forces. Almost all the leading Southern newspapers and many of those of the West protested vigorously. Such great national journals as the New York *Times* and the New York *World* published editorial criticism and printed world opinion opposed to our policy. President William Green of the American Federation of Labor raised his voice against the charge that Mexican labor was bolshevist. Churches and peace organizations mobilized their memberships speedily and effectively. Many Democrats, particularly in the South, denounced the administration, for partisan and other reasons. Borah, La Follette, and Wheeler took a masterful stand in the Senate. Kellogg and Coolidge, Brisbane and Hearst, producers of oil, bananas, and mahogany, and the Knights of Columbus were held in check,[13] but for several months the relations of the United States and Mexico continued to be tense and critical.

[13] *Cf.* New York *Times,* New York *World,* and *Christian Science Monitor,* Jan. 10 to 30, 1927; *Congressional Record,* Jan. 8 to 26, 1927; and the *Nation* and *New Republic* for the same period.

CHAPTER XXIII

THE WORK OF AMBASSADOR MORROW—CONCLUSION

HAVING tried diplomatic coercion without signal achievements and witnessed a demonstration of American public sentiment in connection with the Nicaraguan issue, President Coolidge finally decided to change his procedure. In October, 1927, J. R. Sheffield, whose efforts had long been ineffective in Mexico City, returned to the United States and Dwight W. Morrow, a noted financier with an ingratiating personality, was sent to take his place. Soon afterwards Coolidge announced his new policy in the following words: "A firm adherence to our rights and a scrupulous respect for the sovereignty of Mexico, . . . coupled with patience and forbearance, it is hoped, will resolve all our difficulties without interference with the friendly relationship between the two Governments." [1]

The whole atmosphere changed immediately. Morrow was received (October 29, 1927) with unprecedented demonstrations and began at once to apply his new diplomacy. Will Rogers, our popular humorist, and Charles A. Lindbergh, our aviation idol, were drafted for the occasion. For the first time in years Mexicans began to feel that they had in the United States what Wilson had called a "coöperating friend."

When Morrow took up his work in Mexico City he confronted at least five issues: (1) An alien land law designed gradually to deprive foreigners of ownership of lands on the northern and maritime frontiers of Mexico, as well as to prevent foreign corporations from owning a controlling interest in agricultural lands or water power anywhere in the Republic; (2) complaints of citizens of the United States on account of inadequate compensation for lands taken from their estates and transferred to Indian villages; (3) the resentment of some of the oil companies of the United States because of the attempt of the Mexican government to recover a large measure of the petroleum resources of the country and to increase its revenues by taxes upon this commodity; (4) claims of citizens of the United States against Mexico amounting to millions of dollars were still un-

---

[1] *Cf.* C. W. Hackett, in *Current History,* December, 1927, ff.

settled and little progress was being made toward their adjudication; (5) payments of interest on government and railway bonds to the amount of over P. 232,000,000 (principal and accrued interest) owned by citizens of the United States had been irregular and were on the point of being suspended.[2] Toward the end of his mission Morrow's task was rendered more difficult by a Mexican revolution (March, 1929) and by the somewhat ruthless expulsion by agents of the United States of Mexicans who had emigrated to this country in search of work and a better living standard.[3]

After three years of service, hailed by the press of the United States with perhaps somewhat more applause than he deserved, the Ambassador returned to the United States and entered the Senate. The evidence required for an accurate estimate of his work is not available, but a tentative statement may be ventured.

Probably the most important phase of his achievement was the contribution which he made toward the transformation of Mexican attitude from suspicion and hostility to confidence and a willingness to coöperate in the settlement of outstanding difficulties. This he did by showing the Mexicans that a Yankee—even a Yankee millionaire—could be moderate, genial, and appreciative of the qualities of Mexican character and culture. He also took a long view of the Mexican situation and reached the conviction that some of Mexico's domestic problems would have to be solved before her difficulties with the United States could be taken up with any hope of satisfactory solution.

Shortly after Morrow's arrival, the Supreme Court of Mexico handed down a decision (November 17, 1927) more favorable to the oil interests. The question involved was whether the Department of Industry could properly cancel drilling permits for "tagged" lands (lands with reference to which some positive act looking toward the extraction of petroleum had taken place prior to May 1, 1917) because the owner had not applied for a fifty-year confirmatory concession within the time limit fixed by the petroleum law of 1925. The Court held that drilling permits could not be cancelled on this ground. It maintained that vested rights could not be subjected to partial loss or restriction. The owner possessed acquired rights, not mere *expectancies*, in the oil beneath the lands in question

---

[2] Edgar Turlington's *Mexico and Her Foreign Creditors,* is a good discussion of this important subject.

[3] For a convenient summary of the immigration problem, consult Rippy, "La Inmigración Mexicana en los Estados Unidos," *Universidad de Mexico,* I (December, 1930), 162 ff. *Cf.,* also, Ray L. Garis, *Immigration from Countries of the Western Hemisphere.*

and a confirmatory concession for fifty years would be a restriction upon these rights, which were without limitation as to time. Taking note of this decision, President Calles urged Congress to modify the petroleum law so as to conform with it. The result was an amendment—passed in December, 1927, and promulgated in the following January—requiring that pre-constitutional oil rights be confirmed without cost by the issuance of confirmatory concessions "without limitation of time."

The problem was not yet entirely solved, however; for the task of readjusting the petroleum regulations still remained. "There ensued several weeks of negotiations which were characterized by the utmost friendliness on both sides, and during all of which Ambassador Morrow kept in the closest touch with the local representatives of the leading American oil companies." The negotiations ended in a satisfactory settlement of a very troublesome issue. On March 28, 1928, the Department of State published the following statement:

> The Petroleum Regulations just promulgated by President Calles constitute executive action which completes the process beginning with the decision made by the judicial branch of the Mexican Government on November 17, 1927, and followed by the enactment of the new petroleum law by the legislative branch on December 26 last.
>
> Together these steps voluntarily taken by the Mexican Government would appear to bring to a practical conclusion the discussions which began ten years ago with reference to the effect of the Mexican constitution and laws upon foreign oil companies. The department feels, as does Ambassador Morrow, that such questions, if any, as may hereafter arise can be settled through the due operation of the Mexican administrative departments and the Mexican courts.

Although at first there was some indication [4] that the oil companies would not acquiesce in the settlement, during the course of the next few months they gradually signified their acceptance and their agents and those of other companies appeared in Mexico to solicit from the government new concessions for the exploitation of oil.[5] It is important to point out once more just what each side had gained by the long controversy. Mexico had secured the acceptance of its positive acts doctrine, and the owners of land upon which no such acts looking toward the development of oil had taken place prior to May 1, 1917, were virtually deprived of the right to extract oil from their lands. The main concession which the United States gained for its citizens and companies who had performed positive acts on lands

---

[4] *Cf.* Guy Stevens, *Current Controversies with Mexico*, p. 315 ff. In connection with Stevens's work, an article by J. Reuben Clark, entitled "The Oil Settlement with Mexico" (*Foreign Affairs*, July, 1928), should be consulted.

[5] Hackett, in *Current History*, July, 1930, pp. 768-769.

owned or leased by them was the avoidance of a time limit of fifty years for the extraction of petroleum from these lands. In view of the over-production of petroleum, this concession may be an important one. Moreover, Mexico granted a broad and liberal definition of the term "positive acts"—a definition which accorded with the terms of the agreement of 1923.

Progress was also made with reference to other controversies. Agricultural bonds were slowly issued in payment for lands expro-priated from foreigners, the claims commissions resumed their work, the Mexican government showed a disposition to meet its debt ob-ligations to the extent of its capacity to pay, and commissions deal-ing with the United States–Mexican boundary and the distribution and control of the waters of the Rio Grande advanced harmoniously toward the solution of these problems.

Lastly, it must be noted that Morrow took part in another nego-tiation which, although connected only indirectly with his duties, may turn out in the long run to be the most significant contribution of his mission. He served as a mediator in the settlement of the diffi-culties between the civil and ecclesiastical authorities in Mexico and thus brought to an end, temporarily and perhaps even permanently, the long and tragic struggle between Church and State in that country.

When Morrow began his residence in Mexico, the leaders who had won the social revolution of 1911–1920 were engaged in a rather menacing conflict with the clergy. As a protest against the constitu-tion of 1917 and the laws designed to make effective its religious pro-visions, the churches had been closed, a religious boycott had been declared, armed bands of ardent Catholics were scattered over the country fighting under a banner bearing the inscription, "*Viva Cristo El Rey*," and many acts of brutality were being committed by both sides.

"The crux of the conflict," as Walter Lippmann has remarked, "was whether the Mexican clergy would continue to oppose or would accept and coöperate with the régime resulting from the social rev-olution. . . . For nearly a hundred years they had identified the interests of the Church with a Mexican state dominated by the great landlords and foreign interests; they had regarded the revolutionists against the conservative state, from Father Hidalgo through Benito Juárez to Carranza and Obregón and Calles, as the enemies of the Church. And because the Church was identified with the conserva-tive state and with foreign intervention, the revolutionists became in practice the enemies of the clergy." But due to three years of unsuccessful conflict with the revolutionary leaders, as well as to the influence of Morrow and certain liberal Catholics of the United States, "the Mexican hierarchy achieved a new orientation. It ceased to identify itself with the small class of great landlords who had been overthrown by the revolution, and learned to identify itself with the aspirations of the common people. . . .

"In this new orientation is to be found the significance of the settlement [of June, 1929] and the only possible guarantee that it will last. The Mexican Church has started to become a democratic church. With the change of allegiance, the powers vested in the government by the Constitution and the laws ceased to have any real significance. They were war powers directed against a hierarchy which was inveterately hostile to the new régime and threatened its overthrow. Against a hierarchy which accepts a new régime such as Mexico has now been promised, they will not be used, and in the course of time will either be forgotten or repealed." [6]

Such, in brief outline, were the achievements of Morrow. To many Americans with unpaid interest and claims they doubtless appeared meager enough. But a policy of patience and forbearance applied to a country just recovering from a long and bloody revolution must be viewed with a lengthy perspective. Morrow's mission was too brief to achieve numerous or lasting results. These must depend upon the ability of his successors and continued stability in Mexico. If the United States had sent more men of his type to the Aztec capital the story related in this volume might have been a very different one.

When Morrow left Mexico City (September 17, 1930) President Ortiz Rubio issued a statement praising the Ambassador and declaring that the relations of the two countries had reached the "peak of cordiality." The statement was essentially true, notwithstanding certain friction which had arisen on account of the recent tariff law passed by the United States and the severe treatment of Mexican immigrants in the Southwest.

From this vantage ground of harmony we may appropriately survey a century of Mexican-American relations in search of the fundamental factors which have tended to determine their nature. These factors or forces are at least six in number.

Perhaps the most obvious of them is that of geographical proximity. The United States and Mexico adjoin each other along an immense frontier which has varied in length, with changing boundaries, from more than three thousand to less than two thousand

---

[6] This view appears a bit optimistic, but the brilliant article of Lippmann deserves careful attention ("Church and State in Mexico: The American Mediation," *Foreign Affairs,* VIII (January, 1930), p. 186 ff.).

miles. There have been no natural barriers, the two nations being separated by an imaginary line, a barbed-wire fence, an easily forded river, an undergrowth of mesquite or chaparral. Citizens of both nations have passed back and forth with little difficulty or interruption, or have settled in neighboring states amidst natural surroundings which have not repelled them by their unfamiliar aspect. Bandits, filibusters, and Indians have raided freely back and forth. Smugglers have often plied their trade with relative ease and security. Robbers of stock have sometimes been able to operate on a large and profitable scale. Political insurgents and refugees have often sought and found safety across the international line.

A second factor is the rich natural resources of Mexico. Among these are minerals of every description, superb timbers, fertile soil, an infinitely varied climate adapted to an infinite variety of products, an isthmus for interoceanic communications—absolutely nothing lacking save rainfall in certain areas and great natural waterways. Worthy of special emphasis is the fact that in Mexico are produced three commodities which are deemed of great importance to modern life; namely, rubber, oil, and tropical fruits.

In the third place, Mexico has been a disorderly and bankrupt nation for more than two-thirds of its independent existence. It has been the scene not only of revolutions but also of considerable administrative irregularities and graft. Foreigners residing in Mexico, foreign merchants engaged in Mexican commerce, foreigners holding Mexican securities, have all suffered from these conditions. Many pecuniary claims have arisen, frequent complaints have been made, and foreign governments have often remonstrated or intervened. In the case of the United States, drastic action and threats of coercion have almost always had some connection with the maltreatment of American citizens. Furthermore, Mexican disorders have furnished a benevolent appeal for imperialistic tendencies in both Europe and America. It has been argued that the more "advanced" nations should establish order in Mexico and relieve the misery of the Mexican people as a matter of moral obligation.

Fourth, the people of the United States have always been a very active, enterprising, and aggressive people. With great strength and much confidence in themselves, proud of their power and achievements, with acquisitive tendencies highly developed, they have alarmed Mexicans as often by exaggerated expressions of their ambitions and destiny as by their aggressive acts. Seldom has there been a time when we have not been eager for something belonging to our southern neighbor. Prior to 1860 it was territory and trade. Subsequent to 1865 it has been investment opportunities, subsoil resources, commerce, a port of entry on the Gulf of California, and at times the Peninsula of Lower California itself. In moments of ecstasy we have magnified our ambitions and overstated our sense of destiny. Mexico has been greatly alarmed both by these acts and by these utterances. Distrusted and feared almost from the beginning, the United States soon became *El Coloso* and its citizens *El Peligro Yanqui*. Europeans fomented this fear and distrust. Mexican demagogues often sought popularity by arousing this latent sentiment. Barriers of language, race, and religion made it difficult to remove. And on occasions it became a veritable *Yankeephobia*. The Mexican masses, in moments of reckless abandon, have been led to abuse and persecute the alleged deadly enemy of soul and fatherland. Many an American—whether missionary, laborer, or business man—has suffered on this account. The revolution which overthrew Díaz was in some respects a Boxer movement directed mainly at the Yankees. The character of the American people has unquestionably been an important influence in United States–Mexican relations.

Fifth, the attitude and procedure of Europeans, as already suggested, have always been a potent factor. The Spanish minister in the United States and the British *chargé d'affaires* in Mexico had much to do with the origin of Mexican *Yankeephobia* a century ago. Since that time Europeans have seldom let pass an opportunity to foment fear and suspicion of the United States. Mainly with this end in view they have issued warnings, privately through their legations in the Mexican capital and publicly through the European press and in newspapers which they have established for the purpose in Mexico. The United States has been keenly conscious of the disposition and conduct of European nations and individuals. Rarely have European schemes in Mexico passed unnoticed or failed to exert influence upon American policy. Between 1837 and 1845 apprehensiveness with reference to British and French activities in Texas overcame opposition to its annexation. Exasperation at Europe's apparent disposition to interfere seems to have been a factor in Polk's decision to declare war against Mexico in 1846 and to strike at once. The possibility of European intervention in Mexico in 1858–1860 held a prominent place in Buchanan's proposed intervention at that time. In fact, plans for eliminating European influence figured in nearly all American-Mexican negotiations between 1855 and 1867. For several years subsequent to the withdrawal of the French from the Aztec republic (1867) the European factor ceased to be of importance, but during the recent revolutionary period much was said and written by Americans in regard to the schemes of European companies or powers, particularly Germany. It should also be added that in recent years the Japanese danger frequently has been brought into the foreground. The effect of this fear and jealousy of the Great Powers may be summed up in the exhortation: "Let us act before these nations do," or "Let us proceed while the Europeans and Japanese are busy elsewhere." In a word, the European factor has often served as a goad to drastic action.

The fundamental forces mentioned thus far have usually tended to promote aggression on the part of the United States. There is another factor, however, which has almost always had the opposite tendency. Conflicting interests and ideals of sections and groups in the United States have usually held the government in check. While the slavery issue may have tended to render the government aggressive at certain given moments, on the whole and in the long run it probably saved the Mexican nationality from total extermination prior to 1861. In like manner, a lively bombardment of the Hayes administration by the commercial group and those holding concessions just received from the Díaz government probably saved Díaz from coercion in the interest of old claimants and concessionaires and Texas frontiersmen during the period 1877–1880. Again, it may be seriously doubted whether President Wilson could have avoided a drastic Mexican policy between 1913 and 1920 if he had not been loyally supported by laborers, churchmen, liberal journalists and educators, and many plain people throughout the country. And finally, these same groups, joined by mid-continent oil men and large mercantile interests, probably toned down the demands of the Harding and Coolidge administrations upon the Obregón and Calles governments.

Such are the factors which have tended to determine the relations between the United States and Mexico. Whether Mexico will swing more completely into the orbit of its neighbor will depend largely upon the operation and counter-operation of the forces which have been enumerated. Most of them appear to be constant in nature. The two nations cannot escape the fact of contiguity. Each is bound to be affected by conditions in the other. Mexico's subsoil resources are almost inexhaustible; its supersoil treasures probably capable of indefinite development; its climate and its isthmus bid defiance to the assaults of time. Its natural wealth will always attract Americans. The Mexicans may find a balm for their political maladies and they may not. For the last ten years matters have gone fairly well, however. The growing complexity of the modern world holds out little hope of an isolation that will totally remove the possibility of intimate European and Asiatic contacts. Nor are the Anglo-Saxons of the North likely to change their energetic, aggressive nature. On the contrary, continued increase of population and progressive development of colossal industries will stimulate the desire for economic expansion. But in recent years our utterances and our diplomacy with reference to Mexico are becoming noted for their tact, and our policy has been patient if not generous. The relations of the two countries have rarely been so harmonious as at the present time. For the moment, the more idealistic and less aggressive groups appear to have the upper hand in the determination of Mexican policy.

BIBLIOGRAPHY

I. GUIDES

Ames, John G. *Comprehensive Index to the Publications of the United States Government, 1881–1893.* Washington, 1905. 2 vols.

Bolton, H. E. *Guide to Materials for the History of the United States in the Principal Archives of Mexico.* Washington, 1913.

Catalogue of the Public Documents of the United States. Washington, 1896 ff.

Channing, E., A. B. Hart, and F. J. Turner. *Guide to the Study and Reading of American History.* Boston, 1912.

Hasse, A. R. *Index to United States Documents relating to Foreign Relations 1828–1861.* Washington, 1914–1921. 3 vols.

Library of Congress: Division of Manuscripts. *Check List of Collections of Personal Papers in Historical Societies, University and Public Libraries, and Other Learned Institutions in the United States.* Washington, 1918. *Handbook of Manuscripts in the Library of Congress.* Washington, 1918.

Library of Congress: Periodical Division. *A Check List of American Newspapers in the Library of Congress.* Washington, 1901.

A Check List of Foreign Newspapers in the Library of Congress. Washington, 1904.

New York Public Library. *Manuscript Collections in the New York Public Library,* in its *Bulletin,* Vol. 5.

Newberry Library. *Selected List of Books and Manuscripts Purchased Since January, 1910.* Chicago, 1915–1919. 3 vols.

Poore, Benjamin Perley. *A Descriptive Catalogue of the Government Publications of the United States, September 5, 1774–March 4, 1881.* Washington, 1885.

State Department. *General Index to the Published Volumes of the Diplomatic Correspondence and Foreign Relations of the United States.* Washington, 1902.

Times Index, New York, 1878 (for period 1863–1877); 1913 ff. (Four volumes for each year.)

United States Document Office. *Checklist of United States Public Documents, 1789–1909, Congressional: to close of 60th Congress, Departmental: to end of Calendar Year 1909.* Washington, 1911.

Van Tyne, C. H. and W. G. Leland. *Guide to the Archives of the Government of the United States in Washington.* Washington, 1907.

II. PRIMARY MATERIALS

1. *Manuscripts*

Bolton Collection of Transcripts from the Principal Archives of Mexico. University of California.

Buchanan, James. Papers. Pennsylvania Historical Society.

Extracts from Manuscripts and Printed Matter in the Collection of Mons. Alphonse Pinart. University of California.

Great Britain: Public Record Office, London:
Foreign Office—Mexico, Despatches, vols. 260–335 (1853–1860).
Foreign Office—Mexico, Instructions, vols. 250–342 (1853–1860).

Gwin, William M. Memoirs. University of California.

Marcy, William L. Papers. Library of Congress.

Pickett, John T. Papers. Library of Congress.

Pierce, Franklin. Papers. Library of Congress.

Plumb, Edward Lee. Papers. Library of Congress.

Sherman, General W. T. Records and Papers. Library of Congress.

United States: State Department.
Despatches—Mexico, vols. 12–136 (1849–1898).
Domestic Letters (Only a few of these which related to certain important points were examined).
Instructions—Mexico, vols. 15–23 (1849–1898).
Miscellaneous Letters (Only the letters bearing upon the policy of the United States at certain critical periods were examined).
Notes from the Department to the Mexican Legation, vols. 5–
Notes to the Department from the Mexican Legation, vols. 6–
Special Agents, C. L. Ward, Package.
Special Missions, vol. no. 3, Memorandum of Instructions to C. L. Ward, October 22, 1853.
United States and Mexican Claims Commission, Opinions, vols. 1–3, and A, B, C.

United States: War Department. Correspondence with the Commanders on the Southwestern frontier, 1853–1854.

2. Newspapers

Mexican. (Files of these have been consulted in Bancroft Library, University of California.)
Correo de España. Mexico City, 1854–1855.
Diario de Avisos. Mexico City, 1856–1860.
Eco de España. Mexico City, 1853–1854.
El Español. Mexico City, 1852–1853.   `
La Nación. Mexico City, 1856–1857.
El Omnibus. Mexico City, 1851–1852.
El Siglo Diez y Nueve. Mexico City, 1848–1860.
El Universal. Mexico City, 1848–1860, 1921–1930.
Note: The Ministers of the United States in Mexico often transmitted clippings from the Mexican press bearing upon the relations of the two countries. These were bound with the despatches and sometimes printed in the public documents of the United States. By using these sources I have obtained access, for the period subsequent to 1860, to such important journals as: *Correo de Español; Diario Oficial; The Mexican Herald; El Monitor Republicano; El Nacional; Las Novedades; El Partido Liberal; La Patria; El Tiempo; Trait d'Union; Two Republics; El Universal,* etc., etc.

United States. (In the Library of Congress unless otherwise indicated.)
Alta California. San Francisco, 1851–1860. University of California.
Commercial Advertiser. New York, 1850–1851.
Daily Picayune. New Orleans, 1847–1853.

Herald. New York, 1849–1850, 1852–1860.
Journal of Commerce. New York, 1850–1860.
Evening Post. New York, 1848–1860 (Occasional numbers examined.),
The Sun. New York, 1848–1850.
Texas States Gazette. Austin, 1849–1855. Texas States Library.
Times. New York, 1850–1860, 1876–1878, 1913–1930.
Washington Union. Washington, D. C., 1848–1854.

3. *Official Documents*

(1) United States of America.
A Biographical Congressional Directory, 1774–1911. Washington, 1911.
Bureau of Foreign and Domestic Commerce.
*Commercial Relations of the United States with Foreign Countries during
the Year 1902. House Document* No. 305, 57 Cong. 2 Sess. (Ser. 4520).
(Pp. 443–511 give a report on investments of United States citizens in
Mexico.)
Confidential Bulletin, No. 40, 1921. (Investments of citizens of the United
States in Mexico.)
Monthly Trade and Consular Reports, 1880 ff. (The report for July 18,
1912 contains Consul-General Letcher's estimate of American investments
in Mexico.)
Congress. (Figures in parentheses represent the serial numbers.)
  Congressional Globe, 30 Cong., 1 Sess. to 42 Cong. 3 Sess. *Congressional
    Record,* 43 Cong., Special Sess. to 67 Cong., 1 Sess.
  House Executive Documents.
    30 Cong., 2 Sess., No. 50 (509). (Correspondence regarding the Treaty
    of Guadalupe Hidalgo.)
    31 Cong., 1 Sess., No. 62 (577). (Indians on the Mexican border.)
    32 Cong., 1 Sess., No. 112 (648). (Disorders on the Rio Grande.)
    33 Cong., 1 Sess., No. 109 (726). (Message of President Pierce accom-
    panied by the Gadsden Treaty.)
    33 Cong., 2 Sess., No. 1, Part I (777). (Estimate of Indians in New
    Mexico and adjacent regions.)
    34 Cong., 1 Sess., No. 47 (856). (Commercial matters.)
    34 Cong., 1 Sess., No. 135 (861–862). (Emory's "Report" on the bound-
    ary survey.)
    35 Cong., 1 Sess., No. 64 (955). (Execution of Crabb and his asso-
    ciates.)—No. 88 (956). (Correspondence with Major-General Wool
    concerning California filibusters.)
    36 Cong., 1 Sess., No. 52 (1050), No. 81 (1056). (Difficulties on the
    Southwestern frontier.)
    37 Cong. 2 Sess., No. 100 (1136); 37 Cong., 3 Sess., No. 54 (1162); 39
    Cong., 1 Sess., No. 73 (1261–1262). (French intervention in Mexico.)
    41 Cong. 1 Sess., No. 1 (1412). (U. S. army operations on the Mexican
    frontier.)
    45 Cong., 1 Sess., No. 13 (1773). (Difficulties on the Texas border.)
  House Journal, 30 Cong., 1 Sess. ff. (One volume for each Session.)
  House Miscellaneous Documents.
    33 Cong., 1 Sess., No. 45 (741). (Indian depredations in New Mexico.)
    45 Cong., 2 Sess., No. 64 (1820). ("Texas Border Troubles.")
  House Reports.
    31 Cong., 1 Sess., No. 280 (584). (Indian incursions into Mexico.)

23 Cong., 2 Sess., No. 151 (808). (Indian depredations in Texas.)

44 Cong., 1 Sess., No. 343 (1709). (Disorders along the Mexican border.)

45 Cong., 2 Sess., No. 701 (1824). (Mexican border difficulties.)

Senate Executive Documents.

30 Cong., 1 Sess., No. 40 (507). (Proposed military aid to Yucatán.)

30 Cong., 1 Sess., Nos. 52 and 60 (509). (Action of the Senate on the Treaty of Guadalupe Hidalgo.)

31 Cong., 1 Sess., No. 34 (562). (United States-Mexican boundary commission.)

32 Cong., 1 Sess., No. 60 (620). (Charges against Boundary Commissioner Bartlett.)

32 Cong., 1 Sess., No. 80 (620). (Claim of Samuel A. Belden.)

32 Cong., 1 Sess., No. 89 (620). (McClellan-Bartlett controversy regarding the conduct of the boundary survey.)

32 Cong., 1 Sess. No. 97 (620). (Correspondence regarding the isthmus of Tehuantepec.)

32 Cong., 1 Sess., No. 119 (626). (Correspondence relative to the United States-Mexican boundary controversy.)

32 Cong., 1 Sess., No. 120 (627). (Mexican complaints regarding lack of progress on the determination of the United States-Mexican boundary.)

32 Cong., 1 Sess., No. 121 (627). (Graham's report on the Mexican boundary survey.)

32 Cong., 2 Sess., No. 14 (660). (Report of Secretary of the Interior on the boundary survey.)

32 Cong., 2 Sess., No. 17 (660). (Imprisonment of American citizens at Acapulco.)

32 Cong., 2 Sess., No. 41 (665). (Report of J. R. Bartlett on the boundary.)

33 Cong., Special Sess., No. 6 (688). (Correspondence regarding the United States-Mexican boundary commission.)

33 Cong., 2 Sess., No. 16 (751). (Correspondence regarding California filibustering expeditions into Mexico.)

33 Cong., 2 Sess., No. 38 (752). (Claim of Francis W. Rice.)

33 Cong., 2 Sess., No. 55 (752). (A. B. Gray's report on the boundary survey.)

34 Cong., 1 Sess., No. 57 (821). (Boundary line and indemnity under the Gadsden Treaty.)

34 Cong., 1 Sess., No. 108 (832–834). (Emory's "Report" on the boundary survey.)

35 Cong., 1 Sess., No. 72 (930). (Correspondence regarding the Isthmus of Tehuantepec.)

35 Cong., 2 Sess., No. 18 (981). (Claims of the United States against foreign governments.)

44 Cong., 2 Sess., No. 31 (1720). (Claims of Mexican and American citizens under the convention of July 4, 1868.)

55 Cong., 2 Sess., No. 247 (3612–3614). (Report on the survey of the boundary between the United States and Mexico, 1891–1896.)

Senate Documents.

66 Cong., 1 Sess., No. 1 (7609). (Claims of American citizens against Mexico.)

BIBLIOGRAPHY

'66 Cong., 1 Sess., No. 67 (7610). (*Ibid.*)
66 Cong., 2 Sess., No. 285 (7665–7666). ("Investigation of Mexican Affairs." Fall Committee Report.)
Senate Journal, 30 Cong., 1 Sess. ff. (One volume for each Session.)
Senate Executive Journal. Washington, 1828–1911. 32 vols.
Senate Miscellaneous Documents.
   30 Cong., 2 Sess., No. 50 (533). (Petition of P. A. Hargous in reference to the Tehuantepec grant.)
   32 Cong., 2 Sess., No. 33 (670). (Outrages upon American citizens at Acapulco.)
Senate Reports.
   32 Cong., 1 Sess., No. 355 (631). (The Isthmus of Tehuantepec.)
   41 Cong., 2 Sess., No. 166 (1409). (Smuggling on the southwestern frontier.)
Interior Department: Indian Affairs Office. *Annual Report*, 1849–1896. (Also published in the Serial Set. See checklist.)
State Department.
   Diplomatic Correspondence, 1861–1868.
   Papers Relating to the Foreign Relations of the United States, 1870–1917.
   Statutes at Large of the United States of America. Washington, 1850 ff.
War Department: Secretary of War. *Annual Report*, 1849 ff. (Also published in Serial Set. See checklist.)
United States of Mexico. (Note: The publications of the Mexican government have appeared in such irregular and unsystematic fashion that it will not be worth while to list them save under a single heading and in alphabetical order.)
Archivo Mexicano. Actas de las sesiones de las Cámaras; despacho diario de las ministerios, sucesos notables, documentos oficiales importantes. . . . Mexico, 1852–1853. 2 vols.
El Archivo Mexicano. Colección de leyes, decretos, circulares y otros documentos. . . . Mexico, 1856–1862. 4 vols.
Colección de las leyes fundamentales que han regido en la República Mexicana, y de los planes que han tenido mismo carácter, desde el año de 1821 hasta el de 1856. Mexico, 1856.
Correspondencia de la Legación mexicana en Washington durante la intervención extranjera. Mexico, 1870–1892. 10 vols.
Dictamen de la comisión especial de Tehuantepec del Senado. . . . Mexico, 1851.
Dictamen de la mayoría de la comisión especial de la Cámara de Diputados del Congreso General, sobre el privilegio concedido a D. José Garay, para la apertura de una via de comunicación interoceánica por el Istmo de Tehuantepec. Mexico, 1851.
Informe general de la comisión pesquisidora de la frontera del noroeste al ejecutivo de la unión en cumplimiento . . . de la ley de 30 de setiembre de 1872. Mexico, [1875].
Informe de la comisión pesquisidora del norte al ejecutivo de la unión en cumplimiento . . . de la ley de 30 de setiembre de 1872. Mexico, 1874. An English translation under the title *Report of the Committee of Investigation sent in 1873 by the Mexican Government to the Frontier of Texas.* New York, 1875.
Leyes, decretos y órdenes que forman el Derecho Internacional mexicano o que se relacionan con el mismo. Mexico, 1879.

Mining Law of the United States of Mexico. Mexico, 1901. This publication is supplemented by *New Mining Law of the United States of Mexico* . . . , published in Spanish and in English, Nogales, 1910.

Ministerio de Comunicaciones y Obras Publicas. *Memoria.* Published irregularly, 1899 ff.

Reseña histórica y estadística de los ferrocarriles de jurisdicción federal. Mexico, 1905.

Ministerio de Fomento, Colonización é Industria. *Anales.* Mexico, 1880–1898. 19 vols.

Legislación sobre ferrocarriles . . . *1882–1885.* Mexico, 1882–1885. 3 vols.

Memoria. Published irregularly, 1877 ff.

Ministerio de Guerra y Marina. *Memoria.* Published irregularly, 1830 ff.

Ministerio de Hacienda y Crédito Público. *Memoria.* Irregular numbers, 1843 ff.

Exposición de la Secretaría de Hacienda de 15 de enero 1879, sobre la condición actual de México, y el aumento del comercio con los Estados Unidos, rectificando el informe dirigido por el Honorable John W. Foster, . . . *el 9 de octubre, 1878 al Señor Carlisle Mason de* . . . *Chicago.* Mexico, 1879. English translation, New York, 1880.

Ministerio de Relaciones Exteriores. *Archivo historico mexicano.* Mexico, 1923 ff. 14 numbers to date.

Boletin Oficial. Mexico, 1896–1906. 22 vols.

La Diplomacia mexicana. Mexico, 1910–1913. 3 vols.

Memoria. Published irregularly, Mexico, 1849 ff.

Memoria instructiva de los derechos y justas causas que tiene el gobierno de los Estados-Unidos mexicanos para no reconocer . . . *la subsistencia del privilegio concedido a Don José Garay para abrir una via de comunicación entre los oceanos Atlántico y Pacífico por el Istmo de Tehuantepec.* Mexico, 1852. English translation published same place and same year.

Santa Anna, Antonio López de. *Manifesto del Presidente de la República a la Nación.* Mexico, 1855.

El Presidente de la República a sus conciudadanos, 17 de deciembre de 1853.

Secretaría de Industria, Comercio y Trabajo. *Documentos relacionados con la Legislación Petrolera mexicana.* Mexico, 1919.

4. *Other Printed Sources*

Abel, Annie Heloise, ed. *The Official Correspondence of James A. Calhoun while Indian Agent at Santa Fé, and Superintendent of Indian Affairs in New Mexico.* Washington, 1915.

The Cincinnati and Sonora Mining Company. *Gold and Silver Mining in Sonora, Mexico.* Cincinnati, 1867.

De Bow's Commercial Review. New Orleans, 1846, 1880. 39 vols.

Domenech, Emmanuel Henri Deudonné. *Missionary Adventures in Texas and Mexico. A Personal Narrative of Six Years' Sojourn in those Regions.* London, 1858.

Dublán, Manuel y José María Lozano. *Legislación mexicana o Colección completa de los Disposiciones legislativas expedidas desde le Independencia de la República.* Mexico, 1867–1879. 11 vols.

García, Genaro y Carlos Pereyra. *Documentos inéditos o múy raros para la historia de México.* Mexico, 1903–1911. 36 vols.

Kappler, C. J. *Indian Affairs; Laws and Treaties* (Sen. Doc. No. 319, 58 Cong., 2 Sess., Ser. 4623–4624). Washington, 1904. 2 vols.
Linn, John J. *Reminiscences of Fifty Years in Texas.* New York, 1883.
Malloy, William M., Comp. *Treaties, Conventions, International Acts, Protocols, and Agreements between the United States of America and Other Powers, 1776–1909.* Washington, 1910. 2 vols.
Manero, Vicente E. *Documentos interesantes sobre colonización.* Mexico, 1878.
Maza, Francisco F. de la. *Código de colonización y terrenos baldíos de la República mexicana.* Mexico, 1893.
Moore, John Bassett. *A Digest of International Law.* . . . Washington, 1906. 8 vols.
History and Digest of International Arbitrations to which the United States has been a Party. Washington, 1898. 6 vols.
The Works of James Buchanan. . . . Philadelphia, 1908–1911. 12 vols.
Niles' National Register. Baltimore-Philadelphia, 1811–1849. 75 vols.
Olmstead, Frederick Law. *A Journey through Texas* . . . New York, 1857.
O'Shaughnessy, Mrs. Edith Louise. *Diplomatic Days.* New York, 1917.
A Diplomat's Wife in Mexico. New York, 1916.
Intimate Pages of Mexican History. New York, 1920.
Quaife, Milo Milton. *The Diary of James K. Polk during his Presidency, 1845–1849.* Chicago, 1911. 4 vols.
Richardson, James D. *A Compilation of the Messages and Papers of the Presidents.* Washington, 1896–1899. 10 vols.
A Compilation of the Messages and Papers of the Confederacy . . . Nashville, 1905. 2 vols.
Robinson, Edgar Eugene and Victor J. West. *The Foreign Policy of Woodrow Wilson, 1913–1917.* New York, 1917.
Santa Anna, Antonio López de. *A sus compatriotes.* San Tomás, 1858. "Mi Historia militar y político, 1810–1872," in García, *Documentos* (see above), vol. 2.
Stone, Charles P. *Notes on the State of Sonora.* Washington, 1861.
Walker, William. *The War in Nicaragua.* Mobile, 1860.
Webster, Daniel. *The Writings and Speeches of Daniel Webster.* National ed. Boston, 1903. 18 vols.
Wilson, Woodrow. *Selected Addresses and Public Papers.* Hart, A. B., ed. New York, 1918.
Winkler, E. W., ed. "The Bryan-Hayes Correspondence," in *The Southwestern Historical Quarterly,* XXV ff., *passim.*

III. SECONDARY REFERENCES

Ackerman, Carl W. *Mexico's Dilemma.* New York, 1918.
Álvarez, Ignacio. *Estudios sobre la historia general de México.* Zacatecas, 1869–1877. 6 vols.
Bancroft, Frederic. *Life of William H. Seward.* New York, 1900. 2 vols.
Bancroft, Hubert Howe. *History of Arizona and New Mexico, 1530–1888.* San Francisco, 1889.
History of Mexico, 1516–1887. San Francisco, 1883–1888. 6 vols.
History of the North Mexican States and Texas. San Francisco, 1884–1889. 2 vols.
Bell, Edward I. *The Political Shame of Mexico.* New York, 1914.
Bigelow, John. *Breaches of Anglo-American Treaties.* New York, 1917.
Retrospections of an Active Life. New York, 1909–1913. 5 vols.

Blakeslee, George H., ed. *Mexico and the Caribbean.* New York, 1920.

Bourne, E. G. "The United States and Mexico, 1847–1848," in *Amer. Hist. Review* V (April, 1900), 491 ff.

Bulnes, Francisco. *The Whole Truth about Mexico; President Wilson's Responsibility.* New York, 1916.

Caldwell, R. G. *The López Expeditions to Cuba, 1848–1851.* Princeton, 1915.

Callahan, James Morton. *Cuba and International Relations.* Baltimore, 1889.

"Evolution of Seward's Mexican Policy," in West Virginia University, *Studies in American History,* Series 1, Nos. 4, 5, 6. Morgantown, 1909.

"The Mexican Policy of Southern Leaders under Buchanan's Administration," in American Historical Association, *Annual Report* (1910), Washington, 1912.

Current History, Vols. IV (1916) to date. New York, 1916–

De Bekker, L. J. *The Plot Against Mexico.* New York, 1919.

Dillon, E. J. *Mexico on the Verge.* London, n. d.

President Obregon—A World Reformer. Boston, [1923].

Dodd, William E. *Jefferson Davis.* Philadelphia, 1907.

"The West and the War with Mexico," in Illinois State Historical Society, *Transactions* (1912), pp. 15–23.

Dunning, William Archibald. *The British Empire and the United States; A Review of their Relations during the Century of Peace following the Treaty of Ghent.* New York, 1914.

Fish, Carl Russell. *American Diplomacy.* 4th ed. rev. New York, 1923.

Garber, Paul Neff. *The Gadsden Treaty.* Philadelphia, 1923.

Hart, Albert Bushnell. *The Monroe Doctrine; an Interpretation,* Boston, 1916.

Hendrick, B. J. *Life and Letters of Walter Hines Page,* New York, 1922. 2 vols.

Inman, Samuel Guy. *Intervention in Mexico.* New York, 1919.

Johnson, Willis Fletcher. *America's Foreign Relations.* New York, 1916. 2 vols.

Jones, Chester Lloyd. *Mexico and Its Reconstruction.* New York, 1921.

Kohl, Clayton Charles. *Claims as a Cause of the Mexican War.* New York, 1914.

The Literary Digest. New York, 1914–1930. vols. 48–88.

The Living Age. Boston, 1914–1924. vols. 280–322.

McCormac, Eugene Irving. *James K. Polk, A Political Biography.* Berkeley, 1922.

Manero, Antonio. *México y la Solidaridad americana.* Madrid, [1918].

Manning, William Ray. *Early Diplomatic Relations between the United States and Mexico.* Baltimore, 1916.

Marshall, Thomas Maitland. *A History of the Western Boundary of the Louisiana Purchase.* Berkeley, 1914.

Middleton, P. Harvey. *Industrial Mexico.* New York, 1919.

Mowry, Silvester. *Memoir of the Proposed Territory of Arizona.* Washington, 1857.

The Nation. New York, 1913–1924. vols. 96–118.

The New Republic. New York, 1914–1924. vols. 1–40.

Powell, Fred Wilbur. *The Railroads of Mexico.* Boston, 1921.

Priestley, Herbert I. "The Carranza Debacle," in *University of California Chronicle,* XXIII, 3–17.

"The Relations of the United States and Mexico since 1910," *ibid.,* XXII, 3–16.

"Mexican Literature on the Recent Revolution," in *The Hispanic American Historical Review*, II (May, 1919), 286 ff.

The Mexican Nation, A History. New York, 1923.

Reeves, Jesse S. *American Diplomacy under Tyler and Polk.* Baltimore, 1907.

Rippy, J. Fred. "Literary Yankeephobia in Hispanic America," in *Journal of International Relations* (January and April, 1921), pp. 250 ff., 524 ff.; "Some Contemporary Mexican Reactions to Cleveland's Venezuelan Message," in *Political Science Quarterly*, XXXIX (June, 1924), 280 ff.

Riva Palacio, Vicente, ed. *México á través de los siglos.* Barcelona, 1888–1889. 5 vols.

Rivera Cambas, Manuel. *Historia antigua y moderna de Jalapa.* Mexico, 1869–1871. 5 vols.

Rives, George Lockhart. *The United States and Mexico, 1821–1848.* New York, 1913. 2 vols.

Robinson, Edgar Eugene and Victor J. West. *The Foreign Policy of Woodrow Wilson, 1913–1917.* New York, 1917.

Smith, Justin Harvey. *The Annexation of Texas.* New York, 1911.

The War with Mexico. New York, 1919. 2 vols.

Scroggs, William O. *Filibusters and Financiers. The Story of William Walker and his Associates.* New York, 1916.

Thomas, David Yancey. *One Hundred Years of the Monroe Doctrine.* New York, 1923.

Thompson, Wallace. *The People of Mexico.* New York, 1921.

Travesí, Gonzalo G. *La Revolución de México y el Imperialismo yanqui.* Barcelona, 1914.

Trowbridge, E. D. *Mexico To-day and To-morrow.* New York, 1919.

Tweedie, Ethel B. *Mexico from Diaz to the Kaiser.* New York, 1918.

Williams, Charles Richard. *The Life of Rutherford Birchard Hayes.* Boston and New York, 1914. 2 vols.

Wilson, Howard Lafayette. "President Buchanan's Proposed Intervention in Mexico," *The American Historical Review*, V (1900), p. 687 ff.

Zamacois, Niceto de. *Historia de Méjico desde sus tiempos más remotos hasta nuestros dias.* Mexico, 1877–1882. 18 vols.

SUPPLEMENTARY BIBLIOGRAPHY

Diario Oficial. Mexico, 1925–1926.

United States Daily. Washington, D. C., 1925–1930.

Senate Documents.

   69 Cong., 1 Sess., No. 96.

Proceedings of the United States-Mexican Commission, 1923. Washington, 1925.

Clark, J. Reuben. "The Oil Settlement with Mexico," in *Foreign Affairs*, VI (July, 1928).

American Association for International Conciliation, "The United States and Mexico." No. 187, New York, 1923.

Kendrick, Burton J. *The Life and Letters of Walter H. Page.* New York, 1926.

Wilson, Henry Lane. *Diplomatic Episodes.* New York, 1927.

Foreign Affairs. New York, 1922–1930. vols. 1–8.

Hackett, C. W. *The Mexican Revolution and the United States.* Boston, 1926.
Lippmann, Walter. "Church and State in Mexico: The American Mediation," in *Foreign Affairs*, VIII (January, 1930).
McBride, G. M. *The Land Systems of Mexico.* New York, 1923.
Márquez Sterling, M. *Los Ultimos Dias del Presidente Madero.* Habana, 1917.
Rippy, J. Fred. *Latin America in World Politics.* New York, 1928.
Rippy, J. Fred, José Vasconcelos, and Guy Stevens. *American Policies Abroad: Mexico.* Chicago, 1928.
Stevens, Guy. *Current Controversies with Mexico.* n. p., n. d.
Tannenbaum, Frank. *The Mexican Agrarian Revolution.* New York, 1929.
Turlington, Edgar. *Mexico and her Foreign Creditors.* New York, 1930.

INDEX

A B C powers, 352
Abolitionists, *see* slavery in the U. S.
Acapulco, 44-45, 47
Acayucán, 60
Adams, John Quincy, 10
Adams, Stephen, of Mississippi, 149
Aguas Calientes, 121, 316, 329
Alamán, Lucas Ignacio, 7
Alamo Cattle Co., 313
Alaska, 272
Aldrich, Nelson, 230
Alexander, *Major,* 291
Alien land law (1926), Mexico's, 373
Allen, Philip, 149
Almonte, Juan N., 142, 165, 171, 242-243
Álvarez, Juan, 176
America, Central, 26, 256
 England in, 30, 198-200
 France in, 198-200
 Louis Napoleon's interference, 30
 Mexican rôle in arbitration, 320
 protectorate of England, France, and
  Sardinia, rumored, 199-200
 United States in, 199
  Clayton-Bulwer Treaty hampers
   the policy of, 210
  Houston's resolution for protec-
   torate, 217
America, South
 England in, 30, 200
 France in, 200
"America, Young," 66, 132
 origin of, 26
 U. S. expansion, favor, 27
 see also United States, expansion
American colonization of Mexico, *see*
 Mexico, colonization in
American-Mexican claims commission,
 see claims
American Smelting and Refining Co.,
 313
Americanization of Mexico, *see* Mex-
 ico,

United States in, penetration or
 Americanization
Americans in Mexico, *see* Mexico,
 United States in
Anaconda group, 313
Anglo-Saxons in America, 382, 385
 Mexicans hostile to, 8, 44, 60, 90-
  91, 102, 115, 122-123
 friendly, 36-38
 superior nation (Onis' memoir), 2
Annexation, *see* name of place
Apaches, *see* Indians, tribes
Archibald Gracie, *bark,* 176
Arctic Ocean
 U. S. expansion up to the, 26, 252
Arista, Mariano
 Fillmore letter, reply to, 62-63
 Indian ravages, complaints of, 82
  Larrainzar to Washington, sends,
   63
 Tehuantepec Isthmus project, favors
  the U. S., 56
  conference with Smith on the, 60
 United States, said to favor annexa-
  tion of Mexico to the, 37
Arizona, 194, 233
 lawlessness in, 282
 Sonora annexation wanted by, 194
 territorial organization wanted, 194
Arizona Colonizing Co., 178
Ashhurst, Henry F., 356
Atascador estate, 314
Ávalos, *General,* 89-91, 101
 Indian invasion of Texas, promotes,
  91
Ayutla, 203, 221
 plan of, 168
  California financial aid, 176
Azcarate
 Poinsett's interview with (1822), 5

Bagby, Arthur P., 23
Bagdad, 280
Balance of power, 31

397

Huerta Victoriano (*continued*)
  Wilson, 350-352
Hughes, Charles E., and Mexico, 365-370
Humphrey, William E., 356
Hunker Democrats, 15
Hunter, Robert M. T., 149
Huntington, Collis P., 312, 329
Hyde, *Judge,* 116

Imperialistic tendencies, 361
Illinois, 194
Indian captives,
  to be returned when found (Poinsett's treaty), 8
  Gadsden Treaty, 152, 162
Indians, 172, 174-175, 360
  border, number of, 70
  Commissioner of Indian affairs, 71-72
  conflicts with, inevitable, 68
  description of, 70
  depredations by, 76, 80, 120, 147, 184-185, 192, 282, 285, 287-295
    Bonilla on, 134
  fire-arms necessary for, 69-70
  Gadsden Treaty and, 148
  Mexican measures against, 76-79
    campaigns, number of, 79-80
    ineffective, 79-80
    coöperation with U. S. proposed, 82
  Mexico, Indians go into, because southwest of U. S. is too crowded, 172-173
  Mexico, raids upon, 76
  Poinsett's treaty stipulations, 7-8
  prisoners kept by, 71, 79
    delivery of, 72-74
  reciprocal passing of boundary in pursuit, 175-176, 185
  Texas Indian agent, 72-73
  treaties with, 72-73
    chastisement of, for not carrying out treaties, 73
  tribes of,
    Apache, 68, 70-71, 73, 75, 91, 173
      Gila, 71-72
      Mescalero, 295
    Comanche, 68, 70, 73
    Kickapoo, 173, 288-289

Indians (*continued*)
    Mackenzie-Bullis expedition, 288-290
    removing them to northern side of boundary failed in 1871 and 1872, 289
    Kiowa, 70, 73
    Lipan, 73, 173, 294-295
    Muskogee, 78, 173
    Navajo, 70
    Seminole, 78, 172
    Utah, 70
    Yaquis, expulsion of, 330
    Yuma, 70
  U. S. difficulties in restraining, 70, 185
    1869, Mexico forbids U. S. to cross border in pursuit of, 288
    lack of proper measures, 70-73, 363
    soldiers needed, 74-76, 286
  Yucatán whites threatened by, 20-21
Interior, Department of the, 70, 108, 112, 114, 128
Intervention, *see* Mexico
Isthmus of Darien, *see* Panama
Isthmus of Tehuantepec, *see* Tehuantepec Isthmus
Iturbide, Augustin de, *Emperor of Mexico,*
  Clay admired by, 1
  Mexican revolution led to success (1821) by, 1
  republican government after overthrow, 5
  U. S. fraternal relations with Mexico expected, 1

Jackson, Andrew,
  1837, Congress declines war over claims, 12
  President of the U. S., as, 6
  Texas occupation advocated by, 3, 12
Jackson (Mississippi), 246
Jalisco, 250, 316
James, Charles Tillinghast, 149
Janos, 78 n
Japanese, 326, 330, 350, 358 n